CCNA 200-301 Hands-on Mastery with Packet Tracer

Companion Website and Pearson Test Prep Access Code

Access interactive study tools on this book's companion website, including practice test software, Key Term flash card application, and Packet Tracer lab files!

To access the companion website, simply follow these steps:

1. Go to **www.ciscopress.com/register**.

2. Enter the **print book ISBN**: 9780135313091.

3. Answer the security question to validate your purchase.

4. Go to your account page.

5. Click on the **Registered Products** tab.

6. Under the book listing, click on the **Access Bonus Content** link.

W0050282

When you register your book, your Pearson Test Prep practice test access code will automatically be populated with the book listing under the Registered Products tab. You will need this code to access the practice test that comes with this book. You can redeem the code at **PearsonTestPrep.com**. Simply choose Pearson IT Certification as your product group and log into the site with the same credentials you used to register your book. Click the **Activate New Product** button and enter the access code. More detailed instructions on how to redeem your access code for both the online and desktop versions can be found on the companion website.

If you have any issues accessing the companion website or obtaining your Pearson Test Prep practice test access code, you can contact our support team by going to **ciscopress.com/support**.

CCNA 200-301 Hands-on Mastery with Packet Tracer

Anthony Sequeira, CCIE No. 15626

Ronald Wong

Cisco Press

Hoboken, New Jersey

CCNA 200-301 Hands-on Mastery with Packet Tracer

Anthony Sequeira; Ronald Wong

Copyright© 2025 Pearson Education, Inc.

Published by:
Cisco Press

28 2025

Library of Congress Control Number: 2024945096

ISBN-13: 978-0-13-531309-1
ISBN-10: 0-13-531309-0

Warning and Disclaimer

Trademark Acknowledgments

Microsoft® Windows®, and Microsoft Office® are registered trademarks of the Microsoft Corporation in the U.S.A. and other countries. This book is not sponsored or endorsed by or affiliated with the Microsoft Corporation.

Special Sales

For information about buying this title in bulk quantities, or for special sales opportunities (which may include electronic versions; custom cover designs; and content particular to your business, training goals, marketing focus, or branding interests), please contact our corporate sales department at corpsales@pearsoned.com or (800) 382-3419.

For government sales inquiries, please contact governmentsales@pearsoned.com.

For questions about sales outside the U.S., please contact intlcs@pearson.com.

Feedback Information

At Cisco Press, our goal is to create in-depth technical books of the highest quality and value. Each book is crafted with care and precision, undergoing rigorous development that involves the unique expertise of members from the professional technical community.

Readers' feedback is a natural continuation of this process. If you have any comments regarding how we could improve the quality of this book, or otherwise alter it to better suit your needs, you can contact us through email at feedback@ciscopress.com. Please make sure to include the book title and ISBN in your message.

We greatly appreciate your assistance.

Please contact us with concerns about any potential bias at https://www.pearson.com/report-bias.html.

GM K12, Early Career and Professional Learning: Soo Kang

Alliances Manager, Cisco Press: Caroline Antonio

Director, ITP Product Management: Brett Bartow

Managing Editor: Sandra Schroeder

Development Editor: Chris Zahn

Senior Project Editor: Mandie Frank

Copy Editor: Kitty Wilson

Technical Editor: Wes Bryan

Editorial Assistant: Cindy Teeters

Designer: Chuti Prasertsith

Composition: codeMantra

Indexer: Timothy Wright

Proofreader: Donna E. Mulder

CISCO.

Americas Headquarters
Cisco Systems, Inc.
San Jose, CA

Asia Pacific Headquarters
Cisco Systems (USA) Pte. Ltd.
Singapore

Europe Headquarters
Cisco Systems International BV Amsterdam,
The Netherlands

Cisco has more than 200 offices worldwide. Addresses, phone numbers, and fax numbers are listed on the Cisco Website at **www.cisco.com/go/offices.**

Cisco and the Cisco logo are trademarks or registered trademarks of Cisco and/or its affiliates in the U.S. and other countries. To view a list of Cisco trademarks, go to this URL: www.cisco.com/go/trademarks. Third party trademarks mentioned are the property of their respective owners. The use of the word partner does not imply a partnership relationship between Cisco and any other company. (1110R)

About the Authors

Anthony Sequeira (CCIE No. 15626) began his IT career in 1994 with IBM in Tampa, Florida. He quickly formed his own computer consultancy, Computer Solutions, and then discovered his true passion: teaching and writing about Microsoft and Cisco technologies. Anthony has lectured to massive audiences around the world while working for Mastering Computers. He has never been happier in his career than he is now as a senior technical instructor at ACI Learning. ACI is a leader in audit, cybersecurity, and IT pro training in self-paced and instructor-led formats. Follow Anthony today on X @compsolv or Facebook at facebook.com/compsolv.

Ronald Wong is the Director of Content Development for ACI Learning. He leads teams that are responsible for developing learning content for ACI. They develop courseware, labs, assessments, and ITPRO training. Previously Ronald has led Cisco, Microsoft Windows, CompTIA, and IT security training for the U.S. Army 7th SFG, the U.S. Air Force Special Operations Group, and the DoD at Ft. Lee. Most recently, Ronald was an Edutainer at ACI Learning and loved it. He takes a special interest in Networking Technology, especially Cisco, and tries his best to work as a good generalist in the IT field.

About the Technical Reviewer

Wesley Bryan, with nearly 15 years of experience as a technical instructor, specializes in CompTIA and Microsoft training. He began his journey as an IT student and discovered his passion for helping others launch their IT careers through certification and skills training. Wesley has served as a member of the Board of Directors for the North Florida Association of IT Professionals and participated in Instructor Advisory Boards. He is currently a technical instructor and subject matter expert for ACI Learning. Follow Wesley on Facebook via facebook.com/Wes.ITProTV, YouTube: youtube.com/@wsbryan1, and LinkedIn: linkedin.com/in/wesleyabryan.

Dedications

This book is dedicated to the countless CCNA students I have enjoyed helping over the decades I have worked in this industry. Keep up the inspired work!

—Anthony

To my family, friends, and co-workers, who somewhat pretended to be interested every time I talked about this book I was co-writing. Thanks for faking it so well! Someone owes me 50 bucks!

—Ronald

Acknowledgments

Thanks so much to Brett Bartow of Pearson for sharing our vision for this text. Also, huge thanks to Wes Bryan who meticulously edited every technical detail of this text.

Contents at a Glance

Reader Services

Register your copy of *CCNA 200-301 Hands-on Mastery with Packet Tracer* at www.ciscopress.com/title/ISBN for convenient access to downloads, updates, and corrections as they become available. To start the registration process, go to www.ciscopress.com/register and log in or create an account.* Enter the product ISBN 9780135313091 and click Submit. When the process is complete, you will find any available bonus content under Registered Products.

*Be sure to check the box indicating that you would like to hear from us to receive exclusive discounts on future editions of this product.

Contents

Command Syntax Conventions

The conventions used to present command syntax in this book are the same conventions used in the IOS Command Reference. The Command Reference describes these conventions as follows:

- **Boldface** indicates commands and keywords that are entered literally as shown. In actual configuration examples and output (not general command syntax), boldface indicates commands that are manually input by the user (such as a **show** command).

- *Italic* indicates arguments for which you supply actual values.

- Vertical bars (|) separate alternative, mutually exclusive elements.

- Square brackets ([ ]) indicate an optional element.

- Braces ({ }) indicate a required choice.

- Braces within brackets ([{ }]) indicate a required choice within an optional element.

Preface

Why is this book so valuable? Why is it an excellent resource to use prior to taking the CCNA 200-301 exam? Let us outline it for you here:

- This book balances the two potential areas of expertise you need for each exam topic. You either need to focus on just the theory of a technology or you need to be able to demonstrate a comprehensive understanding of configuration, verification, and troubleshooting in addition to the theory. You can trust this text to guide you through the precise knowledge you need, topic by topic.

- As alluded to above, this text is tightly focused on the exam. Whereas larger texts might provide background or peripheral information about a topic, this book is laser-focused on just those topics you need to comprehend for success in the exam environment. I certainly encourage the reading and study of larger works for those who require it.

- We have specialized in writing about and training candidates in all things CCNA since the inception of the certification in 1998. This book's technical reviewer also possesses vast knowledge in networking and cloud topics.

- We have taken the actual CCNA exam each and every revision since the certification's inception. We are therefore intimately familiar with the exam as well as with Cisco's testing techniques.

- This book is filled with valuable resources to assist you immediately in getting a passing score; these resources include quizzes, review questions, practice exams, and, of course, many hands-on labs using the superb Packet Tracer tool.

Introduction

Welcome to *CCNA 200-301 Hands-on Mastery with Packet Tracer*! This book covers the newly updated CCNA 200-301 certification exam. This new "one CCNA exam to rule them all" is more important than ever before in Cisco's overall certification strategy. It covers the information you need to build a strong foundation for the varied CCNP certification tracks from Cisco Systems.

Whether this is your first or your fifteenth *CCNA textbook*, you'll find information here that will ensure your success as you pursue knowledge, experience, and certification. This Introduction covers how this text can help you prepare for the CCNA exam.

This Introduction discusses the basics of the CCNA exam. Included are sections covering preparation, how to take an exam, a description of this book's contents, how this book is organized, and, finally, author contact information.

Each chapter in this book contains practice questions. There are also two full-length Practice Exams at the end of the book. Practice Exams in this book should help you accurately assess the level of expertise you need in order to pass the test. Answers and explanations are included for all test questions. It is best to obtain a level of understanding equivalent to a consistent pass rate of at least 90% on the Review Questions and Practice Exams in this book before you take the real exam.

Let's begin by looking at preparation for the exam.

How to Prepare for the Exam

This text follows the official exam objectives closely to help ensure your success. The official objectives from Cisco Systems can be found at https://www.cisco.com/c/en/us/training-events/training-certifications/exams/current-list/ccna-200-301.html.

As you examine the numerous exam topics now covered on the CCNA exam, resist the urge to panic! This book you are reading will provide you with the knowledge (and confidence) you need to succeed in taking this new CCNA exam. You just need to make sure you read it and follow the guidance it provides throughout your CCNA journey.

Practice Questions

This book is filled with practice questions to get you ready. Enjoy the following:

- **Chapter pretest questions at the beginning of each and every chapter:** These detailed, open-ended questions ensure that you really know the material. Some readers use these questions to "test out of" reading a particular section.

- **Topic-based quizzes ending each section:** These quizzes provide a chance to demonstrate your knowledge after completing a section.

- **Review questions ending each chapter:** These questions give you a final pass through the material covered in the chapter.

- **Two full practice exams:** The answer keys for the practice exams include explanations and tips for approaching each practice exam question.

- **Packet Tracer practice labs:** Every chapter challenges you with Packet Tracer practice labs. You simply download these labs from the book's companion website. These labs evaluate your progress and grade you when you complete each lab. Working through the practice labs will give you the knowledge and confidence you need in the actual exam.

Taking a Certification Exam

When you have prepared for the CCNA 200-301 exam, you must register with Cisco Systems to take the exam. The CCNA exam is given at Pearson VUE testing centers. Check the Pearson VUE website at www.pearsonvue.com to get specific details.

You can register for an exam online or by phone. After you register, you will receive a confirmation notice. Some areas may have limited testing centers available, so you should schedule your exam in advance to make sure you can get the specific date and time you would like.

Note You can now take the CCNA exam from your home or office. If you choose this option, be sure to review the requirements to ensure that you have no issues taking your exam in the privacy of your home or office.

Arriving at the Exam Location

As with any other examination, you should arrive at the testing center early. Be prepared! You need to bring two forms of identification (one with a picture). The testing center staff requires proof that you are who you say you are and that someone else is not taking the test for you. Arrive early because if you are late, you will be barred from entry and will not receive a refund for the cost of the exam.

Note You'll be spending a lot of time in the exam room. Plan on using the full two hours of time allotted for your exam and surveys. Policies differ from location to location regarding bathroom breaks, so check with the testing center before beginning the exam.

In the Testing Center

You will not be allowed to take into the examination room study materials or anything else that could raise suspicion that you're cheating. This includes practice test material, books, exam prep guides, and other test aids. The testing center will provide you with scratch paper and a pen or pencil—or possibly an erasable whiteboard.

After the Exam

Examination results are available immediately after the exam. If you pass the exam, you will simply receive a passing grade; your exact score will not be provided. Candidates who do not pass will receive a complete score breakdown by domain. This allows those individuals to see what areas they are weak in.

About This Book

The ideal reader for this text is someone seeking the CCNA certification. However, it should be noted that this book is very easily readable, and it rapidly presents facts. Therefore, this book is also extremely useful as a quick reference manual.

This book includes other helpful elements in addition to the actual logical, step-by-step learning progression of the chapters themselves. *There are plenty of quiz and review questions as well as plenty of labs to ensure that you are fully comprehending the material as you go.* This text also includes a very helpful Glossary to assist you.

Note   Bulleted lists, numbered lists, tables, and graphics are also used where appropriate. A picture can paint a thousand words sometimes, and tables can help to associate different elements with each other visually.

Remember that you do not have to build your own Packet Tracer labs when using this book. We have built them for you. Be sure to visit the companion website for this text in order to download the Packet Tracer labs.

The Exam Blueprint

The table that follows outlines the CCNA exam domains and objectives and maps each objective to the chapter in the book that covers it in detail.

Exam Domain	Objective	Chapter in Book That Covers It
Network Fundamentals	Explain the role and function of network components	Appendix A
Network Fundamentals	Describe characteristics of network topology architectures	Appendix A
Network Fundamentals	Compare physical interface and cabling types	Chapter 5
Network Fundamentals	Identify interface and cable issues	Chapter 5
Network Fundamentals	Compare TCP to UDP	Appendix A
Network Fundamentals	Configure and verify IPv4 addressing and subnetting	Chapter 6

Exam Domain	Objective	Chapter in Book That Covers It
Network Fundamentals	Describe the need for private IPv4 addressing	Chapter 6
Network Fundamentals	Configure and verify IPv6 addressing and prefix	Chapter 7
Network Fundamentals	Describe IPv6 address types	Chapter 7
Network Fundamentals	Verify IP parameters for Client OS	Chapter 6
Network Fundamentals	Describe wireless principles	Chapter 8
Network Fundamentals	Explain virtualization fundamentals	Appendix A
Network Fundamentals	Describe switching concepts	Chapter 9
Network Access	Configure and verify VLANs spanning multiple switches	Chapter 10
Network Access	Configure and verify interswitch connectivity	Chapter 10
Network Access	Configure and verify Layer 2 discovery protocols	Chapter 11
Network Access	Configure and verify EtherChannel	Chapter 10
Network Access	Interpret basic operations of Rapid PVST+ Spanning Tree Protocol	Chapter 12
Network Access	Describe Cisco Wireless Architectures and AP modes	Chapter 13
Network Access	Describe physical infrastructure connections of WLAN components	Chapter 13
Network Access	Describe network device management access connections	Appendix A
Network Access	Interpret the wireless LAN GUI configuration for client connectivity, such as WLAN creation, security settings, QoS profiles, and advanced settings	Appendix A
IP Connectivity	Interpret the components of a routing table	Chapter 14
IP Connectivity	Determine how a router makes a forwarding decision by default	Chapter 14
IP Connectivity	Configure and verify IPv4 and IPv6 static routing	Chapter 15
IP Connectivity	Configure and verify single area OSPFv2	Chapter 16

Exam Domain	Objective	Chapter in Book That Covers It
IP Connectivity	Describe the purpose, functions, and concepts of first hop redundancy protocols	Appendix A
IP Services	Configure and verify inside source NAT using static and pools	Chapter 17
IP Services	Configure and verify NTP operating in a client and server mode	Chapter 18
IP Services	Explain the role of DHCP and DNS within the network	Chapter 19
IP Services	Explain the function of SNMP in network operations	Chapter 20
IP Services	Describe the use of syslog features including facilities and levels	Chapter 20
IP Services	Configure and verify DHCP client and relay	Chapter 19
IP Services	Explain the forwarding per-hop behavior for QoS, such as classification, marking, queuing, congestion, policing, and shaping	Appendix A
IP Services	Configure network devices for remote access using SSH	Chapter 20
IP Services	Describe the capabilities and function of TFTP/FTP in the network	Chapter 20
Security Fundamentals	Describe key security concepts	Appendix A
Security Fundamentals	Describe security program elements	Appendix A
Security Fundamentals	Configure and verify device access control using local passwords	Chapter 21
Security Fundamentals	Describe security password policies elements, such as management, complexity, and password alternatives	Chapter 21
Security Fundamentals	Describe IPsec remote access and site-to-site VPNs	Appendix A
Security Fundamentals	Configure and verify access control lists	Chapter 22
Security Fundamentals	Configure and verify Layer 2 security features	Chapter 23
Security Fundamentals	Compare authentication, authorization, and accounting concepts	Appendix A

Exam Domain	Objective	Chapter in Book That Covers It
Security Fundamentals	Describe wireless security protocols	Chapter 24
Security fundamentals	Configure and verify WLAN within the GUI using WPA2 PSK	Chapter 24
Automation and Programmability	Explain how automation impacts network management	Appendix A
Automation and Programmability	Compare traditional networks with controller-based networking	Appendix A
Automation and Programmability	Describe controller-based, software-defined architecture	Appendix A
Automation and Programmability	Explain AI and machine learning in network operations	Appendix A
Automation and Programmability	Describe characteristics of REST-based APIs	Appendix A
Automation and Programmability	Recognize the capabilities of configuration management mechanisms, such as Ansible and Terraform	Appendix A
Automation and Programmability	Recognize components of JSON-encoded data	Appendix A

Other Book Elements

There are various important elements that are not part of the standard chapter format. These elements apply to the book as a whole.

- **Practice Exams:** In addition to including exam-preparation questions at the end of each chapter, this book provides two full Practice Exams.

- **Answers and explanations for practice exams:** An Answer Key follows each practice exam, providing answers to and explanations for the questions in the exams.

- **Glossary:** The Glossary defines important terms used in this book.

- **Companion website:** The companion website for this book allows you to access several digital assets that come with your book:

  - Pearson Test Prep software (both online and Windows desktop versions)

  - Key Terms Flash Cards application

  - A PDF version of the Command Reference

- The Packet Tracer Hands-On Labs

How to Access the Companion Website

Register this book to get access to the Pearson IT Certification test engine and other study materials, as well as additional bonus content. Be sure to check the box indicating that you would like to hear from us to receive updates and exclusive discounts on future editions of this product or related products.

To access this companion website, follow these steps:

Step 1.   Go to **www.ciscopress.com/register** and log in or create a new account.

Step 2.   Enter the ISBN: **9780135313091**.

Step 3.   Answer the challenge question as proof of purchase.

Step 4.   Click the **Access Bonus Content** link in the Registered Products section of your account page to be taken to the page where your downloadable content is available.

Please note that many of our companion content files can be very large, especially image and video files.

If you are unable to locate the files for this title by following the steps above, please visit www.ciscopress.com/support. Our customer service representatives will assist you.

Pearson Test Prep Practice Test Software

As noted previously, this book comes complete with the Pearson Test Prep practice test software, containing two full exams. These practice tests are available to you either online or as an offline Windows application. To access the practice exams that were developed with this book, please see the instructions below.

How to Access the Pearson Test Prep (PTP) App

You have two options for installing and using the Pearson Test Prep application: a web app and a desktop app. To use the Pearson Test Prep application, start by finding the registration code that comes with the book. You can find the code in these ways:

■ You can get your access code by registering the print ISBN (9780135313091) on ciscopress.com/register. Make sure to use the print book ISBN regardless of whether you purchased an eBook or the print book. After you register the book, your access code will be populated on your account page under the Registered Products tab. Instructions for how to redeem the code are available on the book's companion website by clicking the Access Bonus Content link.

Note   After you register your book, your code can always be found in your account on the Registered Products tab.

Once you have the access code, to find instructions about both the Pearson Test Prep web app and the desktop app, follow these steps:

Step 1.   Open this book's companion website, as shown earlier in this Introduction, under the heading, "How to Access the Companion Website."

Step 2.   Click the **Practice Test Software** button.

Step 3.   Follow the instructions listed there for both installing the desktop app and using the web app.

Note that if you want to use the web app only at this point, just navigate to pearsontestprep.com, log in using the same credentials used to register your book, and register this book's practice tests using the registration code you just found. The process should take only a couple of minutes.

Customizing Your Exams

When you are in the exam settings screen, you can choose to take exams in one of three modes:

- **Study mode:** Allows you to fully customize your exams and review answers as you are taking the exam. This is typically the mode you would use first to assess your knowledge and identify information gaps.

- **Practice Exam mode:** Locks certain customization options, as it is presenting a realistic exam experience. Use this mode when you are preparing to test your exam readiness.

- **Flash Card mode:** Strips out the answers and presents you with only the question stem. This mode is great for late-stage preparation when you really want to challenge yourself to provide answers without the benefit of seeing multiple-choice options. This mode does not provide the detailed score reports that the other two modes do, so you should not use it if you are trying to identify knowledge gaps.

In addition to these three modes, you will be able to select the source of your questions. You can choose to take exams that cover all of the chapters, or you can narrow your selection to just a single chapter or the chapters that make up specific parts in the book. All chapters are selected by default. If you want to narrow your focus to individual chapters, simply deselect all the chapters; then select only those on which you wish to focus in the Objectives area.

You can also select the exam banks on which to focus. Each exam bank comes complete with a full exam of questions that cover topics in every chapter. You can have the test engine serve up exams from all banks or just from one individual bank by selecting the desired banks in the exam bank area.

There are several other customizations you can make to your exam from the exam settings screen, such as the time of the exam, the number of questions served up, whether to randomize questions and answers, whether to show the number of correct answers for multiple-answer questions, and whether to serve up only specific types of questions. You can also create custom test banks by selecting only questions that you have marked or questions on which you have added notes.

Updating Your Exams

If you are using the online version of the Pearson Test Prep software, you should always have access to the latest version of the software as well as the exam data. If you are using the Windows desktop version, every time you launch the software while connected to the Internet, it checks if there are any updates to your exam data and automatically downloads any changes that were made since the last time you used the software.

Sometimes, due to many factors, the exam data may not fully download when you activate your exam. If you find that figures or exhibits are missing, you may need to manually update your exams. To update a particular exam you have already activated and downloaded, simply click the **Tools** tab and click the **Update Products** button. Again, this is only an issue with the desktop Windows application.

If you wish to check for updates to the Pearson Test Prep exam engine software, Windows desktop version, simply click the **Tools** tab and click the **Update Application** button. This ensures that you are running the latest version of the software engine.

Packet Tracer Hands-On Labs

Remember, the Packet Tracer labs are available for download from the companion website for this book.

If you do not have Packet Tracer (or if you have an older version that does not work with our files), be sure to register and download the latest free version from Cisco Networking Academy (https://www.netacad.com). As of this writing, Packet Tracer is available at https://skillsforall.com. Chapter 1 of this text walks you through the download and installation of this powerful network simulator.

Once you have Packet Tracer installed, you can simply double-click one of the PKA files to launch the topology and preexisting configurations in your version of Packet Tracer.

Contacting the Authors

Hopefully, this book provides you with the tools you need to pass the CCNA exam. Feedback is appreciated. You can contact the authors at ptracerbook@ajsnetworking.com.

Thank you for selecting our book; we have worked hard to apply the same concepts in this book that we have used in the hundreds of training classes we have taught. Spend your study time wisely and you, too, can become a CCNA. Good luck with the exam, although if you carefully work through this text, you will certainly minimize the amount of luck required!

Credits

Figures 6-4 and 19.1 - © Microsoft 2024

Cover: simonkr/E+/Getty Images

Packet Tracer Fundamentals

This first part of the book covers Packet Tracer basics. The three chapters in Part I walk you through how to access and install Cisco Packet Tracer, how to use it to build simulations, and how to customize your installation of Packet Tracer.

While the authors of this book have created Packet Tracer labs for you (that will grade your performance), this part of the book is still very valuable, especially for those who are brand new to Cisco Packer Tracer. Part I includes the following chapters:

Chapter 1   Introducing Packet Tracer

Chapter 2   Building Your First Simulation

Chapter 3   Customizing Packet Tracer

Introducing Packet Tracer

This chapter covers the following topics:

- Requirements for installing Cisco Packet Tracer
- Accessing the Cisco Packet Tracer download

Packet Tracer (from the Cisco Networking Academy) is a free and powerful network simulator you can use to practice Cisco networking. You can use this tool to practice many physical and logical configurations of popular networking equipment. Every edition of Cisco Packet Tracer gets more advanced, and today's version supports modern technologies like wireless, Internet of Things (IoT), and cybersecurity.

Unlike other hands-on practice tools (such as GNS3 or EVE-NG), Cisco Packet Tracer does not require substantial resources on the host computer where you install it. As you will quickly learn in this chapter, all major operating systems support installation of Cisco Packet Tracer.

Note How is Cisco Packet Tracer able to run on modest computer hardware? Packet Tracer is a simulator, not an emulator. Tools like GNS3 and EVE-NG are networking emulators, which means those tools actually run the network operating systems of the devices in the practice lab. As a result, emulators require robust RAM, disk space, and CPU resources in order to function.

This book focuses on the use of Cisco Packet Tracer to practice skills required for the CCNA exam. Please keep in mind that there are additional skills you can practice with this valuable tool.

Accessing and Installing Cisco Packet Tracer

This text is based on Version 8.2.1 of Cisco Packet Tracer. This version can be installed on the following operating systems:

- macOS 10.14 or later (64-bit)

- Windows 10 or 11 (64-bit)

- Ubuntu LTS 20.04 or later (64-bit)

Notice that for each OS, you must be using an AMD64 (x86-64) CPU. You also need to have at least 4 GB of RAM and 1.4 GB of free disk space.

> **Note**   There is no need for you to try to find the exact 8.2.1 version of Packet Tracer to accompany this text. The many practice labs of this text will operate just fine with later versions of the Packet Tracer software. Version 8.2.1 should be considered the minimum version you need.

You can obtain the Cisco Packet Tracer download by visiting https://skillsforall.com/resources/lab-downloads. Figure 1.1 shows this page.

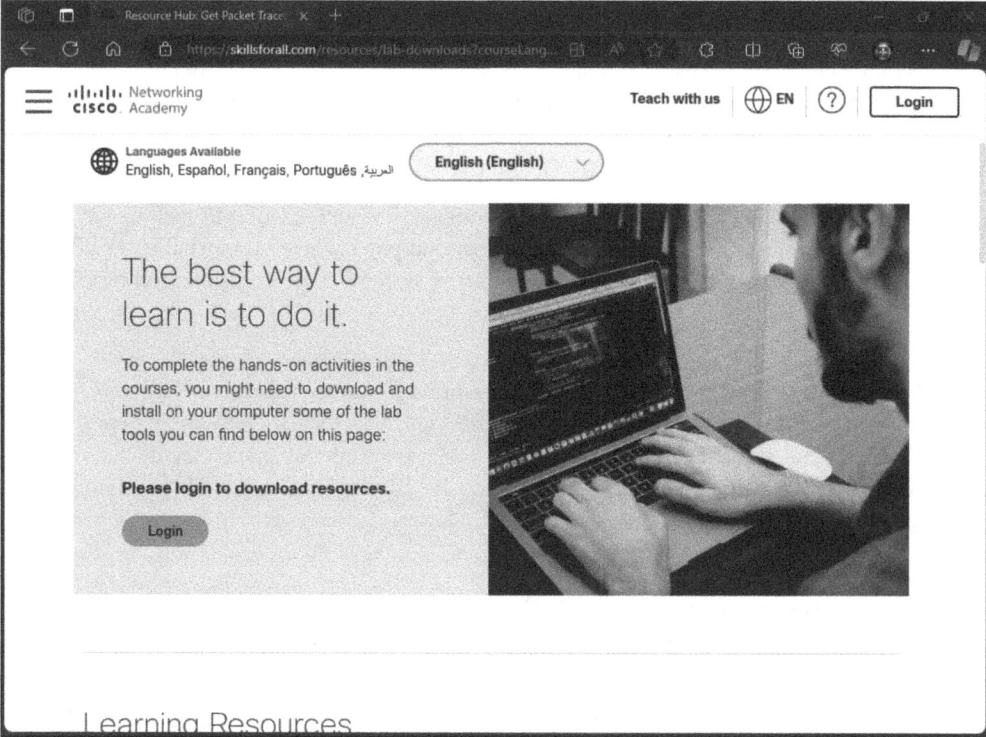

Figure 1.1   *The Networking Academy Resource Download Page*

In order to access the downloads on this page, you must log in. For your login, you can use any of the following free accounts (as shown in Figure 1.2):

■ Cisco.com

■ Cisco Networking Academy account

■ Google account

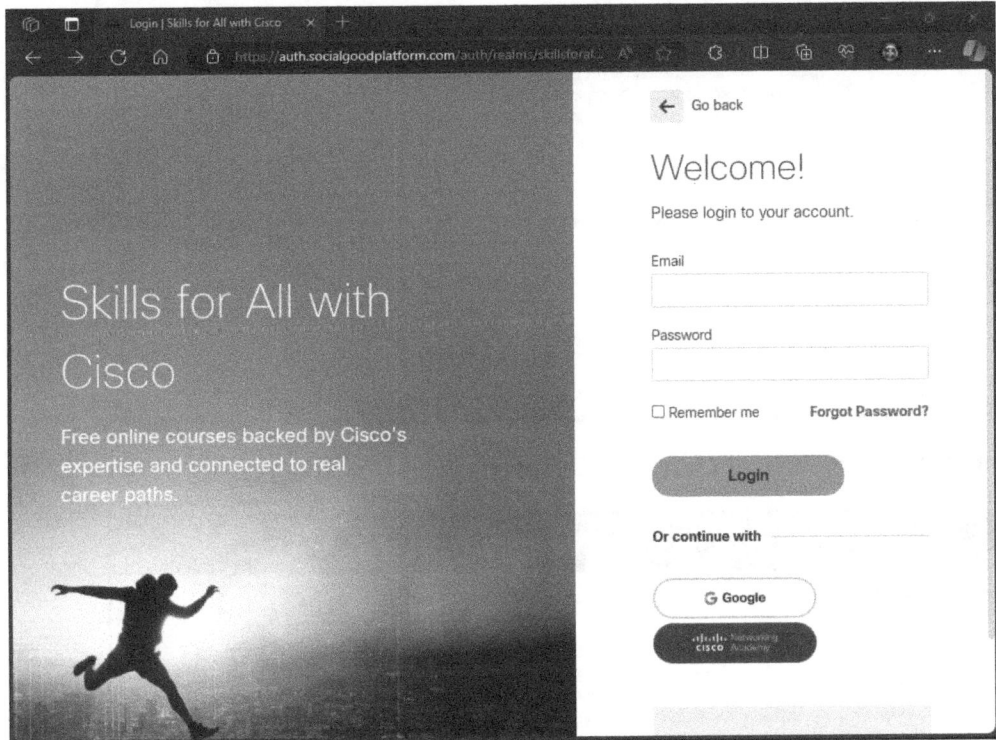

Figure 1.2   *The Login Page for the Networking Academy*

If this is your first login to the Networking Academy, accept the terms and conditions, as shown in Figure 1.3.

From the Networking Academy main page, access the Courses option and select the Beginner filter options and then access the Getting Started with Cisco Packet Tracer course, as shown in Figure 1.4.

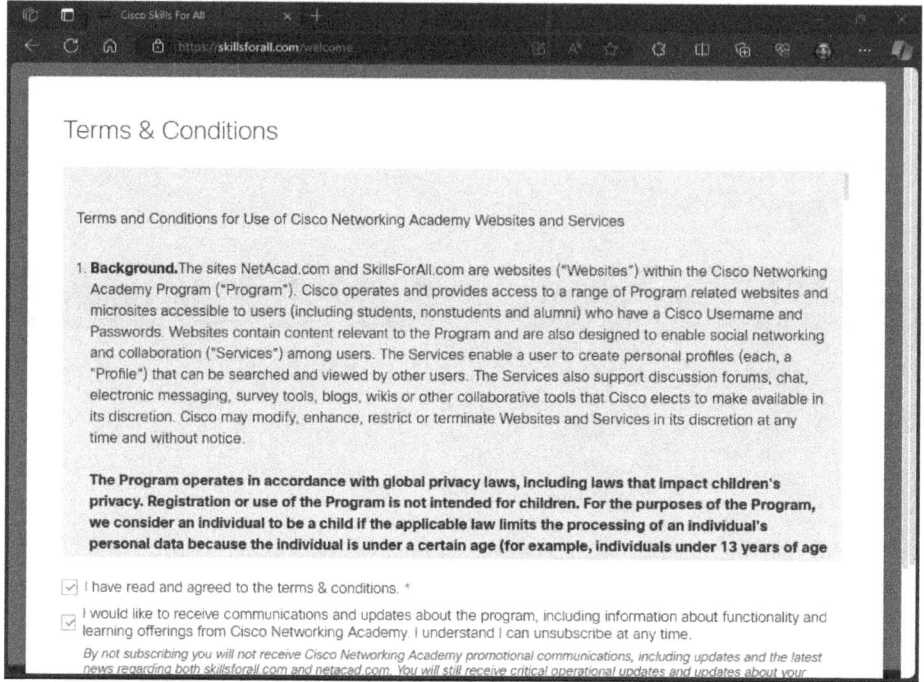

Figure 1.3   *The Terms and Conditions Page*

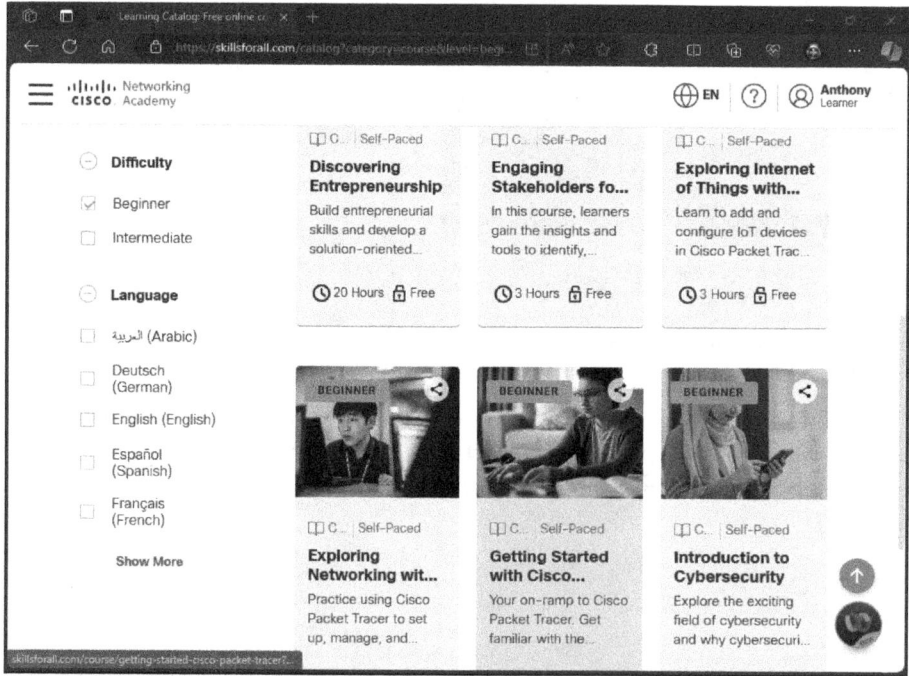

Figure 1.4   *The Courses Page*

Click the Get Started button for the Getting Started with Cisco Packet Tracer course, as shown in Figure 1.5.

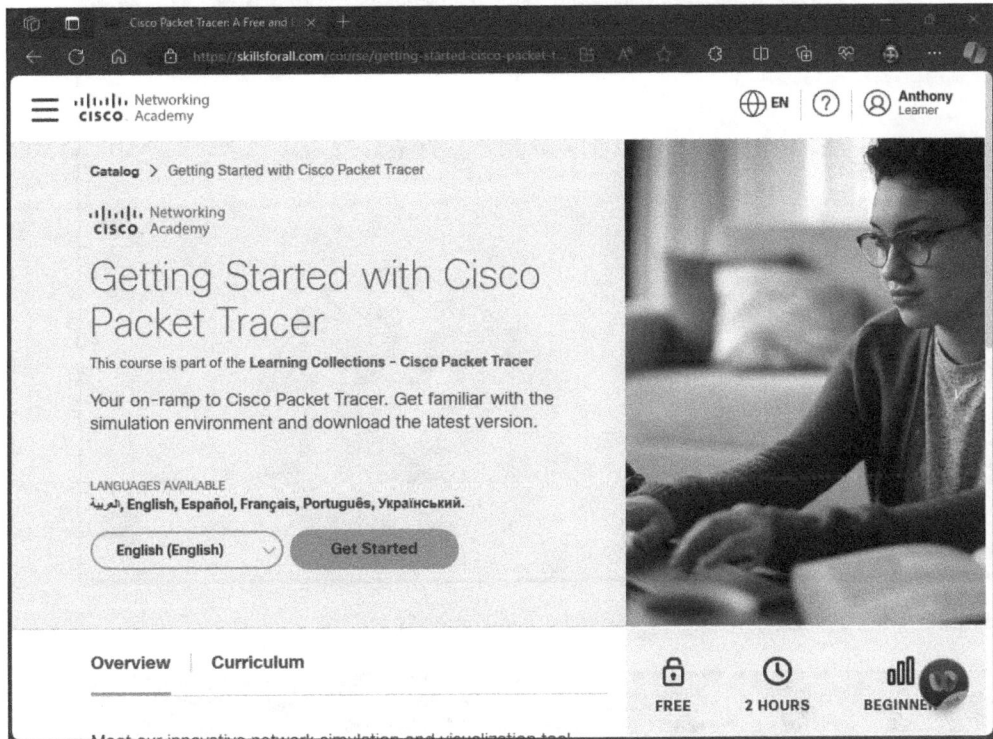

Figure 1.5 *Launching the Getting Started with Cisco Packet Tracer Course*

Inside the course, access the Download the Cisco Packet Tracer lesson, as shown in Figure 1.6.

From the online lesson, select the download link given (https://skillsforall.com/resources/lab-downloads), as shown in Figure 1.7.

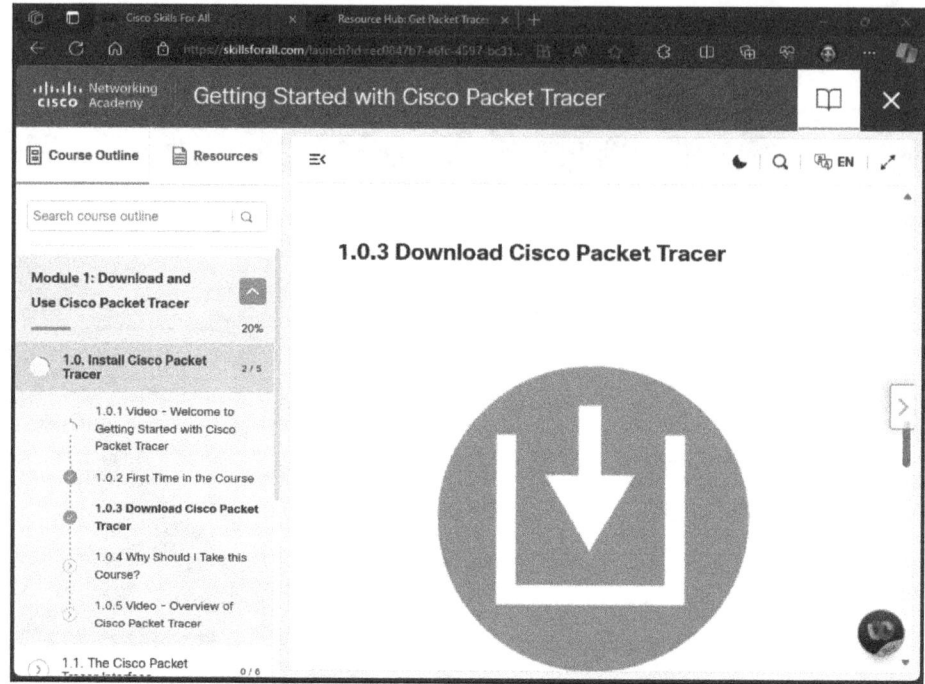

Figure 1.6 *The Download the Cisco Packet Tracer Lesson*

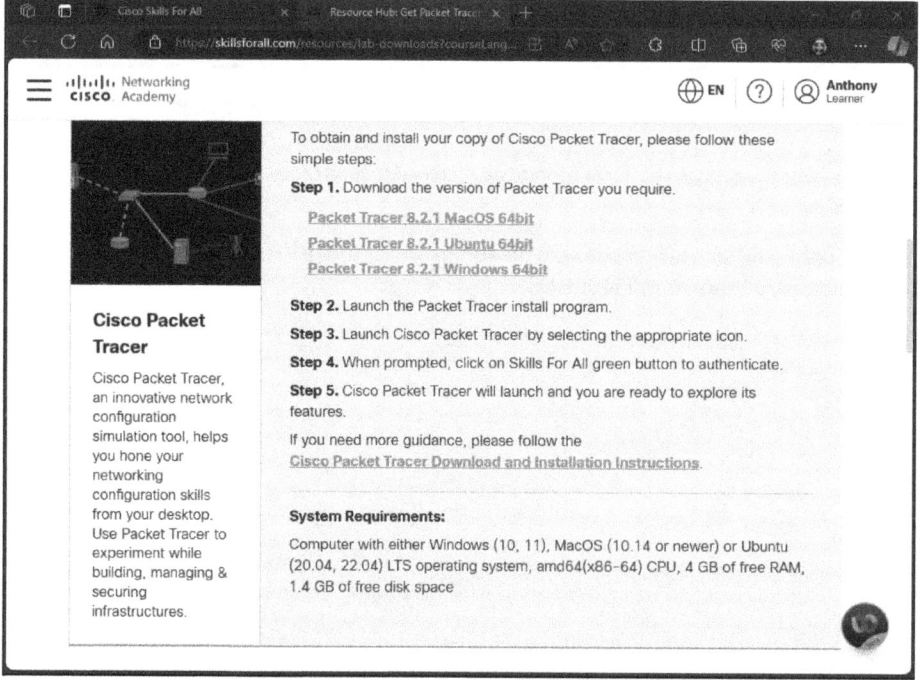

Figure 1.7 *The Cisco Packet Tracer Download Page*

Download the appropriate version of the installation file and install Packet Tracer in your operating system of choice.

Exploring Packet Tracer

Start your newly installed Packet Tracer. You will notice that Packet Tracer launches to a blank logical topology, as shown in Figure 1.8.

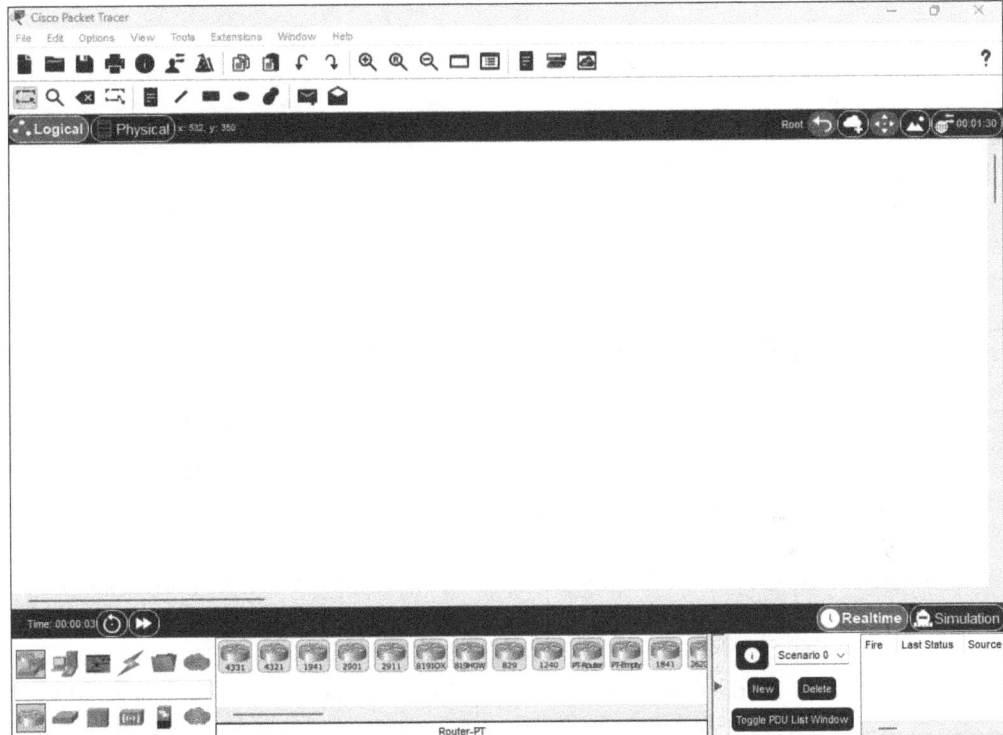

Figure 1.8   *The Initial Launch of Packet Tracer*

Each new version of Packet Tracer ships with updated sample topologies. In order to get familiar with the various interfaces inside Packet Tracer, let's look at one of these sample topologies now:

Step 1.   Inside Packet Tracer, click the **File** menu and choose **Open Samples.** Open the folder **01 Networking** and then the subfolder **DHCP.** Finally, open the Packet Tracer file named **dhcp_reservation.** You now see the sample topology in Packet Tracer, as shown in Figure 1.9.

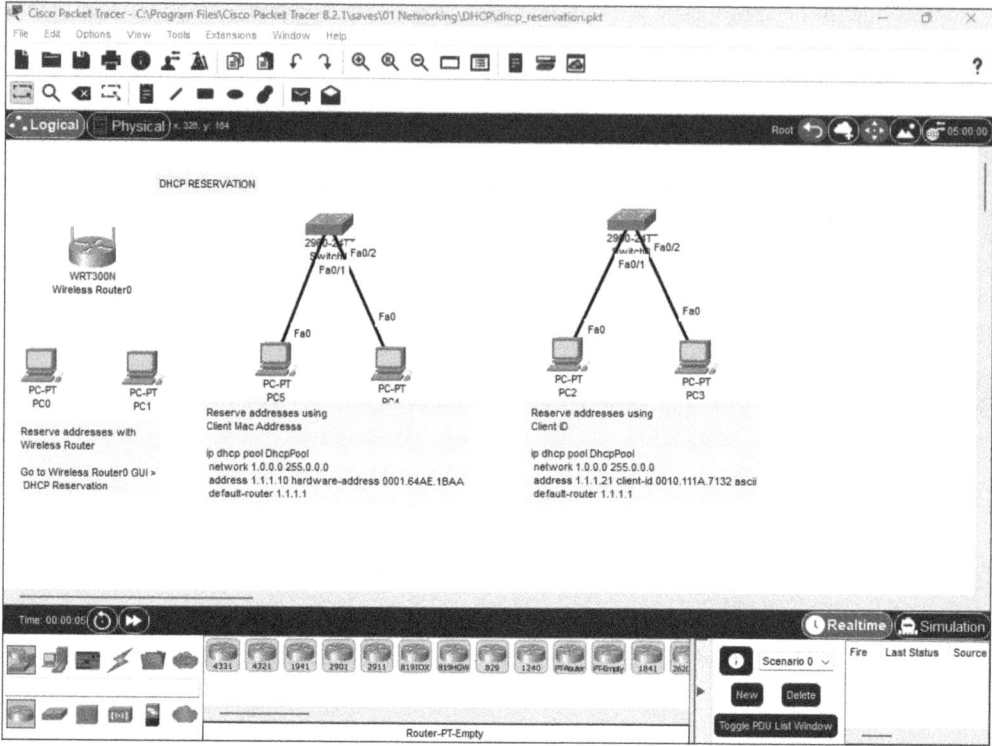

Figure 1.9   *The DHCP Reservation Sample Lab*

Step 2.   To see how Packet Tracer can simulate a graphical user interface (GUI) on a PC, click **PC0** in the topology. The PC0 window appears, with the Physical tab selected, as shown in Figure 1.10.

Step 3.   To see the IP configuration of this PC using the tools of the simulated PC, click the **Desktop** tab. You now see a variety of possible apps, as shown in Figure 1.11.

Step 4.   To view the IP configuration, select the **IP Configuration** app. You now see a window that displays the current IP configuration of PC0, as shown in Figure 1.12.

Step 5.   To examine the command-line interface (CLI) of a typical Cisco switch, close the PC0 window. Click **Switch1** in the topology to launch the Switch1 window, as shown in Figure 1.13. Notice that the Physical tab of the Switch1 window is selected.

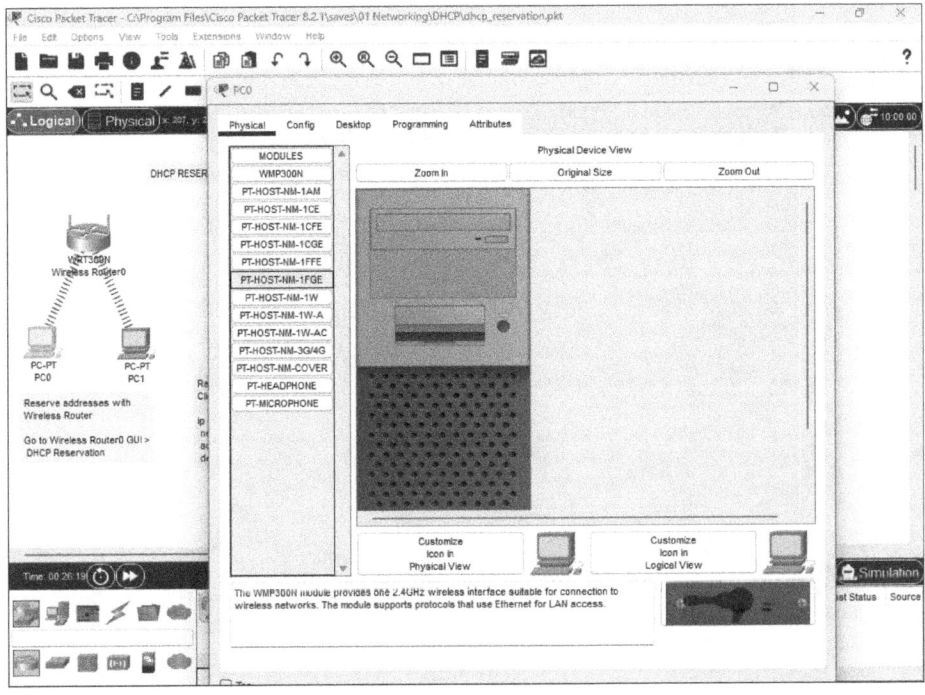

Figure 1.10   *The Physical Tab of PC0*

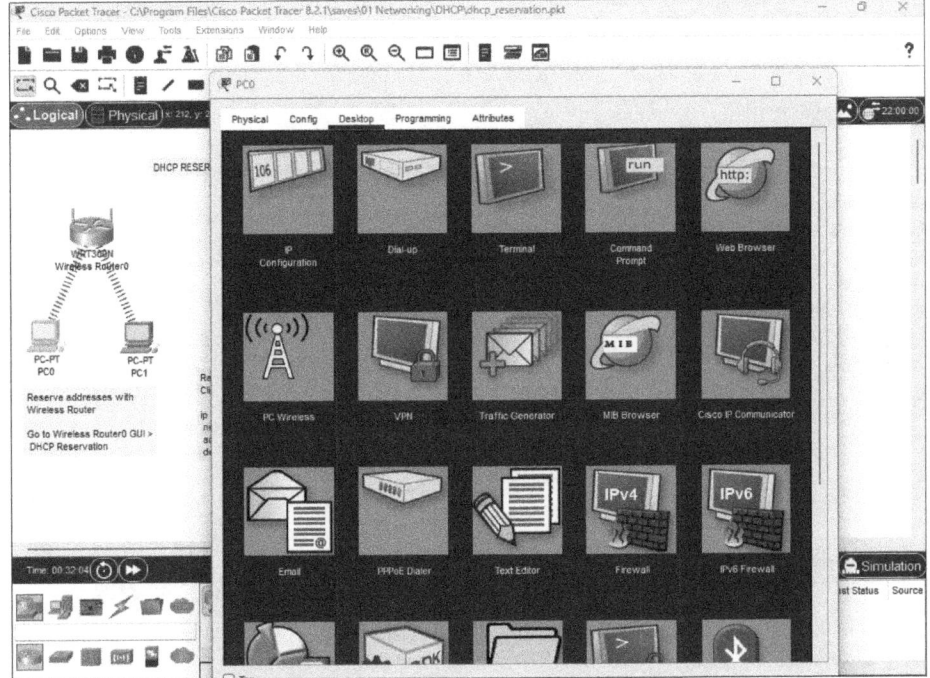

Figure 1.11   *The Various Apps on the PC Desktop*

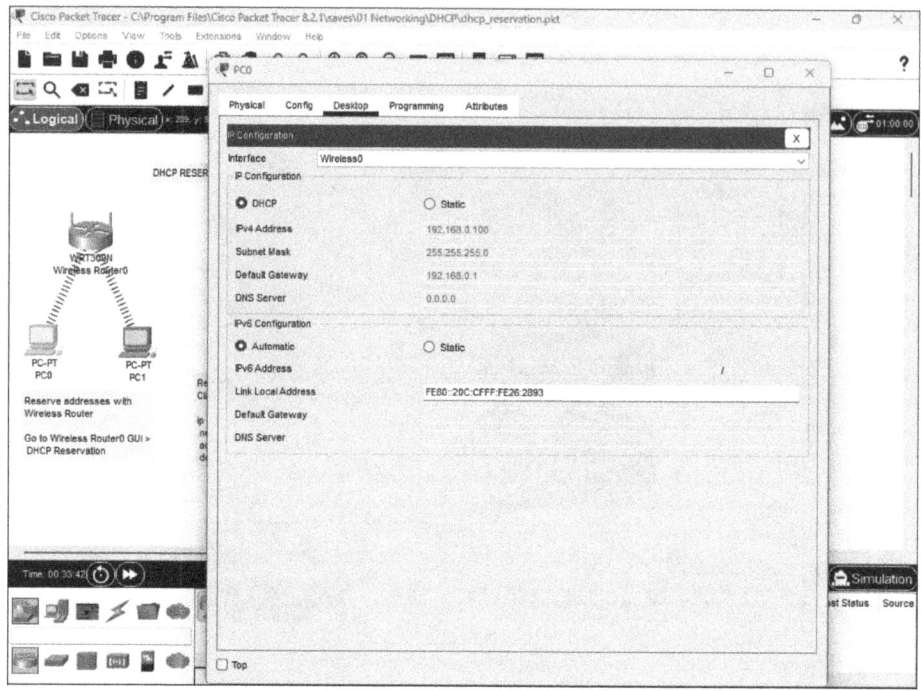

Figure 1.12   *The IP Configuration of PC0*

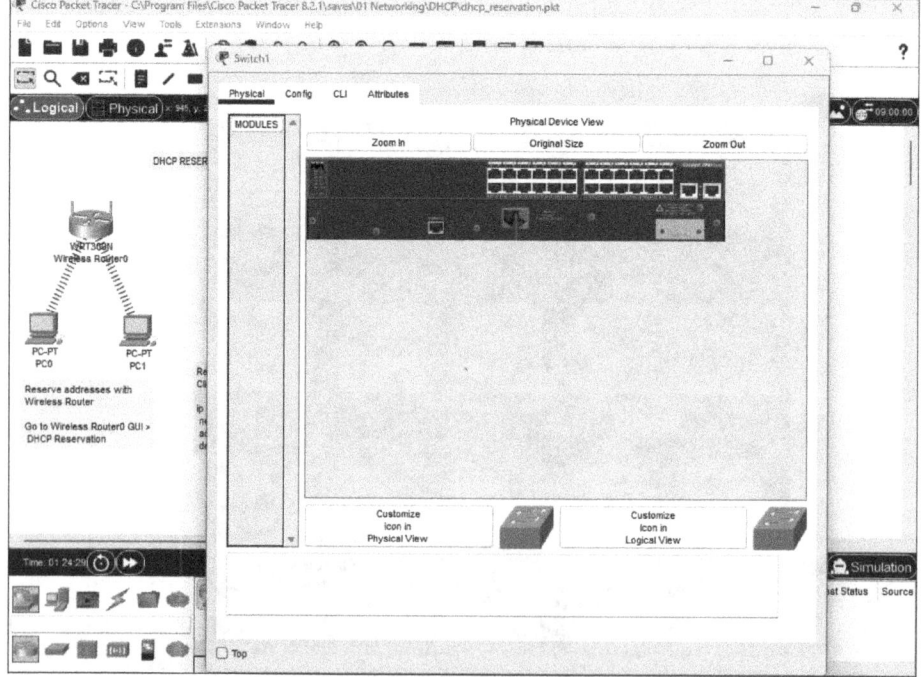

Figure 1.13   *The Switch1 Window in Packet Tracer*

Step 6.   Click the **CLI** tab to view the switch CLI, as shown in Figure 1.14.

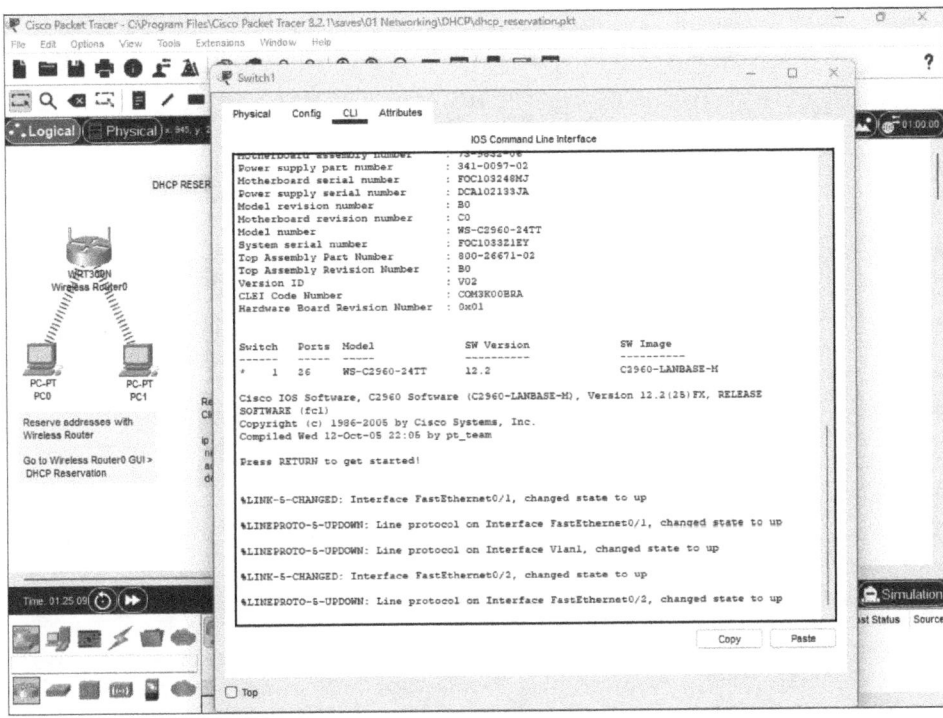

Figure 1.14   *The CLI Window for Switch1*

Step 7.   Press **Enter** on the keyboard to access the Switch prompt in the CLI. Type
enable and press **Enter** in order to enter privileged mode on the Cisco
switch. Now view the configuration of the switch in the CLI by typing **show
running-config** and pressing **Enter**. To see each page of the configuration,
use the spacebar to advance one screen of data at a time.

Step 8.   When you are done viewing the configuration of the switch, close the
Switch1 window and close Packet Tracer. If you are asked to save your
configuration, click **No**.

Chapter Review

In this chapter, we covered how you can obtain the free Cisco Packet Tracer software and
on what devices you can install it. We also examined a sample simulation and explored a
bit of the Packet Tracer interface.

In the next chapter, you will use Packet Tracer to build your first network simulation
from scratch. While, technically, you do not need to build your own simulations with this
text (we provide them), this is a valuable skill for your additional practice with this powerful network simulator. Chapter 2 also helps you learn more about the Cisco Packet Tracer
interface, and you will need those skills to succeed with this text.

Building Your First Simulation

This chapter covers the following topics:

- Building a simple network topology in Cisco Packet Tracer
- Configuring and testing IP reachability

While one of the major selling features of this book is the fact that we do all the work for you when it comes to building Cisco Packet Tracer labs for you to practice and learn with, we believe it would be irresponsible for you not to learn how easy it is for you to build your own network simulations. Learning to build Packet Tracer labs from scratch can be your next step in becoming proficient with the Cisco technologies covered in the Cisco CCNA certification.

In this chapter, you will be guided through the creation of a functional small, simple network. Once we have talked about how to place all of the hardware in the lab and properly connect it, we will then walk through configuring and verifying full IP reachability in this lab.

Building the Lab Topology

In Chapter 1, "Introducing Packet Tracer," you learned how to download and install Cisco Packet Tracer on your choice of PC, Mac, or Linux workstation. It is now time to launch Packet Tracer and get building!

Lab 2.1: Building a Sample Lab

Follow these steps to build your first sample lab topology:

Step 1.   Launch Cisco Packet Tracer by clicking the **Packet Tracer** icon from your installation in Chapter 1. As shown in Figure 2.1, Cisco Packet Tracer launches and provides you with a blank topology window so that you can start building your network simulation.

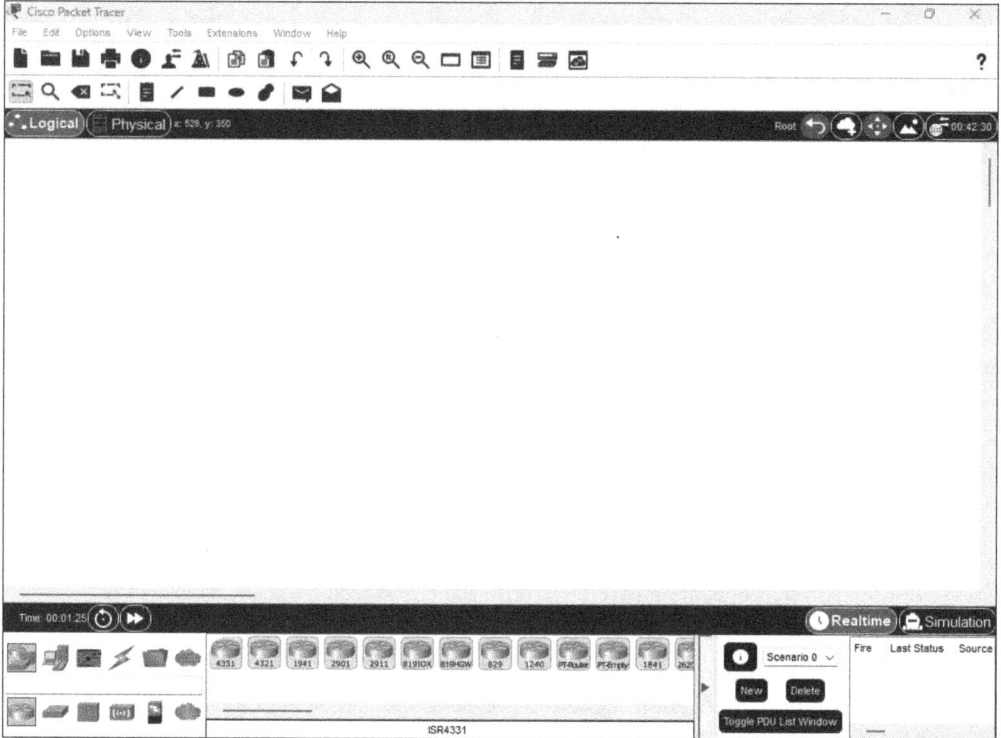

Figure 2.1   *A Blank Topology Window After Launch*

Step 2.   Notice at the bottom of your screen you can see the various Cisco routers you can choose to use in your network simulation. Packet Tracer shows the routers because of the two default selections in the lower-left area of the screen: the [Network Devices] and [Routers] icons. From the list of routers shown, click the **2911** model to select it and then click in the middle of your blank logical topology canvas. As shown in Figure 2.2, you have just placed your first device in the topology.

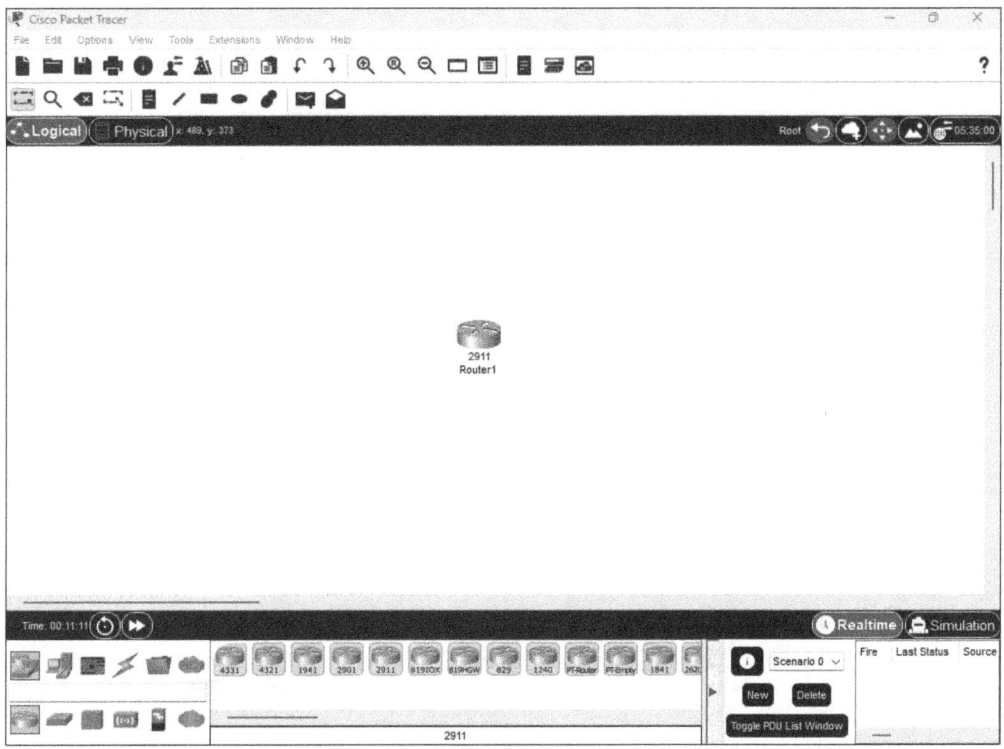

Figure 2.2   *Placing Your First Device in the Topology*

Step 3.   In the bottom left of your Packet Tracer window, click the **[Switches]** icon to display the switches available in the network simulator. Click the **2950-24** switch from the available switch models. Now, just as you did with your router, click in the topology pane to place this switch in your simulation. You are going to use two switches in this simulation, so place this switch to the left of your router.

Step 4.   To place your second switch, click the **2950-24** switch icon again and click in the topology to place your second switch to the right of the router. Figure 2.3 shows what your topology should look like so far.

Step 5.   Now it is time to add in two personal computers to the topology. In the bottom left of the screen, click the **[End Devices]** icon. In the list of available end devices, click **PC** and place a PC to the left of Switch0 and then click the **PC** icon again to place another PC to the right of Switch1. Your topology now has the five devices you will use in this basic network, and you are ready to connect the devices together.

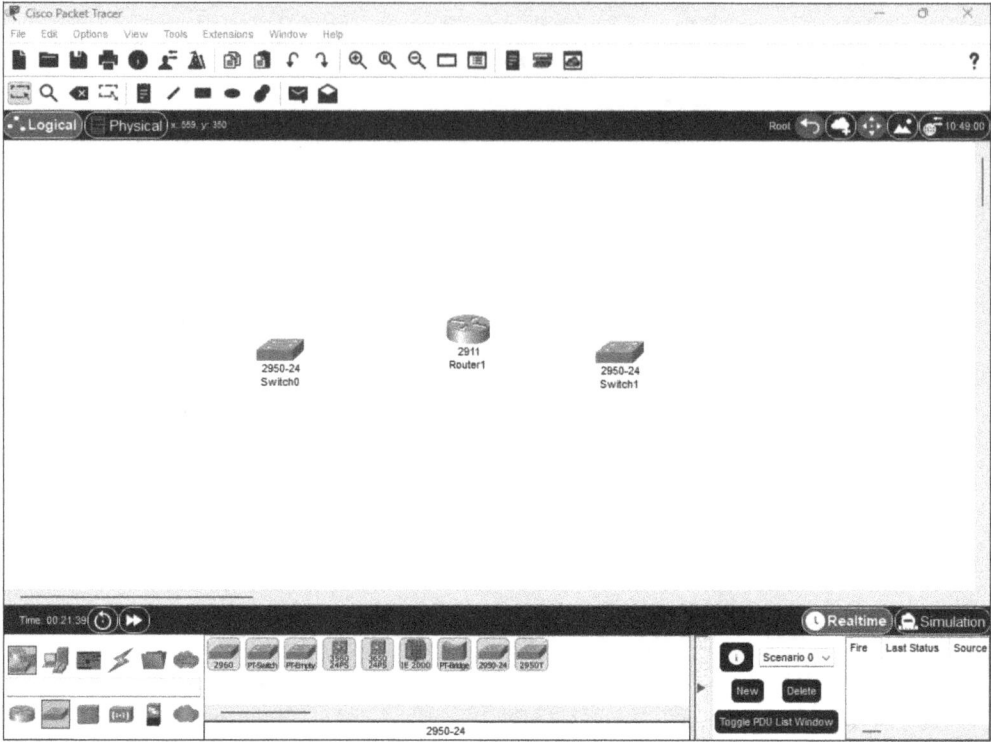

Figure 2.3 *Your Topology with One Router and Two Switches*

Step 6.   In the bottom left, click the **[Connections]** icon, which looks like a lightning bolt. From the available connection types, again choose the **[Connections]** icon. Packet Tracer will now automatically choose the connection type that is appropriate for the devices you are connecting.

Step 7.   Click **PC0** and then click **Switch0** to automatically connect these two devices. Click the **[Connections]** icon again and then click **Switch0** followed by **Router0** to connect those two devices. Repeat this process to connect Router0 to Switch1 and then Switch1 to PC1. Figure 2.4 shows the topology thus far.

Note   Notice how the links between the devices display an LED-like status for each interface. For example, the two interfaces on Router0 have defaulted (correctly) to a shutdown state, so these interfaces as well as the switch interfaces they connect to are displayed with red downward-facing triangles. In the next lab, you will enable the router interfaces to bring up these links.

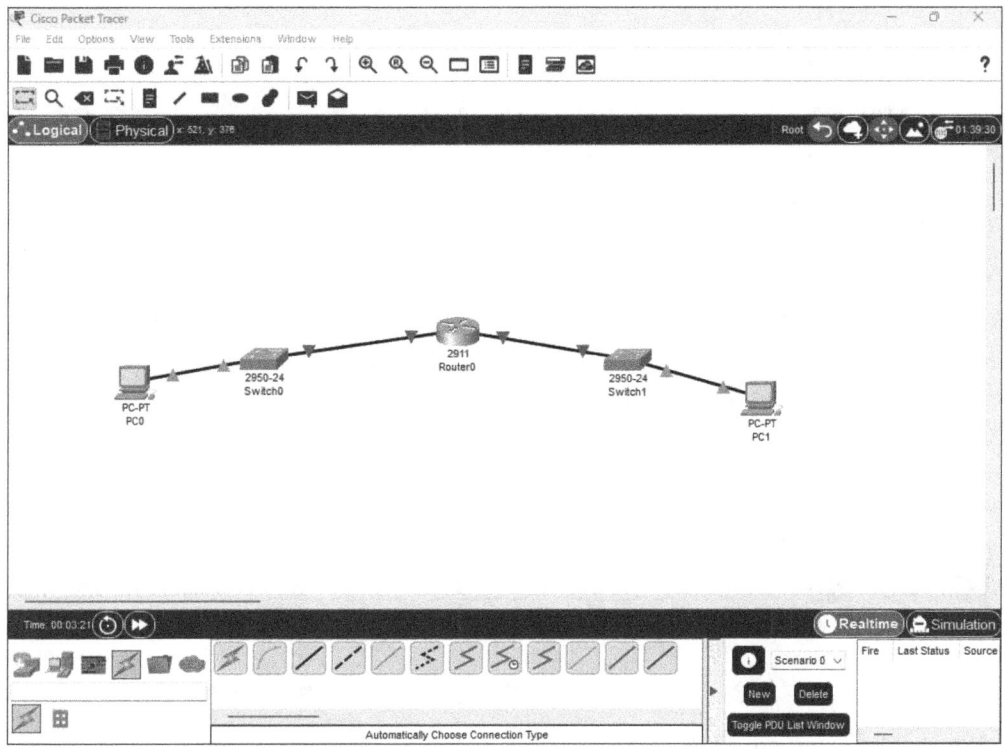

Figure 2.4   *The Topology with Network Connections*

Step 8.   You have worked hard on this first topology, and it is now time to save your work so click **File** and then **Save**. Choose a location to save your Packet Tracer topology and name the file **02 First Network**.

Configuring and Verifying IP Reachability

Congratulations on building your first Packet Tracer topology. Now you are ready to configure and verify IP reachability between your devices.

Lab 2.2: Configuring IP Reachability

Follow these steps to configure and verify IP reachability between your devices:

Step 1.   With your topology from Lab 2.1 open, click **Router0** in your topology to bring up the Router0 window. Click the **CLI** tab. Notice that the router is asking if you would like to enter the initial configuration dialog. Click in the CLI window, type **no**, and press **Enter**. At the Press RETURN to Get Started! prompt, press **Enter** to access the default Router> prompt on your device. Figure 2.5 shows your progress so far.

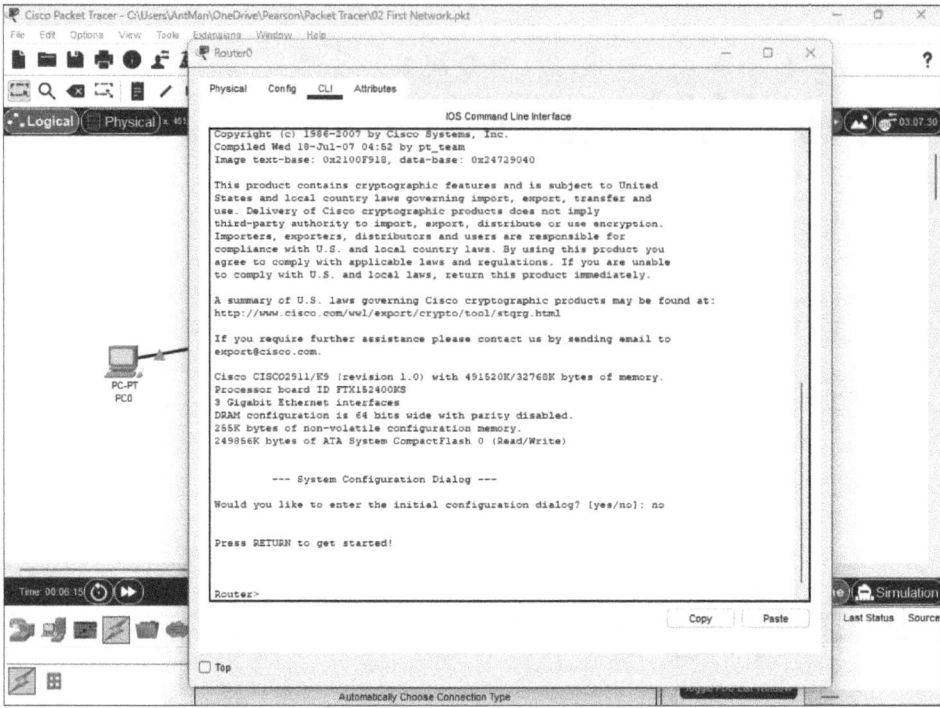

Figure 2.5 *Configuring Router0*

Step 2.   To enable the interfaces on Router0 and provide IP addresses to these interfaces, at the Router> prompt, type `enable` and press **Enter** to launch privileged mode on the router. Now type `configure terminal` and press **Enter** to launch global configuration mode on the device. Next, type `interface gigabitethernet 0/0` and press **Enter** to launch interface configuration mode. (Chapter 4, "Cisco IOS Basics," discusses the commands used in these steps in greater detail.)

Step 3.   Type `no shutdown` and press **Enter** to enable the Gi0/0 interface of Router0. Press **Enter** again to ensure that you are at the interface configuration mode prompt. Type `ip address 192.168.1.1 255.255.255.0` and press **Enter** to assign an IP address and subnet mask to the interface. Type `exit` and press **Enter** to return to global configuration mode.

Step 4.   To enable the second router interface and provide an IP address and subnet mask, type `interface gigabitethernet 0/1` and press **Enter** to launch interface configuration mode. Now type `no shutdown` and press **Enter** to enable the interface. Press **Enter** again to access interface configuration mode. Finally, type `ip address 10.10.10.1 255.255.255.0` and press **Enter** to assign an IP address.

Step 5.   Type `end` and press **Enter** twice to return to privileged mode on the router. Now save your hard work with the command `copy running-config` startup-config and press **Enter**. Press **Enter** again to accept the startup-config destination filename. Close the Router0 window.

Step 6.   To configure IP addresses on the PCs as well as the appropriate default gateway IP addresses, click **PC0** to launch its properties window. Click the **Desktop** tab and then click on the **IP Configuration** icon. In the IPv4 Address field, enter **192.168.1.100**. Click in the **Subnet Mask** field and notice that the 24-bit subnet mask 255.255.255.0 is entered automatically. Next, click in the **Default Gateway** field and erase the 0.0.0.0 entry there. Enter the default gateway address **192.168.1.1**. Figure 2.6 shows the completed configuration. Close the PC0 window.

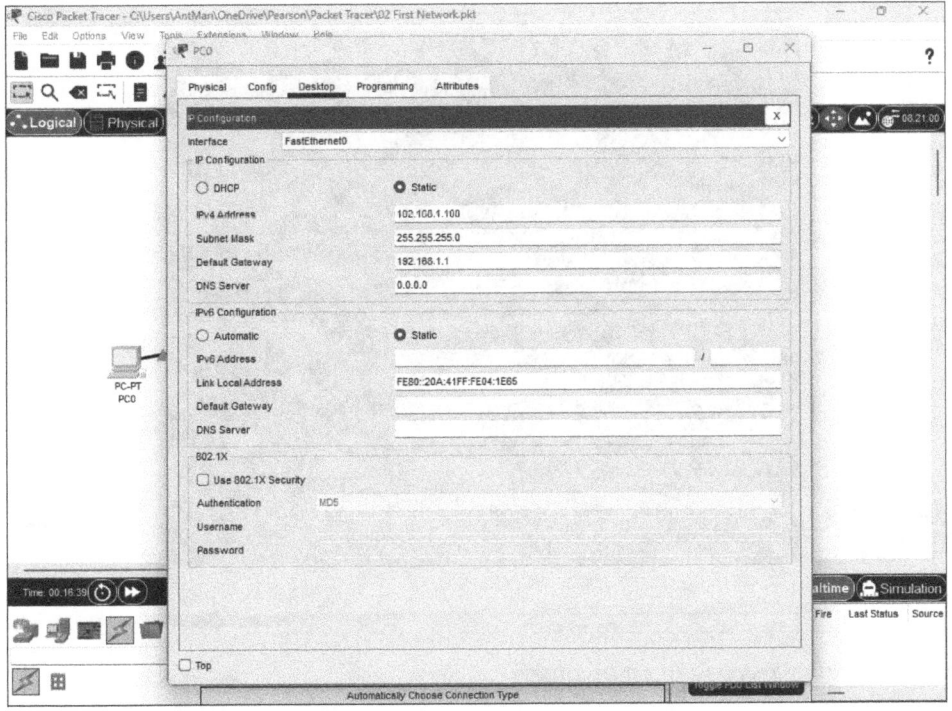

Figure 2.6   *Configuring the IP Address Information on PC0*

Step 7.   Click **PC1** to launch its properties window. Click the **Desktop** tab and then click the **IP Configuration** icon. In the **IPv4 Address** field, enter **10.10.10.100**. Click in the **Subnet Mask** field and erase the default 8-bit subnet mask 255.0.0.0. Enter the 24-bit mask **255.255.255.0** in the Subnet Mask field. Next, click in the **Default Gateway** field and erase the 0.0.0.0 entry there. Enter the default gateway address **10.10.10.1**. Close the IP Configuration window by clicking the X icon in the top right. (Keep the PC1 window open.)

Step 8.   To test connectivity, in the Desktop tab of PC1, click the **Command Prompt** icon to launch a new command prompt session on the PC. Type **ping 192.168.1.100** and press **Enter** to send test packets to PC0 from PC1. Figure 2.7 shows the results of this test. The first test packet fails its round-trip journey as the ARP process works its magic in the topology. The next three test packets succeed. You can now close the PC1 window and close and save your topology in Packet Tracer.

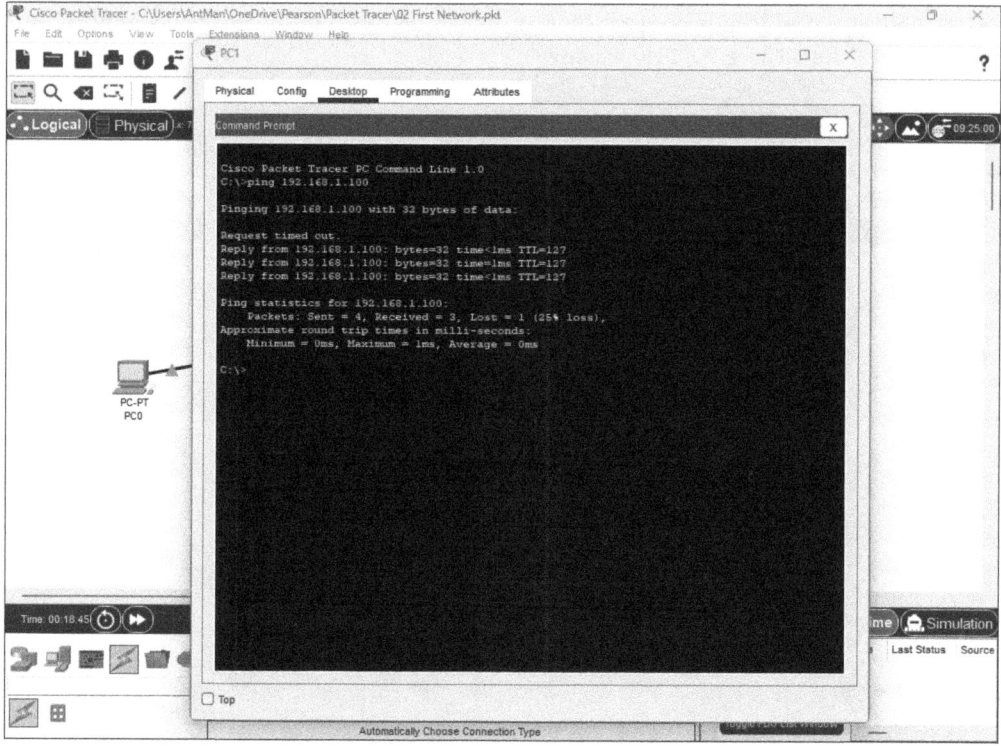

Figure 2.7 *Testing Reachability with* **ping**

Chapter Review

Congratulations on your first Packet Tracer topology. In the sample network you built, you were able to achieve full IP reachability. Each PC was configured with a default gateway (Router0). Router0 is able to route between the two networks you created because it is directly attached to each of them.

Hopefully you enjoyed this network-building experience. If you did, you are in for a lot more excitement throughout this text as you build on what you have done here. In the next chapter, you will work with this topology again to learn about some valuable customizations you can make in Cisco Packet Tracer.

Chapter 3

Customizing Packet Tracer

This chapter covers the following topics:

- Customizing Packet Tracer
- Customizing your first simulation

Without any modifications, Packet Tracer enables you to be up and running with network simulations very quickly. However, many customizations are possible. In fact, there are many customizations that I simply could not live without.

In this chapter, we are going to look at many of the customizations that I love to make to Packet Tracer. We are also going to revisit the network simulation you created in Chapter 2, "Building Your First Simulation," so you can make further customizations to that network. During these customizations, you will learn about many other additional (and exciting) features of Packet Tracer.

Customizing Packet Tracer

Let's begin with some customizations of Packet Tracer. This chapter does not cover all the potential tweaks you can make in the network simulator, but it will give you a huge head start on the many options that are available.

Lab 3.1: Customizing Packet Tracer

In this lab, you will begin by launching the sample network simulation that you built in Chapter 2. You will then dive right into some handy customizations and some cool optional features of Packet Tracer. Follow these steps:

Step 1. Launch Cisco Packet Tracer by clicking the **Packet Tracer** icon.

Step 2.   In Packet Tracer, select **File** and then **Open** to launch the First Network simulation you created in Chapter 2. If your network appears too small for you to see it clearly, select **View** and then **Zoom** or click the **Zoom In** shortcut icon at the top of the Packet Tracer interface.

Step 3.   Notice the Logical and Physical buttons that appear in the blue bar under the shortcut icons at the top of the Packet Tracer interface. The Logical button is selected by default, but you need to look at the physical equipment in the simulation so click the **Physical** button, as shown in Figure 3.1.

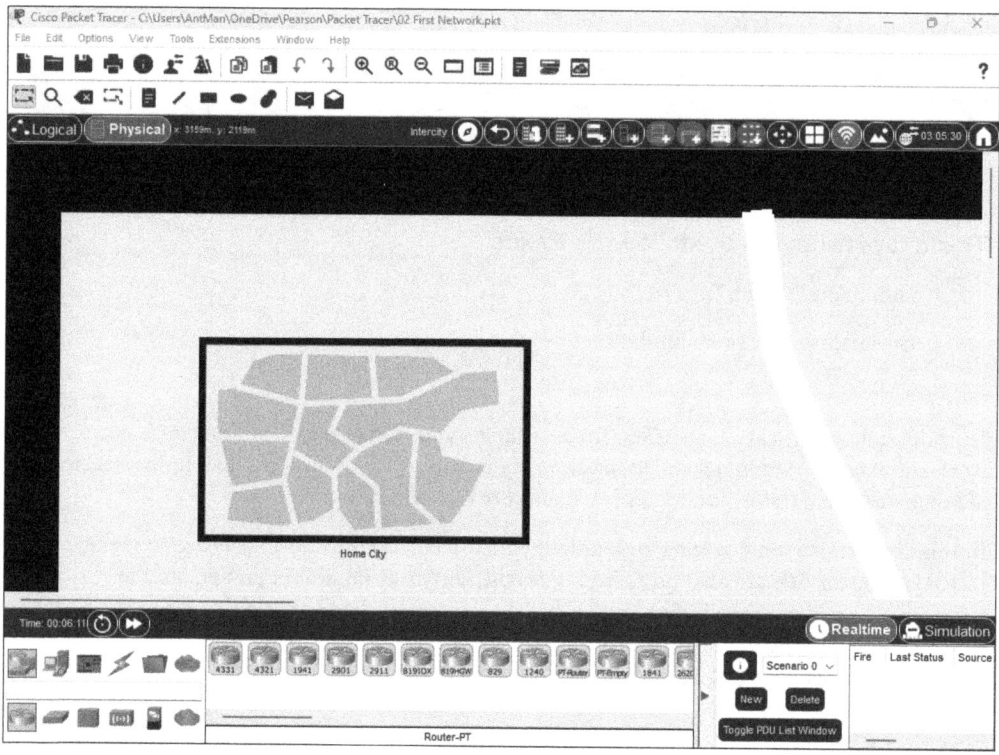

Figure 3.1   *Examining the Physical Topology*

Step 4.   To be able to actually see your physical equipment, click **Home City** to zoom in to that location. Then click **Corporate Office** to zoom in another level. Finally, click **Main Wiring Closet** to zoom in and see the router and switches that make up your first network.

Step 5.   To take a closer look at the router, right-click the router and choose **Inspect Front**. The router expands so you can see it better. Click the zoom-in magnifying class in the Front window so you can see the router even better, as shown in Figure 3.2. When you are done inspecting the router, click the **X** in the top-right corner of the Front window to close it.

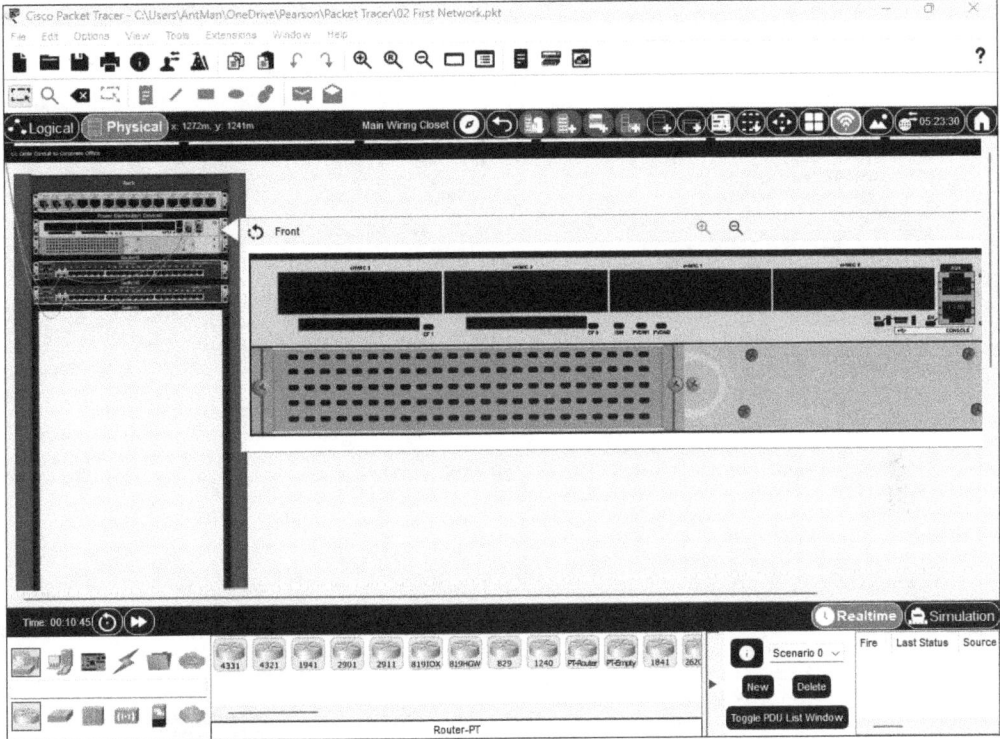

Figure 3.2 *Inspecting the Front of Your Router*

Step 6. To inspect the logical view, click the **Logical** button in the Packet Tracer interface. Notice that there is a blue bar with controls that is located just below the topology pane that contains your network. This bar displays the time your simulation has been running. Next to the time display is the button **Power Cycle Devices**. Click this button to power cycle all five of your network devices. Click **Yes** to confirm that you want to do this.

Step 7. Notice that your switch ports take some time to move to a forwarding state (due to Spanning Tree Protocol, which you'll learn about in Chapter 12, "Configure Rapid PVST+ Spanning Tree Protocol"). You can tell this from the LED indicators that take time to transition from orange to green. You can speed through such convergence delays by clicking the **Fast Forward Time** button located next to the Power Cycle Devices button.

Step 8. To begin making customizations to how Packet Tracer presents simulations and how it operates, go to the Preferences window by clicking **Options** and then **Preferences** if you are using the Windows version of Packet Tracer or **Cisco Packet Tracer** and then **Preferences** if you are on a Mac. Figure 3.3 shows the Preferences window.

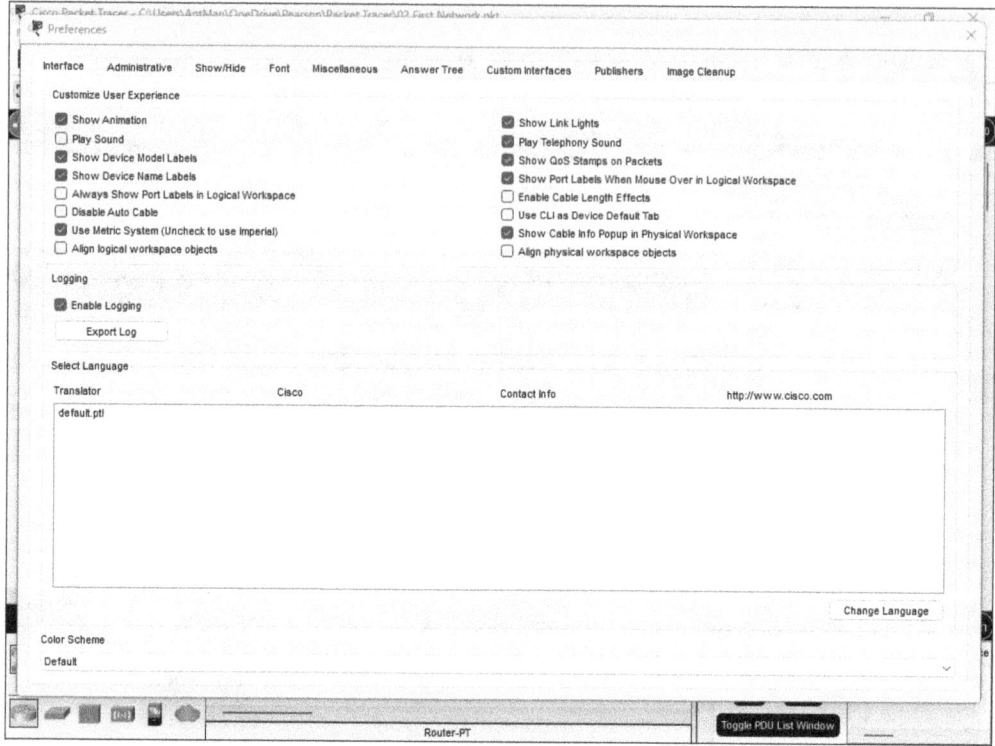

Figure 3.3   *Setting Preferences in Cisco Packet Tracer*

Step 9.   Ensure that the **Interface** tab is selected. You will use this tab to make changes to the user interface display of Packet Tracer. To always display the port labels, select the **Always Show Port Labels in Logical Workspace** checkbox. To turn off the LED link lights, clear the **Show Link Lights** checkbox.

Step 10.   Select the **Font** tab, where you can verify the font and color scheme of the CLI for network devices. The default Packet Tracer font is quite small in the CLI, and it is black text on a white background. You want to ensure that it is instead a white font on a black background. In the **CLI** area under **Dialogs**, change the font size to **20** points. In the **Colors** area, ensure Router IOS Text is set to **White**. Ensure that Router IOS Background is set to **Black**. When you are finished, click the **Apply** button.

Step 11.   Select the **Miscellaneous** tab and notice that, in the General area, you can control how often Cisco Packet Tracer automatically backs up your network simulation. The default is Off for this feature. Change this value to **10 minutes**.

Step 12.   Close the Preferences window.

Customizing Your First Simulation

Now you're ready to have some fun customizing your first simulation network. The steps in this lab will help you understand the vast scope of customizations you can make when working with your Cisco Packet Tracer networks.

Lab 3.2: Customizing Your First Simulation

If your First Network file is not open in Cisco Packet Tracer, be sure to open it now. This lab continues using that five-device topology that you originally created back in Chapter 2. In it, you'll add a server to your topology and take a quick glimpse at the many capabilities you can add to a simulation. Follow these steps:

Step 1.   In the lower-left corner of the Packet Tracer interface, click the **[End Devices]** icon and then click the **Server** icon in the list of available devices. Click above your **Switch0** device to place **Server0** in the topology. Figure 3.4 shows the result.

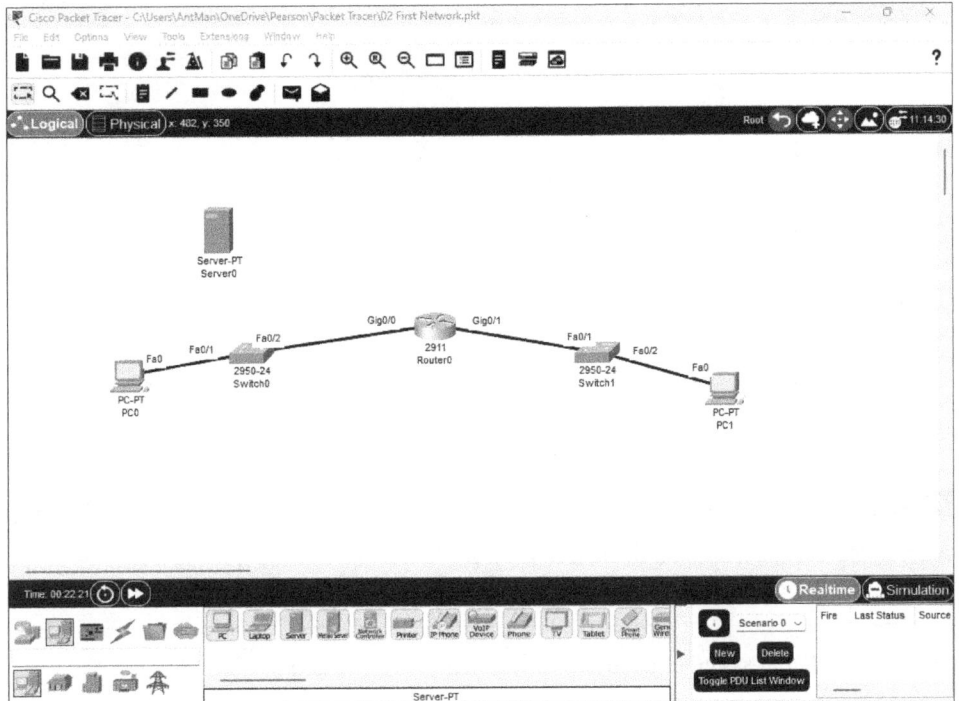

Figure 3.4 *Adding a Server to the Topology*

Step 2.   Click the **[Connections]** icon and then click the **Copper Straight-Through** cable option. Click **Server0** and then click the single port available, **FastEthernet0**. Then click **Switch0** and click the available port **FastEthernet0/3**. You have now connected Server0 to the topology using the ports you specified.

Note   You will not bother to configure full IP reachability for the new devices that you are adding but keep in mind that you certainly could do so if you wanted to continue practicing IP addressing assignment on these various devices. Don't worry, in the chapters that follow, you will be building plenty of "real-world" network configurations.

Step 3.   Click **Server0** to bring up the Server0 window. Click the **Services** tab to see the many services that you can configure for the Packet Tracer server device, as shown in Figure 3.5. Click the **DHCP** button in the list of services to see the many configuration options that are available for your DHCP server. When you are done examining these (and any other services you want to explore), close the **Server0** window.

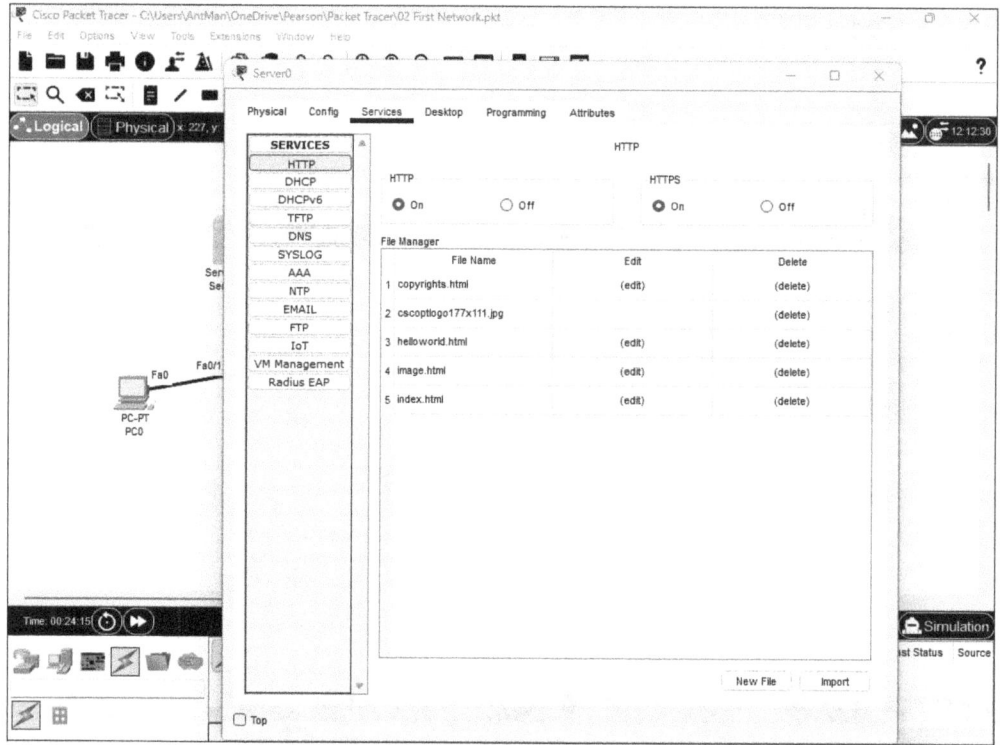

Figure 3.5   *Available Services with the Packet Tracer Server Device Option*

Step 4.   To add a wireless router to the topology, click the **[Network Devices]** icon and then click the **[Wireless Devices]** icon below it. From the available network devices, click the icon for **WRT300N**. Finally, click above Router0 to place **Wireless Router0** in your topology.

Step 5. From the devices area in the lower left of the interface, click the [Connections] icon and then click the **Automatically Choose Connection Type** option. Click **Wireless Router0** and then click **Router0** to connect these two devices.

Step 6. To add a laptop to the topology and install a wireless network interface, click the [End Devices] option and then click **Laptop** from the available network devices area. Place **Laptop0** above the Switch1 device in the topology and then click **Laptop0** to launch its properties window.

Step 7. Click **Zoom In** on the Physical tab to zoom in on the laptop and its interfaces. You might have to scroll in the window to see the installed interfaces. Click the **power button** on the laptop (to the right of the power cable shown connected to the laptop) to power off the laptop. Hover your mouse over the Ethernet port on the laptop (the installed PT-LAPTOP-NM-1CFE network interface). Click and drag this interface to the list of modules available for the laptop in the **Laptop0** window. Now click and drag the **WPC300N** wireless network interface in the list of modules and drop it in the empty laptop slot. Finally, power on Laptop0 by clicking the **power button** and close the Laptop0 window. Notice that wireless connectivity is shown flowing between the wireless router and your laptop. Figure 3.6 shows the updated topology.

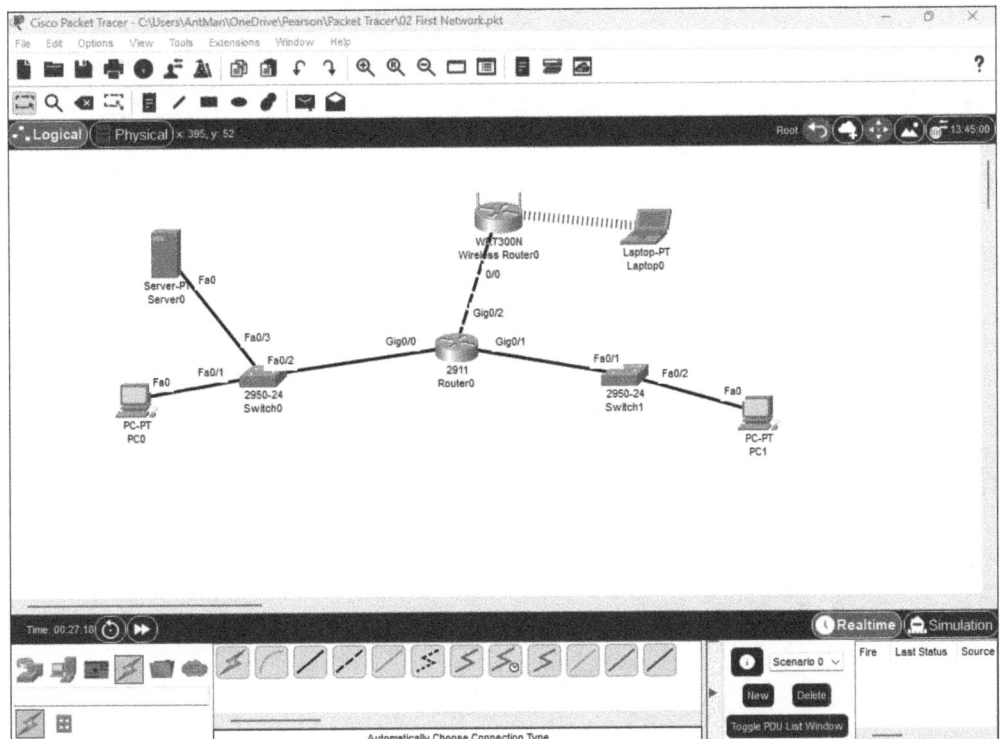

Figure 3.6 *Your Topology with New Devices Added*

Step 8.   To see how you would configure wireless in this lab, click **Wireless Router0** to bring up the device's properties window. Select the **GUI** tab to examine the configuration screens available for the wireless router. When you are done examining these screens, close the Wireless Router0 window.

Step 9.   Close Packet Tracer and save your network topology.

Chapter Review

In this chapter you have gotten a quick look at the impressive customization capabilities in Packet Tracer. You have also gotten a glimpse at a few of the many devices and many potential hardware configurations you can simulate with Cisco Packet Tracer.

In the next chapter you'll start your official CCNA training in Packet Tracer. You'll begin with a tour of the CLI structure and the key administration commands you need in order to be successful when working with Cisco devices.

Network Fundamentals

Networks are so complex today that there are plenty of fundamental concepts we should understand before we launch into more specific technologies. A significant portion of the questions you will face in your exam relate to the six chapters in Part II.

Here you will learn the basics of Cisco IOS and then move into the important topic of network interfaces and cables. You'll dig into the worlds of TCP/IP version 4 and TCP/IP version 6. Both of these protocol suites are already popular today. IPv4 should gradually fade away from use (although perhaps never completely), whereas IPv6 should become predominant in more and more installations and IoT applications. Part II includes the following chapters:

Chapter 4   Cisco IOS Basics

Chapter 5   Physical Interfaces and Cabling Types

Chapter 6   Configure and Verify IPv4 Addressing and Subnetting

Chapter 7   Configure IPv6

Chapter 8   Describe Wireless Principles

Chapter 9   Configure Switching Basics

Cisco IOS Basics

This chapter covers the following official CCNA 200-301 exam topics:

■ The Cisco IOS CLI

■ Configuring Cisco IOS

This is the first chapter of Part II, "Network Fundamentals," and it is an interesting one. If you look for the topics listed above in the CCNA 200-301 exam blueprint, you will not find them! No, Cisco does not call these out as specific objectives, but you will be in big trouble if you do not understand them. In this chapter, you will learn the basics of working with Cisco Internetwork Operating System (IOS). Without knowledge of Cisco IOS, you will be unable to tackle the many objectives in the exam topics that begin with "Configure" and "Verify." Don't worry: I will make sure you have a solid foundation in connecting to and configuring Cisco IOS.

This chapter covers the following essential terms and components:

■ Cisco IOS

■ User mode

■ Privileged mode

■ Password security

■ Command-line interface (CLI) help

■ Command history and editing

■ The show and debug commands

■ Configuration modes

■ Saving configurations

■ Erasing configurations

Chapter Pretest

1. What symbol ends the prompt for user mode on a Cisco IOS router?

   _____

2. What command do you use to enter privileged mode from user mode?

   _____

3. What command do you use to protect privileged mode with the encrypted password P3arson232?

   _____

4. What is the result of entering `conf?` at the CLI?

   _____

5. You would like IOS to recall the last command you entered. What keystroke does this?

   _____

6. What type of Cisco IOS command would you use to see packet activity in near real time?

   _____

7. What is the router prompt format for a device that is in interface configuration mode?

   _____

8. What configuration file is used at boot by a Cisco device?

   _____

9. What command do you use to save your configuration on a Cisco device?

   _____

10. What command can you use to erase your startup configuration?

   _____

Answers

1. `>`

2. `enable`

3. `enable secret P3arson232`

4. The help system displays all commands in the current mode that start with `conf`.

5. Up arrow or Ctrl+P

6. `debug`

7. `R1(config-if)#`

8. startup-config file

9. `copy running-config startup-config`

10. `erase startup-config`

The Cisco IOS CLI

Most Cisco routers and switches use Internetwork Operating System (IOS) as their operating system. You access IOS by using a console connection or Secure Shell (SSH). (Telnet is also an option but is frowned upon because it is a plaintext protocol, which makes it a nightmare for security teams.)

When you access the IOS CLI, you are in user EXEC mode, which is typically called user mode. You can immediately tell you are in user mode because the prompt uses the > symbol.

User mode is for running simple verification commands. It is not designed to permit much device configuration. To begin making intense configurations, you type the **enable** command to access privileged mode in IOS. You can tell you are in privileged mode because your prompt ends with a # symbol. Example 4.1 shows the process of accessing privileged mode on a device and then using the **exit** command to return to user mode.

Example 4.1 *User Mode and Privileged Mode in Cisco IOS*

```
Router>
Router> enable
Router# exit
Router>
```

Note You will not see many Cisco veterans type the full command **enable**. This is because shortcuts are permitted when no other command matches the character pattern. So you can just type **en** and press Enter on the keyboard to enter the **enable** command in user mode. Another frequent veteran move is to use tab autocomplete. If you type **en** and then press tab, the command autocompletes. This is very useful when you are typing in long, multiple-word commands.

Privileged mode on a Cisco device is like the entryway for all more specific configurations. For example, Example 4.2 shows how to set the hostname of a device. Notice that you need to enter global configuration mode with the `configure terminal` (or `config t`) command. You can then configure the hostname of the device.

Example 4.2 *Setting the Device Hostname*

```
Router> enable
Router# configure terminal
Enter configuration commands, one per line. End with CNTL/Z.
Router(config)# hostname R1
R1(config)# exit
R1#
%SYS-5-CONFIG_I: Configured from console by console
R1#
```

Let's now look at how easy it is to protect a Cisco device with a password. Example 4.3 shows how to use the `enable secret` command to set password protection for privileged mode. It also shows how to enter the console port and use the `login` command along with the `password` command to set a password on the console connection.

Example 4.3 *Setting Password Security*

```
R1# configure terminal
Enter configuration commands, one per line. End with CNTL/Z.
R1(config)# enable secret WeL0veP3arson
R1(config)# line console 0
R1(config-line)# login
% Login disabled on line 0, until 'password' is set
R1(config-line)# password Th3yL0veP3arson
R1(config-line)# end
R1#
%SYS-5-CONFIG_I: Configured from console by console
R1#
```

Another wonderful feature of Cisco IOS is its built-in help system. Table 4.1 shows the help commands and features that are available.

Table 4.1 *Cisco IOS Help Commands*

Command	Result
?	Shows help for all commands in the current mode
mycommand ?	Shows all the first parameter options for the given command
mycom?	Shows all the commands that begin with mycom
mycommand par1 ?	Shows all the second parameter options for the given command

As you complete Packet Tracer labs, be sure to take advantage of and experiment with the valuable IOS help system. Even longtime IOS users rely on this convenient and accurate system.

Cisco IOS also offers a command history buffer and command editing capabilities. As you enter commands in Cisco IOS, the operating system retains a history of your commands and allows you to easily recall them and edit them if needed. By default, Cisco IOS retains the last 10 commands. Table 4.2 lists the keystrokes you can use to easily call up previous commands and then quickly edit them, if required.

Table 4.2 *Working with the Command History Buffer*

Keyboard Action	Result
Up arrow or Ctrl+P	Shows the most recently used command; pressing it again moves backward through the list
Down arrow or Ctrl+N	Shows the next command in the history buffer
Left arrow or Ctrl+B	Moves the cursor backward in the currently displayed command
Right arrow or Ctrl+F	Moves the cursor forward in the currently displayed command
Backspace	Moves the cursor backward in the currently displayed command while deleting characters

Lab 4.1: The Cisco IOS CLI

To complete this Hands-On Lab Practice Assignment, download the assigned Packet Tracer file from the book's companion website and perform the lab on your locally installed version of Packet Tracer. You will be following the instructions in the lab, and your performance will be evaluated.

In this lab, you will practice with basic IOS configurations in the topology shown in Figure 4.1.

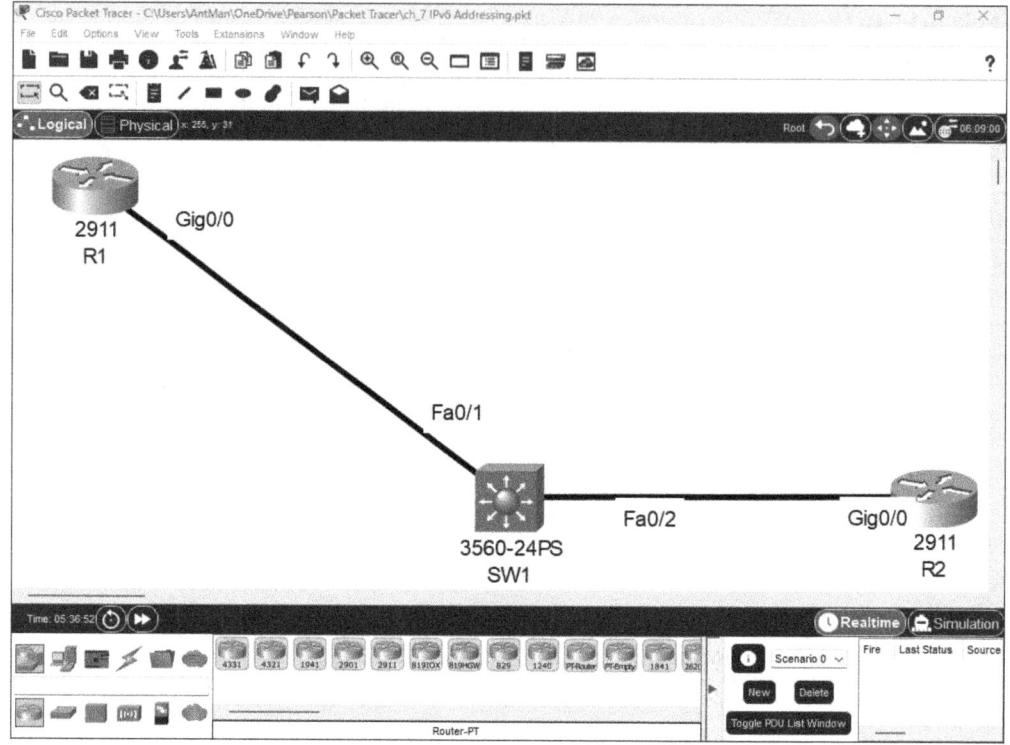

Figure 4.1   *The Cisco IOS CLI*

Topic Quiz

1. What symbol ends the prompt for privileged mode on a Cisco IOS router?

 A. >

 B. :

 C. @

 D. #

2. What command in Cisco IOS do you use to enter global configuration mode?

 A. enable

 B. configure terminal

 C. login

 D. enable secret

3. What Cisco IOS prompt signifies global configuration mode?

   A. `Router#`

   B. `Router(config)#`

   C. `Router>`

   D. `Router(config-if)#`

4. What command is used with the `password` command to configure the checking of passwords in console configuration mode?

   A. `login`

   B. `enable secret`

   C. `configure terminal`

   D. `enable`

5. What character do you enter to see a list of all the commands that are supported in a given Cisco IOS mode?

   A. #

   B. >

   C. ?

   D. *

6. You would like to have the cursor move backward one position in a Cisco IOS command without deleting any characters. Which of the following would you use?

   A. Left arrow or Ctrl+B

   B. Left arrow or Ctrl+1

   C. Left arrow or Ctrl+A

   D. Left arrow or Shift+B

Topic Quiz Answers

1. D is correct. The default IOS prompt for privileged mode is *hostname*#.

2. B is correct. You use the `configure terminal` command in privileged mode to enter global configuration mode.

3. B is correct. You can tell you are in global configuration mode by examining the router prompt. IOS signifies global configuration mode with `Router(config)#`.

4. A is correct. You use the `login` command in console configuration mode to have IOS prompt for a password upon user login.

5. C is correct. You use the `?` character to access the Cisco IOS help system.

6. A is correct. Cisco IOS has shortcuts for quickly editing commands. To move a character backward in a command without deleting a character, press the left arrow key or Ctrl+B.

Configuring Cisco IOS

An expert method of Cisco device configuration involves making small configuration changes and then verifying these changes. When it comes to verifying and exploring Cisco device configurations, the two shining stars are Cisco `show` commands and `debug` commands. Example 4.4 shows the use of the `show ip interface brief` command on a Cisco device to quickly verify the interface statuses and IP address configurations.

Example 4.4   *Using a Sample show Command*

```
R2>show ip interface brief
Interface          IP-Address      OK? Method Status                Protocol
GigabitEthernet0/0   10.10.10.1    YES manual up                    up
GigabitEthernet0/1   unassigned    YES unset  administratively down down
GigabitEthernet0/2   unassigned    YES unset  administratively down down
Vlan1                unassigned    YES unset  administratively down down
R2>
```

While `show` commands are great and give you a look at status at a given moment they don't allow you to see packet or event activity in real time. This is what Cisco `debug` commands are for. Example 4.5 shows the use of `debug ip packet` on a Cisco device. In this example, you can see OSPF hello packets being received from a neighboring device.

Example 4.5   *Using a debug Command on a Cisco Device*

```
R2# debug ip packet
Packet debugging is on
R2#
IP: s=10.10.10.100 (GigabitEthernet0/0), d=224.0.0.5 len 20, rcvd 2

IP: s=10.10.10.100 (GigabitEthernet0/0), d=224.0.0.5 len 20, rcvd 2

IP: s=10.10.10.100 (GigabitEthernet0/0), d=224.0.0.5 len 20, rcvd 2

IP: s=10.10.10.100 (GigabitEthernet0/0), d=224.0.0.5 len 20, rcvd 2
```

```
IP: s=10.10.10.100 (GigabitEthernet0/0), d=224.0.0.5 len 20, rcvd 2

IP: s=10.10.10.100 (GigabitEthernet0/0), d=224.0.0.5 len 20, rcvd 2

IP: s=10.10.10.100 (GigabitEthernet0/0), d=224.0.0.5 len 20, rcvd 2
R2# undebug all
All possible debugging has been turned off
R2#
```

Note   Notice the use of the `undebug all` command to disable the debug activity. This disables any and all debugging that might be running. To disable only the command `debug ip packet`, you can enter `no debug ip packet`.

You make configurations in IOS by using the different modes that are available. Earlier in this chapter you learned about global configuration mode. Another important mode is interface configuration mode. Example 4.6 shows the process of assigning an IP address and setting a description on a Cisco IOS device interface. Notice how the prompt changes as the example moves from mode to mode with these configuration changes.

Example 4.6   *Using Interface Configuration Mode*

```
R1> enable
R1# configure terminal
Enter configuration commands, one per line.  End with CNTL/Z.
R1(config)# interface gigabitethernet0/0
R1(config-if)# ip address 10.10.10.1 255.255.255.0
R1(config-if)# description LINK TO HQ
R1(config-if)# no shutdown

R1(config-if)#
%LINK-5-CHANGED: Interface GigabitEthernet0/0, changed state to up

%LINEPROTO-5-UPDOWN: Line protocol on Interface GigabitEthernet0/0, changed state to up

R1(config-if)# end
R1#
```

IOS configurations are stored in configuration files. For example, the startup-config file is used when a device boots and is stored in the NVRAM of the device. When the device starts, this configuration file is copied into RAM, where it becomes the running-config file. When you have made changes to a Cisco device, verified the changes, and are ready to save the configuration, you issue the `copy running-config startup-config` command, as shown in Example 4.7. The commonly used shortcut for this important command is `copy run star`.

Example 4.7   *Saving an IOS Device Configuration*

```
Router> enable
Router# configure terminal
Enter configuration commands, one per line.  End with CNTL/Z.
Router(config)# hostname R1
R1(config)# exit
R1#
%SYS-5-CONFIG_I: Configured from console by console

R1# copy running-config startup-config
Destination filename [startup-config]?
Building configuration...
[OK]
R1#
```

Note   You can verify configuration files with the appropriate `show` command. For example, to see the startup-config file, you use `show startup-config`. To see the running-config file, you use `show running-config`.

What about erasing these configuration files? Well, with the running-config file stored in RAM, reloading the device does the trick. For the startup-config file, you just use the `erase startup-config` command.

Lab 4.2: Configuring Cisco IOS

To complete this Hands-On Lab Practice Assignment, download the assigned Packet Tracer file from the book's companion website and perform the lab on your locally installed version of Packet Tracer. You will be following the instructions in the lab, and your performance will be evaluated.

In this lab, you will perform configurations and verifications in Packet Tracer, using the topology shown in Figure 4.2.

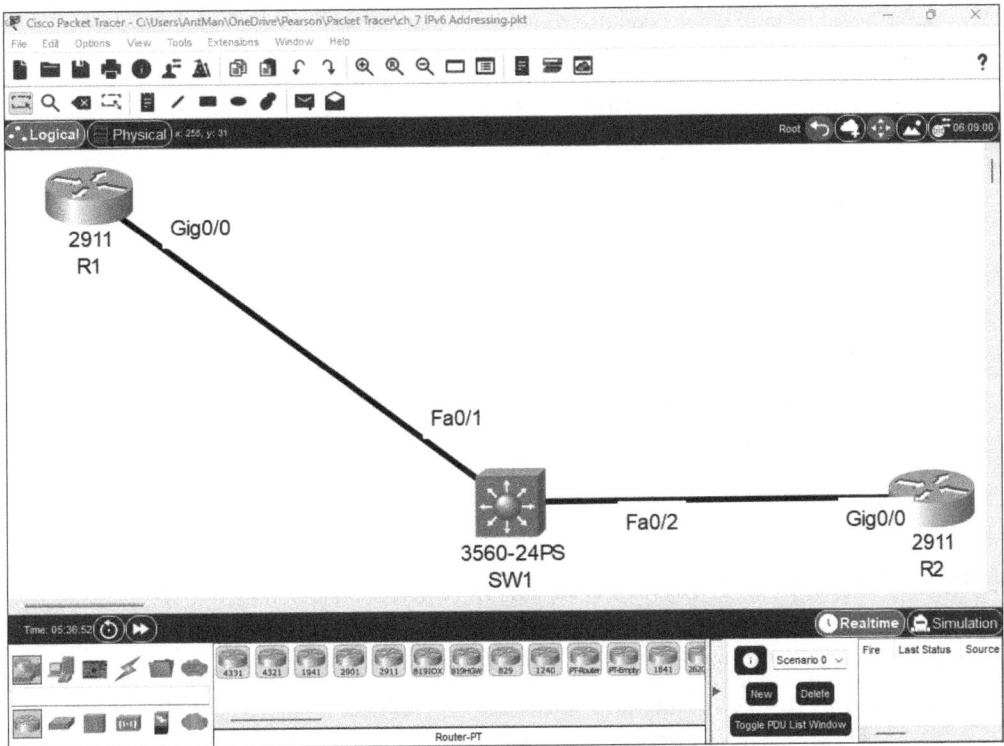

Figure 4.2 *Configuring Cisco IOS*

Topic Quiz

1. What show command would you use to view a summary of your device interfaces and their statuses?

   A. show version

   B. show interface

   C. show ip interface brief

   D. show ip interface

2. What command would you use to enter interface configuration mode for the gigabitethernet0/1 interface?

   A. `interface gigabitethernet0/1`

   B. `ip interface gigabitethernet0/1`

   C. `interface ip gigabitethernet0/1`

   D. `enable interface gigabitethernet0/1`

3. What command can you use to turn off all enabled debug commands on a Cisco router?

   A. `debug off`

   B. `disable debug all`

   C. `stop debug all`

   D. `undebug all`

Topic Quiz Answers

1. C is correct. The `show ip interface brief` command allows you to see a summary of the interfaces on a Cisco device.

2. A is correct. To enter interface configuration mode for gigabitethernet0/1, use the `interface gigabitethernet0/1` command.

3. D is correct. Use `undebug all` to disable all debug commands.

Lab 4.3: Chapter Review

To complete this Hands-On Lab Practice Assignment, download the assigned Packet Tracer file from the book's companion website and perform the lab on your locally installed version of Packet Tracer. You will be following the instructions in the lab, and your performance will be evaluated.

In this lab, you will carry out and verify the various IOS-related tasks described in this chapter. You will perform this review against the topology shown in Figure 4.3.

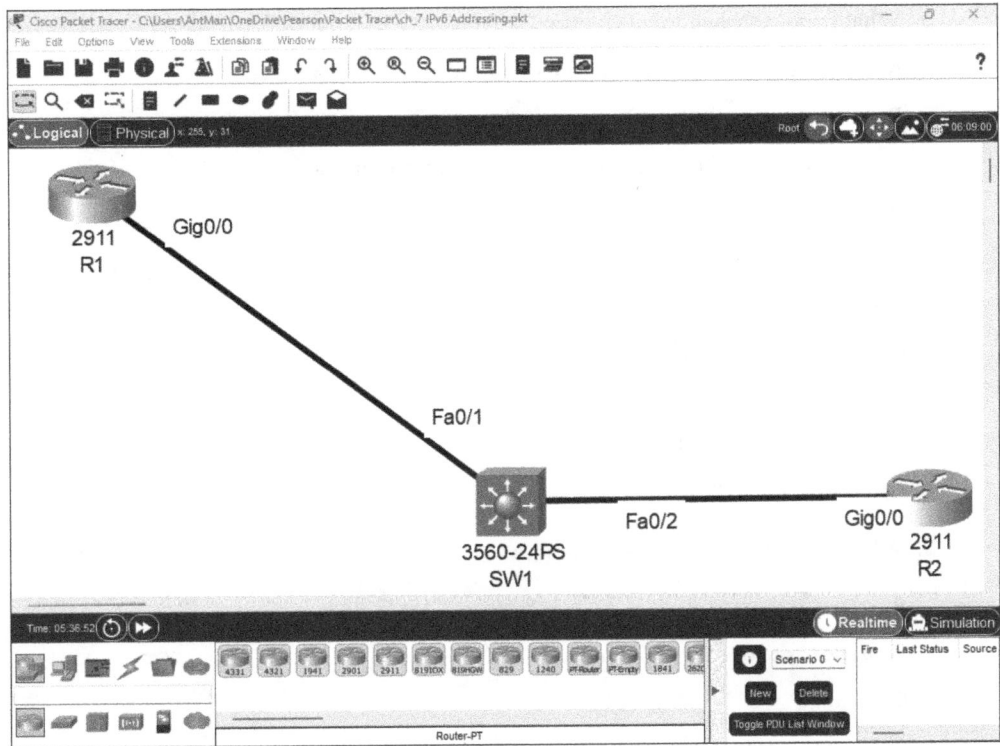

Figure 4.3 *The Cisco IOS Chapter Review Packet Tracer Lab*

Review Questions

1. What command can you use to quickly return to privileged mode from interface configuration mode?

  A. start

  B. home

  C. return

  D. end

2. What prompt signifies global configuration mode?

  A. Router(config)#

  B. Router(global)#

  C. Router(enable)#

  D. Router(edit)#

3. What happens when you type the ? character in user mode?

    A. Nothing. ? is not accepted in user mode.

    B. IOS displays all possible commands.

    C. IOS displays all the commands available in user mode.

    D. IOS enables debugging.

4. When moving through the command history buffer on an IOS device, what do you use to move to the next command?

    A. Right arrow or Ctrl+F

    B. Down arrow or Ctrl+N

    C. Up arrow or Ctrl+P

    D. Left arrow or Ctrl+B

5. What command do you use to assign a description to a Cisco IOS device interface?

    A. `name`

    B. `description`

    C. `enable`

    D. `text`

Answers to Review Questions

1. D is correct. You can use the `end` command to quickly return to privileged mode from interface configuration mode.

2. A is correct. Global configuration uses a `Router(config)#` prompt.

3. C is correct. The context-sensitive help system displays all the commands available in user mode.

4. B is correct. When you are moving through the command history buffer, use the down arrow key or Ctrl+N to move to the next command.

5. B is correct. The `description` command allows you to set a description on an interface.

Chapter 5

Physical Interfaces and Cabling Types

This chapter covers the following official CCNA 200-301 exam topics:

- Single-mode fiber, multimode fiber, copper

- Interface and cable issues

This chapter ensures that you are ready for questions related to these topics in the "Network Fundamentals" section of the CCNA 200-301 exam blueprint from Cisco Systems. Remember that this chapter covers just a portion of the "Network Fundamentals" section.

It is time to get physical in our discussion of networking technologies. As in all other areas of information technology, there have been many advancements in this regard. As our networks have had to deal with more and more data (including audio and video data), we have needed faster and faster physical solutions to move that data.

This chapter covers the following essential terms and components:

- Ethernet

- Copper media

- Unshielded twisted pair (UTP)

- Fiber media

- Cat 5e

- Cat 6

- Auto MDI-X

- PoE

Chapter Pretest

1. Name a category of Ethernet cabling that supports speeds of 10 Gbps.

_____

2. What is the speed of 1000BASE-T?

_____

3. What are the two major categories of fiber-optic technology in network cables today?

_____

_____

4. What is the benefit of PoE in a network?

_____

5. What command allows you to quickly see the various errors that might have occurred on Gi0/1 on a Cisco switch?

_____

6. What is the typical size of a giant frame in a Gigabit Ethernet data center?

_____

7. What is the typical size of a baby giant frame in a modern network?

_____

8. Runts are frames that are smaller than what size?

_____

9. Name the two duplex options.

_____

_____

Answers

1. Cat 6 supports 10 Gbps Ethernet.

2. 1000BASE-T operates at a speed of 1000 Mbps, or 1 Gbps.

3. Single-mode fiber and multimode fiber

4. To provide power over the network cable for devices like VoIP phones, wireless access points, and IP video cameras

5. `show interface gi0/1`

6. A giant frame is an Ethernet frame that has a total size (including all headers and the frame check sequence) of more than 1518 bytes. A giant frame can be up to approximately 9216 bytes in size. Giant frames are also known as jumbo frames.

7. A baby giant frame has a total size of more than 1518 bytes but less than 1600 bytes.

8. 64 bytes

9. Full-duplex and half-duplex

Single-Mode Fiber, Multimode Fiber, and Copper

Ethernet is king today, including when it comes to cabling. Ethernet is no longer made up of just copper at its core. Fiber options also exist within the standards and permit blazing speeds over relatively long distances.

Ethernet continues to evolve and get faster. Table 5.1 list some of the forms you should be aware of.

Table 5.1   *Examples of Ethernet Technologies*

Name	IEEE Standard Number	Speed	Standard Name	Cable Type, Maximum Length
Ethernet	802.3	10 Mbps	10BASE-T	Copper, 100 m
Fast Ethernet	802.3u	100 Mbps	100BASE-T	Copper, 100 m
Gigabit Ethernet	802.3z	1000 Mbps	1000BASE-LX	Fiber, 5,000 m
Gigabit Ethernet	802.3ab	1000 Mbps	1000BASE-T	Copper, 100 m
10-Gigabit Ethernet	802.3an	10 Gbps	10GBASE-T	Copper, 100 m
40-Gigabit Ethernet	802.3ba	40 Gbps	40GBASE-LR4	Fiber, 10,000 m

Note   For a long time, we had to worry about the way in which the copper cables inside a physical Ethernet cable were arranged. There was a straight-through pin-out for connecting unlike devices (a router and a switch, for example). There was a crossover pin-out for connecting like devices (a switch to a switch, for example). Although these pin-outs still exist, they are much less problematic because modern Cisco switches support auto MDI-X, a technology that enables a switch to work correctly with whatever cable is connected between the switch and any other device. By the way, auto MDI-X stands for automatic medium-dependent interface crossover. You can see why Cisco came up with an easier way to say that!

The most popular forms of Ethernet use unshielded twisted pair (UTP). There are many categories of UTP, abbreviated as follows: Cat 1, Cat 2, Cat 3, Cat 4, Cat 5, Cat 5e, Cat 6, Cat 6a, and Cat 7. Each of the UTP cable categories is technologically advanced compared to its predecessor. For example, Cat 5e is capable of carrying 1 Gbps Ethernet, whereas Cat 6 is capable of carrying 10 Gbps Ethernet.

Multimode Versus Single-Mode Fiber

If an Ethernet cable does not have copper in its core, it uses fiber optics. The signals pass through a fiber-optic cable using glass as the transmission medium. The signal is a light that transmits the 0s and 1s that systems use to communicate. While it is strange to think about glass being inside a network cable, keep in mind that the glass used in the core of the cable is a long, thin, flexible "fiber" of glass—not the glass you look through when you drive a car. Even though fiber-optic cable is quite flexible, it is very important for a fiber-optic cable plant installation never to exceed the fiber-optic cable's bend radius.

There are two extremely popular variations of fiber-optic media: multimode fiber and single-mode fiber. Multimode fiber permits multiple angles of light waves, called *modes*, to propagate through the core.

Single-mode fiber has a much smaller diameter core for the network cable. To use this much smaller fiber-optic strand, a laser-based transmitter sends the light at a single angle through the core.

Ethernet Shared Media Versus Point-to-Point

Thankfully, using Ethernet in a "shared media" environment is a thing of the past. *Shared media* refers to Ethernet designs that use hubs (or a coaxial cable run) as networking devices. Hubs force the network devices to operate in half-duplex mode and use CSMA/CD to deal with collisions that occur.

Modern networks use switches with Ethernet and permit the creation of *point-to-point links* that function independently from each other at Layer 1, making collisions extremely rare (or even impossible if all the devices are healthy and configured properly). It is possible to run a system in full-duplex mode with such a configuration. Systems enjoy sending and receiving data at the same time as other systems in the infrastructure, which makes for a wonderful, worry-free, and collision-less network.

Note   Creating a LAN by using Ethernet in this full-duplex, point-to-point manner creates a separate collision domain for each port in the LAN. With only a single endpoint device (PC, server, AP, phone, printer, and so on) in the collision domain, there is no chance of collisions.

Power over Ethernet (PoE)

Your phone calls are not transmitted over a dedicated phone (voice) network the way they were when I was making calls in high school (in the mid-1980s). Today, most voice traffic is transmitted over the same network as data. Wouldn't it be nice if you could plug your voice over IP (VoIP) phone into a switch using an Ethernet cable and not only allow the phone to communicate but also allow it to receive the power it needs to operate? That is exactly what Power over Ethernet (PoE) makes possible!

Note   VoIP phones are not the only devices that benefit from PoE. This solution is also hugely valuable for devices like IP video cameras and wireless access points.

Like the standards for all our other tech today, the PoE standards have evolved over time. Here is a quick recap for you:

- **IEEE 802.3af:** This is the original 2003 standard, which provides up to 15.4 W of DC power per port.

- **IEEE 802.3at:** This 2009 standard (called PoE+) provides 25.5 W of power.

- **IEEE 802.3bu:** This 2016 amendment introduces single-pair Power over Data Lines (PoDL) and is used for industrial applications; power can be set from 0.5 W to 50 W.

- **IEEE 802.3bt:** This 2018 standard provides up to 100 W of power; such great power needs are required by some wireless access points and sophisticated surveillance cameras.

Various network equipment vendors have also deployed their own proprietary PoE implementations, with Cisco leading the pack. These early proprietary implementations drove adoption of PoE and put pressure on the IEEE to standardize it.

Serial Connections

Serial connections are legacy connections for device communication, and you will not see serial connections deployed in new installations today. However, you may still find them in use in data centers to make certain types of WAN connections. Unfortunately, selecting the correct serial cable can be a complicated business. Here are just some of the questions you must answer:

- Is the router being connected to a data terminal equipment (DTE) or data communications equipment (DCE) device?

- Is a male or female connector required on the cable?

- What signaling standard does the device require?

Note   Although there are many types of serial cables that you can implement in a network, there is one critical command you use to check the type and the health of such a cable: `show controllers`. For the CCNA 200-301 exam, you need to know this command and its output.

The following is an example of the output of the `show controllers` command:

```
HD unit 0, idb = 0x29A82C, driver structure at 0x2A1DF0
buffer size 1524 HD unit 0, V.35 DCE cable, clockrate 64000
```

In this output, `DCE cable` indicates that the DCE side of the cable is attached to this particular interface.

Topic Quiz

1. What technology eliminates the major concerns about crossover versus straight-through cables?

   A. STP

   B. RSTP

   C. Auto MDI-X

   D. FabricPath

2. Which of the following is not an example of a question you might need to answer when provisioning a device with the correct serial cable?

   A. Is the router being connected to a DTE or DCE device?

   B. Is the port part of the chassis, or is it modular?

   C. Is a male or female connector required on the cable?

   D. What signaling standard does the device require?

3. What physical medium is used with 40GBASE-LR4?

   A. Copper

   B. Fiber

   C. IR

   D. Radio frequency/radio waves

Topic Quiz Answers

1. **C** is correct. Auto MDI-X permits a switch to adapt to the type of cable connected to the device.

2. **B** is correct. Whether the port you are connecting is part of a module or part of the chassis typically is not relevant to the cable type or connector, whereas the other questions listed here are relevant.

3. **B** is correct. 40GBASE-LR4 uses single-mode fiber as the transmission medium.

Troubleshoot Interface and Cable Issues (Collisions, Errors, Duplex, Speed)

Many things can go wrong when you are dealing with a technology as complex as local-area networking, and there are many issues you should be aware of. Note that many of the following issues are not explicitly listed in the CCNA 200-301 exam blueprint, but they are very likely to be included on the exam:

■ The **show interface** command on a switch displays a ton of potential errors and problems that occur due to interface and cable issues. Notice these errors in the last section of the output shown in Example 5.1.

Example 5.1 *show interface Command Output on a Cisco Switch*

```
Switch# show interface gi0/1
GigabitEthernet0/1 is up, line protocol is up (connected)
  Hardware is iGbE, address is fa16.3eb4.b62b (bia fa16.3eb4.b62b)
  MTU 1500 bytes, BW 1000000 Kbit/sec, DLY 10 usec,
     reliability 255/255, txload 1/255, rxload 1/255
  Encapsulation ARPA, loopback not set
  Keepalive set (10 sec)
  Unknown, Unknown, link type is auto, media type is unknown media type
  output flow-control is unsupported, input flow-control is unsupported
  Auto-duplex, Auto-speed, link type is auto, media type is unknown
  input flow-control is off, output flow-control is unsupported
  ARP type: ARPA, ARP Timeout 04:00:00
  Last input never, output 00:00:00, output hang never
  Last clearing of "show interface" counters never
  Input queue: 0/75/0/0 (size/max/drops/flushes); Total output drops: 32562
  Queueing strategy: fifo
  Output queue: 0/0 (size/max)
  5 minute input rate 0 bits/sec, 0 packets/sec
  5 minute output rate 0 bits/sec, 0 packets/sec
    6783 packets input, 0 bytes, 0 no buffer
    Received 14 broadcasts (0 multicasts)
    0 runts, 0 giants, 0 throttles
    0 input errors, 0 CRC, 0 frame, 0 overrun, 0 ignored
    0 watchdog, 0 multicast, 0 pause input
    108456 packets output, 7107939 bytes, 0 underruns
    0 output errors, 0 collisions, 2 interface resets
    0 unknown protocol drops
    0 babbles, 0 late collision, 0 deferred
    0 lost carrier, 0 no carrier, 0 pause output
    0 output buffer failures, 0 output buffers swapped out
Switch#
```

■ Collisions should not occur in a properly designed switched network. Today, we have the ability to design full-duplex networks using switches that intelligently queue frames to prevent them from being sent simultaneously out an interface.

■ Errors might occur in a network for a wide variety of reasons. For example, there could be electrical interference somewhere or a bad network interface card that is not able to frame things correctly for the network. Remember that checking the frame check sequence (FCS) is often the best way to catch these errors. Each time a router forwards a packet on an Ethernet network, it replaces and rewrites the Layer 2 Ethernet header information and provides a new FCS.

- Duplex used to be a big concern in Ethernet LANs. As described earlier in this chapter, with hubs in a network, in the past you needed to ensure that duplex mismatches did not occur between full-duplex (switched) areas and half-duplex areas. Today autonegotiation to full-duplex between devices is common. For the CCNA 200-301 exam, you need to understand that if an older device is hard coded to half-duplex, and you code the LAN device connected to full-duplex, a duplex mismatch may result. Such errors can be difficult to track down because some packets typically make it through the connection fine, whereas others are dropped. In networks that operate in half-duplex, carrier-sense multiple access with collision detection (CSMA/CD) is used to allow devices to operate on a half-duplex network.

- Speed is another area where conflict can occur, but this is also becoming a less common problem as technologies advance. For example, 1 Gbps interfaces are quite common now and operate with each other seamlessly at 1 Gbps. The issue, again, is that older equipment might default to a slower speed, causing a speed mismatch.

- Runts are Ethernet frames that are less than 64 bytes and may be caused by excessive collisions. Of course, these frames have become rarer as networks have become nearly collision free.

- Today many technologies are enhancing networks by adding information to Ethernet frames. This results in jumbo (or giant) frames—which are typically frames of 9216 bytes for Gigabit Ethernet but technically can refer to anything over the standard IP MTU (maximum transmission unit) of 1500 bytes.

- What if an Ethernet frame is just a little larger than the standard MTU of 1500 bytes? Specifically, what if a frame is 1600 bytes in size? This is what networkers term a baby giant frame.

Although the indicators in the preceding list are by far the most likely to appear on the CCNA 200-301 exam, the following conditions are also often included in **show interface** output:

- **Output hang:** The number of hours, minutes, and seconds since the interface was last reset because of a transmission that took too long.

- **Input drops:** The number of frames dropped on the input interface. Typically, this is a result of congestion on the interface.

- **Output drops:** The number of frames dropped on the output interface.

- **No buffer:** The number of input packets dropped due to a lack of available buffer space.

- **Broadcasts:** The number of broadcasts received on the interface. (Note that this is not an error.)

■ **Throttles:** The number of times the local interface requested another local interface within the switch to slow down.

■ **Input errors:** The total of no buffer, runt, giant, CRC, frame, overrun, ignored, and abort errors.

■ **CRC:** The failure of the cyclic redundancy check on an input packet. This can be detected thanks to the FCS field in the Ethernet header.

■ **Frame:** The number of frames received that did not end on an 8-bit byte boundary.

■ **Overrun:** The number of times the receiver hardware was unable to transfer received data to a hardware buffer because the input rate exceeded the receiver's ability to process the data.

■ **Ignored:** The frames dropped because the interface hardware buffers ran low on internal buffer space.

■ **Abort:** An illegal sequence of 1 bit detected in a frame received.

■ **Dribble condition detected:** A dribble bit error, indicating that a frame is slightly too long. The frame is still accepted in this case.

■ **Underruns:** The number of times the sender has been running faster than the switch can handle.

■ **Interface resets:** The number of times the interface was reset. This is normally the result of missed keepalives from a neighboring device.

■ **Alignment errors:** Misaligned reads and writes.

■ **Babbles:** The number of transmitted frames greater than 1518 bytes in size.

■ **Late collision:** A collision detected after transmitting the first 64 bytes of the frame. According to CSMA/CD and the original Ethernet definition, the time needed to transmit 64 bytes is the maximum time required for a collision to be detected at the furthest interface and a "jamming detected" signal to propagate back to the sender. Under normal conditions, no collision should occur after 64 bytes have been transmitted. If it does, then something is quite wrong. In modern networks, this indicates a manual duplex mismatch (which on Cisco devices would by default be detected by CDP). In older networks, it meant a noncompliant Ethernet implementation or a host being connected on a segment physically longer than the maximum allowed distance.

■ **Deferred:** The number of frames transmitted successfully after waiting because the media was busy.

■ **Lost carrier:** The number of times the carrier was lost during transmission.

■ **No carrier:** The number of times the carrier was not present during the transmission.

■ **Output buffer failures:** The number of times a frame was not output from the output hold queue because of a shortage of shared memory.

■ **Output buffers swapped out:** The number of frames stored in main memory when the output queue is full.

If counters in the output related to FCS, CRC, alignment, or runs are incrementing, check for a duplex mismatch on the device. Duplex mismatch is a situation where the switch is operating at full-duplex and the connected device is operating at half-duplex or vice versa. A duplex mismatch results in extremely slow performance, intermittent connectivity, and loss of connection. Tracking down duplex mismatches can be tough because a variety of symptoms are possible. Note that some problems, such as slow performance, could also be caused by other issues.

Note   Although this section focuses on switches, remember that many of these same conditions appear in **show interface** output from routers as well.

Lab 5.1: Working with Interfaces and Cable Types

To complete this Hands-On Lab Practice Assignment, download the assigned Packet Tracer file from the book's companion website and perform the lab on your locally installed version of Packet Tracer. You will be following the instructions in the lab, and your performance will be evaluated.

In this lab, you will work with interfaces and cables on Cisco routers using the topology shown in Figure 5.1.

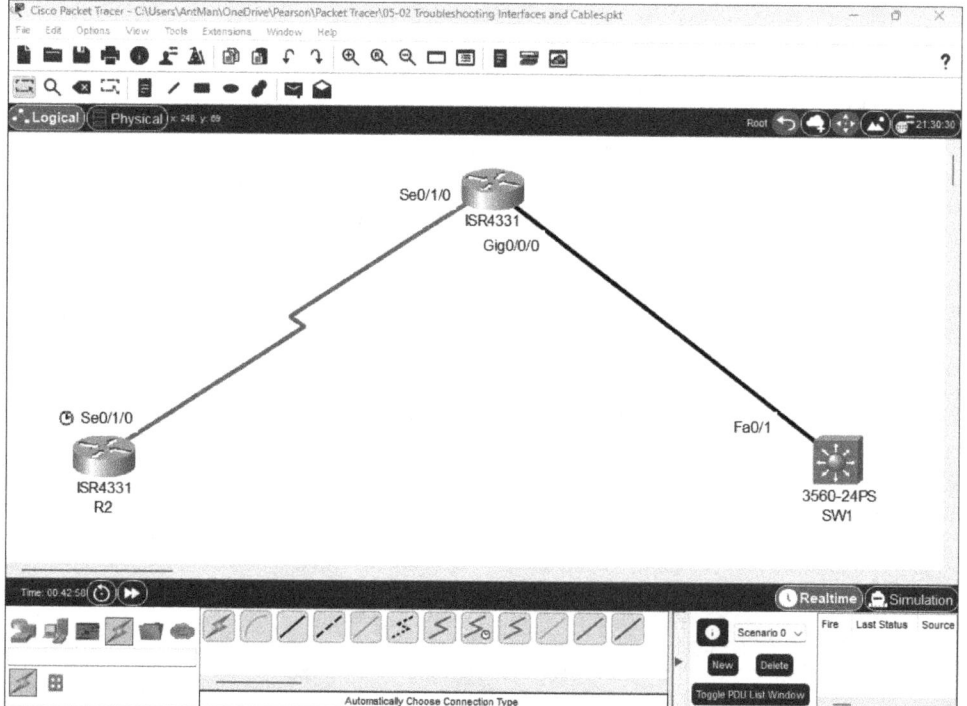

Figure 5.1   *Working with Interfaces and Cables*

Topic Quiz

1. Which of the following is not a valid error typically seen in `show interface` output?

   A. Babble

   B. Late collision

   C. Ignored

   D. Trickle

2. What counter increments if the number of frames transmitted is greater than 1518 bytes in size?

   A. Babble

   B. Late collision

   C. Runt

   D. Ignored

3. What technology attempts to dynamically resolve speed and duplex between two devices?

   A. Negotiation

   B. Autonegotiation

   C. CDP

   D. LLDP

Topic Quiz Answers

1. D is correct. There is no Trickle reported in the output as this is not a valid counter.

2. A is correct. Babble increments when the number of frames over 1518 bytes increases.

3. B is correct. Autonegotiation (auto MDI-X) attempts to resolve to a common duplex and speed between two Ethernet devices.

Lab 5.2: Chapter Review

To complete this Hands-On Lab Practice Assignment, download the assigned Packet Tracer file from the book's companion website and perform the lab on your locally installed version of Packet Tracer. You will be following the instructions in the lab, and your performance will be evaluated.

In this lab, you will work with and troubleshoot various interface and cable types on Cisco routers. You will perform this review against the topology shown in Figure 5.2.

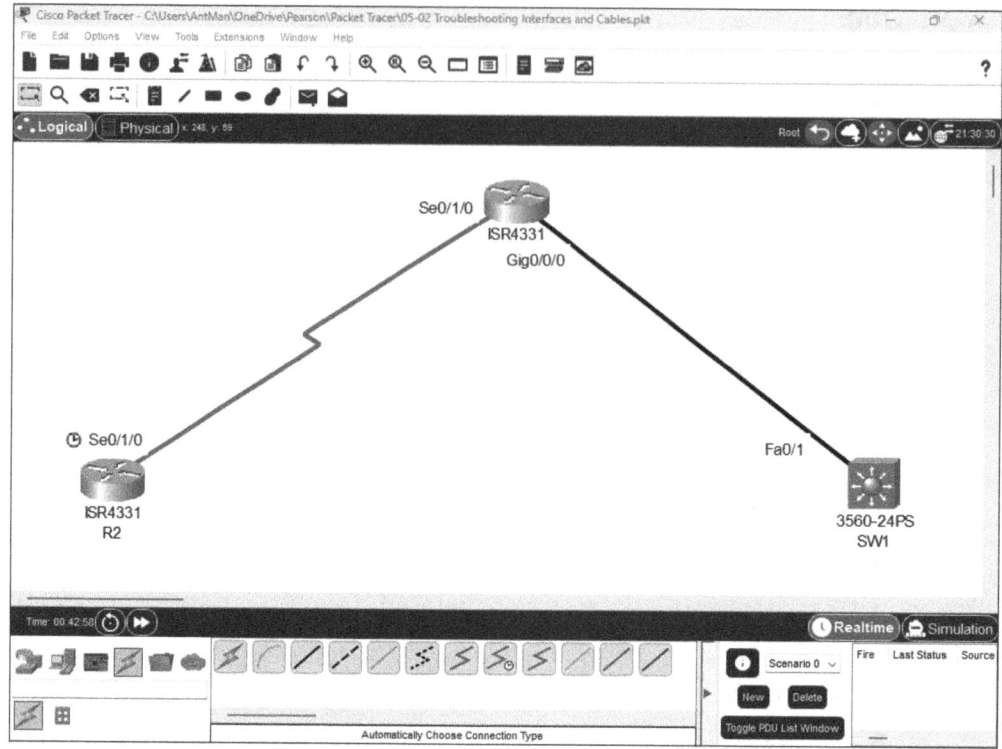

Figure 5.2   *The Interface and Cable Chapter Review Packet Tracer Lab*

Review Questions

1. What is the physical medium used by 802.3an?

   A. Copper

   B. Multimode fiber

   C. Single-mode fiber

   D. Wireless

2. If you are not using auto MDI-X on a Cisco switch, what type of cable is used to connect a Layer 2 switch's port to a PC?

   A. Crossover

   B. Rollover

   C. Console

   D. Straight-through

3. What is the duplex setting used throughout a point-to-point Ethernet network?

   A. Half-duplex

   B. Full-duplex

   C. Main duplex

   D. Dual-duplex

4. What was the original PoE standard designation?

   A. 802.3bt

   B. 802.3at

   C. 802.3af

   D. 802.3bu

5. What command allows you to see what type of serial cable is connected to a device?

   A. `show version`

   B. `show controllers`

   C. `show interface`

   D. `show flash`

6. What type of cable is used to connect a switch to another switch?

   A. Straight-through

   B. Crossover

   C. Null

   D. Dual-band

7. You are analyzing the frames sent and received over a Gigabit Ethernet connection, and you are surprised to see many frames that are approximately 9000 bytes in size. What is the term for these frames?

   A. Error frames

   B. Pico frames

   C. Runts

   D. Jumbo frames

Answers to Review Questions

1. **A** is correct. 802.3an is 10 Gigabit Ethernet (10GBASE-T). This high-speed Ethernet technology uses copper cables (Cat 6 or Cat 6a) as the physical medium.

2. **D** is correct. You connect unlike devices (for example, a switch and a PC) with a straight-through cable. To connect like devices (for example, a switch and a switch), you use a crossover cable.

3. **B** is correct. Modern networks consist of full-duplex links that use a point-to-point Ethernet environment. This eliminates collisions on the LAN.

4. **C** is correct. The first PoE standard adopted, in 2003, is the 802.3af standard. 802.3af has been integrated into 802.3-2012.

5. **B** is correct. The `show controllers` command allows you to see what type of serial cable attaches to the interface.

6. **B** is correct. A crossover cable is used to connect like devices, such as two switches.

7. **D** is correct. Many technologies today require that additional information be added to Ethernet frames. This results in frame sizes up to around 9000 bytes. Technically, any frame over 1500 bytes of payload is called a jumbo frame. These frames are sometimes reported by networking devices as giants.

Chapter 6

Configure and Verify IPv4 Addressing and Subnetting

This chapter covers the following official CCNA 200-301 exam topics:

- Configure, verify, and troubleshoot IPv4 addressing and subnetting
- Compare and contrast IPv4 address types
- Describe the need for private IPv4 addressing
- Verify IP parameters for client OS (Windows, macOS, Linux)

This chapter ensures that you are ready for questions related to these topics in the "Network Fundamentals" section of the CCNA 200-301 exam blueprint from Cisco Systems. Remember that this chapter covers just a portion of the "Network Fundamentals" section. The other chapters in Part II, "Network Fundamentals," also provide information pertinent to the "Network Fundamentals" section.

This chapter covers the following essential terms and components:

- IPv4 addressing
- IPv4 address classes
- Subnet masks
- IPv4 subnetting
- IPv4 address configuration
- Broadcasts
- Unicasts
- Multicasts

- Private IPv4 addressing
- Network Address Translation (NAT)
- Client IP parameters

Chapter Pretest

1. What is 187 converted to binary?

_____

2. What is 10010011 converted to decimal?

_____

3. What class of address is 239.1.2.3?

_____

4. You are using 5 mask bits in an octet. What is the decimal value of the subnet mask in this octet?

_____

5. How many hosts can the 10.0.0.0 255.255.255.128 network support?

_____

6. How many subnets can you create if you borrow 6 bits?

_____

7. What is the broadcast address for the subnet 10.15.2.0 255.255.254.0?

_____

8. What is the usable host range for 10.15.0.224/27?

_____

9. When you send information from one system to another system in a network without intending for the data to reach any other system, what type of traffic is this?

_____

10. What type of traffic uses the destination IP address range with 224–239 in the first octet?

_____

11. What destination MAC address do you find in an ARP frame when it is sent from a workstation that needs Layer 3–to–Layer 2 address resolution?

_____

12. List the Class A private address space.

_____

13. List the Class B private address space.

_____

14. List the Class C private address space.

_____

15. What command can you use at the command prompt on a Windows system in order to see the basic IP configuration on an interface?

_____

16. What command can you use in the terminal on a Linux system in order to view the IP configuration of all interfaces?

_____

Answers

1. 10111011

2. 147

3. Class D

4. 248

5. 126

6. 64

7. 10.15.3.255

8. 10.15.0.225–10.15.0.254

9. Unicast

10. Multicast

11. The broadcast address (ffff.ffff.ffff)

12. 10.0.0.0 to 10.255.255.255

13. 172.16.0.0 to 172.31.255.255

14. 192.168.0.0 to 192.168.255.255

15. `ipconfig`

16. `ifconfig`

Configure, Verify, and Troubleshoot IPv4 Addressing and Subnetting

An IPv4 address is a 32-bit number that is usually represented in dotted-decimal notation.

Consider using a conversion chart for the 8 bits that exist in an octet to help with the various subnetting exercises you might encounter on the CCNA 200-301 exam. Figure 6.1 is a simple chart you can jot down on scratch paper before starting the exam.

2^7	2^6	2^5	2^4	2^3	2^2	2^1	2^0
128	64	32	16	8	4	2	1

Figure 6.1   *A Conversion Chart for IPv4 Addressing and Subnetting Questions*

One task that is simple using this chart is converting a number from decimal to binary or vice versa. For example, to convert 186 to binary, you first note that you can successfully subtract 128 from this number, so you can set the first bit to on (1). The remainder after this subtraction is 58, and you cannot subtract 64 from this number (without having a negative number), so you set the 64 value to off (0) and move to the next number. You then subtract 32 from 58, place a 1 in the 32 column, and end up with 26 as the remainder. You can subtract 16 from 26, so you put a 1 in that column. Continuing with this method, you can easily calculate that 186 in binary is 10111010.

Converting from binary to decimal is even easier: Just examine what bit positions are on (1) and add those decimal values together. So, for example, 11101111 equals 239.

Early on in the development of TCP/IP, the designers created address classes to attempt to accommodate networks of various sizes. They did this by setting the initial bit values. Table 6.1 shows these classes.

Table 6.1   *The IP Version 4 Address Classes*

Address Class	High-Order Bit Setting	First Octet Range in Decimal
A	0	1–127
B	10	128–191
C	110	192–223
D	1110	224–239

Note   It is an important skill to be able to recognize the class of an address based on the decimal value in the first octet. Note that addresses beginning with 127 are reserved for local loopback purposes. Also keep in mind that Class D addresses are for multicasting. Multicasting can be used to send a message to multiple devices across multiple networks and subnetworks.

Another critical memorization point here is the default subnet masks for the address classes. Remember that it is the job of a subnet mask to define what part of a 32-bit address represents the network portion and what part represents the host portion. Table 6.2 defines the classful masks that have been defined.

Table 6.2   *Classful IPv4 Subnet Masks*

Address Class	Classful Mask	Prefix Notation Mask Bits
A	255.0.0.0	/8
B	255.255.0.0	/16
C	255.255.255.0	/24

Notice that subnet masks must use continuous on bits (1), starting from the left (the most significant bit [MSB]). The subnet mask octet 11100000 is valid, whereas 00111111 and 11100011 are not. This results in the only possible values in a subnet mask octet being those shown in Table 6.3.

Table 6.3   *The Possible Values in an IPv4 Subnet Mask Octet*

On Bits	Binary	Value
8	11111111	255
7	11111110	254
6	11111100	252
5	11111000	248
4	11110000	240
3	11100000	224
2	11000000	192
1	10000000	128
0	00000000	0

Note   Some students write out this table on scratch paper, along with other information provided in this chapter, before answering any CCNA 200-301 exam questions. If you can quickly calculate these facts on an as-needed basis during the exam, you can skip this step.

Remember that subnetting is a process of "stealing," or "borrowing," bits from the host portion of a classful IPv4 address in order to create additional subnets. Think of using the following IP address and subnet mask combination in your network:

10.0.0.0/8 or 10.0.0.0 255.0.0.0

This allows you to create only one giant network. Sure, this network can have many host systems (specifically, $2^{24} - 2$), but they all must exist in the same network. With broadcast traffic and other potential issues, this would be terrible for efficient communications. Today, we like to divide networks into small sections (subnetworks) of about 100 computers or fewer.

Note   Notice that to calculate the number of hosts a subnet can support, you take the number of bits remaining for host addressing (h) and make this the exponent for the number 2 and then subtract 2 from this amount. Thus, the formula is $2^h - 2$. You subtract 2 in this formula because you cannot assign a host an IP address with all zeros in the host bits or all ones in the host bits. These addresses are reserved; the all-zeros address identifies the network itself, and the all-ones address is the broadcast address for the subnet. The all-zeros host address is specifically reserved because older (pre-BSD 4.3) IPv4 implementations actually sent directed broadcasts to the all-zeros address.

In the preceding example, say that you decide to borrow 4 bits for subnetting. Now the identifications look like this:

10.0.0.0 255.240.0.0 or 10.0.0.0/12

How many bits are left for host identification? The subnet mask now contains 12 bits, leaving 20 bits available for host identification. This calculation, $2^{20} - 2$, requires a calculator. As a result, you would not see this question on the CCNA 200-301 exam. (The answer, by the way, is an astounding 1,048,574 hosts per subnet.)

How many subnets can you create? The answer is the formula 2^s, where s is the number of subnet bits you are borrowing. In this case, you have 24. If you examine the scratch paper chart from Figure 6.1, you quickly see that the answer is 16 subnets. Note that as you borrow more and more host bits, you can create more and more subnets, but each subnet supports fewer and fewer hosts.

Another important skill you need is to be able to establish the exact subnets to create, given a bit-borrowing scenario. The great news is that you can once again rely on Figure 6.1 for assistance!

Using the preceding scenario, you have:

10.0.0.0 255.240.0.0 or 10.0.0.0/12

To determine the subnets, you find the block size by identifying the least significant bit (rightmost) decimal value that the subnet mask extends to. So in this example, you extend 4 bits into the second octet. In this case, you can use Figure 6.1 to determine that the decimal value (block size) here is 16. Therefore, you start at 0, and then each new subnet increments by 16—so you have subnets numbered 0, 16, 32, 48, 64, 80, and so on. Plugging these values into the IP address given, you have the following subnets:

   10.0.0.0/12

   10.16.0.0/12

   10.32.0.0/12

   10.48.0.0/12

   10.64.0.0/12

   10.80.0.0/12

   and so on.

What if you begin with 10.46.0.0/16 and want to borrow 4 additional bits to create new subnets? No problem. Now this is what you have:

   10.46.0.0/20

   10.46.16.0/20

   10.46.32.0/20

   10.46.48.0/20

   10.46.64.0/20

   10.46.80.0/20

   and so on.

What if you begin with 192.168.1.0/24 and need to create six subnets? Borrowing 3 bits does the job, with some to spare ($2^3 = 8$), and you have these subnets:

   192.168.1.0/27

   192.168.1.32/27

   192.168.1.64/27

   192.168.1.96/27

   192.168.1.128/27

   192.168.1.160/27

There are two more subnets, of course, but you do not care in this case because you need only six.

> **Note** You can further subnet unused subnets! This is known as *variable-length subnet masking*.

What about usable addresses for hosts on a subnet? Look at 192.168.1.0/27 above. That is a reserved address—the subnet ID itself. Add 1 to this address, and you have the first usable host address on this subnet: 192.168.1.1/27. The last address before you get to the next subnet is 192.168.1.31/27. This is reserved for the subnet broadcast. Remember from the earlier discussion that these two reserved addresses are why we subtract 2 in the formula for calculating the number of hosts. Because the last usable address is always the next subnet ID minus 2, the last usable address on the subnet is 192.168.1.30/27.

Here is one more example. If you have 10.10.0.0/16 and want at least 15 new subnets, you can create the scheme 10.10.0.0/20. Here are the usable host address ranges for the first four subnets:

Subnet 10.10.0.0/20: 10.10.0.1 (first usable)–10.10.15.254 (last usable)

Subnet 10.10.16.0/20: 10.10.16.1 (first usable)–10.10.31.254 (last usable)

Subnet 10.10.32.0/20: 10.10.32.1 (first usable)–10.10.47.254 (last usable)

Subnet 10.10.48.0/20: 10.10.48.1 (first usable)–10.10.63.254 (last usable)

> **Note** Be ready to implement all the skills just outlined when you take the CCNA 200-301 exam. Obviously, there are a variety of ways in which questions can be asked, and this chapter provides plenty of examples through practice questions. Although initially these questions might seem like a lot of work, you will eventually crave questions like these in the exam because math questions don't have the challenging gray areas that some multiple-choice questions have.

Lab 6.1: IPv4 Address Configuration and Verification

To complete this Hands-On Lab Practice Assignment, download the assigned Packet Tracer file from the book's companion website and perform the lab on your locally installed version of Packet Tracer. You will be following the instructions in the lab, and your performance will be evaluated.

In this lab, you will configure and verify IPv4 addressing configurations in the topology shown in Figure 6.2.

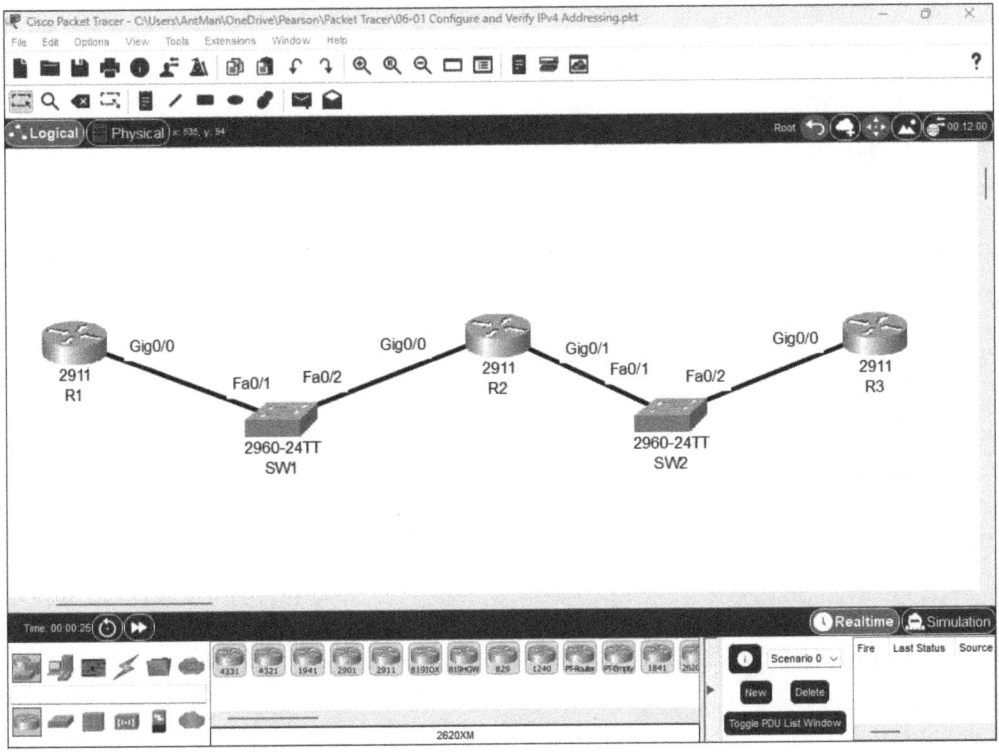

Figure 6.2   *The IPv4 Addressing and Verification Lab*

Topic Quiz

1. What is 203 converted to binary?

   A. 11001011

   B. 11101011

   C. 10101100

   D. 11001000

2. What is 01101111 in decimal?

   A. 112

   B. 111

   C. 120

   D. 110

3. What is the default subnet mask for a Class B network?

    A. 255.255.255.0

    B. 255.0.0.0

    C. 255.255.0.0

    D. 255.255.255.255

4. If a subnet mask has a length of 19 bits, what is the subnet mask in dotted-decimal notation?

    A. 255.255.192.0

    B. 255.255.224.0

    C. 255.255.240.0

    D. 255.255.252.0

5. If you have the mask 255.255.255.240, how many hosts can you support?

    A. 32

    B. 62

    C. 14

    D. 6

6. Your network needs to support 30 subnets. How many bits should you "borrow" from the host portion of the address in order to create the least waste in terms of address space?

    A. 4

    B. 5

    C. 6

    D. 7

7. What is the last usable host address on a subnet where a host has been given the address 172.16.7.1 255.255.254.0?

    A. 172.16.7.255

    B. 172.16.6.1

    C. 172.16.7.128

    D. 172.16.7.254

Topic Quiz Answers

1. **A** is correct. Using the chart in Figure 6.1, you arrive at these decimal values: $128 + 64 + 8 + 2 + 1 = 203$.

2. **B** is correct. The bits you add here are $64 + 32 + 8 + 4 + 2 + 1 = 111$.

3. **C** is correct. 255.255.0.0, or 16 bits, is the default mask for a Class B address.

4. **B** is correct. The /19 indicates 3 bits of subnetting in the third octet, which means a value of $128 + 64 + 32 = 224$.

5. **C** is correct. With this mask, there are only 4 bits left for host addressing. Using the chart in Figure 6.1, you can determine that 2 raised to the 4th power is 16. You subtract 2 from this number to arrive at 14 hosts.

6. **B** is correct. Borrowing 5 bits permits the creation of 32 subnets. You have the 30 subnets you need, plus 2 additional subnets. Borrowing 4 bits only allows for the creation of 16 subnets (which is not enough), but borrowing 6 bits would allow for 64 subnets (with 34 unused subnets, which would be too much waste).

7. **D** is correct. The usable host range here is 172.16.6.1 through 172.16.7.254.

Compare and Contrast IPv4 Address Types

Modern networking systems use three main forms of IPv4 addressing for communication in a network:

- Unicast
- Broadcast
- Multicast

Unicast transmission is most likely what you think of first. Say that you are in a home network with IP address 192.168.1.2, and you want to send data to print to a printer located at 192.168.1.10. You do not intend for any other system to receive this traffic. This is a classic example of unicast IPv4 traffic.

When you have a system that must send a frame to all members of the network, this is termed a *broadcast*. At Layer 2, the destination broadcast address is FF:FF:FF:FF:FF:FF.

Note Do not be confused by the various presentations of MAC addresses in different operating systems. For example, Windows uses FF-FF-FF-FF-FF-FF, Linux uses ff:ff:ff:ff:ff:ff, and macOS uses ffff.ffff.ffff. These are all just different methods of representing the same important address.

At Layer 3, an example of a broadcast IPv4 address is 255.255.255.255. Remember that there is another type of broadcast, however, that is sent when a packet is destined for all the members of a subnet—known as a *directed broadcast*, or *targeted broadcast*. For example, the broadcast address for subnet 10.10.0.0/20 is 10.10.15.255. (Earlier in this chapter, you calculated the broadcast addresses for subnets.)

Note   Because a directed broadcast to a remote subnet can introduce many potential security issues, most routers give you the opportunity to enable or disable directed broadcast capabilities. You can, therefore, ensure that a router will not take a directed broadcast from a remote subnet and forward into another (destination) subnet. Of course, routers can do nothing about directed broadcasts locally generated into the existing local subnet.

What if you want a device to "tune into" traffic in much the same way you tune into a television station in order to enjoy a broadcast of some show? The network equivalent of this is multicasting. Remember that the multicast address range is 224–239 in the first octet. Computers can "subscribe to" or "join" a multicast group by participating in (listening to) this address scheme (in addition to their unicast address). Multicast is a way of sending packets to multiple hosts across multiple networks and subnetworks. Some routing protocols use multicast addressing. When you enable RIPv2 on a router, it starts listening for traffic destined for its 224.0.0.9 address as this is the address used to send traffic to all RIPv2 routers.

Note   Multicast saves bandwidth and server resources because a single traffic stream serves multiple recipients across multiple networks. Contrast this with a traffic stream that must be replicated for every single unicast receiver that needs the traffic.

Lab 6.2: IPv4 Address Types

To complete this Hands-On Lab Practice Assignment, download the assigned Packet Tracer file from the book's companion website and perform the lab on your locally installed version of Packet Tracer. You will be following the instructions in the lab, and your performance will be evaluated.

In this lab, you will explore IPv4 address types in the topology shown in Figure 6.3.

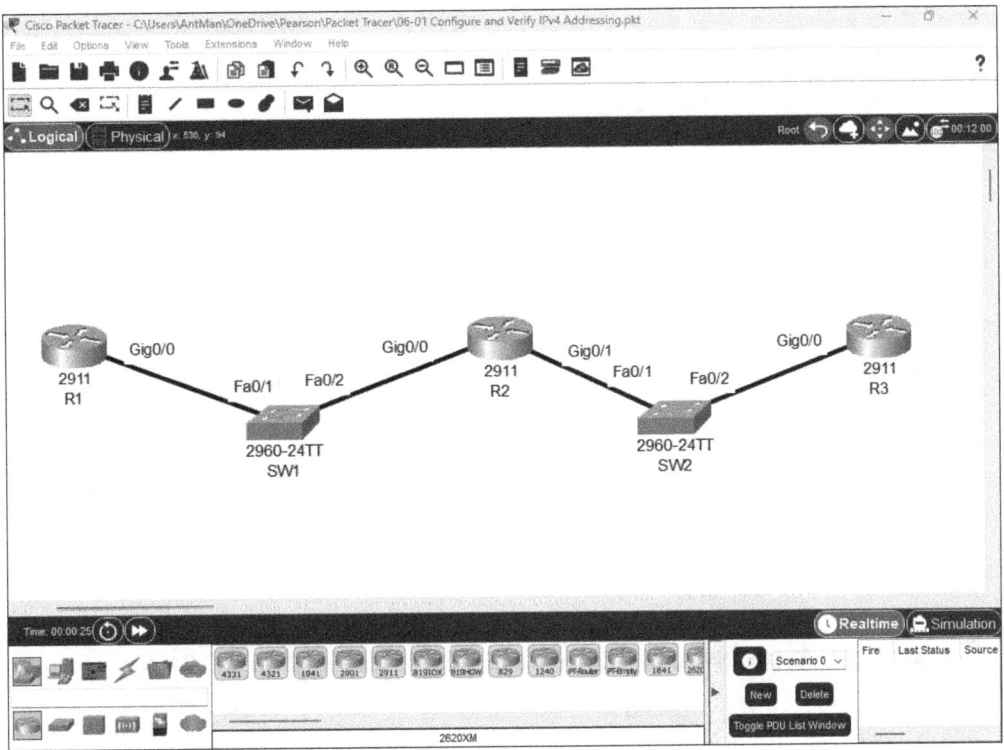

Figure 6.3 *IPv4 Address Types*

Topic Quiz

1. What type of IP traffic is used when communicating directly between two nodes (for example, in exchanging email)?

    A. Broadcast

    B. Multicast

    C. Unicast

    D. Anycast

2. EIGRP uses the IPv4 address 224.0.0.10 in its operation. What type of address is this?

    A. Unicast

    B. Broadcast

    C. Multicast

    D. Anycast

3. What does it mean when you see FF:FF:FF:FF:FF:FF as the destination address in an Ethernet frame?

   A. It means the frame is a multicast frame.

   B. It means the frame is a unicast frame.

   C. It means the frame should be dropped.

   D. It means the frame is a broadcast frame.

Topic Quiz Answers

1. C is correct. Although an ARP broadcast may initially be needed, because these systems have already communicated, the traffic can be sent unicast.

2. C is correct. 224.0.0.10 is the reserved multicast address for *EIGRP routers*. (See https://www.iana.org/assignments/multicast-addresses/multicast-addresses.xhtml.)

3. D is correct. The destination address FF:FF:FF:FF:FF:FF is a reserved MAC address that indicates a broadcast.

Describe the Need for Private IPv4 Addressing

The designers of IPv4 created the private address space to help alleviate the problem of IPv4 addresses being depleted. The private address space is not routed on the public Internet but can be used as needed inside private networks. Thanks to private address space, many different companies can be using exactly the same IP address space without causing things to break badly. This address space can then be translated using Network Address Translation (NAT) to allow access to and through the public Internet.

While it is your responsibility to set up your network correctly and not send the RFC 1918 prefixes to the Internet (via your ISP), understand that ISPs are not in the business of trusting the skills of network architects. ISPs put filters on interfaces that connect to private networks. These filters drop the RFC 1918 advertisements and traffic if they inadvertently appear. It is also interesting to note that these filters filter other addresses as well. These include special use and other addresses that it would not make sense to source from a private network. Packets that should not appear on the Internet are called *Martian* packets or *bogons*.

Note   Whenever you use private address space on an Internet-facing device, you must use NAT in order to enable proper communication with the public Internet.

Because of private addresses and NAT, you tend to see the same address range (typically 192.168.1.X) used in many homes today. Table 6.4 identifies the ranges in the private address space.

Table 6.4 *The IPv4 Private Address Ranges*

Address Class	Range of Private Addresses
A	10.0.0.0 to 10.255.255.255
B	172.16.0.0 to 172.31.255.255
C	192.168.0.0 to 192.168.255.255

Note   Both for success as a network architect and for the CCNA 200-301 exam, you must memorize the private address ranges. Although it is normally not important to memorize Request for Comments (RFC) numbers, the RFC that defined these ranges, RFC 1918, is so famous that you should know it. While I refer to the contents of RFC 1918 as private address ranges, the IETF often refers to these address ranges as "blocks," so do not be confused by that if you see it in the literature on the subject.

Topic Quiz

1. What technology permits many private addresses to communicate on the Internet?

   A. SMTP

   B. POP3

   C. SNMP

   D. NAT

2. Which of the following is not a private address?

   A. 10.10.10.1

   B. 12.34.100.1

   C. 172.16.1.10

   D. 192.168.1.10

3. What famous RFC defines what IP address space is for private use only?

   A. RFC 2020

   B. RFC 2191

   C. RFC 2001

   D. RFC 1918

Topic Quiz Answers

1. **D** is correct. Network Address Translation permits private addresses to communicate with and across the Internet.

2. **B** is correct. 12.X.X.X is part of the public IP address space.

3. **D** is correct. RFC 1918 defines the private address space.

Verify IP Parameters for Client OS (Windows, macOS, Linux)

Regardless of what client OS you use, there is an easy way to verify the IP parameters on network interfaces (unless the OS is administratively locked down to prevent such actions). In fact, in Chapter 7, "Configure IPv6," you will discover that it is also as easy to do this for IPv6 information assigned to interfaces.

Example 6.1 shows the use of `ipconfig` on a Windows 11 system. As you can see, the output of this command provides you with basic configuration parameters. In Chapter 7, you will learn how to obtain even more information by using the `/all` switch after this command.

Example 6.1 *Using `ipconfig` on a Windows 10 System*

```
C:\Users\terry>ipconfig
Windows IP Configuration

...

Wireless LAN adapter Wi-Fi:
   Connection-specific DNS Suffix . :
   IPv6 Address. . . . . . . . . . . :  2603:9000:e70b:5300:340d:2223:70a:4585
   Temporary IPv6 Address. . . . . . :  2603:9000:e70b:5300:44b7:970b:a94b:be24
   Temporary IPv6 Address. . . . . . :  2603:9000:e70b:5300:758e:acd4:c9f0:d24d
   Link-local IPv6 Address . . . . . : fe80::340d:2223:70a:4585%5
   IPv4 Address. . . . . . . . . . . : 192.168.0.8
   Subnet Mask . . . . . . . . . . . : 255.255.255.0
   Default Gateway . . . . . . . . . : fe80::92c7:92ff:fecc:dda7%5
                                       192.168.0.1
```

Keep in mind that you can also obtain this information in the GUI. In Windows 11, you find this information in the GUI by going to **Settings**, clicking the **Network & Internet** option, and clicking **View your network properties**. Figure 6.4 shows an example of this approach.

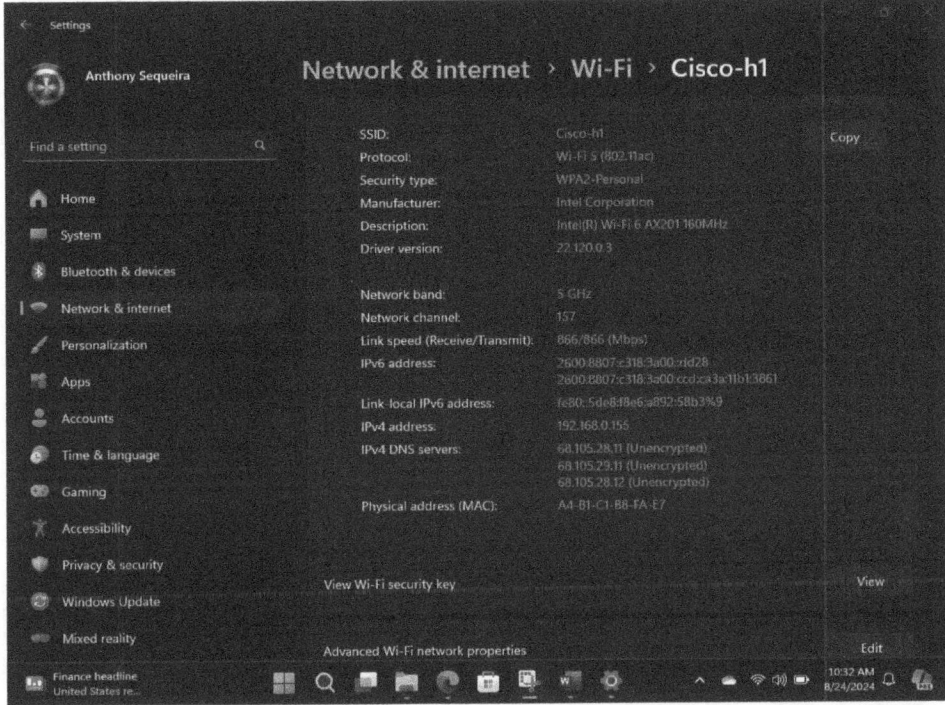

Figure 6.4 *Using the Windows 11 GUI to Obtain IP Address Information*

Note   For the CCNA 200-301 exam, you need to know that you check your IPv4 address settings in macOS or Linux by using `ifconfig`. This command is roughly equivalent to `ipconfig` in Windows. Interestingly, Linux systems are moving away from `ifconfig` in favor of more user-friendly tools.

Lab 6.3: Verify IPv4 on a Client OS

To complete this Hands-On Lab Practice Assignment, download the assigned Packet Tracer file from the book's companion website and perform the lab on your locally installed version of Packet Tracer. You will be following the instructions in the lab, and your performance will be evaluated.

In this lab, you will verify IPv4 on a client OS in the topology shown in Figure 6.5.

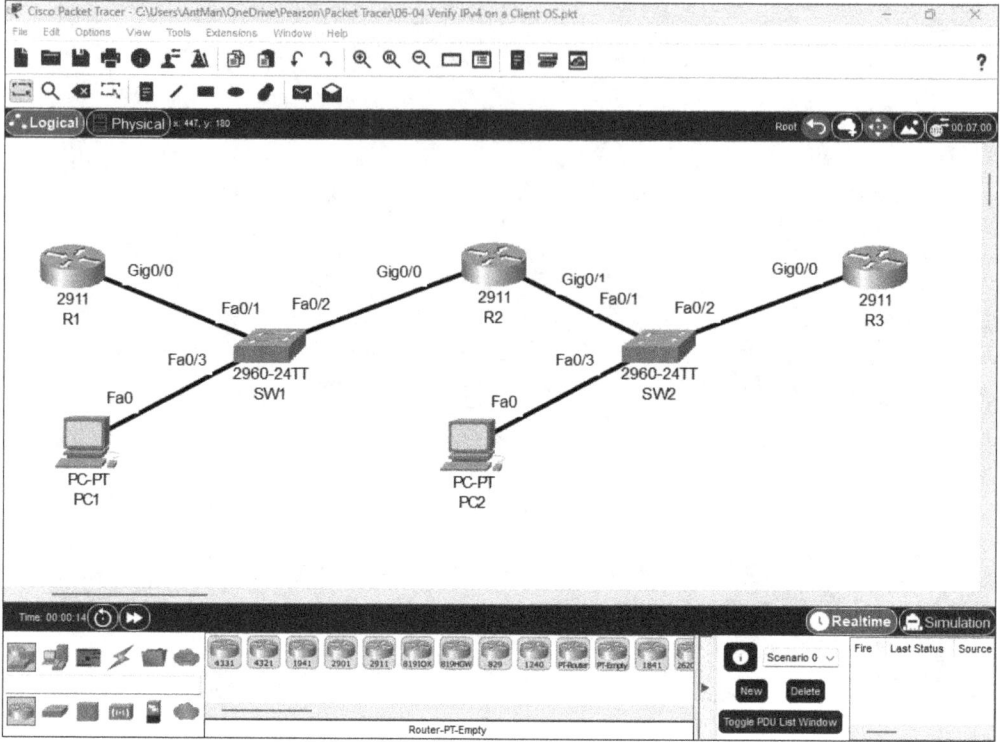

Figure 6.5   *Verify IPv4 on a Client OS*

Topic Quiz

1. You are in the command prompt on a Windows system. What command displays your IP address and default gateway for the local network interface?

   A. `ifconfig`

   B. `ipconfig`

   C. `netconfig`

   D. `testconfig`

2. You are in the terminal on a macOS system. How can you quickly see your IP address and default gateway information?

   A. `netstat`

   B. `intconfig`

   C. `ipconfig`

   D. `ifconfig`

Topic Quiz Answers

1. B is correct. The `ipconfig` command displays this information in Windows.

2. D is correct. Use the `ifconfig` command in Linux or on a macOS system.

Lab 6.4: Chapter Review

To complete this Hands-On Lab Practice Assignment, download the assigned Packet Tracer file from the book's companion website and perform the lab on your locally installed version of Packet Tracer. You will be following the instructions in the lab, and your performance will be evaluated.

In this lab, you will verify IPv4 on a client OS in the topology shown in Figure 6.6.

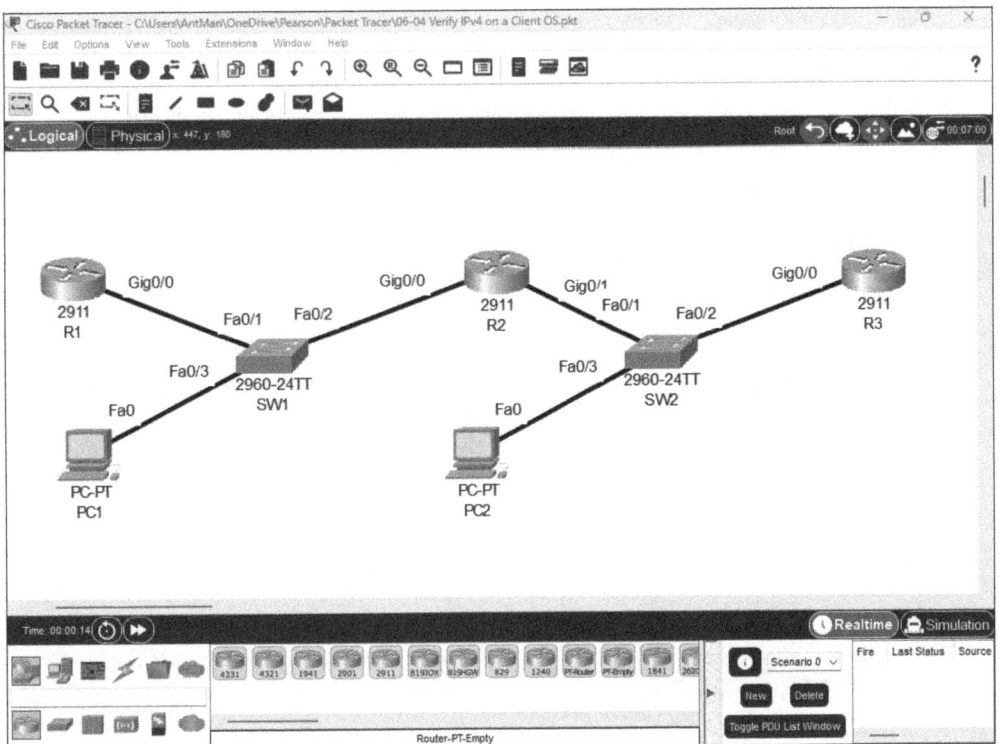

Figure 6.6 *The IPv4 Chapter Review Packet Tracer Lab*

Review Questions

1. What is 2 raised to the 7th power?

  A. 64

  B. 128

  C. 32

  D. 16

2. Which of the following is true of the IP address 127.0.0.1?

  A. This is a multicast address.

  B. This is a Class A unicast address.

  C. This is a loopback address.

  D. This is an invalid IP address.

3. What is the subnet mask if you begin with the default Class A mask and then "borrow" 4 bits for subnetting?

  A. 255.255.128.0

  B. 255.255.240.0

  C. 255.240.0.0

  D. 255.255.255.240

4. If you need to create six subnets and want to waste as little IP address space as possible, how many bits should you "borrow"?

  A. 2

  B. 3

  C. 4

  D. 5

5. Examine the following diagram. What is the most likely reason Host A is unable to ping Host B?

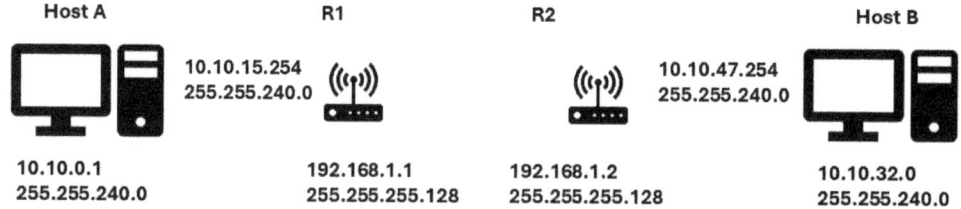

  A. The subnet masks are incorrect for the link between R1 and R2.

  B. Host A has an invalid IP address.

    C. Host B is attempting to use the subnet ID as an IP address.

    D. The R2 interface to R1 is attempting to use a subnet broadcast IP address.

6. What is the Layer 3 broadcast address?

    A. 127.255.255.255

    B. 0.0.0.0

    C. 1.1.1.1

    D. 255.255.255.255

7. What is the range of Class B private addresses?

    A. 172.16.0.0 to 172.16.255.255

    B. 172.0.0.0 to 172.255.255.255

    C. 172.16.0.0 to 172.31.255.255

    D. 172.32.0.0 to 172.36.255.255

8. What parameters is your engineer most likely verifying when they enter `ifconfig` on your Linux system?

    A. Duration of the current interface state

    B. OS version information

    C. Registry settings

    D. IP address settings

Answers to Review Questions

1. B is correct. As shown in the chart in Figure 6.1, $2^7 = 128$.

2. C is correct. 127.0.0.1 is a loopback address.

3. C is correct. The default Class A subnet mask is 255.0.0.0. Borrowing 4 bits from the next octet creates the new mask 255.240.0.0.

4. B is correct. Borrowing 3 bits makes it possible to create eight subnets. Borrowing fewer bits does not allow for as many subnets, and borrowing more than 3 bits wastes addressing space because there will be more unused subnets than when borrowing 3 bits.

5. C is correct. The Host B IP address is the subnet identifier for that subnet and is reserved.

6. D is correct. The IPv4 broadcast address is simply 255.255.255.255.

7. C is correct. The RFC 1918 /20 range is 172.16.0.0 to 172.31.255.255 for Class B networks.

8. D is correct. The `ifconfig` command in Linux displays IP address information.

Chapter 7

Configure IPv6

This chapter covers the following official CCNA 200-301 exam topics:

- Compare and contrast IPv6 address types

- Configure, verify, and troubleshoot IPv6 addressing

- Verify IPv6 parameters for the client OS (Windows, macOS, and Linux)

This chapter ensures that you are ready for questions related to these topics in the "Network Fundamentals" section of the CCNA 200-301 exam blueprint from Cisco Systems. Remember that this chapter covers just a portion of the "Network Fundamentals" section. The other chapters in Part II, also provide information pertinent to the "Network Fundamentals" section.

This chapter covers the following essential terms and components:

- IPv6 addressing

- IPv6 stateless address autoconfiguration (SLAAC)

- Global unicast

- Unique local

- Link local

- IPv6 multicast

- Modified EUI-64

- IPv6 autoconfiguration

- IPv6 anycast

Chapter Pretest

1. How many bits are in an IPv6 IP address?

   _____

2. Rewrite this IPv6 address to shorten it as much as possible: 2001:0000:0011:0100:0000:0000:0001:1AB1.

   _____

3. What is the "standard" host portion for an IPv6 address?

   _____

4. What type of IPv6 address is similar to an RFC 1918 address in IPv6?

   _____

5. What type of IPv6 address enables a variety of IPv6 services to function between two devices on the same network?

   _____

6. For what type of IPv6 address do you configure identical addresses on different devices?

   _____

7. What is the term for running IPv4 and IPv6 on the same network interface?

   _____

8. What command would you use to configure the IPv6 address 2001:aaaa:bbbb::1 on an interface with a 64-bit mask?

   _____

9. What method uses the interface hardware address as part of the IPv6 address?

   _____

10. What is the IPv6 equivalent of the IPv4 command `show ip interface brief`?

    _____

11. What command can you use at a command prompt on a Windows system to see the verbose IPv6 (and IPv4) address configuration?

    _____

12. What command can you use in the terminal on a Linux system to view the IPv4 and IPv6 configurations of all interfaces?

    _____

Answers

1. 128 bits

2. 2001:0:11:100::1:1AB1

3. 64 bits

4. A unique local address

5. A link-local address

6. An anycast address

7. Dual stack

8. `ipv6 address 2001:aaaa:bbbb::1/64`

9. Modified EUI-64

10. `show ipv6 interface brief`

11. `ipconfig /all`

12. `ifconfig`

Compare and Contrast IPv6 Address Types

IPv6 attacks the address exhaustion issues that plague IPv4 head on, expanding the address space from 32 bits to 128 bits. Because IPv6 addresses are long, we represent them using hexadecimal. Hexadecimal is also a convenient choice for summarization and subnetting exercises with IPv6 addresses.

An IPv6 header (shown in Figure 7.1) is larger than an IPv4 header.

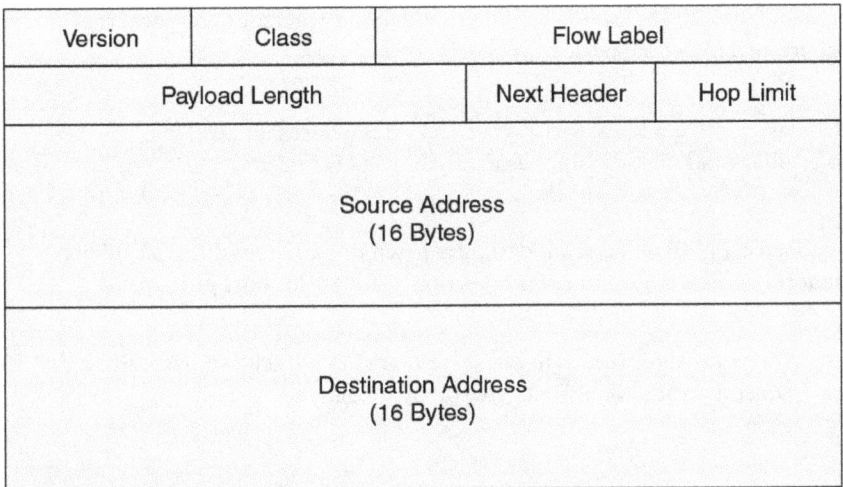

Figure 7.1 *The IPv6 Header*

The IPv6 address format is eight sets of four hex digits (16-bit sections, or hextets). A colon separates each set of four digits. Here is an example:

2001:1111:A231:0001:2341:9AB3:1001:19C3

Keep in mind that there are two rules for shortening IPv6 addresses:

■ You can represent consecutive sections of 0000s with a double colon (::). Note that you can only do this once within an IPv6 address.

■ You can eliminate leading zeros, and you can represent a section of all zeros (0000) with simply 0. You can do this as many times as needed in an address.

For example, say that you start with this address:

2001:0000:0011:0001:0000:0000:0001:1AB1

Using the rules just presented, you can reduce this address to the following shorter version, which is more convenient to read and type:

2001:0:11:1::1:1AB1

Another trick is to present the subnet mask in prefix notation only. For example, an IPv6 address that uses the first 64 bits to represent the network could be shown like this:

2001:0:11:1::1:1AB1/64

This section of the chapter focuses on the global unicast address space for IPv6. Global unicast IPv6 addresses function like the public IPv4 addresses that you are accustomed to. Other types of IPv6 addresses are elaborated on later in this chapter.

The Internet Assigned Numbers Authority (IANA) is responsible for managing the IPv6 address space. IANA assigns blocks of address spaces to regional registries, which then allocate address space to network service providers. Your organization then requests address space from a service provider. For example, a company may be assigned an address space similar to 2001:DB8:6783::/48. From that network address space, the company can create and use subnets.

Note   With the massive IPv6 address space your service provider can give you, you should have more subnet and host capabilities than you will ever need.

To simplify subnetting in IPv6, network designers often use a /64 mask for all subnets. Remember that this means a 64-bit network portion and a 64-bit host portion.

Note   Although a lot of the information in the section might sound like "real-world-only" information, it is frequently tested on the CCNA 200-301 exam.

For success on the CCNA 200-301 exam regarding IPv6, it is critical that you fully comprehend the following terms related to IPv6 addresses:

■ **Global unicast:** This is a unique IPv6 address that may be used on the Internet.

■ **Unique local:** This address is similar to a private-use-only address (RFC 1918) in IPv4 in that it is not routed on the Internet. In IPv6, this type of address begins with FC or FD. For example, FDE4:8DBA:82E1::1/64 is an example of a unique local address.

■ **Link-local unicast:** As the name makes clear, this type of address functions only on the local link. IPv6 devices automatically generate these addresses in order to perform many automated functions between devices. A link-local address has the prefix FE80::/10.

■ **Multicast:** Just as in an IPv4 environment, multicast traffic is beneficial in IPv6. Remember that multicasting means a packet is sent to a group of devices interested in receiving the information. In IPv6, multicasting completely replaces the IPv4 approach of broadcasting. In IPv6, if a device wants to reach all devices on the local network segment, it sends traffic to the IPv6 multicast address FF02::1.

■ **Modified EUI-64:** A device can use this approach to assign itself its 64-bit-long host portion of the IPv6 address.

■ **IPv6 autoconfiguration:** This refers to an IPv6 address derived through the *stateless address autoconfiguration* (SLAAC) process.

■ **IPv6 anycast:** This feature allows you to configure *identical* IPv6 addresses on your devices. When clients attempt to reach an IPv6 anycast address, IPv6 routers can send the traffic to the nearest anycast device. In Cisco IOS, the configuration is simple for this addressing feature: It simply requires the addition of the `anycast` keyword following the IPv6 address configuration.

Note Be sure to commit to memory the prefixes (including the mask length) used for these IPv6 address types:

■ **Unique local:** FC00::/7

■ **Link-local unicast:** FE80::/10

■ **Multicast:** FF00::/8

Remember that creating flash cards for such information can help you study for the CCNA 200-301 exam.

Topic Quiz

1. What is the size of the source address field in an IPv6 header?

   A. 6 bytes

   B. 8 bytes

   C. 12 bytes

   D. 16 bytes

2. What are two rules you can use to shorten an IPv6 address? (Choose two.)

   A. You can trim all trailing zeros in all sections.

   B. You can trim all leading zeros in all sections.

   C. You can use :: twice in an address.

   D. You can use :: once in an address.

3. How large is the typical network portion of an IPv6 global unicast address?

   A. 32 bits

   B. 48 bits

   C. 64 bits

   D. 128 bits

4. What does a link-local address begin with?

   A. FD80::/10

   B. FE80::/10

   C. FF80::/10

   D. FC80::/10

5. What address does IPv6 use in order to multicast traffic to all devices on a network segment?

   A. FF02::1

   B. FF02::2

   C. FF02::5

   D. FF02::6

6. When troubleshooting an IPv6 network, you notice that two devices have identical IPv6 addresses. If the network is configured correctly, why might this occur?

   A. The devices are using broadcasts for routing protocol traffic.

   B. The devices are using anycast.

C. The devices are using matching link-local addresses for the purpose of SLAAC.

D. The devices are using unique local addresses.

Topic Quiz Answers

1. **D** is correct. The source and destination address fields are 16 bytes in length to accommodate the IPv6 addresses.

2. **B** and **D** are correct. You can trim all leading zeros in all sections. In addition, you can use :: to represent consecutive sections of all zeros.

3. **C** is correct. The network portion is typically 64 bits, and the host portion is 64 bits as well.

4. **B** is correct. The FE80::/10 space is reserved for link-local addressing.

5. **A** is correct. This is the all-nodes IPv6 multicast address. The other multicast addresses listed in this question are valid but are used for other purposes. For example, FF02::2 is for all routers.

6. **B** is correct. If the devices are properly configured and have matching configured addresses, they must be using anycast addresses.

Configure, Verify, and Troubleshoot IPv6 Addressing

IPv6 address configuration in general is pleasantly simple. Examine the configuration shown in Example 7.1. Note that this interface is dual stacked—that is, it runs IPv4 and IPv6 simultaneously. Dual stacking is used often because IPv4 may be around for the rest of our lifetimes and beyond. (Keep in mind that IPv4 is not required for the configuration of IPv6.)

Example 7.1   *A Sample IPv6 Address Configuration*

```
R1(config)# interface fastethernet0/0
R1(config-if)# ip address 10.10.10.1 255.255.255.0
R1(config-if)# ipv6 address 2001:aaaa:bbbb::1/64
R1(config-if)# no shutdown
```

Note   A global configuration command you will often use is `ipv6 unicast-routing`. This command permits a router to route IPv6 traffic between its interfaces and to run IPv6 routing protocols such as EIGRP for IPv6 or OSPF version 3. This command is not shown in Example 7.1 because it is not required for the configuration of IPv6 addresses.

What about address verification with IPv6? No problem. Example 7.2 shows two different approaches.

Example 7.2 *Two Sample IPv6 Address Verifications*

```
R1# show ipv6 interface brief
FastEthernet0/0              [up/up]
    FE80::C801:6FF:FE65:0
    2001:AAAA:BBBB::1
R1# show ipv6 interface fa0/0
FastEthernet0/0 is up, line protocol is up
   IPv6 is enabled, link-local address is FE80::C801:6FF:FE65:0
   No Virtual link-local address(es):
   Global unicast address(es):
     2001:AAAA:BBBB::1, subnet is 2001:AAAA:BBBB::/64
   Joined group address(es):
     FF02::1
     FF02::1:FF00:1
     FF02::1:FF65:0
   MTU is 1500 bytes
   ICMP error messages limited to one every 100 milliseconds
   ICMP redirects are enabled
   ICMP unreachables are sent
   ND DAD is enabled, number of DAD attempts: 1
   ND reachable time is 30000 milliseconds (using 30000)
R1#
```

Lab 7.1: IPv6 Address Configuration and Verification

To complete this Hands-On Lab Practice Assignment, download the assigned Packet Tracer file from the book's companion website and perform the lab on your locally installed version of Packet Tracer. You will be following the instructions in the lab, and your performance will be evaluated.

In this lab, you will configure and verify IPv6 addressing configurations in the topology shown in Figure 7.2.

Many engineers do not want the extra work of manually assigning host addresses to systems. For such engineers, IPv6 offers an excellent feature: modified EUI-64. Modified EUI-64 uses the MAC address from a device to automatically generate a 64-bit-long host portion. Example 7.3 shows the configuration and verification of an IPv6 address using this very groovy approach.

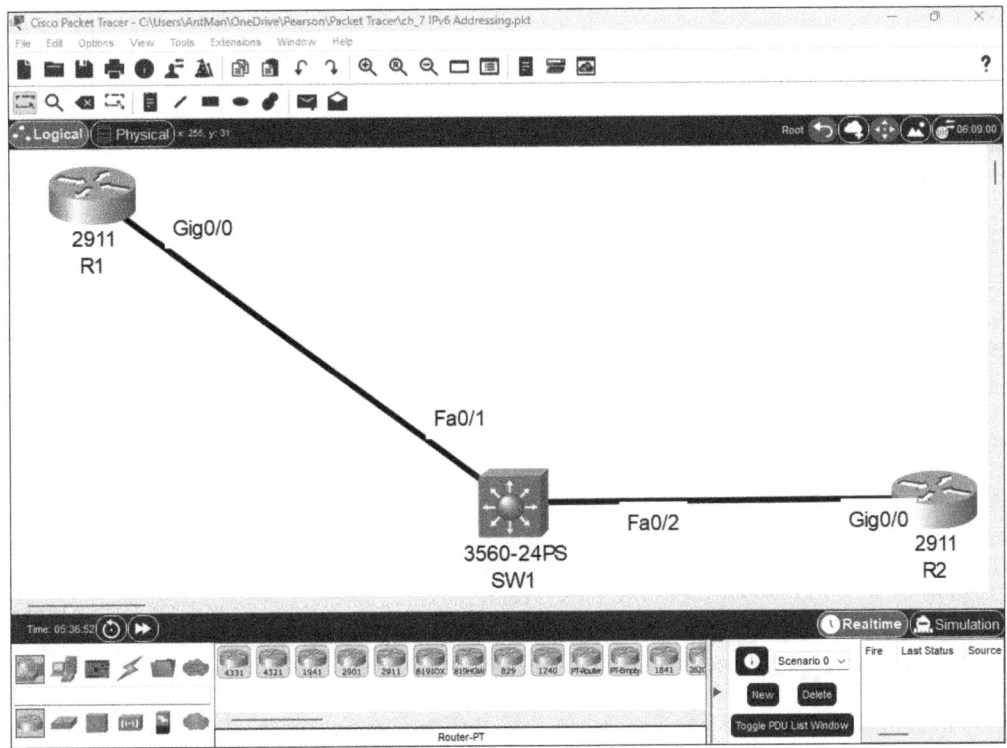

Figure 7.2 *The IPv6 Addressing and Verification Lab*

Example 7.3 *Modified EUI-64 Host Portion Assignment and Verification*

```
R1(config)# interface fastEthernet 0/0
R1(config-if)# ipv6 address 2001:AAAA:BBBB::/64 eui-64
R1(config-if)# no shutdown
R1(config-if)# end
R1#
%SYS-5-CONFIG_I: Configured from console by console
R1# show ipv6 interface brief
FastEthernet0/0            [up/up]
    FE80::C801:6FF:FE65:0
    2001:AAAA:BBBB:0:C801:6FF:FE65:0
R1# show ipv6 interface fa 0/0
FastEthernet0/0 is up, line protocol is up
  IPv6 is enabled, link-local address is FE80::C801:6FF:FE65:0
  No Virtual link-local address(es):
  Global unicast address(es):
   2001:AAAA:BBBB:0:C801:6FF:FE65:0, subnet is 2001:AAAA:BBBB::/64 [EUI]
```

```
Joined group address(es):
 FF02::1
 FF02::1:FF65:0
MTU is 1500 bytes
ICMP error messages limited to one every 100 milliseconds
ICMP redirects are enabled
ICMP unreachables are sent
ND DAD is enabled, number of DAD attempts: 1
ND reachable time is 30000 milliseconds (using 30000)
R1#
```

Note   A confusing command for many students is the interface command `ipv6 enable`. This command is not required to enable IPv6 on an interface, but it autoconfigures a link-local address and enables processing of IPv6 packets on the interface.

Lab 7.2: IPv6 EUI-64 Address Configuration and Verification

To complete this Hands-On Lab Practice Assignment, download the assigned Packet Tracer file from the book's companion website and perform the lab on your locally installed version of Packet Tracer. You will be following the instructions in the lab, and your performance will be evaluated.

In this lab, you will configure and verify EUI-64 IPv6 addressing configurations in the topology shown in Figure 7.3.

The ability to have an IPv6 network device configure the host portion of its IPv6 address (using modified EUI-64) on its own is pretty awesome. What is even more exciting is having one network device assist another in the assignment of the entire address. This is stateless address autoconfiguration (SLAAC). *Stateless* simply means that an external device is not keeping track of the address assignments for every device on a network. For example, in IPv4 and IPv6, you can use a DHCP server in a "stateful" manner. A DHCP device provides the address information that devices need and tracks this information in a database. Obviously, there is a fair amount of overhead involved in this process for the DHCP server. Fortunately, in IPv6, you can use SLAAC to provide a host with all the information it might need, including things like the IPv6 prefix, the prefix length, the default gateway address, and the DNS server(s) address. An alternative to using SLAAC in IPv6 networks is to use stateful or stateless DHCPv6.

With SLAAC, an IPv6 device learns its prefix information automatically over the local link from another device (such as the router), and then it can randomly assign its own host portion of the address or use the modified EUI-64 method discussed earlier in this chapter.

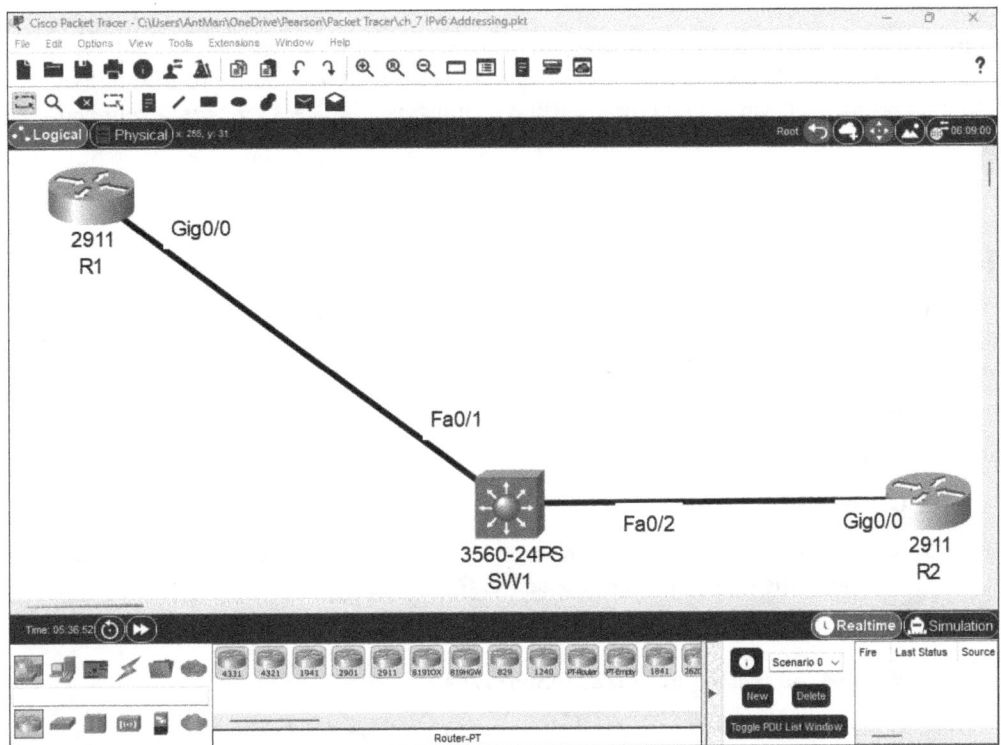

Figure 7.3   *The EUI-64 IPv6 Addressing and Verification Lab*

> **Note**   How does a SLAAC host communicate with its neighbor if it does not yet possess the IPv6 address information it needs? This is the job of the link-local address in IPv6.

Example 7.4 shows an example of configuring a Cisco router to acquire a global unicast IPv6 address using SLAAC. As you can see, the process is simple.

Example 7.4   *Using SLAAC for Address Assignment on a Cisco Router*

```
R1(config)# interface fa0/0
R1(config-if)# ipv6 address autoconfig
```

R1 in Example 7.4 will detect a global unicast prefix using the IPv6 Neighbor Discovery (ND) protocol—but only if a router present on the interface's segment is offering this information. If there is no router attached to the segment, the `ipv6 address auto-config` command will only manage to autoconfigure a link-local IPv6 address, making it equivalent to the `ipv6 enable` command. On the other hand, if a router advertising the link's subnet prefix is present, the local router autoconfigures both a link-local address and (unlike with the `ipv6 enable` command) a global unicast address.

> **Note** Cisco routers that support IPv6 are ready for any of the IPv6 interface addressing methods, with no special configuration required. However, if a router needs to run IPv6 routing protocols (such as OSPF or EIGRP), you must use the `ipv6 unicast-routing` command, as mentioned earlier in this chapter.

Topic Quiz

1. What command do you use to enable IPv6 routing capabilities on a Cisco router?

   A. `ipv6 unicast-routing`

   B. `ipv6 routing`

   C. `ipv6 routing enable`

   D. `ipv6 unicast-enable`

2. What command configures IPv6 on an interface and eliminates the need to manually configure the host portion of the address?

   A. `ipv6 address 2001:aaaa:bbbb::/64 auto`

   B. `ipv6 address 2001:aaaa:bbbb::/64`

   C. `ipv6 address 2001:aaaa:bbbb::/64 eui-64`

   D. `ipv6 address 2001:aaaa:bbbb::/64 slaac`

3. Which commands could you use to verify your IPv6 interface address? (Choose two.)

   A. `show ipv6 interface brief`

   B. `show interface ipv6 details`

   C. `show ipv6 interface`

   D. `show interface ipv6 info`

Topic Quiz Answers

1. A is correct. The command required to enable IPv6 routing capabilities on a Cisco router is `ipv6 unicast-routing`.

2. C is correct. Use the `eui-64` keyword with the `ipv6 address` command to have a device automatically generate its host portion.

3. A and C are correct. The `show ipv6 interface brief` and `show ipv6 interface` commands are the equivalents of the `show ip interface brief` and `show ip interface` commands.

Verify IPv6 Parameters for the Client OS (Windows, macOS, Linux)

All the popular operating systems today make it very simple to verify the IPv6 parameters of systems. Example 7.5 shows the use of `ipconfig /all` on a Windows 11 system. Notice the wealth of IPv6 address information it displays. Keep in mind that I (as the admin of this machine) did not initiate any of this configuration manually. All this IPv6 configuration transpired by default.

Example 7.5 *Using* `ipconfig /all` *on a Windows 10 System*

```
C:\Users\terry>ipconfig /all

...

Wireless LAN adapter Wi-Fi:

   Connection-specific DNS Suffix . :
   Description . . . . . . . . . . . : Killer Wireless-n/a/ac 1435 Wireless Network
   Adapter
   Physical Address. . . . . . . . . : 9C-B6-D0-66-BE-C9
   DHCP Enabled. . . . . . . . . . . : Yes
   Autoconfiguration Enabled . . . . : Yes
   IPv6 Address. . . . . . . . . . . : 2603:9000:e70b:5300:340d:2223:
   70a:4585(Preferred)
   Temporary IPv6 Address. . . . . . : 2603:9000:e70b:5300:fcf7:2f3d:
   3d15:3a7(Preferred)
   Link-local IPv6 Address . . . . . : fe80::340d:2223:70a:4585%5 (Preferred)
   IPv4 Address. . . . . . . . . . . : 192.168.0.8(Preferred)
   Subnet Mask . . . . . . . . . . . : 255.255.255.0
   Lease Obtained. . . . . . . . . . : Saturday, October 19, 2023 9:13:17 AM
   Lease Expires . . . . . . . . . . : Sunday, October 20, 2023 3:43:56 AM
   Default Gateway . . . . . . . . . : fe80::92c7:92ff:fecc:dda7%5
                                       192.168.0.1
   DHCP Server . . . . . . . . . . . : 192.168.0.1
   DHCPv6 IAID . . . . . . . . . . . : 43824848
   DHCPv6 Client DUID. . . . . . . . : 00-01-00-01-21-B3-15-5F-A4-4C- C8-73-F0-66
   DNS Servers . . . . . . . . . . . : 209.18.47.62
                                       209.18.47.61
   NetBIOS over Tcpip. . . . . . . . : Enabled

...
```

Notice in the output in Example 7.5 the Temporary IPv6 Address value. While this information should not appear on the CCNA 200-301 exam, it is super interesting. This address is created by newer operating systems. Instead of generating the host portion of the address using a MAC address, the OS randomly creates the host portion and regenerates a new one after a short time period (typically hours). It is considered more secure than other approaches because approaches tied to the MAC address could enable computer criminals or noncriminal websites to uniquely identify and track users on the network or the public Internet based on the host portion of their IPv6 address.

While there is no denying the convenience of the command-line output in Example 7.5, keep in mind that you can also check this information by using Windows GUI tools. In fact, there are even GUI tools for verifying IPv6 settings on Linux and macOS client systems.

> **Note**   For the CCNA 200-301 exam, you need to know that the terminal method of checking IPv6 address settings in Linux is to use `ifconfig`. This command is roughly equivalent to the Windows command `ipconfig`. The `ifconfig` utility permits the configuration and querying of IPv4 and IPv6 parameters.

Lab 7.3: IPv6 on a Client OS

To complete this Hands-On Lab Practice Assignment, download the assigned Packet Tracer file from the book's companion website and perform the lab on your locally installed version of Packet Tracer. You will be following the instructions in the lab, and your performance will be evaluated.

In this lab, you will configure and verify a client IPv6 configuration using the topology shown in Figure 7.4.

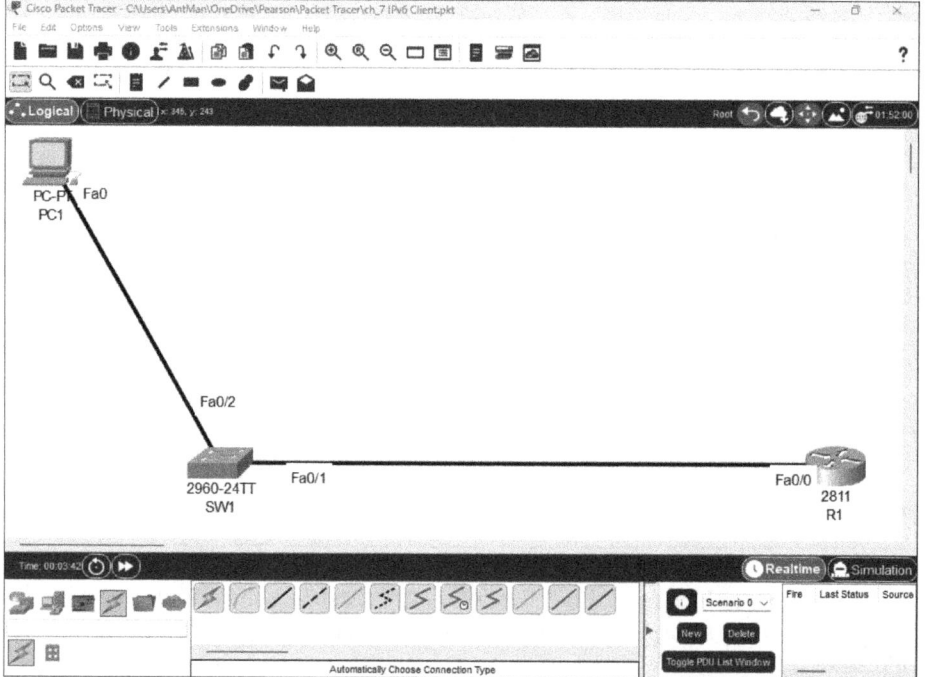

Figure 7.4   *The IPv6 on a Client OS Lab*

Topic Quiz

1. You run `ipconfig` on your Windows system and see an IPv6 address that starts with FE80. What type of address is this?

    A. Global unicast

    B. Multicast

    C. Anycast

    D. Link local

2. What `ipconfig` switch ensures that you can see the IPv6 parameters of your interface?

    A. `/verbose`

    B. `/ipv6`

    C. `/all`

    D. `/new`

Topic Quiz Answers

1. **D** is correct. A link-local address begins with FE80.

2. **C** is correct. The `/all` switch permits verbose output regarding the interface. This includes the IPv6 address information.

Lab 7.4: Chapter Review

To complete this Hands-On Lab Practice Assignment, download the assigned Packet Tracer file from the book's companion website and perform the lab on your locally installed version of Packet Tracer. You will be following the instructions in the lab, and your performance will be evaluated.

In this lab, you will configure and verify various IPv6-related tasks discussed in this chapter. You will perform this review against the topology shown in Figure 7.5.

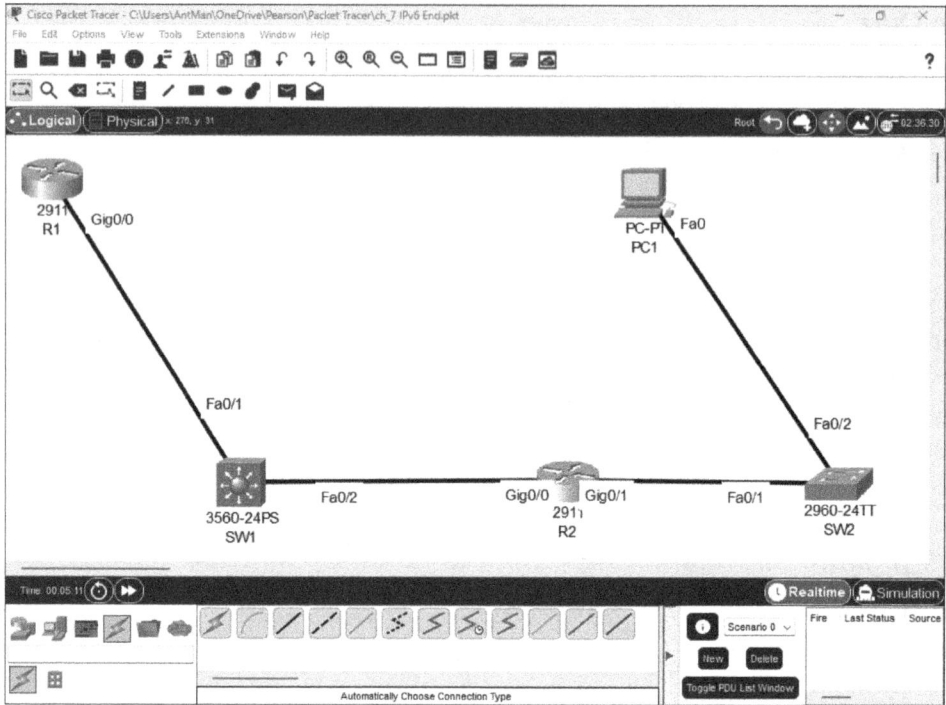

Figure 7.5 *The IPv6 Chapter Review Lab*

Review Questions

1. How many more bits are used in an IPv6 address than in an IPv4 address?

   A. 96

   B. 128

   C. 48

   D. 64

2. What is the significance of :: in the IPv6 address 2001:0:11:1::1:1AB1/64?

   A. It is used to represent a single section of 0000.

   B. It is used to represent consecutive sections of 0000.

   C. It is used to represent a single section of 1111.

   D. It is used to represent consecutive sections of 1111.

3. What command causes a router interface to autoconfigure its host portion of the address?

   A. `ipv6 address 2001:aaaa:bbbb::1/64 auto`

   B. `ipv6 address 2001:aaaa:bbbb::1/64 eui-64`

C. `ipv6 address 2001:aaaa:bbbb::/64 eui-64`

D. `ipv6 address 2001:aaaa:bbbb::/64 auto`

4. What command allows you to see the multicast addresses that an interface has joined in IPv6?

   A. `show ipv6 interface brief`

   B. `show ipv6 interface`

   C. `show ipv6 interface multicast`

   D. `show multicast ipv6`

5. If you are using DHCP combined with the SLAAC feature in IPv6, you are most likely using what form of DHCP?

   A. Stateful

   B. Stateless

   C. Headless

   D. Auto

6. If you use the `ipv6 enable` command on an interface, what address do you have on that interface?

   A. Global unicast

   B. Autoconfiguration

   C. Unique local

   D. Link local

Answers to Review Questions

1. A is correct. An IPv4 address is 32 bits, and an IPv6 address is 128 bits.

2. B is correct. The :: may be used once in an address in order to represent consecutive sections of 0000.

3. C is correct. The modified EUI-64 method is used in this example.

4. B is correct. The `show ipv6 interface` command provides this level of detail. It shows the multicast and link-local addressing joined.

5. B is correct. Stateless DHCP is often used with SLAAC.

6. D is correct. The `ipv6 enable` command ensures that a link-local address exists.

Chapter 8

Describe Wireless Principles

This chapter covers the following official CCNA 200-301 exam topic:

■ Describe wireless principles

Here is another important chapter that covers information in the "Network Fundamentals" section of the CCNA 200-301 exam blueprint from Cisco Systems. Wireless networking has become incredibly common today, especially as more and more of us have become heavily dependent on cloud-based resources. For example, most students now use office suites accessed using a web browser and cloud-based applications. For such individuals, Wi-Fi is the key to productivity. In fact, I am currently composing this book using an online version of Microsoft Word as I sit in my local coffee shop, enjoying the complimentary wireless signal that takes me to the Internet.

This chapter covers the following essential terms and components:

■ Radio frequencies

■ SSIDs

■ Wi-Fi channel overlap

Chapter Pretest

1. What two RF bands are most commonly in use today for Wi-Fi communications?

_____

2. What are the nonoverlapping channels in the 2.4 GHz RF band?

_____

Answers

1. 2.4 GHz and 5 GHz

2. 1, 6, and 11

Wireless Principles

Remember that wireless technologies send data by using ranges of radio frequencies (RF) rather than physical cables. A range of frequencies is typically called a *band*. Do you remember AM radio? It operates using 530 kHz to 1710 kHz, known as the AM band.

You should know about two main bands that are used for wireless: the 2.4 GHz band and the 5 GHz band. You often see these bands included in wireless AP SSID names. For example, your AP might provide the default names CoolCableCo-2.4G and CoolCableCo-5G as part of the default configuration suggested. (If you are fuzzy on what an SSID is, no worries: We will review that in this chapter.)

Inside the 2.4 GHz and 5 GHz bands, the radio frequencies are gathered into *channels*. In the 5 GHz band, there are no overlapping channels. This is wonderful, and it means you do not have to worry about an AP that uses one channel interfering with a neighboring AP that uses an overlapping channel. Unfortunately, the 2.4 GHz band does include some overlapping channels.

To avoid problems when you are setting up wireless access points in the 2.4 GHz band, you should be sure to use the nonoverlapping channels: 1, 6, and 11. Memorize these channels if you have not already.

Over the years, many IEEE 802.11 standards have emerged to take advantage of new wireless technology that operates in the 2.4 GHz and 5 GHz bands. Table 8.1 recaps them for you.

Table 8.1   *IEEE 802.11 Wireless Standards*

Standard	Year	2.4 GHz/5 GHz/Both	Maximum Speed
802.11	1997	2.4 GHz	2 Mbps
802.11b	1999	2.4 GHz	11 Mbps
802.11a	1999	5 GHz	54 Mbps
802.11g	2003	2.4 GHz	54 Mbps
802.11n	2009	Both	600 Mbps
802.11ac	2013	5 GHz	6.93 Gbps
802.11ax	2019	Both	Up to 30% faster than 802.11ac

A wireless device can support more than one of the standards shown in Table 8.1, but your device and wireless client must agree on and use a single standard as they communicate.

Each wireless network has a service set identifier (SSID), which is a string of characters used to uniquely identify that network. Most people simply think of it as the wireless network name, and that certainly works.

In low-security environments—perhaps your home—the SSID is typically broadcast by the AP. You can fire up a computer, have the computer dynamically scan for available SSIDs, and then pick a wireless network to join.

More secured environments may not broadcast the SSID; this is known as *network cloaking*. Keep in mind that network cloaking does not increase the security of a wireless network. It does, however, mean that client devices must be configured with the precise name of the network as they will not be able to dynamically scan and find it.

Note   Eliminating the SSID broadcast is actually a small step in wireless security. Modern tools do not need to be very sophisticated to find the SSID that is being sent through the air in a certain location. This is why wireless security practices ensure that information transmitted in wireless networks is encrypted.

Topic Quiz

1. What 2009 Wi-Fi standard uses both the 2.4 and 5 GHz bands?

   A. 802.11g

   B. 802.11n

   C. 802.11b

   D. 802.11ac

2. How do you identify a wireless network?

   A. Using the RF band and AP MAC combination

   B. Using the IP address of the AP

   C. Using the SSID

   D. Using the passphrase

Topic Quiz Answers

1. B is correct. 802.11n, which was released in 2009, features the use of both the 2.4 GHz and 5 GHz bands.

2. C is correct. You typically locate and connect to a wireless network by using its name, technically known as the SSID.

Lab 8.1: Chapter Review

To complete this Hands-On Lab Practice Assignment, download the assigned Packet Tracer file from the book's companion website and perform the lab on your locally installed version of Packet Tracer. You will be following the instructions in the lab, and your performance will be evaluated.

In this lab, you will configure and verify various wireless tasks presented in this chapter. You will perform this review against the topology shown in Figure 8.1.

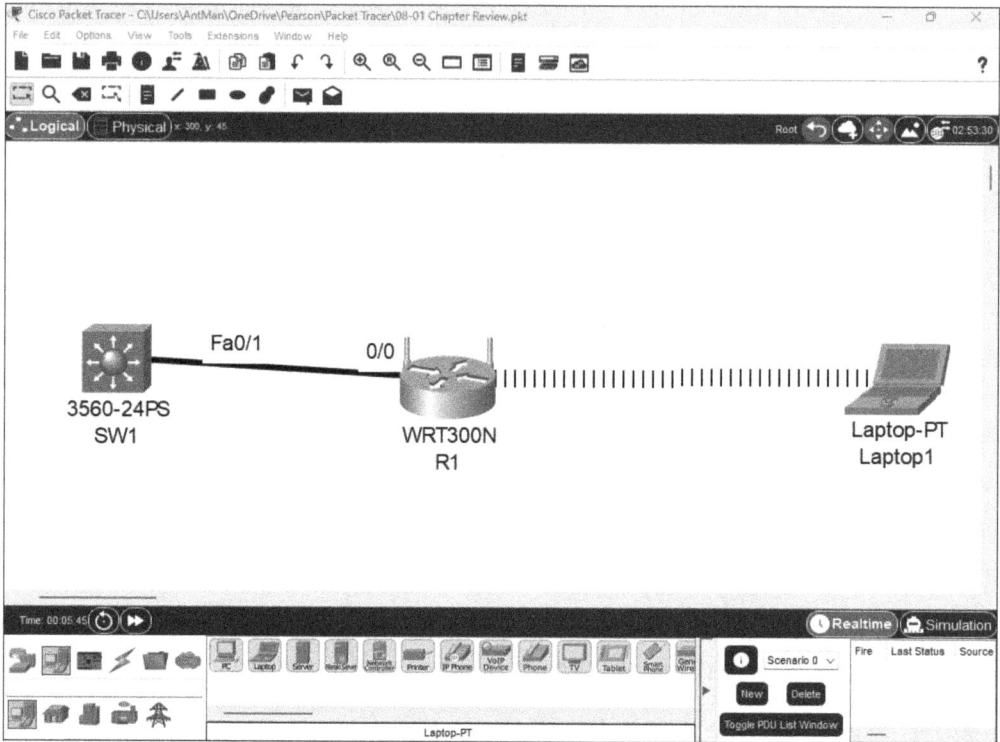

Figure 8.1   *The Wireless Principles Chapter Review Lab*

Review Questions

1. What is a basic security measure used in some wireless networks?

    A. Network cloaking

    B. RF cloaking

    C. SSID broadcasting

    D. MAC masking

2. What wireless standard introduced in 2013 permits a maximum speed of 6.93 Gbps?

   A. 802.11ax

   B. 802.11g

   C. 802.11ac

   D. 802.11n

Answers to Review Questions

1. **A** is correct. A simple security measure that is sometimes used in combination with stronger measures is to prevent the broadcast of the SSID; this is known as network cloaking.

2. **C** is correct. 802.11ac, which was introduced in 2013, shattered previous maximum throughput limits. This technology uses the 5 GHz band and allows a maximum speed of 6.93 Gbps.

Chapter 9

Configure Switching Basics

This chapter covers the following official CCNA 200-301 exam topics:

- Describe switching concepts

- Interpret Ethernet frame format

This chapter ensures that you are ready for questions related to these topics in the "Network Fundamentals" section of the CCNA 200-301 exam blueprint from Cisco Systems. Remember that this chapter covers just a portion of the "Network Fundamentals" section.

This chapter covers the following essential terms and components:

- Ethernet switching

- MAC learning

- MAC aging

- Frame switching

- Frame flooding

- MAC address table

- Ethernet frame format

Chapter Pretest

1. What specific field of an Ethernet frame does a switch learn from inbound frames and then record in a database?

    _____

2. What is the name of the process that occurs when a MAC address that is no longer communicating on the network is removed from the switch database?

    _____

3. What happens when a frame enters a switch, and the destination MAC address is known by the switch?

    _____

4. What happens when a frame enters a switch, and the destination MAC address is not known by the switch?

    _____

5. What Ethernet frame field is 2 bytes in length and is used to determine the protocol carried within the frame's Data field?

    _____

6. What is the first field of the common Ethernet frame format that is in use today?

    _____

7. What is the last field of the common Ethernet frame format that is in use today?

    _____

8. What is the job of the SFD field in an Ethernet frame?

    _____

Answers

1. The switch learns and records the source MAC address.

2. This process of removing stale MAC addresses is termed *aging*, or *aging out*.

3. When the destination MAC address is known by a switch, the switch can intelligently forward the information out the correct port, filtering the traffic from all other ports.

4. Frame flooding occurs when the destination MAC address is unknown; in this process, the frame is sent out all ports (for the same VLAN) except the port on which the frame entered.

5. The Length/Type field is 2 bytes in length and permits the signaling of the upper-layer protocol encapsulated in the frame. For example, 0x0800 indicates an IPv4 packet.

6. Preamble

7. Frame Check Sequence (FCS)

8. The Start Frame Delimiter (SFD) field is 1 byte in length. It has a simple job: It marks the end of the Preamble field and indicates the beginning of the Ethernet frame fields to follow.

Describe Switching Concepts

Figure 9.1 and the list that follows provide the context for the discussion of several fundamental Ethernet switching concepts that you must review for the CCNA 200-301 exam:

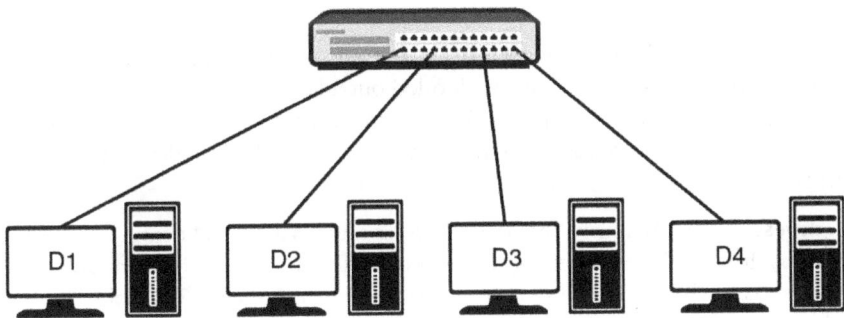

Figure 9.1 *A Simple Switch Layout*

- **MAC learning and MAC aging:** One of the responsibilities of a switch is to learn MAC addresses. The switch transparently observes incoming frames. It records the source MAC addresses of these frames in its MAC address table. It also associates the specific port with a source MAC address. The source MAC address is unique for each connected device. Based on this information, the switch can make intelligent frame-forwarding (switching) decisions. Notice that a host system could be turned off or moved at any point. As a result, a switch must also age MAC addresses and remove them from the table after they have not been seen for some duration.

  In the network shown in Figure 9.1, it will not take long before all four systems send some traffic. Keep in mind that many protocols broadcast information periodically. When these frames enter the switch, it records the source MAC address and port information in its MAC address table.

Note   You can manipulate the aging of MAC addresses on a Cisco switch. Depending on the model of the switch, the range of time you can set is from 0 to 1,000,000 seconds. The default on most Cisco switches is 300 seconds. You can even disable MAC address aging on some switches.

- **Frame switching:** Along with building a MAC address table (mapping MAC addresses to ports), a switch also forwards (switches) frames intelligently from port to port. This is sort of the opposite of how a Layer 1 hub works. The hub takes in a frame and always forwards that frame out all other ports. In a hub-based network, every port is part of the same collision domain. A switch is too smart for that. If its MAC address table is fully populated for all ports, the switch filters the frame from being forwarded out ports unnecessarily. It forwards the frame to the correct port, based on the destination MAC address. Using Figure 9.1 as an example, if D1 sends a unicast frame destined for D4, the switch examines the MAC address table, finds the destination MAC address in that table, and forwards the frame out only the port that connects to D4.

- **Frame flooding:** What happens when a frame has a destination address that is not in the MAC address table? The frame is flooded out all ports other than the port on which the frame was received. This is called *unknown unicast flooding*, and it also happens when the destination MAC address in the frame is the broadcast address (ffff.ffff.ffff).

- **MAC address table:** Obviously, the MAC address table is a critical component in a switch today. It really is the brains of the operation. It contains the MAC address-to-port mappings that allow the switch to work its network magic. Example 9.1 shows how easy it is to examine the MAC address table of a Cisco switch.

Example 9.1   *Examining a Real MAC Address Table*

```
Switch# show mac address-table
          Mac Address Table
-------------------------------------------

Vlan    Mac Address      Type        Ports
----    -----------      --------    -----
 1      e213.5864.ab8f   DYNAMIC     Gi0/0
 1      fa16.3ee3.7d71   DYNAMIC     Gi1/0
```

Note   A switch dynamically learns MAC address entries by default. You can also program a switch with static MAC address entries.

Remember that a switch learns based on source MAC information but then switches frames from port to port, based on the destination MAC information. Switches typically use one of three switching methods to forward frames:

- **Store-and-forward switching:** This means the LAN switch copies each complete frame into the switch memory buffers and computes the cyclic redundancy check (CRC) checksum over the frame's data and compares the calculated value with the value carried within the FCS field for detecting any errors before forwarding the frame. Store-and-forward adds some delay for each frame, but it guarantees that any frames forwarded out of the switch are error free.

- **Cut-through switching:** As soon as the LAN switch copies into its memory just the destination MAC address, which is located in the first 6 bytes of the frame following the preamble, the switch looks up the destination MAC address in its switching table, determines the outgoing interface port, and starts forwarding the frame on to its destination through the designated switch port. The key point here is that the switch starts forwarding the first bits of the frame before having received the entire frame on the inbound port. In reality, cut-through tries to minimize the number of received bits before starting to copy the frame onto the outgoing port.

- **Fragment-free switching:** This works like cut-through switching with the exception that a switch in fragment-free mode stores the first 64 bytes of the frame before forwarding. Fragment-free switching can be viewed as a compromise between store-and-forward switching and cut-through switching. Note that many errors (such as collisions and runts) can be detected in the first 64 bytes of the frame. Fragment-free switching works best when forwarding frames received on an Ethernet segment where collisions might occur. Unlike cut-through switching, it only adds delay in the network shown in Figure 9.1 but does not protect against transmission errors.

Finally, please remember that port LEDs on a switch indicate the health status of ports (when in port status mode). Blinking green indicates that the port is sending and receiving data. Alternating green and amber indicates errors on the link. Amber indicates that a port is blocked by Spanning Tree Protocol.

Topic Quiz

1. What is the default aging time for MAC address entries on a typical Cisco switch?

   A. 60 seconds

   B. 120 seconds

   C. 300 seconds

   D. 1200 seconds

2. If the MAC address fa16.3ee3.7d71 exists in the MAC address table of a switch and is associated with the port gi0/1, which statement is true?

   A. Traffic with source MAC address fa16.3ee3.7d71 entering the switch is forwarded out port gi0/1.

   B. Traffic with source MAC address fa16.3ee3.7d71 entering the switch resets the aging timer.

   C. Traffic with destination MAC address fa16.3ee3.7d72 entering the switch is forwarded out port gi0/1.

   D. Traffic with destination MAC address fa16.3ee3.7d71 entering the switch is flooded.

3. What happens to a frame with destination MAC address ffff.ffff.ffff?

   A. The frame is dropped.

   B. The frame is forwarded out the gi0/0 port only.

   C. The frame is buffered.

   D. The frame is flooded out all ports except for the port on which the frame entered the switch.

4. Which statement about an Ethernet switch is true?

   A. The switch must use dynamic learning only.

   B. The switch records the destination MAC address from received frames.

   C. The switch drops broadcast frames by default.

   D. The MAC address aging process can be disabled.

Topic Quiz Answers

1. C is correct. The default aging time on most Cisco switches is 300 seconds.

2. B is correct. The aging timer is reset when traffic enters the switch with a known source MAC address.

3. D is correct. Notice that the MAC address shown is the broadcast MAC address. This triggers switch flooding behavior.

4. D is correct. It is possible to disable the switch aging process by setting the aging time to 0.

Interpret Ethernet Frame Format

Figure 9.2 shows the most common Ethernet frame format.

Preamble	SFD	Dest. MAC	Source MAC	Type	Data and Pad	FCS

Figure 9.2 *The Ethernet Frame Format*

Here is information you should know regarding this format:

- The fields before the Data and Pad field are collectively termed the *header*.

- The field after the Data and Pad field is known as the *trailer*.

- The Preamble field is 7 bytes in length. It is simply a pattern of alternating 1 and 0 bits that allows devices on the network to easily synchronize their receiver clocks.

- The Start Frame Delimiter (SFD) field is 1 byte in length. It also has a simple job: It marks the end of the Preamble field and indicates the beginning of the Destination MAC field.

- The Destination MAC field is 6 bytes in length and is used to store the frame's destination MAC address.

- The Source MAC address field is also 6 bytes in length. It stores the appropriate source MAC address.

- The Length/Type field is 2 bytes in length and identifies the protocol carried in the frame. For example, this field might indicate an IPv4 or IPv6 payload in a network. You might see this field described as Ether Type instead of just Type.

- The Data and Pad field ranges from 46 to 1500 bytes. The padding might exist so that the field can meet the minimum length requirement of 46 bytes. Of course, the data portion represents the actual data being sent from a higher layer of the OSI model. Some Cisco switches have the capability to support larger-than-default frames. These frame sizes include baby giants (from 1502 up to 1600 bytes) and jumbo frames (from 1601 up to 9216 bytes), depending on the switch model.

- The Frame Check Sequence (FCS) field is 4 bytes in length and holds the result of the cyclic redundancy check calculation on the frame's fields (except with the Preamble, SFD, and FCS fields). The purpose of this field is to determine whether the frame experienced transmission errors in its journey through the network.

Topic Quiz

1. What field of the Ethernet frame ensures that the frame was not damaged in transit?

   A. SFD

   B. Type

   C. FCS

   D. Preamble

2. What field of the Ethernet frame indicates whether IPv4 or IPv6 is in use?

   A. SFD

   B. Type

   C. FCS

   D. Preamble

3. What is the default MTU of the Data and Pad field of the Ethernet frame?

   A. 1200

   B. 900

   C. 1500

   D. 1600

Topic Quiz Answers

1. C is correct. The Frame Check Sequence field determines whether an error occurred during the transmission of the frame.

2. B is correct. The Type field indicates the protocol being carried in the frame's Data field.

3. C is correct. The default MTU for Ethernet is 1500 bytes.

Lab 9.1: Chapter Review

To complete this Hands-On Lab Practice Assignment, download the assigned Packet Tracer file from the book's companion website and perform the lab on your locally installed version of Packet Tracer. You will be following the instructions in the lab, and your performance will be evaluated.

In this lab, you will explore the basic switching concepts covered in this chapter. You will perform this review against the topology shown in Figure 9.3.

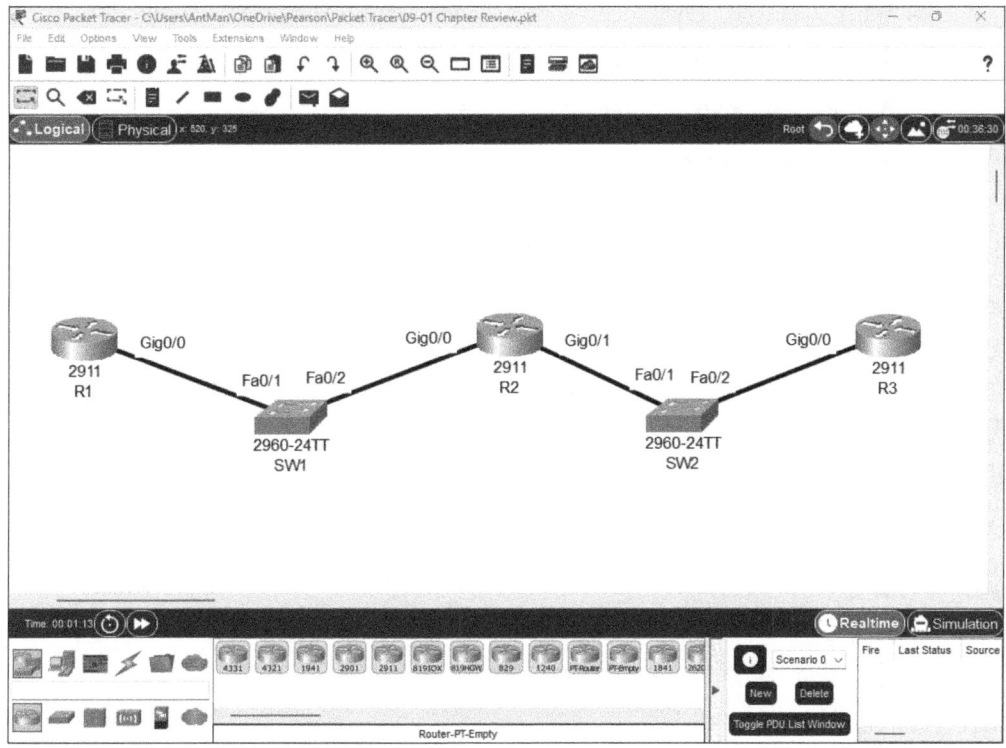

Figure 9.3   *The Basic Switching Chapter Review Lab*

Review Questions

1. When a frame enters a Cisco switch, what field does the switch learn from?

   A. Preamble

   B. FCS

   C. Source MAC

   D. Destination MAC

2. What is the name of the database that stores address information in a Cisco switch?

   A. MAC address table

   B. Routing table

   C. Interface table

   D. Buffer table

3. What command allows you to view the addresses learned by a Cisco switch?

   A. `show mac-address-table`

   B. `show mac address-table`

   C. `show addresses`

   D. `show mac addresses`

4. Why might padding be used in an Ethernet frame?

   A. To bring the entire length of the frame to 1500 bytes

   B. To bring the length of the Data field to 46 bytes

   C. To bring the length of the FCS field to 64 bytes

   D. To bring the length of the SFD field to 1 byte

5. If a switch has five workstations attached, how many collision domains are created?

   A. 1

   B. 0

   C. 5

   D. 6

Answers to Review Questions

1. C is correct. The switch examines and learns the source MAC addresses of incoming frames.

2. A is correct. The database is termed the MAC address table.

3. B is correct. The command is `show mac address-table`.

4. B is correct. Padding might be used in the Data and Pad field in order to bring it to the required minimum length of 46 bytes.

5. C is correct. Each of the five workstations connected to a switch is in its own collision domain.

Network Access

Welcome to another action packed section of this text. In this part, you'll learn about switching technologies, Layer 2 discovery protocols, and wireless technologies. Part III includes the following chapters:

Chapter 10

Configure and Verify VLANs and Interswitch Connectivity

This chapter covers the following official CCNA 200-301 exam topics:

- Configure, verify, and troubleshoot VLANs (normal/extended range) spanning multiple switches

- Configure, verify, and troubleshoot interswitch connectivity

- Configure, verify, and troubleshoot (Layer 2/Layer 3) EtherChannel

This is a critical chapter. Your ability to build the Layer 2 logical structure of a LAN is very important. This structure includes VLANs, trunks, and sometimes EtherChannels. All of these technologies are tackled in this chapter.

This chapter covers the following essential terms and components:

- Virtual local-area networks (VLANs)

- Data access ports

- Voice access ports

- The default VLAN

- Interswitch links

- Trunk ports

- 802.1Q

- The native VLAN

- EtherChannel

- LACP

- PAgP

Chapter Pretest

1. From an IP perspective, what does a VLAN equate to?

_____

2. What is the default VTP mode on a Cisco switch?

_____

3. What VTP mode effectively disables VTP?

_____

4. What command would you use to create VLAN 30?

_____

5. What is the default VLAN on a Cisco switch?

_____

6. What protocol allows a Cisco IP phone to function properly with the voice VLAN and the Cisco switch?

_____

7. What is the most common Ethernet trunking protocol in use today?

_____

8. What is the name of the VLAN that is not tagged on an Ethernet trunk?

_____

9. What is the default native VLAN on Cisco IOS switches?

_____

10. Why are administrators typically concerned about the native VLAN?

_____

11. What technology aggregates multiple physical links so they can act as one link?

_____

12. What are three options for EtherChannel configuration?

_____

Answers

1. A VLAN equates to an IP subnet.

2. The default VTP mode is Server.

3. VTP Transparent mode effectively disables VTP. Some switches also support the Off mode in addition to Server, Client, and Transparent modes.

4. The command `vlan 30` creates VLAN 30. The creation of the VLAN occurs when exiting VLAN configuration mode.

5. VLAN 1

6. Cisco Discovery Protocol (CDP)

7. 802.1Q is the most common Ethernet trunking protocol in use today.

8. The native VLAN is not tagged.

9. The default native VLAN is VLAN 1.

10. The native VLAN brings up security concerns.

11. Layer 2 and Layer 3 EtherChannel

12. Static, LACP, and PAgP

Configure, Verify, and Troubleshoot VLANs (Normal Range) Spanning Multiple Switches

A virtual local-area network (VLAN) is a broadcast domain you create on a switch. This domain also corresponds to a TCP/IP subnet. Figure 10.1 shows an example of VLANs created on a Cisco switch.

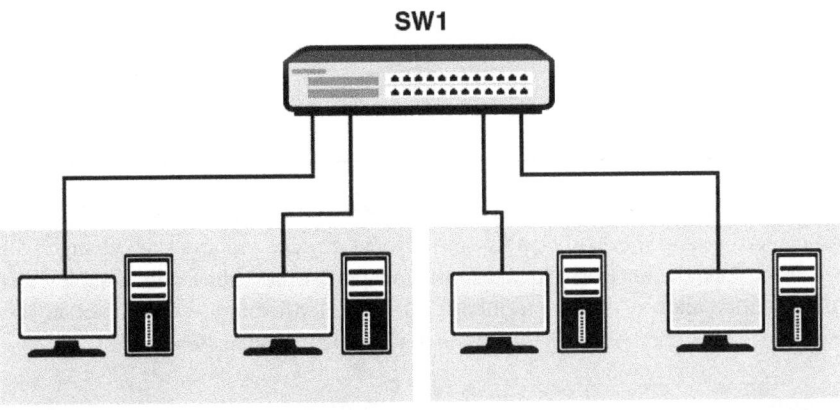

SW1

VLAN 20–EAST–10.20.20.0/24   **VLAN 30–WEST–10.30.30.0/24**

Figure 10.1 *VLANs on a Cisco Switch*

Cisco provides *VLAN Trunking Protocol* (*VTP*) to assist with VLAN creation and synchronization across many switches. In fact, this is why the word *Trunking* appears in the name. In order for VLAN creation to automatically span switches, the switches must be connected with special interswitch links called *trunks*. (The next section of this chapter focuses on trunks.)

Note *Trunk* is the term Cisco uses for a port that can carry traffic for more than one VLAN. Other equipment vendors use different terms, such as *tagged port*.

Example 10.1 shows the default VTP status of a Cisco switch.

Example 10.1   *The Default VTP Status for a Cisco Switch*

```
Switch# show vtp status
VTP Version capable        : 1 to 3
VTP version running        : 1
VTP Domain Name            :
VTP Pruning Mode           : Disabled
VTP Traps Generation       : Disabled
Device ID                  : fa16.3ebb.cb23
Configuration last modified by 0.0.0.0 at 0-0-00 00:00:00
Local updater ID is 0.0.0.0 (no valid interface found)


Feature VLAN:
--------------
VTP Operating Mode             : Server
Maximum VLANs supported locally : 1005
Number of existing VLANs       : 5
Configuration Revision         : 0
MD5 digest                     : 0x57 0xCD 0x40 0x65 0x63 0x59 0x47 0xBD
                                 0x56 0x9D 0x4A 0x3E 0xA5 0x69 0x35 0xBC
Switch#
```

In Example 10.1, note that VTP Operating Mode is set to Server by default. This means you can create and modify VLANs on this local device, and any such change will propagate throughout the network. In addition, Transparent mode basically disables VTP, whereas Client mode allows switches to inherit the VLAN information from a server(s). Note that you cannot create VLANs locally on a VTP client device.

Example 10.2 shows the creation of a VLAN on a Cisco switch.

Example 10.2   *Creating a VLAN on a Cisco Switch*

```
Switch(config)# vlan 20
Switch(config-vlan)# name EAST
Switch(config-vlan)# end
Switch#
%SYS-5-CONFIG_I: Configured from console by console
Switch#
```

Example 10.3 demonstrates several critical points that are likely to be tested on the CCNA 200-301 exam. Notice that one powerful command for verifying VLANs is **show vlan brief**. Also notice that the new VLAN WEST does not appear in the output because you have not exited config-vlan mode. Also, if you want to configure a hostname for the switch itself, you use the **hostname** command from global configuration mode. The limits for the hostname are 63 characters, letters, numbers, or hyphens and no spaces. The name also must begin and end with a letter or number.

Example 10.3 *Configuring and Verifying a VLAN*

```
Switch# configure terminal
Enter configuration commands, one per line. End with CNTL/Z.
Switch(config)# vlan 30
Switch(config-vlan)# name WEST
Switch(config-vlan)# do show vlan brief
VLAN Name                             Status     Ports
---- -------------------------------- ---------- -------------------
1    default                          active     Gi0/0, Gi0/1, Gi0/2,
                                                 Gi0/3
                                                 Gi1/0
20   EAST                             active
1002 fddi-default                     act/unsup
1003 token-ring-default               act/unsup
1004 fddinet-default                  act/unsup
1005 trnet-default                    act/unsup
Switch(config-vlan)#
```

Notice that there is a VLAN 1 by default on a Cisco switch and that all non-trunk ports are listed as participants of this VLAN. This is termed the *default VLAN*. It is a best practice to remove all ports from the default VLAN. Typically, engineers create a special unused VLAN for any ports they are not using on the switch. By default, two hosts connected to the same switch are in separate collision domains (one per port), but they are both part of the same Layer 2 broadcast domain and VLAN.

What good is a VLAN if interfaces (ports) are not participating in it? Example 10.4 demonstrates the configuration of an interface for participation in a data VLAN as well as the simple verification.

Example 10.4 *Configuring and Verifying an Interface for a VLAN*

```
Switch# configure terminal
Enter configuration commands, one per line. End with CNTL/Z.
Switch(config)# interface gi0/1
Switch(config-if)# switchport mode access
Switch(config-if)# switchport access vlan 20
Switch(config-if)# end
```

```
Switch#
%SYS-5-CONFIG_I: Configured from console by console
Switch# show vlan brief
VLAN Name                      Status     Ports
---- -------------------- --------- ----------------------
1    default              active    Gi0/0, Gi0/2, Gi0/3, Gi1/0
20   EAST                 active    Gi0/1
30   WEST                 active
40   TEST                 active
1002 fddi-default         act/unsup
1003 token-ring-default   act/unsup
1004 fddinet-default      act/unsup
1005 trnet-default        act/unsup
Switch#
```

Another big concern for the CCNA 200-301 exam is the configuration of a voice
VLAN for IP phones to use. Example 10.5 demonstrates voice VLAN configuration and
verification. Note that Cisco Discovery Protocol (CDP) is required for Cisco IP phones to
function properly with this configuration. Because CDP is running and enabled on every
port by default on Cisco switches, no configuration for CDP is shown here.

Example 10.5 *Configuring and Verifying a Voice VLAN*

```
Switch# configure terminal
Enter configuration commands, one per line. End with CNTL/Z.
Switch(config)# vlan 50
Switch(config-vlan)# name VOICE
Switch(config-vlan)# exit
Switch(config)# interface gi0/2
Switch(config-if)# switchport mode access
Switch(config-if)# switchport access vlan 30
Switch(config-if)# switchport voice vlan 50
Switch(config-if)# end
Switch#
%SYS-5-CONFIG_I: Configured from console by console
Switch# show vlan brief
VLAN Name                           Status      Ports
---- ------------------------------ ---------- -------------------
1    default                        active     Gi0/0, Gi0/3, Gi1/0,
20   EAST                           active     Gi0/1
30   WEST                           active     Gi0/2
40   TEST                           active
50   VOICE                          active     Gi0/2
```

```
1002 fddi-default                    act/unsup
1003 token-ring-default              act/unsup
1004 fddinet-default                 act/unsup
1005 trnet-default                   act/unsup
Switch# show interface gi0/2 switchport
Name: Gi0/2
Switchport: Enabled
Administrative Mode: static access
Operational Mode: static access
Administrative Trunking Encapsulation: negotiate
Operational Trunking Encapsulation: native
Negotiation of Trunking: Off
Access Mode VLAN: 30 (WEST)
Trunking Native Mode VLAN: 1 (default)
Administrative Native VLAN tagging: enabled
Voice VLAN: 50 (VOICE)
Administrative private-vlan host-association: none
Administrative private-vlan mapping: none
Administrative private-vlan trunk native VLAN: none
Administrative private-vlan trunk Native VLAN tagging: enabled
Administrative private-vlan trunk encapsulation: dot1q
Administrative private-vlan trunk normal VLANs: none
Administrative private-vlan trunk associations: none
Administrative private-vlan trunk mappings: none
Operational private-vlan: none
Trunking VLANs Enabled: ALL
Pruning VLANs Enabled: 2-1001
Capture Mode Disabled
Capture VLANs Allowed: ALL


Protected: false
Appliance trust: none
Switch#
```

Notice in the output in Example 10.5 that the `show interface switchport` command is used to verify the voice VLAN configuration.

Lab 10.1: Configuring VLANs

To complete this Hands-On Lab Practice Assignment, download the assigned Packet Tracer file from the book's companion website and perform the lab on your locally installed version of Packet Tracer. You will be following the instructions in the lab, and your performance will be evaluated.

In this lab, you will configure and verify VLANs in the topology shown in Figure 10.2.

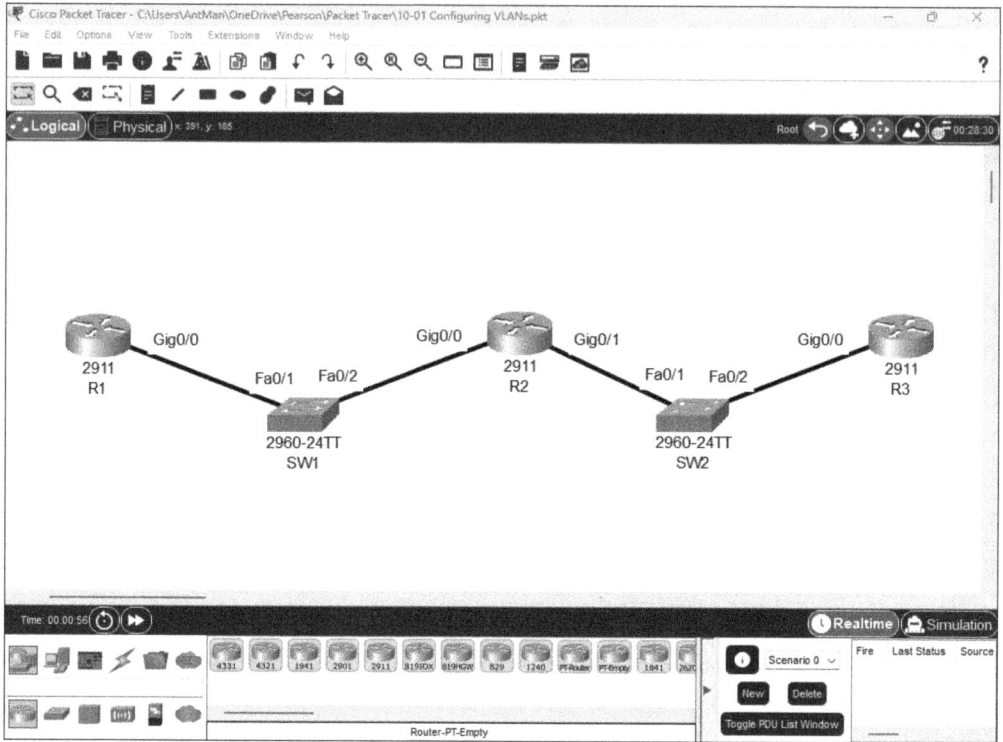

Figure 10.2 *The VLAN Configuration Lab*

Topic Quiz

1. Your 48-port Cisco switch has been configured with five different VLANs. How many broadcast domains exist on the switch?

A. 0

B. 1

C. 5

D. 48

2. What command allows you to easily verify the VTP mode?

A. show vtp mode

B. show vtp status

C. show vtp server

D. show vtp brief

3. What VTP mode would prevent you from creating a VLAN on the local switch?

   A. Client

   B. Server

   C. Transparent

   D. Off

4. What command allows you to view the VLANs and interface assignments on a switch?

   A. `show vlan brief`

   B. `show vlan status`

   C. `show vlan summary`

   D. `show vlan database`

5. What command assigns an access port to VLAN 20?

   A. `switchport vlan 20`

   B. `switchport mode vlan 20`

   C. `switchport assign vlan 20`

   D. `switchport access vlan 20`

6. What command assigns voice VLAN 10 on a switch access port?

   A. `switchport voice vlan 10`

   B. `switchport access vlan 10 voice`

   C. `switchport vlan 10 voice`

   D. `switchport access vlan 10`

7. What command allows you to verify the voice VLAN configuration?

   A. `show interface gi0/1 voice`

   B. `show interface gi0/1 switchport`

   C. `show interface gi0/1 vlan`

   D. `show interface gi0/1 vlan assign`

Topic Quiz Answers

1. **C is correct.** Each VLAN is a broadcast domain. If there are five VLANs defined on the switch, you have five broadcast domains.

2. **B is correct.** The `show vtp status` command allows you to verify many basic VTP parameters.

3. **A is correct.** Client mode prevents local VLAN creation.

4. **A** is correct. The `show vlan brief` command allows you to easily verify the VLANs and the interface assignments.

5. **D** is correct. The command is `switchport access vlan 20`.

6. **A** is correct. The command is `switchport voice vlan 10`.

7. **B** is correct. The command `show interface gi0/1 switchport` is very powerful and displays verbose information regarding the interface configuration, including the voice VLAN.

Configure, Verify, and Troubleshoot Interswitch Connectivity

How does traffic from different VLANs move from switch to switch? It moves over a trunk link—specifically, an 802.1Q trunk link.

Cisco originally created its own method of marking traffic with a VLAN ID for transport over an interswitch link. It was called Inter-Switch Link (ISL), and it took an interesting approach: ISL fully encapsulated the frame in order to add a VLAN marking. 802.1Q takes a different approach: It injects a 32-bit tag in the existing frame. Figure 10.3 shows the 802.1Q approach, which is inserted between the Source MAC and Type fields of the Ethernet header. 802.1Q allows multiple VLANs to be supported over a single trunk interface.

16 Bits	3 Bits	1 Bit	12 Bits
TPID	TCI		
	PCP	DEI	VID

Figure 10.3   *The 802.1Q Tag*

Here is the breakdown of these values:

- **Tag protocol identifier (TPID):** A 16-bit field set to the value 0x8100 in order to identify the frame as an IEEE 802.1Q-tagged frame.

- **Tag control information (TCI):** This section consists of the following:

  - **Priority code point (PCP):** A 3-bit field that refers to the IEEE 802.1p class of service and maps to the frame priority level.

  - **Drop eligible indicator (DEI):** A 1-bit field that may be used separately or in conjunction with PCP to indicate frames eligible to be dropped in the presence of congestion.

  - **VLAN identifier (VID):** A 12-bit field specifying the VLAN to which the frame belongs.

Example 10.6 demonstrates the configuration and verification of 802.1Q trunking on a Cisco switch.

Example 10.6 *Configuring and Verifying Trunking*

```
Switch# configure terminal
Enter configuration commands, one per line. End with CNTL/Z.
Switch(config)# interface gi1/0
Switch(config-if)# switchport trunk encapsulation dot1q
Switch(config-if)# switchport mode trunk
Switch(config-if)# end
Switch#
%SYS-5-CONFIG_I: Configured from console by console
Switch# show interface gi1/0 switchport
Name: Gi1/0
Switchport: Enabled
Administrative Mode: trunk
Operational Mode: trunk
Administrative Trunking Encapsulation: dot1q
Operational Trunking Encapsulation: dot1q
Negotiation of Trunking: On
Access Mode VLAN: 1 (default)
Trunking Native Mode VLAN: 1 (default)
Administrative Native VLAN tagging: enabled
Voice VLAN: none
Administrative private-vlan host-association: none
Administrative private-vlan mapping: none
Administrative private-vlan trunk native VLAN: none
Administrative private-vlan trunk Native VLAN tagging: enabled
Administrative private-vlan trunk encapsulation: dot1q
Administrative private-vlan trunk normal VLANs: none
Administrative private-vlan trunk associations: none
Administrative private-vlan trunk mappings: none
Operational private-vlan: none
Trunking VLANs Enabled: ALL
Pruning VLANs Enabled: 2-1001
Capture Mode Disabled
Capture VLANs Allowed: ALL
Protected: false
Appliance trust: none
Switch# show interface trunk


Port    Mode    Encapsulation  Status      Native vlan
Gi1/0   on      802.1q         trunking    1


Port    Vlans allowed on trunk
Gi1/0   1-4094
```

```
Port    Vlans allowed and active in management domain
Gi1/0   1,20,30,40,50

Port    Vlans in spanning tree forwarding state and not pruned
Gi1/0   1,20,30,40,50
Switch#
```

By default, there is a very special VLAN in the 802.1Q infrastructure: the *native VLAN*. This VLAN is not tagged. It is the only untagged VLAN on a trunk link. By default, the native VLAN is VLAN 1—the default VLAN. Why would Cisco introduce a native VLAN feature? The idea is to use it for management traffic so that this critical traffic can still flow between devices, even if a link loses its trunking status. CDP messages (as well as DTP and VTP messages) are sent over the native VLAN by default.

Lab 10.2: Configuring Interswitch Connectivity

To complete this Hands-On Lab Practice Assignment, download the assigned Packet Tracer file from the book's companion website and perform the lab on your locally installed version of Packet Tracer. You will be following the instructions in the lab, and your performance will be evaluated.

In this lab, you will configure and verify interswitch connectivity in the topology shown in Figure 10.4.

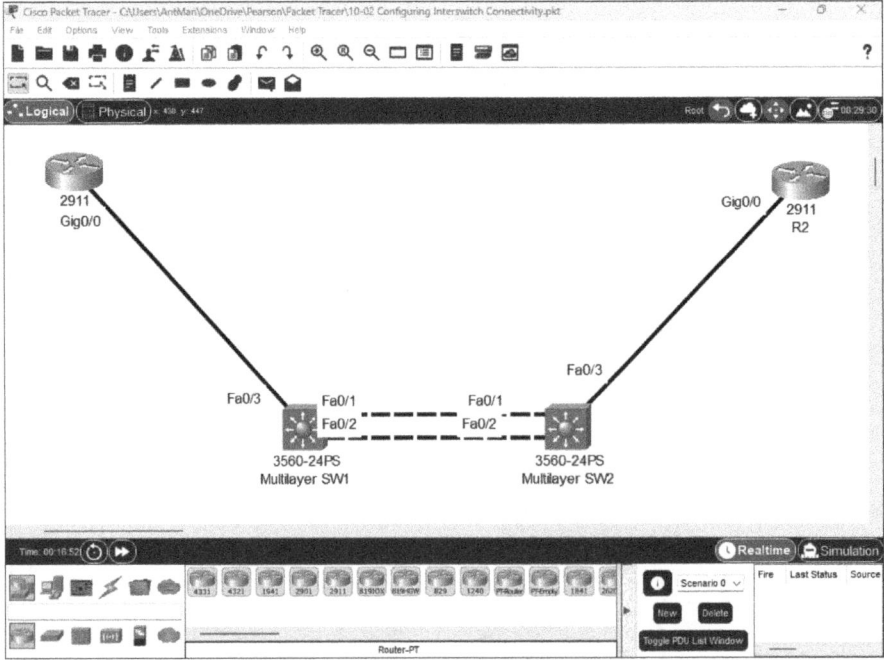

Figure 10.4 *The Configuring Interswitch Connectivity Lab*

Topic Quiz

1. Where is an 802.1Q tag inserted in a frame?

   A. Between the Preamble and SFD fields

   B. Between the Source and Destination MAC fields

   C. Between the Source MAC and Type fields

   D. Between the Source MAC and FCS fields

2. What command configures an interface to trunk?

   A. `switchport trunk`

   B. `switchport trunk dot1q`

   C. `switchport mode trunk`

   D. `switchport trunk enable`

3. What command allows you to quickly view all the trunks on a switch?

   A. `show vlans trunk`

   B. `show interface trunk`

   C. `show trunk interface`

   D. `show trunk all`

4. What is the native VLAN feature intended to carry?

   A. Security traffic

   B. Monitoring traffic

   C. Voice VLAN traffic

   D. Management traffic

5. What methods can a network engineer use to stop security issues with the native VLAN? (Choose two.)

   A. Eliminate VLAN 1.

   B. Disable VLAN 1.

   C. Tag the native VLAN.

   D. Use an unused VLAN for the native VLAN.

Topic Quiz Answers

1. C is correct. The tag is inserted between the Source MAC and Type fields.

2. C is correct. The command is `switchport mode trunk`.

3. B is correct. The command is `show interface trunk`.

4. D is correct. The native VLAN is intended to carry management traffic in the event that the 802.1Q trunking function fails.

5. C and D are correct. Today, engineers should tag the native VLAN or use an unused VLAN for the native VLAN. Doing so reduces some vulnerabilities.

Configure, Verify, and Troubleshoot (Layer 2/Layer 3) EtherChannel

The EtherChannel capability of Cisco switches is often included as part of Spanning Tree Protocol discussions. Why? Because EtherChannel tricks Spanning Tree Protocol and solves a similar problem. EtherChannel involves bundling together multiple links between two Cisco switches to act as a single link. Spanning Tree Protocol gets tricked by this, and it does not block any link within an EtherChannel bundle. Of course, Spanning Tree Protocol might need to block the entire bundle in order to avoid Layer 2 loops, but bundles that are not blocked enjoy the redundancy and increased bandwidth that EtherChannel provides.

To create EtherChannels, you must use interfaces that are of the same type and capabilities from a physical perspective. You should also ensure that they are configured identically.

The number of EtherChannels that a switch supports varies from device to device. A typical number supported for many Cisco switches is eight total EtherChannels. Figure 10.5 shows a topology used in this chapter for configuring, verifying, and troubleshooting the various EtherChannel configurations.

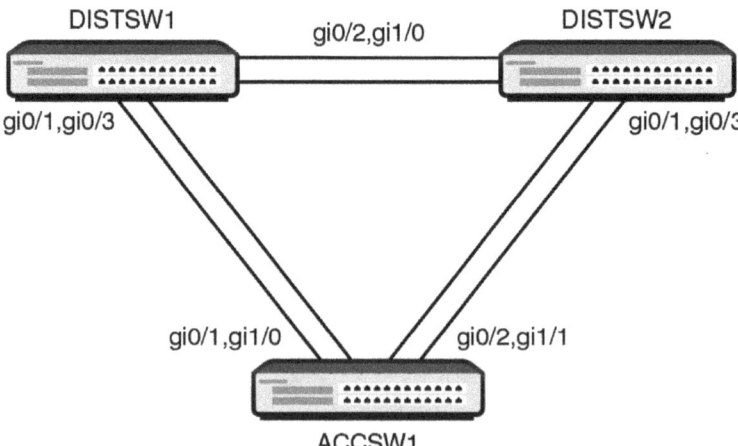

Figure 10.5 *A Sample EtherChannel Topology*

Example 10.7 demonstrates the configuration of a static Layer 2 EtherChannel.

Example 10.7 *Configuring a Static EtherChannel*

```
DISTSW1# configure terminal
Enter configuration commands, one per line. End with CNTL/Z.
DISTSW1(config)# interface range gi0/1 , gi0/3
DISTSW1(config-if-range)# shutdown
DISTSW1(config-if-range)#
%LINK-5-CHANGED: Interface GigabitEthernet0/1, changed state to administratively down
%LINK-5-CHANGED: Interface GigabitEthernet0/3, changed state to administratively down
DISTSW1(config-if-range)# channel-group 1 mode on
DISTSW1(config-if-range)# end
DISTSW1#
DISTSW1#


ACCSW1#
ACCSW1# configure terminal
Enter configuration commands, one per line. End with CNTL/Z.
ACCSW1(config)# interface range gi0/1 , gi1/0
ACCSW1(config-if-range)# channel-group 1 mode on
Creating a port-channel interface Port-channel 1

ACCSW1(config-if-range)# end
ACCSW1#

DISTSW1#
DISTSW1# configure terminal
Enter configuration commands, one per line. End with CNTL/Z.
DISTSW1(config)# interface range gi0/1 , gi0/3
DISTSW1(config-if-range)# no shutdown
DISTSW1(config-if-range)# end
DISTSW1#
```

Notice the following about the configuration shown in Example 10.7:

- The `interface range` command configures the two interfaces simultaneously.

- Issuing the `shutdown` command first prevents EtherChannel misconfiguration errors as the other side of this link defaults to the use of PAgP for dynamically configuring an EtherChannel. When statically configuring an EtherChannel, neither LACP nor PAgP is used.

- The `channel-group` command creates the EtherChannel; the ID 1 is locally significant only, and the mode on indicates a static configuration.

- When the other side of the link (ACCSW1) possesses the same configuration, you issue the command `no shutdown` for the interfaces on DISTSW1.

But does the configuration in Example 10.7 work? Example 10.8 demonstrates how easy it is to verify the EtherChannel.

Example 10.8 *Verifying a Static EtherChannel*

```
DISTSW1#
DISTSW1# show etherchannel 1 summary
Flags: D - down         P - bundled in port-channel
       I - stand-alone  s - suspended
       H - Hot-standby (LACP only)
       R - Layer3       S - Layer2
       U - in use       N - not in use, no aggregation
       f - failed to allocate aggregator

       M - not in use, minimum links not met
       m - not in use, port not aggregated due to minimum links not met

       u - unsuitable for bundling
       w - waiting to be aggregated
       d - default port


       A - formed by Auto LAG

Number of channel-groups in use: 1
Number of aggregators:           1
Group  Port-channel  Protocol    Ports
------+-------------+-----------+----------------------------
1      Po1(SU)          -         Gi0/1(P) Gi0/3(P)
DISTSW1#
```

Notice the following from the output in Example 10.8:

- The configuration creates a logical port channel interface with an ID of 1.

- The port channel interface is Layer 2 (S) and in use (U).

- The physical interfaces are labeled as bundled in a port channel (P).

Next, let's look at the creation of a Layer 2 EtherChannel using the built-in and default dynamic method Port Aggregation Protocol (PAgP). There are two settings possible here: **auto** and **desirable**. Example 10.9 demonstrates this configuration and verification.

Example 10.9   *Using PAgP to Form a Layer 2 EtherChannel*

```
ACCSW1#
ACCSW1# configure terminal
Enter configuration commands, one per line. End with CNTL/Z.
ACCSW1(config)# interface range gi0/2 , gi1/1
ACCSW1(config-if-range)# channel-group 2 mode desirable
Creating a port-channel interface Port-channel 2

ACCSW1(config-if-range)# end
ACCSW1#


DISTSW2#
DISTSW2# configure terminal
Enter configuration commands, one per line. End with CNTL/Z.
DISTSW2(config)# interface range gi0/1 , gi0/3
DISTSW2(config-if-range)# channel-group 2 mode desirable
Creating a port-channel interface Port-channel 2

DISTSW2(config-if-range)# end
DISTSW2#
DISTSW2# show etherchannel summary
Flags: D - down          P - bundled in port-channel
       I - stand-alone   s - suspended
       H - Hot-standby (LACP only)
       R - Layer3        S - Layer2
       U - in use        N - not in use, no aggregation
       f - failed to allocate aggregator
       M - not in use, minimum links not met
       m - not in use, port not aggregated due to minimum links not met
       u - unsuitable for bundling
       w - waiting to be aggregated
       d - default port


       A - formed by Auto LAG

Number of channel-groups in use: 1
Number of aggregators:           1

Group  Port-channel  Protocol    Ports
------+-------------+-----------+------------------------
2      Po2(SU)       PAgP         Gi0/1(P)  Gi0/3(P)

DISTSW2#
```

Example 10.10 shows the creation of a Layer 2 EtherChannel using Link Aggregation Control Protocol (LACP) for automatic negotiation. This mode uses **active** or **passive** settings. Notice that you again use the shutdown approach on the interfaces to avoid the misconfiguration errors that occur with the default mode of PAgP for some Cisco switches.

Example 10.10   *Using PAgP to Form a Layer 2 EtherChannel*

```
DISTSW1#

DISTSW1# configure terminal
DISTSW1(config)# interface range gi0/2 , gi1/0
DISTSW1(config-if-range)# shutdown
DISTSW1(config-if-range)# channel-group 3 mode active
Creating a port-channel interface Port-channel 3

DISTSW1(config-if-range)# end
DISTSW1#


DISTSW2#
DISTSW2# configure terminal
Enter configuration commands, one per line. End with CNTL/Z.
DISTSW2(config)# interface range gi0/2 , gi1/0
DISTSW2(config-if-range)# channel-group 3 mode active
Creating a port-channel interface Port-channel 3

ISTSW2(config-if-range)# end
DISTSW2#


DISTSW1#
DISTSW1# configure terminal
DISTSW1(config)# interface range gi0/2 , gi1/0
DISTSW1(config-if-range)# no shutdown
DISTSW1(config-if-range)# end
DISTSW1#
DISTSW1#
DISTSW1# show etherchannel 3 summary
Flags: D - down P - bundled in port-channel
       I - stand-alone s - suspended
       H - Hot-standby (LACP only)
       R - Layer3 S - Layer2
       U - in use N - not in use, no aggregation
       f - failed to allocate aggregator

    M - not in use, minimum links not met
    m - not in use, port not aggregated due to minimum links not met
```

```
        u - unsuitable for bundling
        w - waiting to be aggregated
        d - default port

        A - formed by Auto LAG

Number of channel-groups in use: 1
Number of aggregators:           2

Group  Port-channel  Protocol    Ports
------+-------------+-----------+------------------------------
3      Po3(SU)       LACP        Gi0/2(P)      Gi1/0(P)

DISTSW1#
```

Configuring a Layer 3 EtherChannel is also simple. Example 10.11 demonstrates this configuration after all previous configurations to DISTSW1 have been removed. Remember that static, LACP, and PAgP options all still exist. Also keep in mind that you create the port channel interface first and then assign it an IP address in the case of the Layer 3 EtherChannel.

Example 10.11 *Configuring a Layer 3 EtherChannel*

```
DISTSW1#
DISTSW1# configure terminal
DISTSW1(config)# interface port-channel 1
DISTSW1(config-if)# no switchport
DISTSW1(config-if)# ip address 10.10.10.1 255.255.255.0
DISTSW1(config-if)# exit
DISTSW1(config)# interface range gi0/1 , gi0/3
DISTSW1(config-if-range)# no switchport
DISTSW1(config-if-range)# shutdown
DISTSW1(config-if-range)# channel-group 1 mode on
DISTSW1(config-if-range)# no shutdown
DISTSW1(config-if-range)# end
DISTSW1#
```

Lab 10.3: Configuring EtherChannel

To complete this Hands-On Lab Practice Assignment, download the assigned Packet Tracer file from the book's companion website and perform the lab on your locally installed version of Packet Tracer. You will be following the instructions in the lab, and your performance will be evaluated.

In this lab, you will configure and verify EtherChannel connectivity in the topology shown in Figure 10.6.

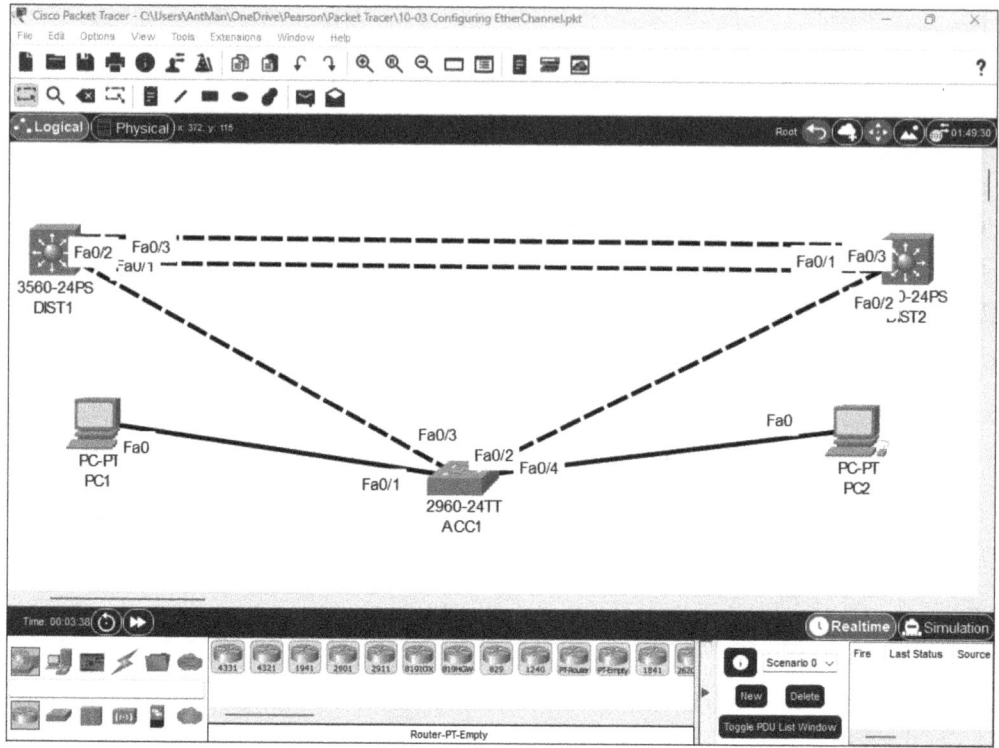

Figure 10.6   *The Configuring EtherChannel Lab*

Topic Quiz

1. What is the default EtherChannel mode on a Cisco switch?

A. PAgP

B. LACP

C. Static

D. NULL

2. Where do you assign the IP address in a Layer 3 EtherChannel?

A. The physical interfaces

B. The port channel interface

C. The NVI interface

D. Global configuration mode

3. What command creates an LACP EtherChannel with local ID 10?

A. `channel-group 10 mode active`

B. `channel-group 10 mode desirable`

C. `channel-group 10 mode on`

D. `channel-group 10 mode enable`

Topic Quiz Answers

1. **A** is correct. The default mode is PAgP.

2. **B** is correct. The IP address is configured at the port channel interface.

3. **A** is correct. The LACP options are `active` and `passive`.

Lab 10.4: Chapter Review

To complete this Hands-On Lab Practice Assignment, download the assigned Packet Tracer file from the book's companion website and perform the lab on your locally installed version of Packet Tracer. You will be following the instructions in the lab, and your performance will be evaluated.

In this lab, you will configure and verify the topics from this chapter in the topology shown in Figure 10.7.

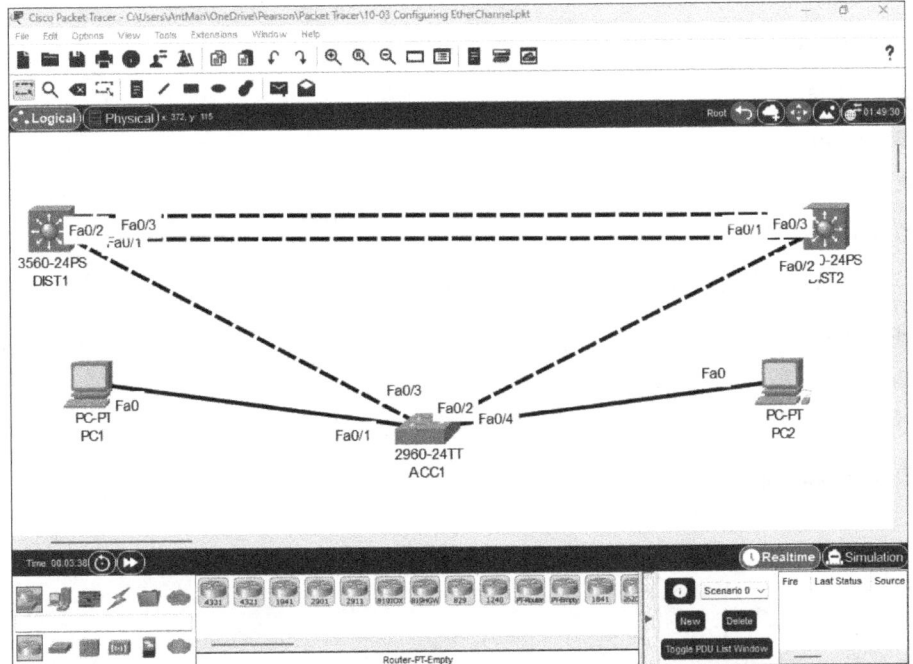

Figure 10.7   *The VLANs and Interswitch Connectivity Chapter Review Lab*

Review Questions

1. What protocol helps you create VLANs across different devices with ease?

  A. VTP

  B. Spanning Tree Protocol

  C. SPAN

  D. CDP

2. What must you do in order to place VLAN 20 in the VLAN database on your local device?

  A. Exit `config-vlan` mode.

  B. Restart the device.

  C. Place the device in Client mode.

  D. Save the running configuration.

3. What is the default VLAN in Cisco networking?

  A. VLAN 10

  B. VLAN 0

  C. VLAN 4092

  D. VLAN 1

4. How big is the VID field inside the 802.1Q tag?

  A. 12 bits

  B. 16 bits

  C. 32 bits

  D. 64 bits

5. Which keyword is used to statically configure an EtherChannel?

  A. `auto`

  B. `active`

  C. `on`

  D. `desirable`

Answers to Review Questions

1. **A** is correct. VTP allows you to configure or modify VLANs on a central device and then have the configurations synchronize across multiple switches.

2. **A** is correct. To complete a VLAN configuration, you must exit `config-vlan` mode.

3. **D** is correct. VLAN 1 is the default VLAN in Cisco.

4. **A** is correct. The VID field is 12 bits in size.

5. **C** is correct. Use the **on** keyword when creating the EtherChannel in order to statically configure the bundle. Note that this avoids the use of both PAgP and LACP.

Chapter 11

Configure and Verify Layer 2 Discovery Protocols

This chapter covers the following official CCNA 200-301 exam topics:

- Configure and verify Cisco Discovery Protocol (CDP)
- Configure and verify Link Layer Discovery Protocol (LLDP)

This chapter ensures that you are ready for questions related to two simple but important topics from the Network Access section of the CCNA 200-301 exam blueprint from Cisco Systems.

This chapter covers the following essential terms and components:

- Layer 2 protocols
- Cisco Discovery Protocol (CDP)
- Link Layer Discovery Protocol (LLDP)

Chapter Pretest

1. What is the Cisco Layer 2 protocol for discovering neighbors?

   _____

2. What is the default status on a switch or router for Cisco's proprietary Layer 2 neighbor discovery protocol?

   _____

3. What is the open standard Layer 2 protocol for discovering neighbors?

_____

4. What is the global configuration command to ensure that a Cisco device speaks LLDP?

_____

Answers

1. Cisco Discovery Protocol (CDP)

2. CDP is enabled by default.

3. Link Layer Discovery Protocol (LLDP)

4. `lldp run`

Configure and Verify Cisco Discovery Protocol (CDP)

Cisco Discovery Protocol is a Layer 2 protocol that allows Cisco devices to communicate information about each other to their directly connected neighbors. This can be useful when you are unsure of the topology. Cisco IP phones also use it to communicate their capabilities and VLAN information to their local switch. CDP messages from a Cisco router are not forwarded by a directly connected Cisco switch. Two routers connected to the same switch would not see each other's CDP messages. On Ethernet, CDP messages are encapsulated within standard Ethernet frames, and the destination MAC address is a multicast MAC address. This actually means that non-Cisco standards-based switches flood CDP frames out all their interfaces. So, Cisco switches are not standards compliant when it comes to CDP frames, but Cisco devices connected by a non-Cisco switch will successfully exchange CDP messages.

CDP is enabled by default on all interfaces of Cisco routers and switches. To ensure that it has not been disabled globally on a device or to ensure that it has not been "trimmed" off an interface, you can use the commands shown in Example 11.1.

Example 11.1 *Ensuring That CDP Is Running on a Device and on an Interface*

```
Switch# configure terminal
Enter configuration commands, one per line. End with CNTL/Z.
Switch(config)# cdp run
Switch(config)# interface gi1/0
Switch(config-if)# cdp enable
Switch(config-if)# end
Switch#
%SYS-5-CONFIG_I: Configured from console by console
Switch#
```

To verify that CDP is running globally, use the `show cdp` command. To verify that CDP is indeed enabled on an interface, use the `show cdp interface` command. To view the information collected by CDP about neighboring devices, use the `show cdp neighbors detail` command.

Administrators might disable CDP globally or on certain interfaces if they are concerned about a device sharing information with an unauthorized neighbor. This concern is legitimate and often leads to disabling CDP on specific public-facing interfaces.

Note Remember that CDP is its own Layer 2 protocol. It does not rely on other protocols. To quote Cisco: "Cisco Discovery Protocol is a Layer 2, media-independent, and network-independent protocol that networking applications use to learn about nearby, directly connected devices."

Topic Quiz

1. What technology does CDP rely on in its operation?

   A. TCP

   B. UDP

   C. ICMP

   D. Layer 2

2. What modern technology heavily relies on CDP?

   A. Cisco VoIP phones

   B. Webex

   C. Catalyst switches

   D. DTP

Topic Quiz Answers

1. D is correct. CDP operates at Layer 2 and does not use TCP, UDP, or ICMP.

2. A is correct. Cisco VoIP phones rely on CDP for neighbor discovery and capabilities exchange.

Configure and Verify Link Layer Discovery Protocol (LLDP)

CDP is obviously a Cisco-specific solution. The open standard protocol for discovering network neighbors is Link Layer Discovery Protocol (LLDP). Note that CDP and LLDP basically serve the same purpose: They provide a method for network devices to communicate information about themselves.

Unlike CDP, LLDP is not enabled globally by default on IOS. When enabled globally, however, it is also by default enabled to both transmit and process incoming LLDP frames on all Ethernet interfaces. Example 11.2 shows the commands that may be used to configure LLDP.

Example 11.2   *Ensuring That LLDP Is Running Globally and on an Interface*

```
Switch# configure terminal
Enter configuration commands, one per line. End with CNTL/Z.
Switch(config)# lldp run
Switch(config)# interface gi1/0
Switch(config-if)# lldp transmit
Switch(config-if)# lldp receive
Switch(config-if)# end
Switch#
%SYS-5-CONFIG_I: Configured from console by console
Switch#
```

To verify that LLDP is running globally, use the `show lldp` command. To verify that LLDP is indeed enabled on an interface, use the `show lldp interface` command. To view the information collected by LLDP about neighboring devices, use the `show lldp neighbors detail` command.

Because LLDP is defined as part of the Ethernet standard, it is available only on Ethernet interfaces. If you need to discover neighbors over non-Ethernet interfaces, your only option is to run CDP.

Topic Quiz

1. What interface-level command ensures that an interface will process incoming LLDP frames?

   A. lldp receive

   B. lldp enable

   C. lldp run

   D. lldp all

2. Which statement regarding LLDP is false in relation to Cisco devices?

   A. LLDP is not enabled by default on IOS devices.

   B. Cisco invented LLDP.

   C. LLDP is compatible with CDP.

   D. After being enabled globally, LLDP must be enabled on specific interfaces.

Topic Quiz Answers

1. **A** is correct. You use the `lldp receive` command on an interface in order to ensure that the device processes incoming LLDP frames on that interface.

2. **B** is correct. LLDP is an open standard protocol that is specified in the IEEE 802.3 standard; it was not invented by Cisco Systems.

Lab 11.1: Chapter Review

To complete this Hands-On Lab Practice Assignment, download the assigned Packet Tracer file from the book's companion website and perform the lab on your locally installed version of Packet Tracer. You will be following the instructions in the lab, and your performance will be evaluated.

In this lab, you will configure and verify the various Layer 2 discovery tasks covered in this chapter. You will perform this review against the topology shown in Figure 11-1.

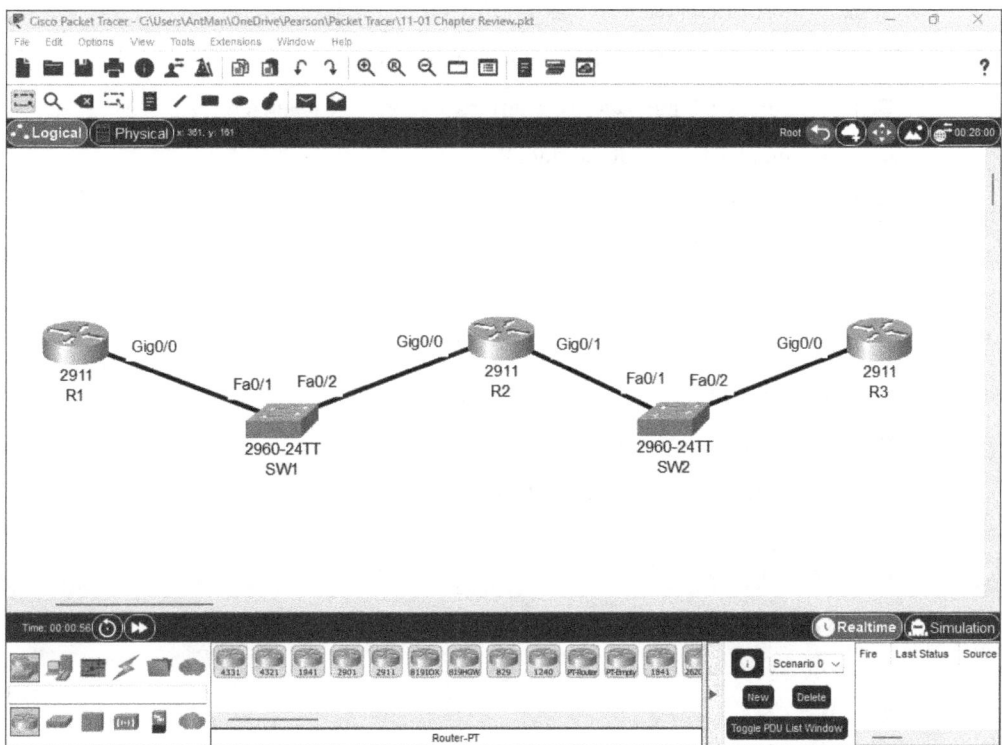

Figure 11.1 *The Layer 2 Discovery Chapter Review Lab*

Review Questions

1. What command disables CDP globally on a device?

    A. `no cdp run`

    B. `no cdp enable`

    C. `cdp disable`

    D. `cdp stop`

2. What command ensures that CDP is running on a specific interface?

    A. `cdp enable`

    B. `cdp on`

    C. `cdp run`

    D. `cdp accept`

3. What is most often meant by the term "trimming" CDP?

    A. Using version 1 of CDP to make it more efficient

    B. Forwarding CDP messages to a different subnet by using a relay

    C. Not running CDP on all interfaces

    D. Globally disabling CDP

4. Which statement about CDP is correct?

    A. CDP relies on TCP.

    B. CDP is disabled by default.

    C. CDP is disabled on all serial interfaces by default.

    D. CDP is a Layer 2 protocol.

5. On a Cisco device, what command would you use on an interface to ensure that the interface is sending LLDP frames?

    A. `lldp run`

    B. `lldp forward`

    C. `lldp transmit`

    D. `lldp send`

Answers to Review Questions

1. A is correct. You use the `no cdp run` command to globally disable CDP on a device. The `cdp disable` and `cdp stop` commands do not exist.

2. A is correct. You use the `cdp enable` command on an interface to run CDP on that specific interface.

3. C is correct. Trimming CDP refers to disabling it selectively on certain interfaces.

4. D is correct. CDP is a media- and protocol-independent Layer 2 protocol.

5. C is correct. On an interface on a Cisco device, you can use the `lldp transmit` command to ensure that the interface sends LLDP frames.

Chapter 12

Configure Rapid PVST+ Spanning Tree Protocol

This chapter covers the following official CCNA 200-301 exam topic:

■ Understand Rapid PVST+ Spanning Tree Protocol

Spanning Tree Protocol has existed for decades for a very good reason. Without this protocol, frames could potentially loop endlessly around a LAN if the LAN had physical paths that could permit this—and it is very common to create such paths to ensure redundancy in a LAN. For example, you want a server to be able to send traffic using an alternate path if there is an issue with the primary path. While Spanning Tree Protocol has been with us for decades, it has undergone many improvements, including the current versions of the protocol, Rapid PVST+.

This chapter covers the following essential terms and components:

■ Spanning Tree Protocol

■ PVST+

■ RPVST+

■ Spanning Tree Protocol root bridge selection

■ Spanning Tree Protocol optional features

Chapter Pretest

1. What two values make up the bridge ID for Spanning Tree Protocol purposes?

_____

2. How does the `show spanning-tree` command indicate that a Cisco switch is using PVST+?

_____

3. What is the converged state of a non-designated port?

_____

4. What value does Spanning Tree Protocol use to calculate the root port?

_____

5. What optional Spanning Tree Protocol feature permits ports to quickly transition from blocking to forwarding?

_____

Answers

1. The bridge ID is made up of the priority value and the system ID.

2. It shows `ieee`.

3. Blocking

4. The root cost value is used to calculate a root port.

5. PortFast

Understand Rapid PVST+ Spanning Tree Protocol

Spanning Tree Protocol is one technology of many that allows you to add redundancy to your switched infrastructure without causing Layer 2 switching loops. There are several different versions of Spanning Tree Protocol in use today. The classic version, termed 802.1D, might be the default on a Cisco Layer 2 switch today. If so, it is implemented on a per-VLAN basis, using a mode Cisco calls Per VLAN Spanning Tree Plus (PVST+).

Note Because classic Spanning Tree Protocol is an older technology, switches are called *bridges* in the Spanning Tree Protocol standards. Do not be confused by this terminology. When you are reading about Spanning Tree Protocol and you read *bridge*, just think of your modern switch.

This classic version of Spanning Tree Protocol operates as follows:

1. Spanning Tree Protocol elects a root bridge. Ports on this device are called *designated ports*, and each one is placed in a forwarding state.

2. Each nonroot switch calculates which one of its ports has the least cost between itself and the root bridge. This cost value is the switch's *root cost*. Spanning Tree Protocol makes this port the *root port* and puts it in the forwarding state.

3. Obviously, many switches can attach to the same Ethernet segment. When two non-root switches connect to a shared segment, the switch with the lowest root cost is selected as the segment's designated bridge. That switch's forwarding interface on that shared link is the designated port for that segment.

4. Nonroot and non-designated ports in the topology are placed in a blocking state.

Note   To find the lowest bridge ID (BID) for the root switch election, remember that the MAC address is represented in hexadecimal and is the least significant part of the BID. The hex numbering system is as follows: 0, 1, 2, 3, 4, 5, 6, 7, 8, 9, A, B, C, D, E, F.

Notice that the key first step in this process is the election of the root bridge. To elect the root bridge, switches use Spanning Tree Protocol bridge protocol data units (BPDUs) to carry their bridge ID information. The device with the lowest bridge ID becomes the root bridge. This bridge ID is an 8-byte value that is unique for each switch. This identi-fier consists of three parts (in descending order of significance): a 4-bit priority value, a 12-bit VLAN ID, and a 6-byte system ID. The 6-byte system ID is based on the built-in MAC address for the switch.

Note   Notice that if you do not modify the priority values on your switches, the election of the root bridge is based on the switch with the lowest built-in MAC address in your topology.

Figure 12.1 provides the topology used to study Spanning Tree Protocol further in this chapter.

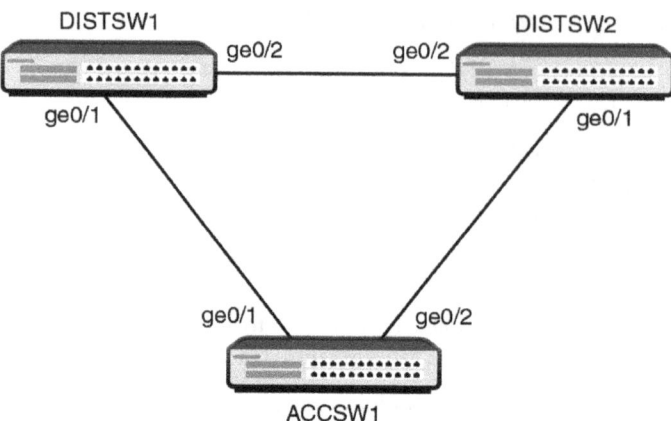

Figure 12.1 *A Classic Sample Spanning Tree Protocol Topology*

Example 12.1 shows a key verification and troubleshooting command for Spanning Tree Protocol: `show spanning-tree.`

Example 12.1 *Verifying Spanning Tree Protocol*

```
DISTSW1#
DISTSW1# show spanning-tree

VLAN0001
  Spanning tree enabled protocol ieee
  Root ID    Priority    32769
             Address     fa16.3e2c.8b4f
             Cost        4
             Port        2 (GigabitEthernet0/1)
             Hello Time  2 sec Max Age 20 sec Forward Delay 15 sec

  Bridge ID  Priority    32769 (priority 32768 sys-id-ext 1)
             Address     fa16.3e3e.8330
             Hello Time  2 sec Max Age 20 sec Forward Delay 15 sec
             Aging Time  300 sec


Interface        Role Sts   Cost   Prio.Nbr Type
---------------- ---- ---    ------ ------   ----------------
Gi0/1            Root FWD    4      128.2    Shr
Gi0/2            Desg FWD    4      128.3    Shr

DISTSW1#
```

From this command output, you can determine some important details regarding this spanning tree topology, including the following:

- The VLAN running Spanning Tree Protocol in the topology is VLAN0001.

- The Spanning Tree Protocol mode that is running by default on this device is ieee; this means PVST+ (Cisco's per-VLAN flavor of 802.1D).

- The root bridge in this topology has the MAC address fa16.3e2c.8b4f and priority value 32769 (which is the default value 32768 plus the VLAN ID 1).

- The local bridge ID is fa16.3e3e.8330, with a bridge priority of 32769; therefore, this is not the root bridge.

- Both of the local switch ports are in the forwarding state. One port is the root port, and the other port is a designated port.

Where is the root bridge? It must be the device off the gi0/1 interface (the root port): ACCSW1. You can confirm this by running **show spanning-tree** on that device, as shown in Example 12.2.

Example 12.2   *Verifying Spanning Tree Protocol on ACCSW1*

```
ACCSW1#
ACCSW1# show spanning-tree

VLAN0001
  Spanning tree enabled protocol ieee
  Root ID  Priority    32769
           Address     fa16.3e2c.8b4f
           This bridge is the root
           Hello Time  2 sec Max Age 20 sec Forward Delay 15 sec

  Bridge ID Priority    32769 (priority 32768 sys-id-ext 1)
           Address     fa16.3e2c.8b4f
           Hello Time  2 sec Max Age 20 sec Forward Delay 15 sec
           Aging Time  300 sec


Interface       Role Sts Cost      Prio.Nbr Type
--------------- ---- --- --------- -------- ----------------
Gi0/1           Desg FWD 4         128.2    Shr
Gi0/2           Desg FWD 4         128.3    Shr

ACCSW1#
```

From this output, you can determine the following:

■ Because this is the root bridge, you can see that the root ID information matches the bridge ID information; also, there is additional output that clearly states This bridge is the root.

■ As described earlier, all the ports on this device are forwarding and are designated ports.

So where is the blocking taking place in this topology? It must be on the device DISTSW2, as the output in Example 12.3 confirms.

Example 12.3   *Verifying Spanning Tree Protocol on DISTSW2*

```
DISTSW2#
DISTSW2# show spanning-tree

VLAN0001
 Spanning tree enabled protocol ieee
 Root ID  Priority    32769
          Address     fa16.3e2c.8b4f
          Cost        4
          Port        2 (GigabitEthernet0/1)
          Hello Time  2 sec Max Age 20 sec Forward Delay 15 sec

 Bridge ID Priority    32769 (priority 32768 sys-id-ext 1)
           Address     fa16.3edb.e1e9
           Hello Time  2 sec Max Age 20 sec Forward Delay 15 sec
           Aging Time 300 sec

Interface        Role Sts  Cost      Prio.Nbr Type
---------------- ---- ---  --------- -------- ---------------
Gi0/1            Root FWD  4         128.2    Shr
Gi0/2            Altn BLK  4         128.3    Shr

DISTSW2#
```

Notice the following on DISTSW2:

■ The root port (gi0/1) is in a forwarding state and connects directly to the root bridge of ACCSW1.

■ The non-designated port is gi0/2 and is in the blocking state; this port connects to the nonroot bridge of DISTSW1.

How can you reconfigure this topology so that the root bridge is DISTSW1? The answer is simple: Lower the priority value on that device. This causes a recomputation of the Spanning Tree Protocol topology. Example 12.4 demonstrates this configuration.

Example 12.4   *Configuring the Spanning Tree Protocol Priority Value*

```
DISTSW1#
DISTSW1# configure terminal
Enter configuration commands, one per line. End with CNTL/Z.
DISTSW1(config)# spanning-tree vlan 1 priority 4096
DISTSW1(config)# end
DISTSW1#
```

If this reconfiguration worked, verification should be simple on DISTSW1, thanks to show spanning-tree, as demonstrated in Example 12.5.

Example 12.5   *Verifying That DISTSW1 Is the New Root Bridge*

```
DISTSW1#
DISTSW1# show spanning-tree

VLAN0001
 Spanning tree enabled protocol ieee
 Root ID    Priority    4097
            Address     fa16.3e3e.8330
            This bridge is the root
            Hello Time   2 sec Max Age 20 sec Forward Delay 15 sec

 Bridge ID Priority    4097 (priority 4096 sys-id-ext 1)
           Address fa16.3e3e.8330
           Hello Time 2 sec Max Age 20 sec Forward Delay 15 sec
           Aging Time 300 sec


Interface       Role Sts  Cost      Prio.Nbr Type
--------------- ---- ---   --------- -------- ----------------
Gi0/1           Desg FWD  4         128.2    Shr
Gi0/2           Desg FWD  4         128.3    Shr

DISTSW1#
```

Although PVST+ does a decent job, it can be fairly slow to converge. Rapid Spanning Tree Protocol (RSTP) was invented to improve convergence time. Cisco implements RSTP with a VLAN-by-VLAN version named Rapid Per VLAN Spanning Tree Plus (RPVST+). It is simple to make this change on a device, as shown in Example 12.6.

Example 12.6   *Configuring a Switch for RPVST+*

```
DISTSW1#
DISTSW1# configure terminal
Enter configuration commands, one per line. End with CNTL/Z.
DISTSW1(config)# spanning-tree mode rapid-pvst
DISTSW1(config)# end
DISTSW1#
```

To verify this change, once again you can rely on **show spanning-tree**, as Example 12.7 demonstrates.

Example 12.7   *Verifying RPVST+*

```
DISTSW1#
DISTSW1# show spanning-tree

VLAN0001
 Spanning tree enabled protocol rstp
 Root ID   Priority   4097
           Address    fa16.3e3e.8330
           This bridge is the root
           Hello Time 2 sec Max Age 20 sec Forward Delay 15 sec

 Bridge ID Priority   4097 (priority 4096 sys-id-ext 1)
           Address    fa16.3e3e.8330
           Hello Time 2 sec Max Age 20 sec Forward Delay 15 sec
           Aging Time  300 sec

Interface        Role Sts Cost     Prio.Nbr Type
---------------- ---- --- --------- -------- ----------------
Gi0/1            Desg FWD 4         128.2    Shr Peer(STP)
Gi0/2            Desg FWD 4         128.3    Shr Peer(STP)

DISTSW1#
```

In a production environment, be sure that you make this change to your other switches as well so that you can take advantage of the faster convergence with Rapid PVST+.

You should also understand the enhancements made available with Rapid PVST+. Here is a summary of those enhancements:

- Convergence is much faster with Rapid PVST+, thanks to a proposal and agreement handshake process between point-to-point connected switches.

- Rapid PVST+ does not rely on timers to control convergence; many changes now trigger immediate convergence events.

- Rapid PVST+ has two new port roles: alternate port and backup port. The alternate port is a port that converges quickly in the event of the loss of a root port. The backup port is a fast-converging port to replace a designated port.

- Port states have been simplified. Specifically, the listening state has been removed completely. Ports can exist in one of the following four states: blocking, learning, forwarding, and disabled.

Spanning Tree Protocol has many powerful optional features you should consider. For the purposes of the CCNA 200-301 exam, you are responsible for understanding PortFast, Root Guard, Loop Guard, BPDU Filter, and BPDU Guard.

PortFast reduces the time it takes a port to move from blocking to forwarding in a Spanning Tree Protocol topology. This feature is used on ports connected to servers and workstations. PortFast should not be used on ports that connect to switches because it can cause switching loops. Example 12.8 demonstrates how easy it is to configure this powerful optional feature.

Example 12.8 *Configuring PortFast*

```
ACCSW1#
ACCSW1# configure terminal
Enter configuration commands, one per line. End with CNTL/Z.
ACCSW1(config)# interface gi0/3
ACCSW1(config-if)# spanning-tree portfast
%Warning: portfast should only be enabled on ports connected to a single host.
  Connecting hubs, concentrators, switches, bridges, etc... to this interface
  when portfast is enabled, can cause temporary bridging loops. Use with CAUTION

%Portfast has been configured on GigabitEthernet0/3 but will only
 have effect when the interface is in a non-trunking mode.
ACCSW1(config-if)# end
ACCSW1#
```

The Root Guard feature in Spanning Tree Protocol is an optional security measure that helps protect the stability of a network by preventing devices not designated as the root bridge from becoming the root bridge. If a device tries to become the root bridge by sending superior BPDUs, Root Guard places the port in a "root-inconsistent" state, blocking it until the superior BPDUs stop. This ensures that the intended network topology is maintained and prevents potential disruptions caused by unauthorized or misconfigured devices.

The Loop Guard feature is a preventive measure designed to avoid network loops that can occur when a switch stops receiving BPDUs on a non-designated port, possibly due to a unidirectional link failure or other issues. If BPDUs are no longer received on a port where they are expected, Loop Guard places the port into a "loop-inconsistent" state, preventing it from transitioning to the forwarding state. This action helps maintain network stability by preventing the formation of loops, which can cause significant network disruptions and degraded performance.

The BPDU Filter feature is used to control the transmission and reception of BPDUs on a network port. When enabled, BPDU Filter can prevent a port from sending or receiving BPDUs, effectively isolating it from participating in STP processes. This can be useful in specific scenarios where network administrators want to ensure that certain ports do not influence the STP topology or are used for devices that do not support STP. However, caution is required when using this feature, as it can lead to network loops if not properly managed.

Finally, the BPDU Guard feature is a protective measure that helps maintain network stability by automatically disabling a port if it receives a BPDU. This feature is typically applied to ports connected to end devices, such as computers or printers, which should not participate in the STP process. By shutting down the port upon receiving a BPDU, BPDU Guard prevents potentially misconfigured or unauthorized devices from disrupting the network's STP topology.

Topic Quiz

1. What is the first step of the Spanning Tree Protocol convergence process?

   A. Block non-designated ports.

   B. Calculate designated ports.

   C. Elect a root bridge.

   D. Calculate root ports.

2. What is the default Spanning Tree Protocol priority value?

   A. 0

   B. 32768

   C. 8192

   D. 4098

3. What command allows you to see the current Spanning Tree Protocol parameters on a Cisco switch?

   A. `show 802dot1d`

   B. `show topology spanning-tree`

   C. `show redundancy`

   D. `show spanning-tree`

4. What command sets the priority to 4096 for VLAN 10?

A. `spanning-tree vlan 10 priority 4096`

B. `spanning-tree priority 4096 vlan 10`

C. `spanning-tree 4096 10`

D. `spanning-tree priority 4096 vlan-id 10`

5. What optional STP feature seeks to preserve the root bridge selection by dynamically disabling ports receiving superior BPDUs?

A. BPDU Filtering

B. BPDU Guard

C. Loop Guard

D. Root Guard

Topic Quiz Answers

1. C is correct. The first step of the Spanning Tree Protocol convergence process is to elect a root bridge.

2. B is correct. The default Spanning Tree Protocol priority on Cisco switches is 32768.

3. D is correct. The `show spanning-tree` command is extremely valuable for checking the Spanning Tree Protocol parameters and status.

4. A is correct. The `spanning-tree vlan 10 priority 4096` command sets the priority value for the switch in VLAN 10.

5. D is correct. The Root Guard feature is an optional security measure that helps protect the stability of the network by preventing devices that are not designated as the root bridge from becoming the root bridge.

Lab 12.1: Chapter Review

To complete this Hands-On Lab Practice Assignment, download the assigned Packet Tracer file from the book's companion website and perform the lab on your locally installed version of Packet Tracer. You will be following the instructions in the lab, and your performance will be evaluated.

In this lab, you will configure and verify the RSTP tasks from this chapter. You will perform this review against the topology shown in Figure 12.2.

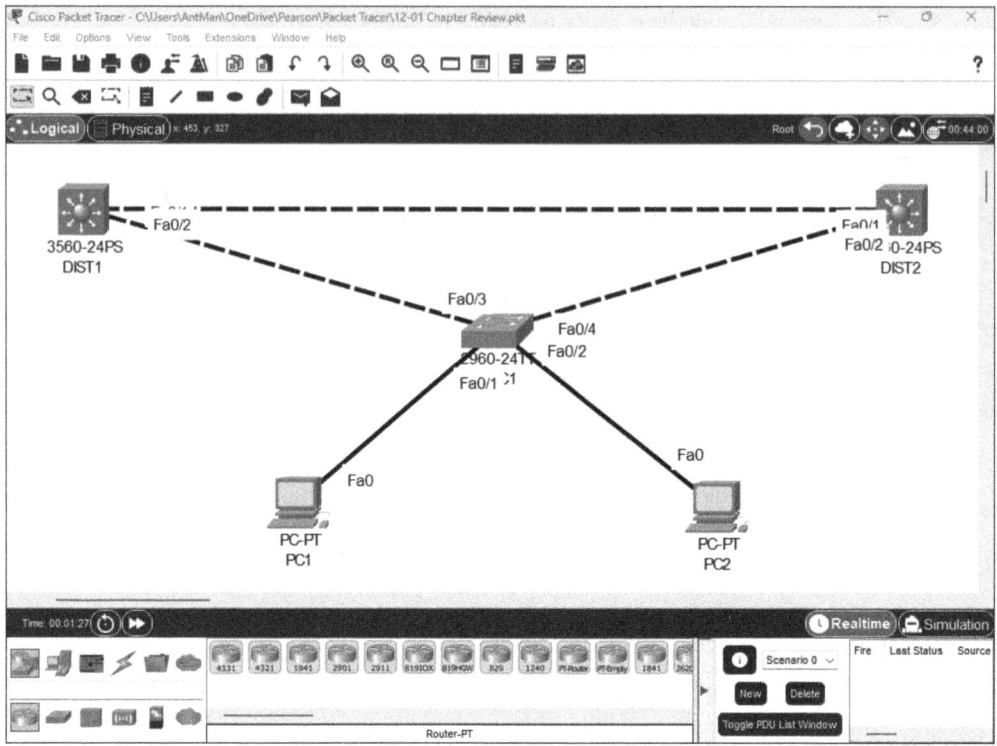

Figure 12.2   *The STP Chapter Review Lab*

Review Questions

1. What version of STP on a Cisco device implements classic IEEE 802.1D?

  A. MST

  B. PVST+

  C. TRILL

  D. RPVST+

2. What Spanning Tree Protocol feature is recommended for ports that connect to workstations or servers?

  A. PortFast

  B. UplinkFast

  C. BPDU Guard

  D. BackboneFast

3. What command allows a port to more quickly transition from blocking to forwarding?

A. `spanning-tree portfast`

B. `spanning-tree convergefast`

C. `spanning-tree rstp`

D. `spanning-tree port-fast enable`

4. What new port roles were introduced with Rapid PVST+? (Choose two.)

A. Alternate

B. Designated

C. Root

D. Backup

5. What STP optional feature is triggered by a switch no longer receiving BPDUs on a non-designated port?

A. BPDU Filtering

B. BPDU Guard

C. Loop Guard

D. Root Guard

Answers to Review Questions

1. B is correct. PVST+ uses classic Spanning Tree Protocol on a Cisco device.

2. A is correct. The optional PortFast feature for ports that connect to workstations or servers improves convergence time.

3. A is correct. The `spanning-tree portfast` command is applied in interface configuration mode and enables PortFast.

4. A and D are correct. The alternate and backup ports are new roles that exist to speed up convergence after topology changes (including failures).

5. C is correct. The Loop Guard feature is triggered by a non-designated port no longer receiving BPDUs.

Chapter 13

Compare Cisco Wireless Architectures and AP Modes

This chapter covers the following official CCNA 200-301 exam topic:

■ Using Cisco wireless architectures and AP modes

Cisco is a market leader in wireless technologies. It is therefore not surprising to see emphasis on Cisco wireless technologies in the CCNA 200-301 exam. This chapter helps you become very familiar with the basics of wireless according to Cisco. It also examines the ports and interfaces that are typical with wireless LAN controllers (WLCs) and access points. This chapter also discusses how to connect to and manage these devices. While Chapter 24, "Configure Wireless Security Protocols," details the various security options available for securing wireless networks, this chapter discusses the settings available on a modern WLC from Cisco Systems.

This chapter covers the following essential terms and components:

■ LAG

■ WLAN security profiles

■ WLAN QoS profiles

■ CAPWAP

■ AP modes

Chapter Pretest

1. Name at least three protocols supported for permitting management traffic communication with a Cisco wireless LAN controller.

_____

_____

_____

2. How many APs would be supported on a Cisco 9800 series controller?

_____

Answers

1. Telnet, SSH, HTTP, HTTPS, console, and TACACS+/RADIUS

2. 250

Using Cisco Wireless Architectures and AP Modes

What would a typical midmarket Cisco wireless LAN controller consist of these days? The Cisco Catalyst 9800-L wireless controller, shown in Figure 13.1, offers the following features and hardware:

Figure 13.1   *Cisco Catalyst 9800-L Wireless Controller*

- Support for 5 Gbps throughput
- Support for 250 APs
- Support for 5000 clients

- 2x 10G/Multigigabit copper or 2x 10G/Multigigabit fiber

- 4x 2.5G/1G copper physical ports

- Console port

- Several deployment modes: Centralized (local), Distributed Branch (Cisco FlexConnect), and SD-Access Wireless (fabric)

- A maximum of 4096 supported VLANs

- A maximum of 4096 WLANs

- High-availability support with Stateful Switchover (SSO)

- Link aggregation (LAG) for physical ports on the controller. (You configure an EtherChannel on the upstream switch to support the local LAG.)

This impressive controller from Cisco Systems offers many management options. For example, you can use a web-based GUI, the CLI, Cisco DNA Center, Netconf/YANG, or Cisco Prime Infrastructure to manage the WLC.

Note DNA Center provides a powerful single-pane-of-glass option for advanced deployment, provisioning, and management of many Cisco devices, including Cisco's many wireless products.

This controller supports all of your favorite management protocols and options, including Telnet, SSH, HTTP, HTTPS, and the console (serial). The Cisco WLC also supports the TACACS+ and RADIUS security protocols.

While the information listed here applies to the physical WLC appliance, keep in mind that you can also deploy the WLC functionality embedded in a Cisco switch, and there is also a virtualized cloud version.

When configuring a wireless LAN controller, you need to configure a profile for each of the following:

- WLAN

- Policy

- Site

- RF

You then configure the following tags for identification:

- Policy

- Site

- RF

Finally, you associate the appropriate tags with the appropriate access points in your infrastructure.

A major portion of your work on a controller involves configuring the wireless LAN. As mentioned earlier, you can create a whopping 4096 WLANs on the device. Each WLAN has a separate WLAN ID, a separate profile name, and a WLAN SSID.

A WLC can publish up to 16 WLANs to each connected access point. However, you can create the maximum number of supported WLANs and then selectively publish them (using access point groups) to different access points for managing your wireless network. Each WLAN can feature a different SSID, or multiple WLANs can all have the same SSID.

In addition to setting required parameters such as the RF band in use for the WLAN, you can set many advanced properties. For example, you can set various session timeout values, and you can even configure Cisco Compatible Extensions (CCX) so that you can have your WLC work with products from vendors other than Cisco.

Important quality of service (QoS) settings are available to help keep your wireless clients happy and productive. You can configure the following in this regard:

- SSID and client policies on wireless QoS targets

- Marking and policing of wireless traffic

- Mobility support for QoS

- The precious metal policies that come preconfigured on the controller, including the following:

  - Platinum for VoIP clients

  - Gold for video clients

  - Silver for traffic that can be considered best effort

  - Bronze for non-real-time (NRT) traffic

As you might guess, WLAN security profiles are critical configurations that you make on a WLC for your wireless infrastructures. Example 13.1 shows how such a profile is configured using the CLI on a WLC.

Example 13.1 *Configuring WLAN Security Settings*

```
Device# configure terminal
Device(config)# wlan mywlan 1 ajsnetworking
Device(config-wlan)# security wpa
Device(config-wlan)# security wpa wpa2 ciphers aes
Device(config-wlan)# end
```

How does the WLC connect to the various access points it manages in a secure fashion? Control and Provisioning of Wireless Access Points (CAPWAP) is the standard typically used. CAPWAP is based on Lightweight Access Point Protocol (LWAPP).

Remember that the access points that Cisco offers can typically operate in one of two modes:

- **Autonomous:** In autonomous mode, the access point does not need a wireless LAN controller for its operations. It possesses all the control plane intelligence it needs to function on the network and provide wireless services. Unfortunately, the feature set available and your ability to monitor and control the device are more limited. Notice that while "autonomous" sounds great, in the context of Cisco wireless solutions, it is actually not the preferred method. It might, however, be the perfect solution for very small office deployments where the power of a WLC is not needed.

- **Lightweight:** In lightweight mode, the access point requires a WLC in order to function properly on the network. Lightweight APs from Cisco can run in a number of different operational modes, as follows:

  - **Local:** This is the default mode in most deployments.

  - **REAP/H-REAP/FlexConnect:** Remote Edge Access Point (REAP) is used to address scalability issues with local mode when accommodating multiple remote locations.

  - **Bridge:** This mode permits bridging of the wired and wireless infrastructures.

  - **SE-Connect:** SE-Connect mode allows you to connect to the lightweight access point using Cisco Spectrum Expert and gather vital information about the RF spectrum surrounding the LAP.

  - **Sniffer:** A LAP operating in Sniffer mode is strictly for troubleshooting purposes.

  - **Rogue Detector:** Rogue Detector mode connects to the wired infrastructure, usually over a trunk link, and watches the traffic traversing the VLANs.

Topic Quiz

1. Up to how many WLANs can a Cisco 9800 series WLC publish to an AP?

   A. 16

   B. 64

   C. 225

   D. 1000

2. Which of the following is not an item for which you configure profiles when first setting up a WLC?

   A. Site

   B. RF

   C. Node

   D. WLAN

Topic Quiz Answers

1. A is correct. A WLC can publish up to 16 WLANs to a single AP.

2. C is correct. When you first set up a WLC, you configure profiles for the site, the RF, the WLAN, and the policy.

Lab 13.1: Chapter Review

To complete this Hands-On Lab Practice Assignment, download the assigned Packet Tracer file from the book's companion website and perform the lab on your locally installed version of Packet Tracer. You will be following the instructions in the lab, and your performance will be evaluated.

In this lab, you will configure and verify some key settings on a Wireless LAN Controller in Packet Tracer using the topology shown in Figure 13.2.

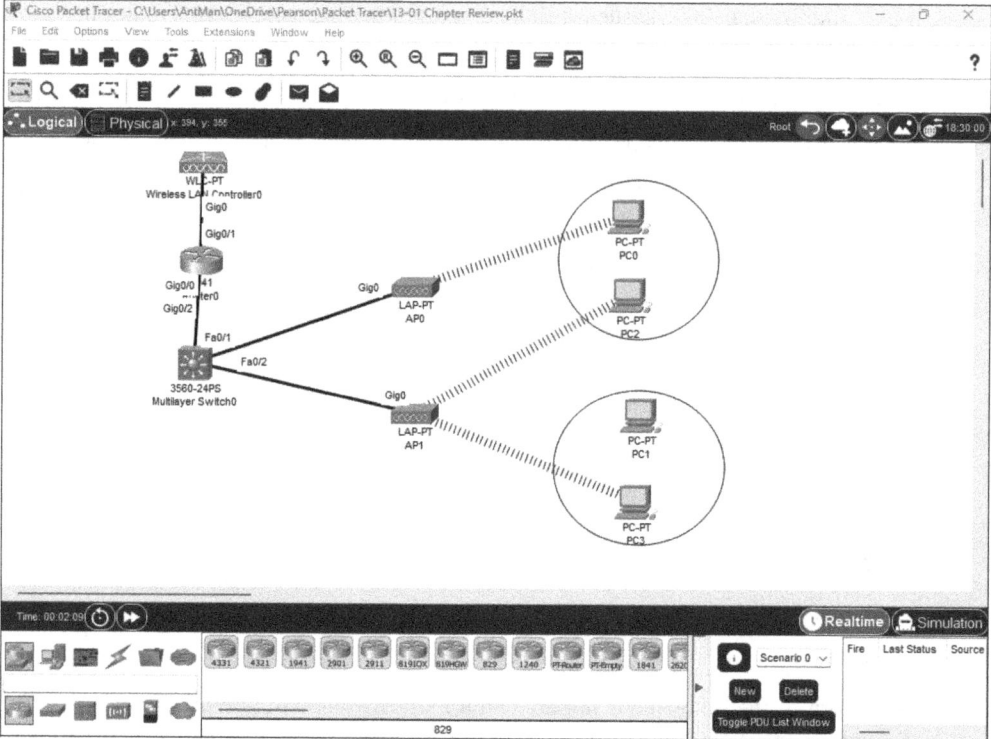

Figure 13.2 *The Cisco Wireless Chapter Review Lab*

Review Questions

1. What is a popular single-pane-of-glass approach to managing a Cisco WLC and other key Cisco components of the network infrastructure?

   A. Cisco Configuration Manager

   B. Cisco GUI Manager

   C. DNA Center

   D. CiscoWorks

2. What is the total throughput possible with a Cisco 9800 series WLC?

   A. 5 Gbps

   B. 10 Gbps

   C. 40 Gbps

   D. 80 Gbps

3. What technology permits high-availability configurations with physical ports on Cisco wireless LAN controllers?

   A. VTP

   B. STP

   C. LAG

   D. PoE

4. Which of the following are supported QoS settings for a WLAN built by a WLC? (Choose two.)

   A. Mobility support

   B. Buffered queuing

   C. Dynamic buffer expansion

   D. Marking and policing

Answers to Review Questions

1. **C** is correct. Cisco DNA Center is a single-pane-of-glass solution for the management of Cisco WLCs and other Cisco devices.

2. **A** is correct. 9800 series devices offer total throughput of 5 Gbps.

3. **C** is correct. WLCs support link aggregation (LAG), which permits the link bandwidth to be bundled together. LAG promotes high availability because even in the face of a failure of one link, the bundle can continue to forward traffic using surviving link members.

4. **A** and **D** are correct. QoS settings are possible through profiles. You can configure mobility support, marking and policing, and even prebuilt settings based on traffic classes.

IP Connectivity

In today's world that is so heavily reliant on the Internet, IP connectivity is more important than ever. This part begins with a high-level overview of routing concepts and quickly moves into details of router configurations, including IPv4 and IPv6 static routing and single area OSPF. Part IV includes the following chapters:

Chapter 14   Interpret the Components of a Routing Table

Chapter 15   Configure and Verify IPv4 and IPv6 Static Routing

Chapter 16   Configure and Verify Single Area OSPFv2

Chapter 14

Interpret the Components of a Routing Table

This chapter covers the following official CCNA 200-301 exam topics:

- Describe routing concepts

- Interpret the components of a routing table

- Describe how a routing table is populated by different routing information sources

This chapter ensures that you are ready for questions related to these topics from the "IP Connectivity" section of the CCNA 200-301 exam blueprint from Cisco Systems. This chapter is very important because routing is a critical function in networks.

This chapter covers the following essential terms and components:

- Packet handling

- Route lookups

- Frame rewriting

- Routing tables

- Prefixes

- Network masks

- Next hops

- Routing protocol code

- Administrative distances

- Metrics

- Gateways of last resort

Chapter Pretest

1. What criterion is used to determine the best match in a routing table lookup?

   _____

2. What does a router rewrite in a packet when forwarding data on Ethernet networks?

   _____

3. In a routing table, what does the IP address immediately following the word "via" indicate?

   _____

4. What does the routing protocol code EX stand for?

   _____

5. In a routing table entry, what do the two numbers in [120/1] mean?

   _____

6. What metric value does RIP use?

   _____

7. What is the gateway of last resort?

   _____

8. What is the meaning of an administrative distance value?

   _____

9. Which is preferred: a lower administrative distance or a higher administrative distance?

   _____

10. What is the default administrative distance value for a static route?

    _____

11. What is the default administrative distance value for Internal BGP?

    _____

Answers

1. The best match is the longest match prefix in the routing table.

2. The router rewrites the Layer 2 header, including the source and destination MAC addresses, along with a new frame check sequence (FCS), as part of the trailer in a newly encapsulated frame.

3. The word "via" indicates the next hop IP address. This is the IP address of the next router for forwarding packets to the destination indicated by the prefix before "via."

4. EIGRP External

5. 120 is the administrative distance, and 1 is the entry's metric.

6. RIP uses hop count as the metric.

7. The gateway of last resort is the default gateway for any unknown prefixes. The prefix entry of the gateway of last resort is 0.0.0.0/0, and it matches all destination addresses for which there is no more specific routing entry. In addition, there can be no less specific entry than the 0.0.0.0/0 entry.

8. Administrative distance is a measure of the trustworthiness of the routing information source. Note that a directly connected prefix is by far the most believable to the router.

9. A router prefers lower administrative distances.

10. 1

11. 200

Describe Routing Concepts

Let's begin with a discussion of how routing really works. You know a packet enters a router, and a routing lookup is done, but what does this really mean? What are the details of the packet-handling process?

When an IPv4 packet arrives on a router interface, the router de-encapsulates the Layer 2 frame and examines the Layer 3 IPv4 header. The router identifies the destination IPv4 address and proceeds through the route lookup process. The router scans the routing table to find a best match for the destination IPv4 address. The best match is the longest match in the table. For example, if the destination IPv4 address is 172.16.0.10, and the entries in the routing table are for 172.16.0.0/12, 172.16.0.0/18, and 172.16.0.0/26, the longest match and the entry used for the packet is 172.16.0.0/26. Remember that for any of these routes to be considered a possible match, there must be at least the number of matching bits indicated by the subnet mask of the routing table prefix. For example, the routing entries 192.168.5.0/24 and 192.168.0.0/16 are both matches for destination address 192.168.5.55, while routing entry 10.65.0.0/16 is not.

Another critical aspect to understand is the frame rewrite procedure used by a router. In order to do its job, a router needs to encapsulate the IP packet without substantially modifying the IP header (except the TTL value) into a new Layer 2 frame. The source MAC address in the outgoing frame is the MAC address of the forwarding interface of the local router. The destination MAC address is the MAC address of the receiving interface of the next hop device. An FCS is also added as the trailer. This process continues from hop to hop on Ethernet networks until the packet reaches the destination host. Even though this process essentially involves discarding the inbound L2 header and creating a brand-new L2 header, it is called an *L2 header rewrite*.

> **Note**   A technique that Cisco routers use to dramatically improve routing performance is to use Cisco Express Forwarding (CEF). CEF stores all the information required to route traffic in specialized hardware. CEF uses a Forwarding Information Base (FIB) for the routing information and an adjacency table with required MAC address information.

Topic Quiz

1. Given the following routing table entries, what is the next router (or hop) to be used for a packet destined for 172.16.1.23?

   ```
   172.16.0.0/16 via 10.10.10.1
   0.0.0.0/0 via 192.168.1.1
   172.16.1.0/24 via 10.20.20.2
   172.16.2.0/24 via 10.30.30.3
   ```

   A. 10.30.30.3

   B. 192.168.1.1

   C. 10.10.10.1

   D. 10.20.20.2

2. When performing a Layer 2 rewrite, what does the router use for the source MAC address?

   A. The next hop interface's MAC address

   B. The sending interface's MAC address

   C. The MAC address of the previous hop's sending interface

   D. The MAC address of the previous hop's receiving interface

Topic Quiz Answers

1. **D** is correct. Here the longest match entry is 172.16.1.0/24 via 10.20.20.2 for the destination IP address 172.16.1.23. Routing table entries 172.16.0.0/16 and 0.0.0.0/0 both match the destination address, but both have a shorter prefix length than 172.16.1.0/24. Entry 172.16.2.0/24 does not match address 172.16.1.23.

2. **B** is correct. During this rewrite process, the router changes the source MAC address to its own sending interface MAC address.

Interpret the Components of a Routing Table

It is time to examine in great detail the vast amount of information communicated in a key network data structure: the IP routing table of a Cisco router. Example 14.1 shows a sample table.

Example 14.1   *IP Routing Table on a Cisco Router*

```
R1# show ip route
Codes: L - local, C - connected, S - static, R - RIP, M - mobile, B – BGP
       D - EIGRP, EX - EIGRP external, O - OSPF, IA - OSPF inter area
       N1 - OSPF NSSA external type 1, N2 - OSPF NSSA external type 2
       E1 - OSPF external type 1, E2 - OSPF external type 2
        i - IS-IS, su - IS-IS summary, L1 - IS-IS level-1, L2 - IS-IS level-2
       ia - IS-IS inter area, * - candidate default, U - per-user static route
        o - ODR, P - periodic downloaded static route, + - replicated route

Gateway of last resort is not set

     10.0.0.0/8 is variably subnetted, 2 subnets, 2 masks
C       10.10.10.0/24 is directly connected, FastEthernet0/0
L       10.10.10.1/32 is directly connected, FastEthernet0/0
     172.16.0.0/24 is subnetted, 3 subnets
R       172.16.1.0 [120/1] via 10.10.10.3, 00:00:19, FastEthernet0/0
R       172.16.2.0 [120/1] via 10.10.10.3, 00:00:19, FastEthernet0/0
R       172.16.3.0 [120/1] via 10.10.10.3, 00:00:19, FastEthernet0/0
     192.168.1.0/32 is subnetted, 1 subnets
O       192.168.1.2 [110/2] via 10.10.10.2, 00:00:37, FastEthernet0/0
     192.168.2.0/32 is subnetted, 1 subnets
O       192.168.2.2 [110/2] via 10.10.10.2, 00:00:37, FastEthernet0/0
R1#
```

Specifically, in this output, it is important to understand the meanings and locations of the following components:

- **Prefix:** Notice that the routing table lists the parent and child prefixes that are reachable in the table. For example, in the table shown in Example 14.1, the entry 172.16.0.0/24 is subnetted, 3 subnets lists the classful network prefix, the subnet length for all subnets, and the specific subnet prefixes 172.16.1.0, 172.16.2.0, and 172.16.3.0. In the case where a classful network is variably subnetted, the classful network prefix length is shown, using CIDR notation (which is the case with the first network shown: 10.0.0.0/8).

- **Network mask:** Notice that the parent prefix lists the network mask in prefix notation. So for the 172.16.0.0 example above, the network mask is /24. Remember that in subnet mask notation, this is 255.255.255.0.

- **Next hop:** The next hop IP address follows the via word for a subnet prefix entry. Note that it is 10.10.10.3 for the 172.16.0.0/24 entries. The *next hop* refers to the IP address of the next router in the path when forwarding packets to a remote destination.

- **Routing protocol code:** Located at the very beginning of a routing table entry is the routing protocol code. Cisco IOS is kind enough to provide a legend at the beginning of the show output to explain what each value indicates:

  - **L:** Local

  - **C:** Connected

  - **S:** Static

  - **R:** RIP

  - **M:** Mobile

  - **B:** BGP

  - **D:** EIGRP

  - **EX:** EIGRP External

  - **O:** OSPF

  - **IA:** OSPF inter-area

  - **N1:** OSPF NSSA External Type 1

  - **N2:** OSPF NSSA External Type 2

  - **E1:** OSPF External Type 1

  - **E2:** OSPF External Type 2

  - **i:** IS-IS

  - **su:** IS-IS summary

  - **L1:** IS-IS Level 1

  - **L2:** IS-IS Level 2

  - **ia:** IS-IS inter-area

  - ***:** Candidate default

  - **U:** Per-user static route

  - **o:** ODR

  - **P:** Periodic downloaded static route

  - **+:** Replicated route

- **Administrative distance:** The routing table shows the administrative distance (AD) for the prefix. (AD is covered in more detail later in this chapter.) In Example 14.1, the AD associated with the 172.16.0.0/24 prefixes is 120. This is because these routes were learned through RIP, and 120 is the default administrative distance for RIP.

- **Metric:** The metric varies depending on the dynamic routing protocol involved. It is a measure of the "distance" to reach the prefix. In the 172 prefixes, the metric is a *hop count*. RIP uses this simple metric, which indicates how many routers you must cross to reach the destination prefix in question.

- **Gateway of last resort:** Notice that Example 14.1 indicates that there is no gateway of last resort set. This means there is no default route 0.0.0.0/0 that allows the router to send traffic somewhere if it does not have a specific prefix entry for the destination IP address. The gateway of last resort can be dynamically learned, or it can be set using any of three different commands: `ip default-gateway`, `ip default-network`, and `ip route 0.0.0.0 0.0.0.0`.

Note   Yes, you must memorize small details like the routing protocol codes. Making and using flash cards can really help you learn such details, especially for non-obvious codes (such as D for EIGRP).

Topic Quiz

1. What is the network mask in dotted-decimal notation for a prefix length of /22?

   A. 255.255.252.0

   B. 255.255.254.0

   C. 255.255.248.0

   D. 255.255.240.0

2. What is the routing protocol code for a connected prefix?

   A. S

   B. L

   C. C

   D. i

3. What aspect of the routing table is affected by the command `ip route 0.0.0.0 0.0.0.0`?

   A. Network mask

   B. Metric

   C. Administrative distance

   D. Gateway of last resort

Topic Quiz Answers

1. **A** is correct. 255.255.252.0 equates to /22.

2. **C** is correct. C is used for connected prefixes.

3. **D** is correct. Using `ip route 0.0.0.0 0.0.0.0` is one way to set the default route and gateway of last resort.

Lab 14.1: Interpret a Routing Table

To complete this Hands-On Lab Practice Assignment, download the assigned Packet Tracer file from the book's companion website and perform the lab on your locally installed version of Packet Tracer. You will be following the instructions in the lab, and your performance will be evaluated.

In this lab, you will interpret the components of a routing table in the topology shown in Figure 14.1.

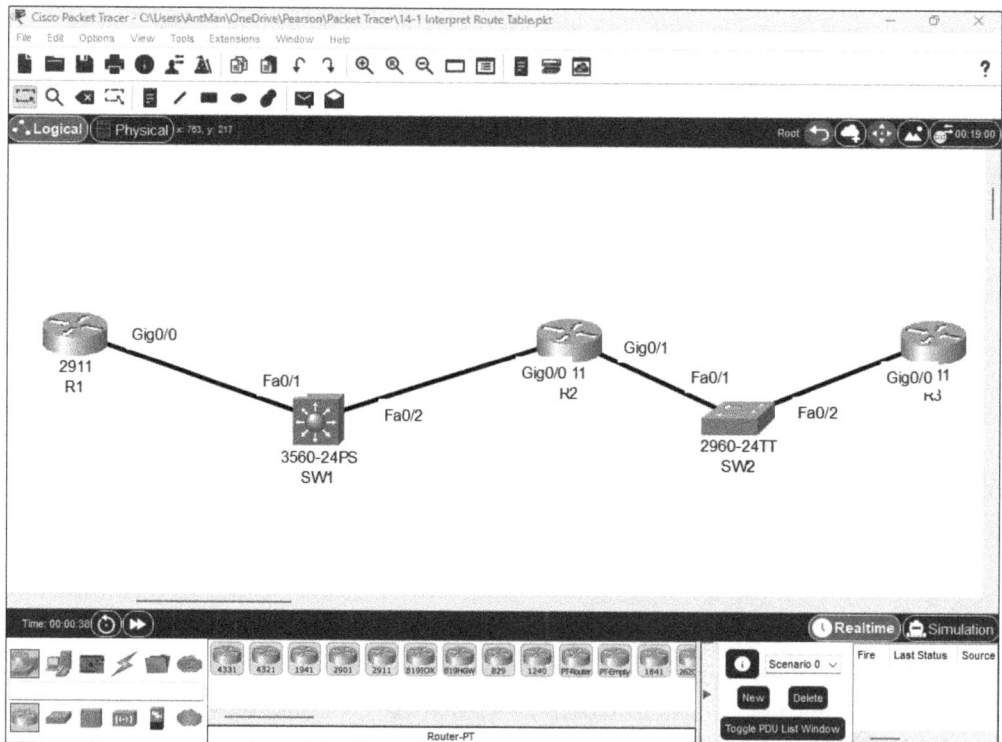

Figure 14.1   *The Interpret a Routing Table Lab*

Describe How a Routing Table Is Populated by Different Routing Information Sources

What happens when multiple different routing sources indicate that they know how to reach a network/prefix? The router needs to be able to break this "tie" between routing information sources. To do so, the router uses administrative distance (AD). This can be a bit of a misleading term since the value has nothing to do with actual distance of any kind. Some administrators like to call it *administrative trustworthiness*. Cisco ranks the trustworthiness of the various routing information sources. A lower score is better, just as in golf and routing protocol metrics.

Table 14.1 shows the default administrative distance values. As you can see, Cisco rates its own protocols, IGRP and EIGRP, as being very trustworthy.

Table 14.1 *Default Administrative Distance Values*

Routing Information Source	Default Administrative Distance
Connected interface	0
Static route	1
EIGRP summary route	5
External BGP	20
Internal EIGRP	90
IGRP	100
OSPF	110
IS-IS	115
RIP	120
EGP	140
External EIGRP	170
Internal BGP	200
Unknown	255

Note   On Cisco gear, the maximum configurable administrative distance for a route is 255, although this AD makes the route unusable. If the administrative distance is 255, the router does not believe the source of that route and does not install the route in the routing table.

Note You should have the values listed in Table 14.1 memorized before you take the CCNA 200-301 exam. If you don't have a lot of experience using the command line, remembering these values can be tough. I recommend that you make flash cards to aid in memorizing information like this. Also consider the logic in these values. For example, RIP scores relatively poorly because it is very prone to problems.

Note Remember that you can see the administrative distance shown in the prefix entries in the routing table by using the `show ip route` command.

Topic Quiz

1. What is the default administrative distance value for RIP?

   A. 100

   B. 60

   C. 200

   D. 120

2. What is the default administrative distance value for External BGP?

   A. 60

   B. 20

   C. 110

   D. 200

3. What is the default administrative distance value for OSPF?

   A. 100

   B. 110

   C. 120

   D. 140

4. What is the administrative distance value for a connected interface?

   A. 5

   B. 1

   C. 0

   D. 20

Topic Quiz Answers

1. **D** is correct. RIP features a default administrative distance of 120.

2. **B** is correct. External BGP features an excellent administrative distance of 20.

3. **B** is correct. OSPF features an AD of 110.

4. **C** is correct. A directly connected interface has the best possible AD, 0, and it cannot be changed.

Lab 14.2: Chapter Review

To complete this Hands-On Lab Practice Assignment, download the assigned Packet Tracer file from the book's companion website and perform the lab on your locally installed version of Packet Tracer. You will be following the instructions in the lab, and your performance will be evaluated.

In this lab, you will demonstrate skills acquired in this chapter using the topology shown in Figure 14.2.

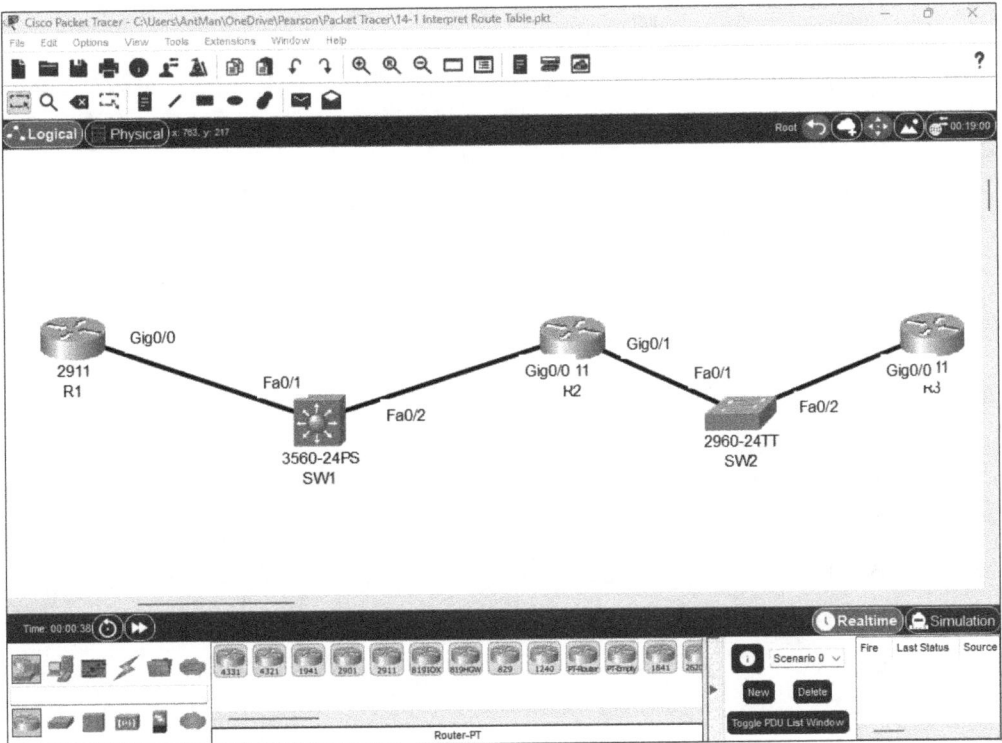

Figure 14.2 *The Routing Table Chapter Review Lab*

Review Questions

1. If a router cannot find a better match, what might the router use to route traffic?

  A. 255.255.255.255/0

  B. 127.0.0.1/32

  C. 0.0.0.0/32

  D. 0.0.0.0/0

2. When a router forwards packets onto Ethernet, what is rewritten?

  A. The source and destination IP addresses

  B. Only the source IP address

  C. Only the source MAC address

  D. The source and destination MAC addresses

3. What does the routing protocol code B in a routing table indicate?

  A. EIGRP

  B. IGRP

  C. RIP

  D. OSPF

  E. BGP

4. What is the administrative distance of Internal EIGRP routes?

  A. 5

  B. 20

  C. 90

  D. 100

5. What is the unreachable AD?

  A. 0

  B. 100

  C. 200

  D. 255

Answers to Review Questions

1. **D** is correct. Routers use the default route (0.0.0.0/0) to send packets that have no other better match in the routing table.

2. **D** is correct. The router must rewrite the source and destination MAC addresses in the Ethernet header before forwarding a frame.

3. **E** is correct. B indicates BGP.

4. **C** is correct. Internal EIGRP routes are installed in the routing table with an AD of 90.

5. **D** is correct. An AD of 255 indicates an unreachable prefix.

Chapter 15

Configure and Verify IPv4 and IPv6 Static Routing

This chapter covers the following official CCNA 200-301 exam topic:

■ Configure, verify, and troubleshoot IPv4 and IPv6 static routing

This chapter ensures that you are ready for questions related to this topic from the "IP Connectivity" section of the CCNA 200-301 exam blueprint from Cisco Systems. While you might think that static routing is silly, especially when there are exciting dynamic routing protocols available for both IPv4 and IPv6 networking, your understanding of static routing is actually critical. For example, production networks often require static routes in order to accommodate default routing to unknown destinations. This is often how you route traffic to the Internet, in fact.

This chapter covers the following essential terms and components:

■ Static routing

■ Default routes

■ Network routes

■ Host routes

■ Floating static routes

Chapter Pretest

1. What is the command to configure a static route to 10.40.40.0/24 with a next hop of 10.10.10.2?

   _____

2. What is the command to configure an IPv6 static route to 2001:aaaa::/64 using the Serial 0/0 interface?

   _____

3. What is a floating static route?

   _____

Answers

1. `ip route 10.40.40.0 255.255.255.0 10.10.10.2`

2. `ipv6 route 2001:aaaa::/64 serial 0/0`

3. A floating static route is a static route that is not installed in the routing table initially, thanks to an artificially high (untrustworthy) AD.

Configure, Verify, and Troubleshoot IPv4 and IPv6 Static Routing

By using static routing, you can create default routes, network routes, and host routes. Remember that a default route references a quad-zero IP address and mask (0.0.0.0 0.0.0.0) and is used to direct traffic to a destination such as the Internet when a more specific route entry does not exist in the routing table. A network route is a static route to a specific prefix, and a host route is a prefix that has a 32-bit network mask, which means you must specify the host address exactly.

Example 15.1 shows the configuration of network, host, and default routes using static routing in IPv4.

Example 15.1   *Configuring Static Network Routes and Host Routes in IPv4*

```
R1# configure terminal
Enter configuration commands, one per line. End with CNTL/Z.
R1(config)# ip route 192.168.1.0 255.255.255.0 10.10.10.2
R1(config)# ip route 172.16.1.3 255.255.255.255 10.10.10.2
R1(config)# ip route 0.0.0.0 0.0.0.0 10.20.20.200
R1(config)# end
R1#
%SYS-5-CONFIG_I: Configured from console by console
R1#
```

Note With a point-to-point link, you can specify just the *outgoing interface*, also referred to as the exit interface, on the local router as part of the `ip route` command (for example, `ip route 192.168.1.0 255.255.255.0 serial 0/0`, where Serial 0/0 is the exit interface of the local router). This is a nice timesaver. Just be careful not to configure an Ethernet exit interface; doing so is not recommended because it leads to excessive ARP requests.

Notice in Example 15.1 how simple the static route creation is. It is just as easy in an IPv6 environment, as shown in Example 15.2.

Example 15.2 *Configuring a Static Route in IPv6*

```
R1# configure terminal
R1(config)# ipv6 route 2001:aaaa::/64 serial 0/0
```

Example 15.3 demonstrates the use of the **show ip route** and **show ipv6 route** commands to verify static routes.

Example 15.3 *Verifying Static IPv4 and IPv6 Routes*

```
R1# show ip route
Codes: L - local, C - connected, S - static, R - RIP, M - mobile, B - BGP
       D - EIGRP, EX - EIGRP external, O - OSPF, IA - OSPF inter area
       N1 - OSPF NSSA external type 1, N2 - OSPF NSSA external type 2
       E1 - OSPF external type 1, E2 - OSPF external type 2
       i - IS-IS, su - IS-IS summary, L1 - IS-IS level-1, L2 - IS-IS level-2
       ia - IS-IS inter area, * - candidate default, U - per-user static route
       o - ODR, P - periodic downloaded static route, + - replicated route
Gateway of last resort is 10.10.10.2 to network 0.0.0.0
S*     0.0.0.0/0 [1/0] via 10.10.10.2
                is directly connected, FastEthernet0/0
       10.0.0.0/8 is variably subnetted, 2 subnets, 2 masks
C         10.10.10.0/24 is directly connected, FastEthernet0/0
L         10.10.10.1/32 is directly connected, FastEthernet0/0
       172.16.0.0/32 is subnetted, 1 subnets
S         172.16.1.3 [1/0] via 10.10.10.2
S      192.168.1.0/24 [1/0] via 10.10.10.2

R1#
R1# show ipv6 route
IPv6 Routing Table - default - 2 entries
```

```
Codes: C - Connected, L - Local, S - Static, U - Per-user Static route
       B - BGP, M - MIPv6, R - RIP, I1 - ISIS L1
       I2 - ISIS L2, IA - ISIS interarea, IS - ISIS summary, D - EIGRP
       EX - EIGRP external, ND - Neighbor Discovery
       O - OSPF Intra, OI - OSPF Inter, OE1 - OSPF ext 1, OE2 - OSPF ext 2
       ON1 - OSPF NSSA ext 1, ON2 - OSPF NSSA ext 2
S    2001:AAAA::/64 [1/0]
       via Serial 0/0, directly connected
L    FF00::/8 [0/0]
       via Null0, receive
R1#
```

Another interesting use of a static route is as a floating static route. A floating static route "floats" above a prefix learned by a dynamic routing protocol. The static route kicks in when the dynamic routing protocol removes the prefix. To create a floating static route, you set the administrative distance (AD) artificially high (numerically higher than other existing routing sources) for the static route. Specifically, you set the AD greater than— so that it is less believable than—the dynamic route.

Example 15.4 shows the creation of a floating static route that could be used with OSPF as the dynamic routing protocol. Notice that the AD is one notch higher (worse) than the default AD of OSPF, which is 110. This newly created static route won't be placed in the routing table as long as 10.60.60.0/24 is being learned via OSPF. If the router stops learning of this route through OSPF, then the static route, with its AD of 111, will be placed in the routing table.

Example 15.4   *Configuring a Floating Static Route*

```
R3#
R3# configure terminal
Enter configuration commands, one per line. End with CNTL/Z.
R3(config)# ip route 10.60.60.0 255.255.255.0 10.20.20.2 111
R3(config)# end
R3#
```

Lab 15.1: IPv4 and IPv6 Static Routes

To complete this Hands-On Lab Practice Assignment, download the assigned Packet Tracer file from the book's companion website and perform the lab on your locally installed version of Packet Tracer. You will be following the instructions in the lab, and your performance will be evaluated.

In this lab, you will configure and verify IPv4 and IPv6 static routes using the topology shown in Figure 15.1.

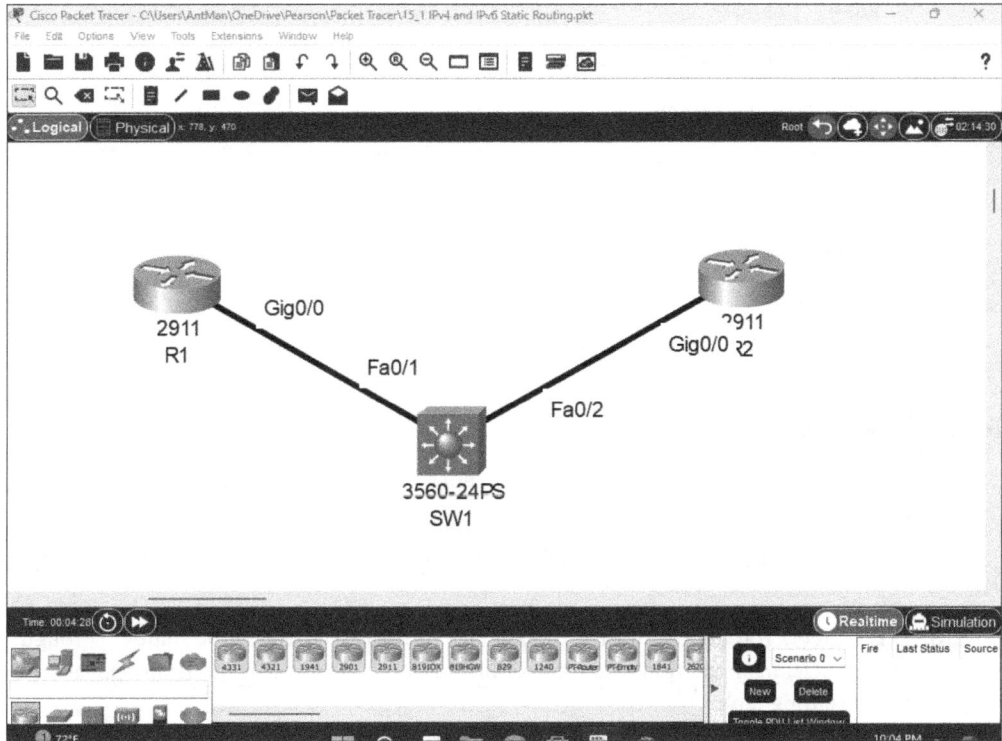

Figure 15.1 *The IPv4 and IPv6 Static Routes Lab*

Topic Quiz

1. What parameters of a static route can be included as part of the `ip route` command to indicate where traffic should be sent? (Choose two.)

   A. Next hop IP address

   B. RE ID

   C. Destination MAC address

   D. Outgoing interface

2. What command enables you to verify that a static route is in the routing table?

   A. `show static`

   B. `show ip route`

   C. `show routing table static`

   D. `show admin routes`

3. What feature do you use in order to create a floating static route?

   A. Metric

   B. Dampening

   C. Route suppression

   D. Administrative distance

Topic Quiz Answers

1. A and D are correct. You can specify the next hop IP address and/or the outgoing interface.

2. B is correct. The `show ip route` command allows you to view static routes (if they exist) in the routing table.

3. D is correct. You use administrative distance to create floating static routes. Through the artificial manipulation of trustworthiness, you prevent the route from appearing in the routing table.

Lab 15.2: Chapter Review

To complete this Hands-On Lab Practice Assignment, download the assigned Packet Tracer file from the book's companion website and perform the lab on your locally installed version of Packet Tracer. You will be following the instructions in the lab, and your performance will be evaluated.

In this lab, you will demonstrate skills acquired in this chapter using the topology shown in Figure 15.2.

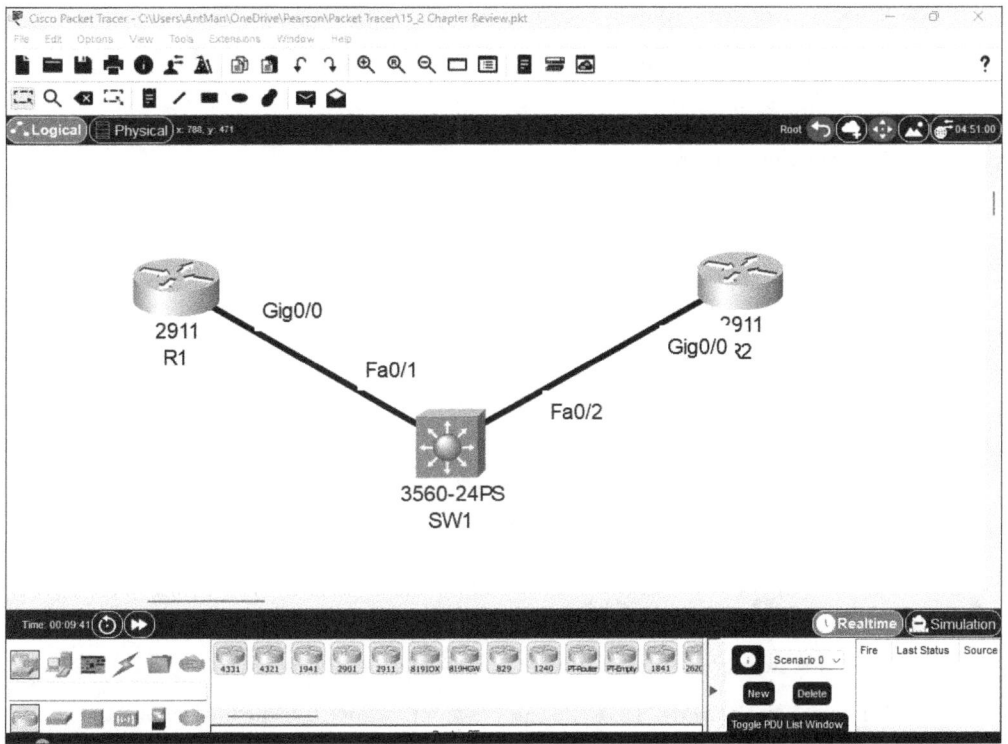

Figure 15.2   *The Static Routing Chapter Review Lab*

Review Questions

1. What is the mask length for a host route?

    A. 0

    B. 64

    C. 16

    D. 32

2. What command permits you to view the IPv6 routing table?

    A. `show route ipv6`

    B. `show route new`

    C. `show ipv6 route`

    D. `show route`

3. What type of static route is shown in the following example?

```
ip route 172.16.1.0 255.255.255.0 192.168.2.100
```

A. A static host route

B. A floating static route

C. A default route

D. A network static route

4. What is the default administrative distance of a static route that references a next hop IP address?

A. 0

B. 1

C. 2

D. 10

Answers to Review Questions

1. D is correct. A host route in IPv4 features a mask of 32 bits.

2. C is correct. The `show ipv6 route` command is the equivalent of `show ip route` but shows the IPv6 routing table.

3. D is correct. This static route is for a network that needs to be reached. The network is 172.16.1.0/24, and the next hop address to reach that network is 192.168.2.100.

4. B is correct. The default administrative distance of a static route is 1, regardless of whether it is referencing a next hop IP address or an exit interface.

Chapter 16

Configure and Verify Single Area OSPFv2

This chapter covers the following official CCNA 200-301 exam topic:

■ Configure, verify, and troubleshoot single area OSPFv2 for IPv4

This chapter ensures that you understand OSPFv2 for the CCNA 200-301 exam from Cisco Systems. It is wonderful to see Cisco Systems finally bidding farewell to RIP when it comes to dynamic routing protocol coverage in the CCNA exam. Instead, the focus now is on a very scalable, exciting, and popular modern routing protocol option: OSPF version 2. This is the OSPF version designed for IPv4.

This chapter covers the following essential terms and components:

■ OSPFv2

■ **network** command

■ Process ID

■ Router ID

■ Designated router (DR)

■ Backup designated router (BDR)

■ Point-to-point network type

■ Broadcast network type

■ Point-to-multipoint network type

■ Non-broadcast network type

■ Point-to-multipoint non-broadcast network type

Chapter Pretest

1. What aspect of OSPF makes the protocol hierarchical and permits the creation of very scalable networks?

———————

2. What single OSPF router configuration command allows the assignment of OSPF area 0 to all interfaces in the range 10.0.0.0 to 10.255.255.255?

———————

Answers

1. OSPF areas

2. `network 10.0.0.0 0.255.255.255 area 0`

Configure, Verify, and Troubleshoot Single Area OSPFv2 for IPv4

Open Shortest Path First (OSPF) is a beloved link-state routing protocol that is extremely configurable and scalable. It uses *areas* to reduce the size of convergence domains in the topology and ensure that scalability can be maintained. Remember that a convergence domain describes the set of routers that need to update their routing information whenever there is a change within that set.

OSPF version 2 is the current IPv4-only version of OSPF. OSPF version 3 is a standard for routing either IPv4 or IPv6 or both IPv4 and IPv6 simultaneously.

Figure 16.1 shows a sample topology, and Example 16.1 shows the configuration of OSPF in a single area of this topology, using the **network** command.

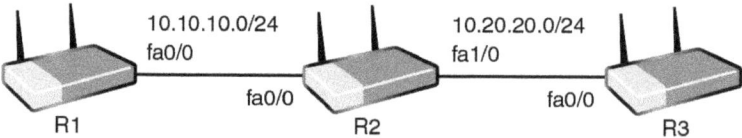

Figure 16.1　*Sample OSPF Topology*

Example 16.1　*Configuring Single Area OSPFv2 Using the* `network` *Command*

```
R1#
R1# configure terminal
R1(config)# router ospf 1
R1(config-router)# network 10.10.10.1 0.0.0.0 area 0
R1(config-router)# network 1.1.1.1 0.0.0.0 area 0
R1(config-router)# end
```

```
R1#
R2#
R2# configure terminal
R2(config)# router ospf 1
R2(config-router)# network 10.0.0.0 0.255.255.255 area 0
R2(config-router)# network 2.2.2.2 0.0.0.0 area 0
R2(config-router)# end
R2#
R3#
R3# configure terminal
R3(config)# router ospf 1
R3(config-router)# network 10.20.20.3 0.0.0.0 area 0
R3(config-router)# network 3.3.3.3 0.0.0.0 area 0
R3(config-router)# end
R3#
```

Notice the following details in the configuration in Example 16.1:

- **router ospf 1:** This command enters router configuration mode for OSPFv2 and sets a process ID of 1; this number is locally significant and does not need to match on the neighboring router.

- **network 10.10.10.1 0.0.0.0 area 0:** The **network** command sets the interface(s) that will run OSPF for this process; note that the wildcard mask 0.0.0.0 indicates that OSPF will run on the specific interface that has the IP address 10.10.10.1 (fa0/0); notice also that this interface participates in area 0, which is the backbone or core area for OSPF; all other areas must have contact with this backbone.

Example 16.2 shows how to easily verify OSPF.

Example 16.2 *Verifying Single Area OSPF*

```
R1#
R1# show ip ospf neighbor
Neighbor ID  Pri    State      Dead Time Address   Interface
2.2.2.2       1     FULL/BDR  00:00:37  10.10.10.2 FastEthernet0/0
R1# show ip route
Codes: L - local, C - connected, S - static, R - RIP, M - mobile, B - BGP
       D - EIGRP, EX - EIGRP external, O - OSPF, IA - OSPF inter area
       N1 - OSPF NSSA external type 1, N2 - OSPF NSSA external type 2
       E1 - OSPF external type 1, E2 - OSPF external type 2
        i - IS-IS, su - IS-IS summary, L1 - IS-IS level-1, L2 - IS-IS level-2
       ia - IS-IS inter area, * - candidate default, U - per-user static route
        o - ODR, P - periodic downloaded static route, + - replicated route
```

```
Gateway of last resort is not set

    1.0.0.0/8 is variably subnetted, 2 subnets, 2 masks
C      1.1.1.0/24 is directly connected, Loopback0
L      1.1.1.1/32 is directly connected, Loopback0
    2.0.0.0/32 is subnetted, 1 subnets
O      2.2.2.2 [110/2] via 10.10.10.2, 00:32:13, FastEthernet0/0
    3.0.0.0/32 is subnetted, 1 subnets
O      3.3.3.3 [110/3] via 10.10.10.2, 00:19:12, FastEthernet0/0
    10.0.0.0/8 is variably subnetted, 3 subnets, 2 masks
C      10.10.10.0/24 is directly connected, FastEthernet0/0
L      10.10.10.1/32 is directly connected, FastEthernet0/0
O      10.20.20.0/24 [110/2] via 10.10.10.2, 00:32:33, FastEthernet0/0
R1# ping 3.3.3.3


Type escape sequence to abort.
Sending 5, 100-byte ICMP Echos to 3.3.3.3, timeout is 2 seconds:
!!!!!
Success rate is 100 percent (5/5), round-trip min/avg/max = 20/52/64 ms
R1#
```

Example 16.2 includes the following commands:

- **show ip ospf neighbor:** This command permits you to verify that you have an OSPF adjacency with your neighbor(s).

- **show ip route:** This command permits you to see the OSPF learned route information.

- **ping 3.3.3.3:** This command tests for full reachability; notice in Example 16.2, the R1 device is pinging an OSPF learned route from R3.

Note   Several parameters must match in order for an OSPF neighborship to form:

- The area ID
- Authentication settings
- Hello and dead intervals
- Stub flag
- MTU size

The hello and dead intervals are manipulated in interface configuration mode with the following commands:

```
(config-if)# ip ospf hello-interval 10
(config-if)# ip ospf dead-interval 30
```

The values used here indicate seconds.

Example 16.3 demonstrates single area OSPF configuration without the use of the `network` command.

Example 16.3 *Configuring Single Area OSPF Without the Use of the* `network` *Command*

```
R1#
R1# configure terminal
R1(config)# interface fa0/0
R1(config-if)# ip ospf 1 area 0
R1(config-if)# interface lo0
R1(config-if)# ip ospf 1 area 0
R1(config-if)# end
R1#
R2#
R2# configure terminal
R2(config)# interface fa0/0
R2(config-if)# ip ospf 1 area 0
R2(config-if)# interface fa1/0
R2(config-if)# ip ospf 1 area 0
R2(config-if)# interface loopback 0
R2(config-if)# ip ospf 1 area 0
R2(config-if)# end
R2#
R3#
R3# configure terminal
R3(config)# interface fa0/0
R3(config-if)# ip ospf 1 area 0
R3(config-if)# interface loopback 0
R3(config-if)# ip ospf 1 area 0
R3(config-if)# end
R3#
```

Notice how simple it is to configure OSPF under the appropriate interfaces. As you can see, you do not have to enter OSPF router configuration mode at all for a basic configuration.

If you examine the `show ip ospf neighbor` command closely, you will notice some very interesting details in the output. First, note that the neighbor ID is listed. In Example 16.2, the neighbor ID value is 2.2.2.2. This is actually the router ID value for the OSPF speaker. This value is very important for various functions in OSPF. In fact, the router ID can be used in the election process of the DR and BDR devices in certain types of OSPF network configurations. This concept is discussed later in this chapter.

You can manually set a router ID for an OSPF router by using the `router-id` command, or you can allow the router to self-assign this value. How does the router choose its own router ID? It follows this order:

1. Use the manually configured router ID (if you configured it).

2. Use the numerically highest IP address on a loopback interface.

3. Use the numerically highest IP address on a non-loopback interface.

The `show ip ospf neighbor` command also indicates the current state of the neighbor. If you examine the output shown in Example 16.2, you will notice the state listed as FULL/BDR.

OSPF uses the following states in its operation in order to build and maintain neighbor relationships:

- Down

- Attempt

- Init

- 2-Way

- Exstart

- Exchange

- Loading

- Full

If there is a problem with a configuration or the underlying network, you might run your neighbor verification command and learn that your OSPF routers are stuck in one of the states that was supposed to be a transition state from Down to Full. Obviously, such information can help you dramatically in your troubleshooting.

What about the BDR indication in the output in Example 16.2? This indicates that the peer router is fulfilling the role of the backup designated router (BDR). The designated router (DR) and the BDR are used in certain types of network configurations for OSPF. They try to make the operation of OSPF more efficient by reducing the number of advertisements that must be made when sharing network information. Here is a list of the network types that are possible in OSPF and whether each one uses a DR and BDR in the operations of the protocol:

- **Broadcast:** DR/BDR used

- **Non-broadcast:** DR/BDR used

- **Point-to-point:** No DR/BDR

- **Point-to-multipoint:** No DR/BDR

- **Point-to-multipoint non-broadcast:** No DR/BDR

Lab 16.1: OSPFv2

To complete this Hands-On Lab Practice Assignment, download the assigned Packet Tracer file from the book's companion website and perform the lab on your locally installed version of Packet Tracer. You will be following the instructions in the lab, and your performance will be evaluated.

In this lab, you will configure and verify OSPFv2 using the topology shown in Figure 16.2.

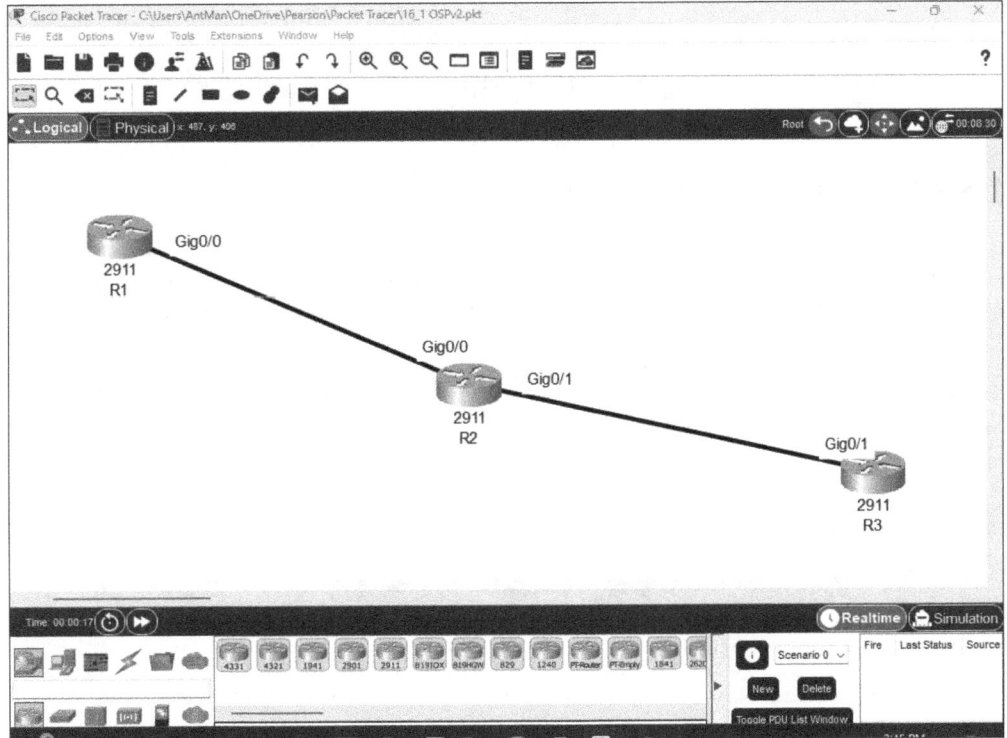

Figure 16.2 *The OSPFv2 Lab*

Topic Quiz

1. Which statement about OSPFv2 is true?

    A. The dead timers do not need to match between neighbors.

    B. The hello timers do not need to match between neighbors.

    C. The area ID must match between neighbors.

    D. The `network` command must be used.

2. What command can you use to verify neighbors in OSPFv2?

   A. `show ospf neighbors`

   B. `show ip ospf neighbors`

   C. `show ospf database neighbors`

   D. `show ospf peers`

Topic Quiz Answers

   1. C is correct. Area ID and hello and dead timers must match between neighbors.

   2. B is correct. The `show ip ospf neighbors` command permits the verification of OSPF peerings.

Lab 16.2: Chapter Review

To complete this Hands-On Lab Practice Assignment, download the assigned Packet Tracer file from the book's companion website and perform the lab on your locally installed version of Packet Tracer. You will be following the instructions in the lab, and your performance will be evaluated.

In this lab, you will demonstrate the skills covered in this chapter using the topology shown in Figure 16.3.

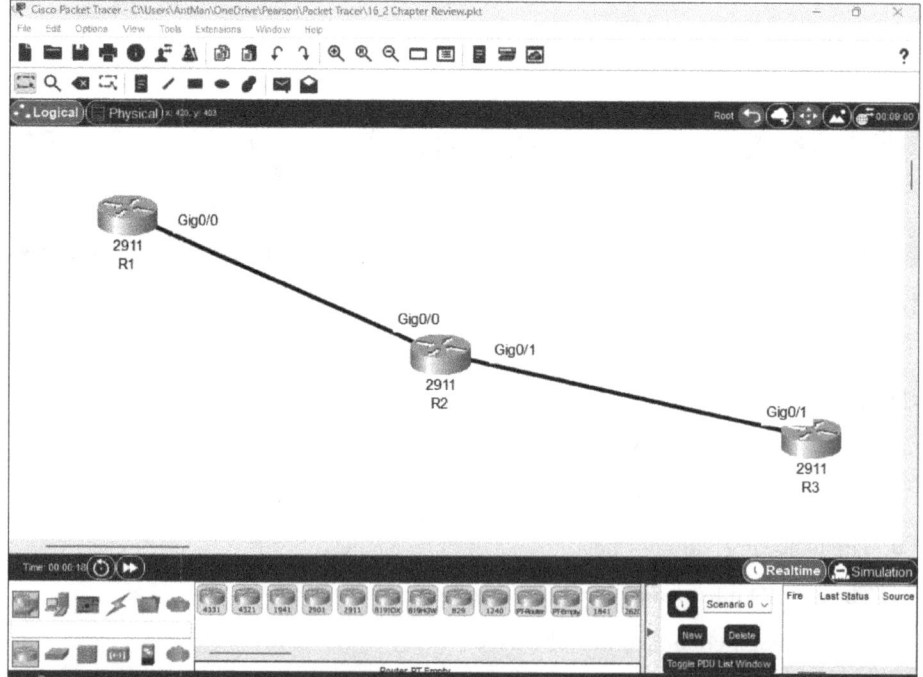

Figure 16.3   *The OSPFv2 Chapter Review Lab*

Review Questions

1. What command enters router configuration mode for OSPF version 2?

    A. `router ospf 1`

    B. `router ospf version 2`

    C. `ospf router version 1`

    D. `router ospf process 1 version 2`

2. You have configured OSPF on a router by using the command `network 10.10.0.0 0.0.255.255 area 0`. On which interface is OSPF running?

    A. Gi0/0: 10.0.0.1 255.255.0.0

    B. Gi0/1: 10.10.100.1 255.255.255.0

    C. Gi0/2: 10.1.10.100 255.0.0.0

    D. Gi0/3: 10.100.100.1 255.255.255.0

3. What does not have to match in order for an OSPF neighborship to form?

    A. Area ID

    B. MTU size

    C. Hello and dead intervals

    D. Use of the `network` command versus the `ip ospf` command

4. You have allowed a router to self-assign its router ID. What is the first option considered for the assignment on the device?

    A. A random router ID assignment

    B. The IP address on the highest-numbered interface name

    C. The highest IP address on a physical interface

    D. The highest IP address on a loopback interface

5. Which network type in OSPF features the use of a DR and a BDR?

    A. Point-to-point

    B. Broadcast

    C. Point-to-multipoint

    D. Point-to-multipoint non-broadcast

Answers to Review Questions

1. **A** is correct. The `router ospf 1` command enters router configuration mode for OSPF. It uses the local process ID 1.

2. **B** is correct. The `network 10.10.0.0 0.0.255.255 area 0` command ensures that OSPF runs on any interfaces that have IP addresses that have 10.10 in the first two octets. This is the Gi0/1 interface in this question.

3. **D** is correct. Neighborships can form in OSPF if one router uses the `network` command and the other uses the interface-level `ip ospf` command. Process IDs do not need to match between routers either.

4. **D** is correct. If you do not manually configure a router ID, the highest IP address on a loopback interface is used as the router ID. If there are no loopback interfaces, the router uses the highest IP address on a physical interface. If OSPF cannot find a configured IPv4 address, the OSPF process does not start.

5. **B** is correct. The DR and BDR devices are used in the broadcast and non-broadcast network types.

IP Services

IP connectivity is wonderful, but we also rely on important IP services every day we use our networks. This part's four chapters all deal with the wonderfully diverse world of IP services.

Part V begins by examining the important Network Address Translation (NAT) that is critical in most IPv4 networks today. It then covers Network Time Protocol (NTP), Dynamic Host Configuration Protocol (DHCP), Domain Name System (DNS), and many more important protocols and services. Part V includes the following chapters:

Chapter 17

Configure and Verify Inside Source NAT

This chapter covers the following official CCNA 200-301 exam topic:

■ Configure, verify, and troubleshoot inside source NAT

This chapter ensures that you are ready for questions related to Network Address Translation (NAT) on the CCNA 200-301 exam from Cisco Systems. NAT is a critical protocol that is used in almost every IPv4 network you can find.

This chapter covers the following essential terms and components:

■ NAT

■ Source NAT

■ Static NAT

■ Unidirectional NAT

■ Bidirectional NAT

■ NAT pools

■ Dynamic NAT

■ PAT

Chapter Pretest

1. What is a classic example of using unidirectional, or one-way, NAT?

————————

2. With inside source dynamic NAT, what is the pool used for?

————————

3. Examine the topology and configuration shown here. In this topology, 10.2.2.0/24 is the inside segment, and 10.1.1.0/24 is the outside segment. R1 (10.2.2.1) cannot trigger a NAT translation on R2 when pinging R3. The configuration should also permit PAT, if needed. What are four issues with the NAT configuration on R2?

————————

————————

————————

————————

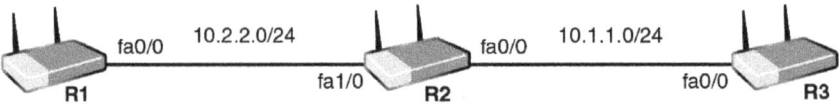

```
R2#
R2# show running-config
Building configuration...
Current configuration : 1406 bytes
!
...
!
hostname R2
!
...
!interface FastEthernet0/0
 ip address 10.1.1.2 255.255.255.0
 ip nat inside
 ip virtual-reassembly
 !
 !
interface FastEthernet1/0
 ip address 10.2.2.2 255.255.255.0
 ip nat outside
 ip virtual-reassembly
 !
 !
```

```
interface FastEthernet1/1 no
 ip address
 shutdown
 duplex auto
 speed auto
 !
 !
router rip
 version 2
 network 10.0.0.0
 no auto-summary
 !
 ...
 !
ip nat inside source list 10 interface FastEthernet0/0
 !
access-list 1 permit host 10.2.1.1
access-list 1 permit host 10.2.1.100
no cdp log mismatch duplex
 !
 ...
R2#
```

Answers

1. Allowing many private IP addresses on an inside network to dynamically access public IP addresses on an outside Internet network

2. The NAT pool is used to specify the outside addresses to be used in the translation.

3. The `inside` and `outside` interface commands are reversed.

The access list specifies the incorrect internal device.

The NAT statement is missing the `overload` keyword.

The incorrect list is specified in the NAT statement.

Configure, Verify, and Troubleshoot Inside Source NAT

The RFC 1918 address space we reviewed in Chapter 6, "Configure and Verify IPv4 Addressing and Subnetting," helped delay the depletion of IPv4 address space. But private addresses that aren't routable over the Internet, combined with the slow adoption of IPv6, necessitated another change: the introduction of Network Address Translation (NAT). A private IP address must be converted to a public IP address to allow communication on the public Internet. Specifically, the private inside source IP address must be converted to an address that is valid on the Internet. When configuring NAT on a device in such a case, you specify interfaces as "inside" and "outside" as part of the configuration.

Although there are many different variations of NAT, the CCNA exam focus is very specific to inside source NAT. This involves starting with IPv4 packets sourced from inside devices and translating the source IP addresses for public communication. Keep in mind that the reverse process is also applied to return traffic.

Note Unidirectional NAT, or *one-way NAT*, permits devices on the inside to initiate connections and communicate to devices on the public network, but devices on the public network cannot initiate connections with devices on the inside network. If you configure NAT to permit connections initiated from the Internet as well, you are configuring bidirectional NAT. Many applications running on inside hosts that require discovery from the outside (for example, BitTorrent, Skype, multiplayer games, botnet malware) use UPnP to automatically configure bidirectional NAT.

The first configuration approach we examine is static NAT. With static NAT, you configure a manual mapping from an inside address to an outside address. Figure 17.1 shows the topology used for the examples in this chapter. This bidirectional translation allows connections to be initialized by devices on the inside or outside.

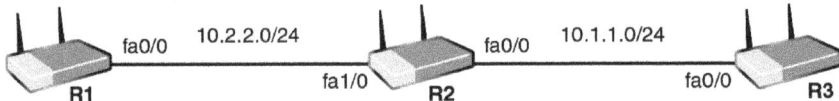

Figure 17.1 *The NAT Topology*

The configuration begins by identifying the inside network. In this case, you can pretend that 10.2.2.0/24 is the inside segment. Next, you identify the outside segment. You can pretend that the outside network is the 10.1.1.0/24 segment. You are now ready for the configuration shown in Example 17.1.

Example 17.1 *Configuring Inside Source Static NAT*

```
R2#
R2# configure terminal
Enter configuration commands, one per line. End with CNTL/Z.
R2(config)# interface fa1/0
R2(config-if)# ip nat inside
R2(config-if)# exit
R2(config)# interface fa0/0
R2(config-if)# ip nat outside
R2(config-if)# exit
R2(config)# ip nat inside source static 10.2.2.1 10.1.1.100
R2(config)# end
R2#
```

Notice the commands that this configuration requires:

- **ip nat inside:** Configures the inside interface for the device and enables NAT there.

- **ip nat outside:** Configures the outside interface for the device and enables NAT there.

- **ip nat inside source static 10.2.2.1 10.1.1.100:** Provides the static instructions for translation; 10.2.2.1 is the source IP address from the inside for translation, and 10.1.1.100 is the new source IP address for the translated packet.

For verification of this configuration, you ping from R1 (10.2.2.1) to R3 (10.1.1.3). This creates the translation on R2 that you can view with **show ip nat translation** (see Example 17.2).

Example 17.2 *Verifying the Inside Source Static NAT Configuration*

```
R1#
R1# ping 10.1.1.3
Type escape sequence to abort.
Sending 5, 100 byte ICMP Echos to 10.1.1.3, timeout is 2 seconds:
!!!!!
Success rate is 100 percent (5/5), round-trip min/avg/max = 200/221/244 ms
R1#
R2#
R2# show ip nat translation
Pro Inside global Inside local Outside local Outside global
icmp 10.1.1.100:0 10.2.2.1:0 10.1.1.3:0 10.1.1.3:0
--- 10.1.1.100 10.2.2.1 --- ---
R2#
```

Notice from the output in Example 17.2 that your exact NAT instructions were followed. The inside local source address of 10.2.2.1 was translated to the global address 10.1.1.100.

Note   It is interesting that the ping succeeds since there is no device with the IP address 10.1.1.100 in this topology! This is because when the traffic returns to R2 (the NAT device), it sees that 10.1.1.100 actually maps to the device at 10.2.2.1, and it replaces the original source address.

In addition to static NAT, there is also dynamic NAT. Example 17.3 demonstrates a dynamic NAT configuration on R2, using the topology in Figure 17.1. Note that before Example 17.3 can be run, all previous NAT commands must have been removed from R2.

> **Note**   A simple method to check for NAT configurations in a running configuration is to use **show run | include nat**. This returns any commands that include *nat*.

Example 17.3   *Configuring Inside Source Dynamic NAT*

```
R2#
R2# configure terminal
Enter configuration commands, one per line. End with CNTL/Z.
R2(config)# interface fa1/0
R2(config-if)# ip nat inside
R2(config-if)# exit
R2(config)# interface fa0/0
R2(config-if)# ip nat outside
R2(config-if)# exit
R2(config)# access-list 1 permit 10.2.2.1
R2(config)# access-list 1 permit 10.2.2.100
R2(config)# ip nat pool MYNATPOOL 10.1.1.100 10.1.1.101 netmask 255.255.255.0
R2(config)# ip nat inside source list 1 pool MYNATPOOL
R2(config)# end
R2#
```

Notice what is unique about this configuration:

- **access-list 1:** This access list defines the inside source addresses that can be translated.

- **ip nat pool MYNATPOOL:** This NAT pool defines the starting IP address and ending IP address to which R2 will translate the source address.

- **ip nat inside source list 1 pool MYNATPOOL:** This is the NAT instruction that ties the access list to the NAT pool you created.

With Example 17.3, verification occurs in exactly the same way as in Example 17.2. A ping from R1 to R3 results in the translation of 10.2.2.1 to 10.1.1.100. Of course, this time there is a dynamic element to the translation. For example, if there were another host on the inside network at 10.2.2.100, and this device were to communicate first across the R2 device, it could translate to 10.1.1.100, which is the first address in the pool.

But even inside source dynamic NAT is not the most popular form of NAT. What is then? It is Port Address Translation (PAT), also sometimes termed *NAT overloading*.

With PAT, you permit many inside devices to communicate on the outside network, using the single public address on the outside address. The IP address on the outside interface can even be used. This is possible because a unique port number is assigned to each translation entry. Example 17.4 shows this configuration, based on the topology shown in Figure 17.1, which takes place after all previous NAT configurations have been removed.

Example 17.4   *The Inside Source Dynamic PAT Configuration*

```
R2#
R2# configure terminal
Enter configuration commands, one per line. End with CNTL/Z.
R2(config)# interface fal/0
R2(config-if)# ip nat inside
R2(config-if)# exit
R2(config)# interface fa0/0
R2(config-if)# ip nat outside
R2(config-if)# exit
R2(config)# access-list 1 permit 10.2.2.1
R2(config)# access-list 1 permit 10.2.2.100
R2(config)# ip nat inside source list 1 interface fa0/0 overload
R2(config)# end
R2#
```

What is different about this configuration compared to inside source dynamic NAT? Not much, really. Notice that the `ip nat inside source` command now specifies `interface fa0/0 overload`. This instructs NAT to translate each source address to the IP address that is on the physical outside interface and allows it to be used over and over again for the source address translation of multiple inside devices.

Example 17.5 shows the verification of this configuration. The IP address on R2 fa0/0 is 10.1.1.2.

Example 17.5   *Verifying the Inside Source Dynamic PAT Configuration*

```
R1#
R1# ping 10.1.1.3
Type escape sequence to abort.
Sending 5, 100-byte ICMP Echos to 10.1.1.3, timeout is 2 seconds:
!!!!!
Success rate is 100 percent (5/5), round-trip min/avg/max = 200/221/ 244 ms
R1#
R2#
R2# show ip nat translation
Pro Inside global Inside local Outside local Outside global
icmp 10.1.1.2:2 10.2.2.1:2 10.1.1.3:2 10.1.1.3:2
R2#
```

Notice that this time R1's source address of 10.2.2.1 is translated to 10.1.1.2. Other inside hosts could translate to this same address. This type of configuration and functionality helped hold off the public IPv4 address shortage. This is also a common NAT configuration in home networks today—and it is why each of your home devices has an IP address from the 192.168.x.x range, and yet when you examine your public IP address (by typing "what is my IP address" in a search engine, for example) you invariably get an address that is not 192.168.x.x.

What about NAT troubleshooting? What can go wrong? The most common misconfigurations are failure to assign NAT inside and outside interfaces and incorrect assignment of inside versus outside interfaces.

Here are some items you should be sure to watch out for:

- With static inside NAT, ensure that the `ip nat inside source static` command lists the inside and outside addresses in the correct order.

- With dynamic NAT, make sure the IP address is constructed properly and matches the appropriate source addresses for translation.

- With PAT, don't forget the `overload` keyword.

Lab 17.1: NAT

To complete this Hands-On Lab Practice Assignment, download the assigned Packet Tracer file from the book's companion website and perform the lab on your locally installed version of Packet Tracer. You will be following the instructions in the lab, and your performance will be evaluated.

In this lab, you will configure and verify NAT using the topology shown in Figure 17.2.

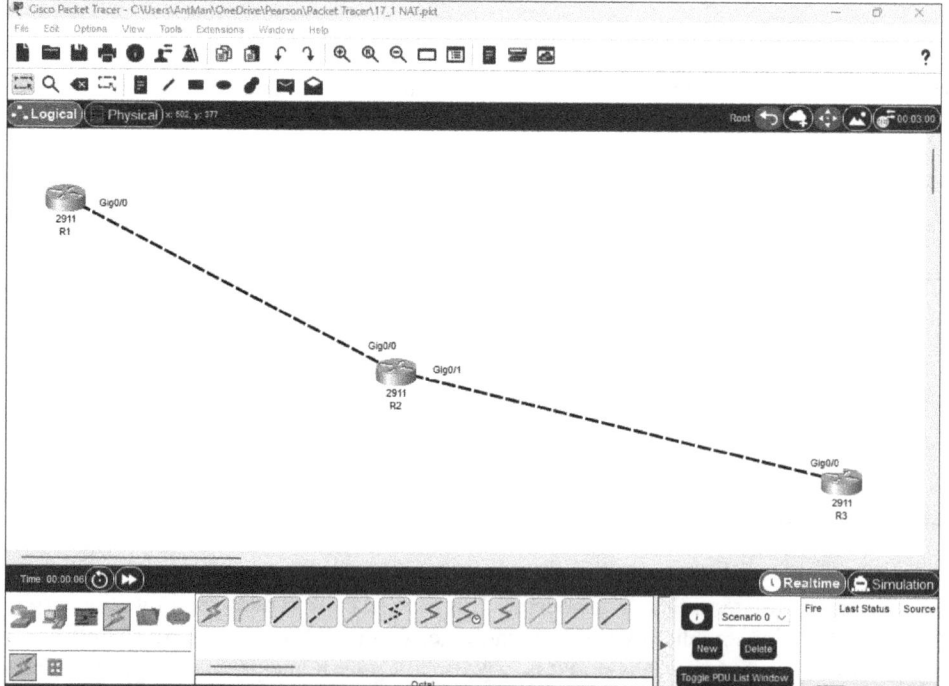

Figure 17.2   *The NAT Lab*

Topic Quiz

1. What was the main motivation for NAT?

   A. To increase the number of possible IPv4 addresses

   B. To allow the RFC 1918 private address space to communicate on the Internet

   C. To secure private networks from outside attackers

   D. To increase the visibility possible with Internet connections

2. What is the purpose of static NAT?

   A. To ensure that the destination IP address remains unchanged during translation

   B. To translate a single specific inside address to a single specific outside address

   C. To ensure that multiple inside addresses can translate to a single outside address

   D. To pull inside addresses for translation from a pool of addresses

3. What is another name commonly used for unidirectional NAT?

   A. One-way NAT

   B. Synchronous NAT

   C. Dual NAT

   D. Static NAT

Topic Quiz Answers

1. **B is correct.** The primary motivation for NAT was to allow RFC 1918 addresses to be used on inside networks while providing these private networks with Internet connectivity.

2. **B is correct.** Inside source static NAT translates a single specific inside address to a single specific outside address.

3. **A is correct.** The terms *one-way NAT* and *unidirectional NAT* are used interchangeably.

Lab 17.2: Chapter Review

To complete this Hands-On Lab Practice Assignment, download the assigned Packet Tracer file from the book's companion website and perform the lab on your locally installed version of Packet Tracer. You will be following the instructions in the lab, and your performance will be evaluated.

In this lab, you will verify the skills covered in this chapter using the topology shown in Figure 17.3.

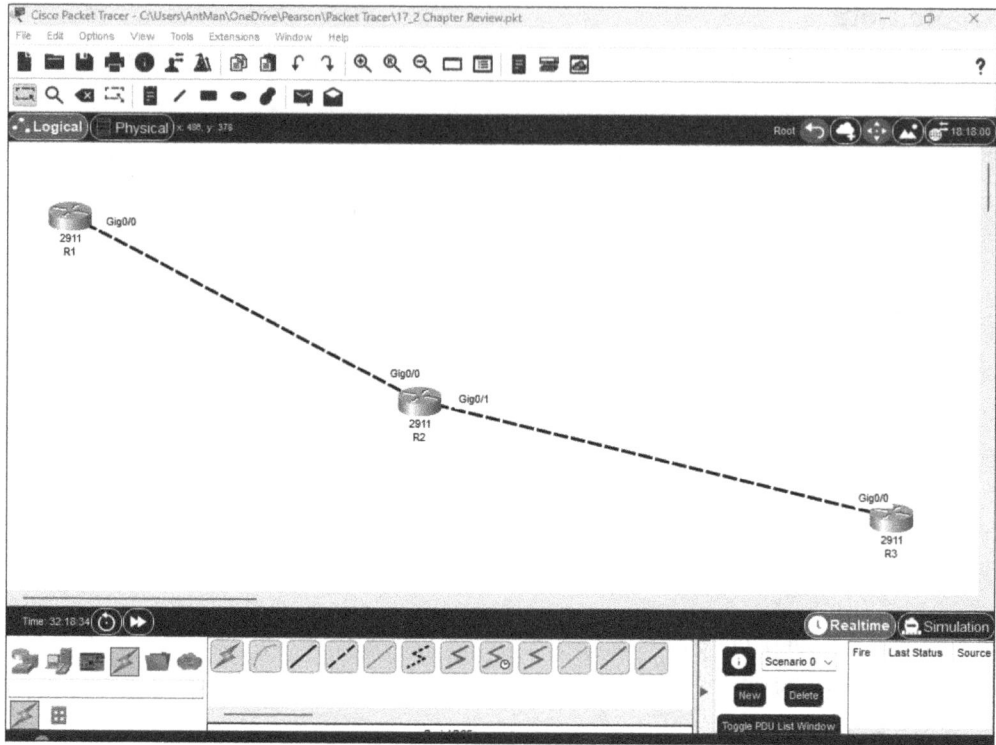

Figure 17.3   *The NAT Chapter Review Lab*

Review Questions

1. What command identifies the inside NAT interface?

A. `nat inside`

B. `nat ip inside`

C. `inside`

D. `ip nat inside`

2. What command allows you to view the NAT translations at the CLI?

A. `show ip nat translations`

B. `show nat usage`

C. `show nat statistics`

D. `show nat all`

3. Examine the following command: `ip nat inside source list 1 interface fa0/0 overload`. What is the inside global address for translation?

   A. The IP address on interface fa0/0

   B. The virtual address on interface fa0/0

   C. The address in access list 1

   D. The address in the NAT pool named `interface`

Answers to Review Questions

1. D is correct. The `ip nat inside` command identifies the inside NAT interface.

2. A is correct. The `show ip nat translations` command allows you to see all the translations currently on the device.

3. A is correct. The IP address on the interface specified here is the inside global address.

Chapter 18

Configure and Verify NTP

This chapter covers the following official CCNA 200-301 exam topic:

- Configure and verify NTP operating in client/server mode

At first, you might think of the time set on your Cisco device as just a bit of a "nice to have" but not something that is very important. In reality, having the super-accurate time on your networking devices can be very, very important—for several reasons. For example, you might have policies that take effect at certain times (such as permitting no gaming traffic during work hours). You might also need accurate time so you can accurately monitor and understand security breaches that have been logged by devices.

Network Time Protocol (NTP) is a proven effective protocol for sharing the correct time between devices and ensuring that the devices stay in sync with accurate time.

This chapter covers the following essential terms and components:

- NTP server
- NTP client
- Stratum

Chapter Pretest

1. What command configures a Cisco router to be an authoritative reference clock source with a stratum of 3?

_____

2. What command confirms an NTP client/server relationship in tabular form?

_____

Answers

1. `ntp master 3`

2. `show ntp association`

> **Note**   Use of the terms *master* and *slave* is ONLY in association with the official termi-
> nology used in industry specifications and standards and in no way diminishes Pearson's
> commitment to promoting diversity, equity, and inclusion and challenging, countering,
> and/or combating bias and stereotyping in the global population of the learners we serve.

Configure and Verify NTP Operating in Client/Server Mode

It is critical—for a number of reasons—to have accurate time on your network devices. Network Time Protocol (NTP) enables you to automate this synchronization process. The current version of the protocol, NTPv4, uses the transport layer protocol UDP and port 123.

NTP uses the concept of a stratum value to gauge the accuracy of time values carried by NTP. A lower stratum value is preferred. The stratum value indicates the NTP hop count from an authoritative reference clock source. Ideally, this reference time source should be an atomic clock. An NTP server that is directly attached to an atomic clock has a stratum of 1.

Example 18.1 shows how to configure R1 to use its internal clock as a reference clock source. Notice that it selects a stratum value of 2.

Example 18.1   *Configuring the NTP Master in a Network*

```
R1# configure terminal
Enter configuration commands, one per line. End with CNTL/Z.
R1(config)# ntp master ?
  <1-15> Stratum number
  <cr>
```

```
R1(config)# ntp master 2
R1(config)# end
R1#
```

Note   The default stratum value for the `ntp master` command is 8.

How do you configure an NTP client to receive the correct time from an NTP server (master)? You use the command `ntp server ntp-server-ip-address-or-dns-name`. You will almost always see a DNS name used in actual production environments. Example 18.2 shows this configuration in our lab.

Example 18.2   *Configuring an NTP Client*

```
R2#
R2# configure terminal
Enter configuration commands, one per line. End with CNTL/Z.
R2(config)# ntp server 10.1.1.1
R2(config)# end
R2#
```

Note   There are several other NTP configuration options available (such as broadcasting NTP updates), but you don't need to understand them for the CCNA 200-301 exam.

Note that once an IOS device synchronizes with a clock source (an internal clock or an external NTP server), it acts as a lower-stratum NTP server, without any additional configuration. The `ntp master` command is necessary only when the IOS device has no external clock source to synchronize to. If you have access to the Internet and wish to synchronize your entire network to the public time, you can have two or three border routers synchronize to public NTP servers with the `ntp server` command and then have your entire internal network synchronize to those border routers (now NTP servers themselves), again using the same `ntp server` command.

There are two key commands for verifying NTP. Example 18.3 shows one of them: the `show ntp associations` command. Note how this command allows you to easily verify the association with the configured NTP master device.

Example 18.3   *Verifying NTP Configuration with* `show ntp associations`

```
R2# show ntp associations

 address     ref clock     st  when poll reach delay offset  disp
*~10.1.1.1 127.127.1.1  2    0    64    275 19.784 40129.7 68.951
 * sys.peer, # selected, + candidate, - outlyer, x falseticker, ~ configured
R2#
```

Example 18.4 shows another frequently used verification command: **show ntp status**.

Example 18.4   *Using* `show ntp status` *to Verify NTP*

```
R2# show ntp status
Clock is synchronized, stratum 3, reference clock is 10.1.1.1
nominal freq is 250.0000 Hz, actual freq is 250.0000 Hz, precision is 2**24
reference time is DA5E7147.56CADEA7 (19:54:31.339 EST Thu Feb 4 2022)
clock offset is 0.0986 msec, root delay is 2.46 msec
root dispersion is 16.27 msec, peer dispersion is 5.33 msec
loopfilter state is 'CTRL' (Normal Controlled Loop), drift is 0.000000009 s/s
system poll interval is 64, last update was 530 sec ago.
R2#
```

> **Note**   Be ready to be patient when you are verifying an NTP configuration. Even in a small practice lab with two devices, it can take many minutes before the NTP synchronization fully takes place. This is by design in the workings of the protocol. Quite impressively, simulators like Packet Tracer take this into account and properly delay the synchronization to add realism.

Lab 18.1: NTP

To complete this Hands-On Lab Practice Assignment, download the assigned Packet Tracer file from the book's companion website and perform the lab on your locally installed version of Packet Tracer. You will be following the instructions in the lab, and your performance will be evaluated.

In this lab, you will configure and verify NTP using the topology shown in Figure 18.1.

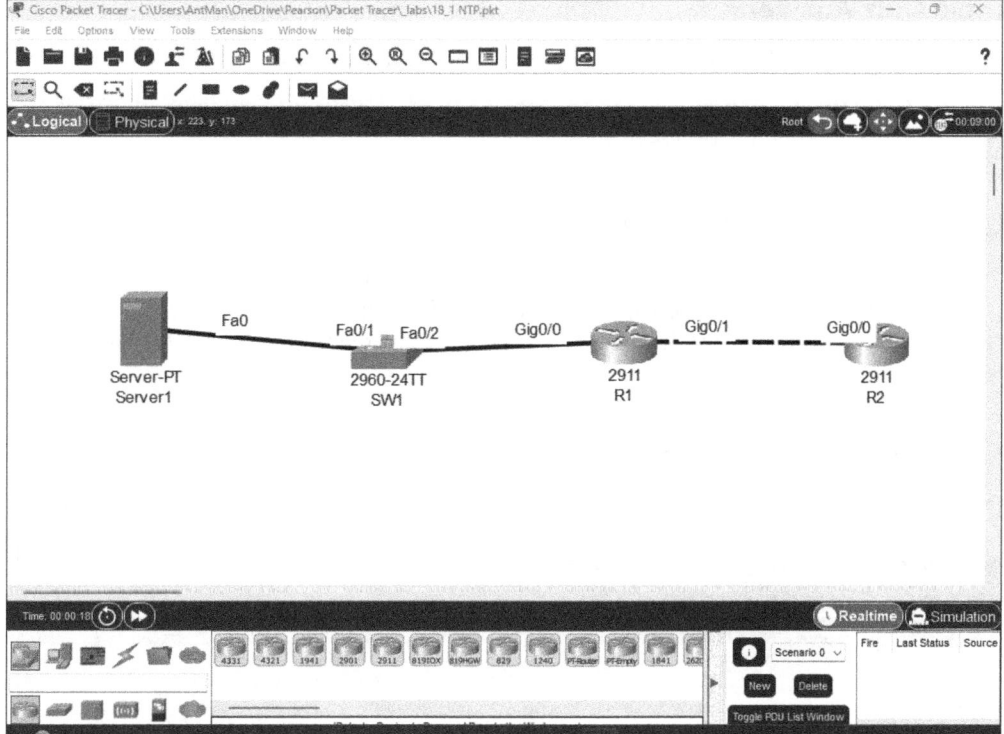

Figure 18.1 *The NTP Lab*

Topic Quiz

1. What is a stratum in NTP?

   A. A measure of the proximity to the reference clock

   B. A measure of a clock's accuracy

   C. A measure of the number of total NTP clients

   D. A measure of the number of NTP queries per minute

2. What command configures a Cisco device as an NTP client of 10.1.1.1?

   A. `ntp client 10.1.1.1`

   B. `ntp master 10.1.1.1`

   C. `ntp server 10.1.1.1`

   D. `ntp 10.1.1.1`

Topic Quiz Answers

1. A is correct. The stratum value indicates how far a device is from the reference clock.

2. C is correct. The `ntp server` command is used on a client to configure the NTP server's IP address or hostname.

Lab 18.2: Chapter Review

To complete this Hands-On Lab Practice Assignment, download the assigned Packet Tracer file from the book's companion website and perform the lab on your locally installed version of Packet Tracer. You will be following the instructions in the lab, and your performance will be evaluated.

In this lab, you will demonstrate your comprehension of the topics in this chapter using the topology shown in Figure 18.2.

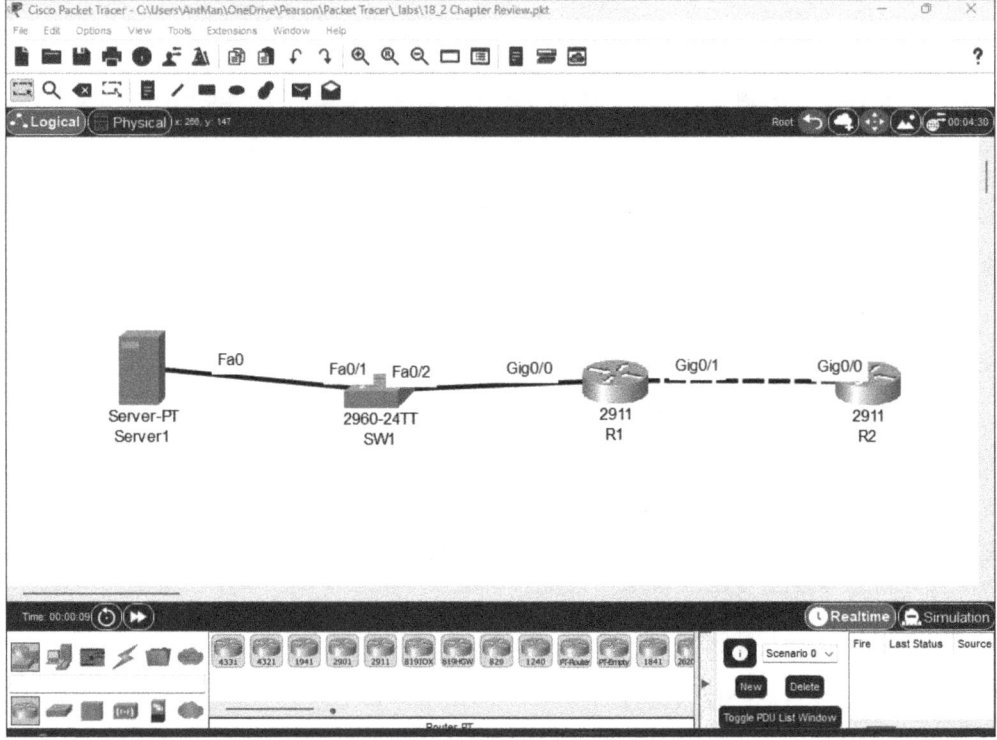

Figure 18.2 *The NTP Chapter Review Lab*

Review Questions

1. What protocol does NTP use, and what port number does it use? (Choose two.)

A. TCP

B. UDP

C. 123

D. 412

2. What is the best possible stratum value that a Cisco NTP server can advertise?

A. 0

B. 1

C. 5

D. 15

3. What command would you use to cause your local router to retrieve the correct time from an NTP master in your network at 10.10.10.100?

A. `ntp receive 10.10.10.100`

B. `ntp fetch 10.10.10.100`

C. `ntp server 10.10.10.100`

D. `ntp client 10.10.10.100`

4. What command produced the output shown here?

```
Clock is synchronized, stratum 3, reference clock is 10.1.1.1

nominal freq is 250.0000 Hz, actual freq is 250.0000 Hz, precision
is 2**24

reference time is DA5E7147.56CADEA7 (19:54:31.339 EST Thu Feb 4
2022)

clock offset is 0.0986 msec, root delay is 2.46 mse

croot dispersion is 16.27 msec, peer dispersion is 5.33 mse

cloopfilter state is 'CTRL' (Normal Controlled Loop), drift is
0.000000009 s/s

system poll interval is 64, last update was 530 sec ago.
```

A. `show ntp status`

B. `show ntp associations`

C. `show ntp peers`

D. `show ntp masters`

Answers to Review Questions

1. B and C are correct. NTP uses UDP and port 123.

2. B is correct. The stratum range is from 1 to 15. The lower the stratum value, the more preferred. Therefore, the best stratum is 1.

3. C is correct. Remember that the `ntp server` command is the command you use to specify the time source for a local device.

4. A is correct. A very powerful `show` command for verifying NTP is **show ntp status.** It provides easy-to-read and easy-to-interpret details about the NTP settings that are in place.

Chapter 19

Configure DNS and DHCP

This chapter covers the following official CCNA 200-301 exam topics:

■ Describe DNS lookup operation

■ Troubleshoot client connectivity issues involving DNS

■ Configure and verify DHCP on a router

■ Troubleshoot client- and router-based DHCP connectivity issues

Domain Name System (DNS) and Dynamic Host Configuration Protocol (DHCP) are important services we cannot live without today. DNS makes it possible to use friendly names like www.ajsnetworking.com for our popular blog sites (shameless plug) instead of having to type hard-to-memorize IP addresses like 209.18.47.62.

One could argue that DHCP is even more critical than DNS. This service ensures that all your connected devices automatically receive the IP address information (including the DNS server address) they need to communicate properly on the local network and beyond, to the Internet. This is an even bigger big deal when you realize that you need to connect many devices these days, including laptops, smartphones, tablets, TV streaming gadgets, smart lights, and the list goes on.

This chapter covers the following essential terms and components:

■ DNS

■ DNS lookups

■ Client DNS configurations

■ DHCP

■ DHCP servers

- DHCP relays
- DHCP clients
- Other DHCP assigned parameters

Chapter Pretest

1. What service resolves "friendly names" like www.certgym.com to IP addresses?

_____

2. Name two types of DNS records.

_____

_____

3. What Windows CLI command allows you to see the configured IP address information as well as the DNS server IP address?

_____

4. What Windows CLI tool allows you to learn information regarding a DNS lookup, including the DNS server name, address, non-authoritative response, and resolved addresses and aliases?

_____

5. What command specifies one or more DNS servers for a Cisco device to use?

_____

6. What is the default lease duration offered by an IOS DHCP server?

_____

7. Which feature allows a router to forward a client's DHCP request to a remote DHCP server?

_____

8. What command allows you to easily verify the lease assignments from the DHCP server?

_____

Answers

1. Domain Name System (DNS) resolves friendly names to IP addresses.

2. Common record types include:

- Start of authority (SOA)
- IP addresses (A and AAAA)

- SMTP mail exchangers (MX)

- Name servers (NS)

- Pointers for reverse DNS lookups (PTR)

- Domain name aliases (CNAME)

3. `ipconfig /all`

4. `nslookup`

5. `ip name-server`

6. The default lease duration is 1 day, which is 86,400 seconds.

7. The DHCP relay agent feature permits this.

8. `show ip dhcp server bindings`

Describe DNS Lookup Operation

Imagine being able to communicate with devices on the Internet (or your company's intranet) only by using the IP addresses of systems. The task would be nearly impossible because memorizing IP addresses for so many devices would be incredibly difficult. DNS prevents this nightmare.

DNS resolves a "friendly" name like www.pearsonvue.com to the IP address that devices truly need to reach that particular remote system. We use DNS every day, as you might guess. Notice that what I've just referred to as a "friendly name" is actually a domain name. It is a structured name consisting of three parts: www, pearsonvue, and com.

DNS can refer to a private RFC 1918 address space inside your organization or to the public, globally routable IPv4 address space on the Internet. You can also have your internal private DNS servers interact with public DNS servers.

DNS delegates the responsibility for assigning domain names and mapping those names to Internet resources by designating *authoritative* name servers for each domain. Network administrators may delegate authority over subdomains of their allocated namespaces to other name servers. This approach provides a fault-tolerant design and eliminates the need for everyone to rely on one single huge database.

Remember that *DNS* refers to this structure of naming (for example, www versus com in www.example.com) as well as the technical details of the protocol itself (for example, what messages are exchanged and how data is processed in the system).

Remember that DNS provides translation services between the domain name hierarchy and the address spaces. A DNS name server is a server that stores the DNS records for a domain; a DNS name server responds with answers to queries against its database.

The most common types of records stored in the DNS database are as follows:

- Start of authority (SOA)

- IP addresses (A and AAAA)

- SMTP mail exchangers (MX)

- Name servers (NS)

- Pointers for reverse DNS lookups (PTR)

- Domain name aliases (CNAME)

DNS databases are traditionally stored in structured files called *zone files*. These zone files contain the records that are the lifeblood of DNS.

Topic Quiz

1. Which statement about DNS is false?

A. DNS operates thanks to one primary central database.

> **Note**   Use of the terms *master* and *slave* is ONLY in association with the official terminology used in industry specifications and standards and in no way diminishes Pearson's commitment to promoting diversity, equity, and inclusion and challenging, countering, and/or combating bias and stereotyping in the global population of the learners we serve.

B. DNS resolves domain names to IP addresses.

C. DNS uses many types of records to do its job.

D. Multiple DNS servers are typically available for a client.

2. What device is responsible for each DNS domain?

A. Primary DNS database

B. Authoritative name server

C. Zone file server

D. DNS client

Topic Quiz Answers

1. A is correct. DNS creates a distributed database to prevent reliance on one primary central database. Note the tricky nature of this question. Choice D is semi-true and semi-false. While it is true that multiple DNS servers are often available to clients, many clients are often configured with just one DNS server. In many (if not most) home networks, the home gateway also acts as the only DNS server available to all the home network's devices; this is the case in Example 19.1, later in this chapter. At the same time, public DNS servers are available to all these same devices (Cloudflare's 1.1.1.1, or Google's 8.8.8.8, for example). So while the falsehood of the D choice hinges on the definitions of the words *typically* and *available*, and the statement could be interpreted as being conditionally either true or false, choice A is outright and unequivocally false, making it the *best*, and therefore right, choice.

2. B is correct. For each domain there is an authoritative name server that helps manage the domain.

Troubleshoot Client Connectivity Issues Involving DNS

Ensuring that your clients are properly configured to use DNS is important for full functionality on the Internet today.

On a Windows client system, you can check the DNS settings by using `ipconfig` with the `/all` switch, as shown in Example 19.1.

Example 19.1   *Examining DNS Settings on a Windows Client*

```
C:\Users\terry>ipconfig /all

Windows IP Configuration

  Host Name . . . . . . . . . . . . : DESKTOP-ABC123
  Primary Dns Suffix . . . . . . . :
  Node Type . . . . . . . . . . . . : Hybrid
  IP Routing Enabled. . . . . . . . : No
  WINS Proxy Enabled. . . . . . . . : No
  DNS Suffix Search List. . . . . . : my-router.home

Ethernet adapter Ethernet:

  Connection-specific DNS Suffix  . : my-router.home
  Description . . . . . . . . . . . : Realtek PCIe GBE Family Controller
  Physical Address. . . . . . . . . : 84-8F-69-F5-5F-3D
  DHCP Enabled. . . . . . . . . . . : Yes
  Autoconfiguration Enabled . . . . : Yes
  Link-local IPv6 Address . . . . . : fe80::bc5e:a448:8dcc:72ce%3 (Preferred)
  IPv4 Address. . . . . . . . . . . : 192.168.1.191(Preferred)
  Subnet Mask . . . . . . . . . . . : 255.255.255.0
  Lease Obtained. . . . . . . . . . : Monday3:33:08 AM
  Lease Expires . . . . . . . . . . : Friday 3:33:19 AM
  Default Gateway . . . . . . . . . : 192.168.1.1
```

```
DHCP Server . . . . . . . . . . . : 192.168.1.1
DHCPv6 IAID . . . . . . . . . . . : 59019113
DHCPv6 Client DUID. . . . . . . . : 00-01-00-01-1E-72-89-C7-84-8F-69-F5-5F-3D
DNS Servers . . . . . . . . . . . : 192.168.1.1
NetBIOS over Tcpip. . . . . . . . : Enabled
C:\Users\terry>
```

Notice from the output in Example 19.1 that this client will send DNS requests to 192.168.1.1. This is, of course, a private-use-only address inside the network. This router receives public DNS server addresses automatically from the ISP so that it can resolve public website names that you want to visit.

Figure 19.1 shows the actual configuration for this Windows client in the Control Panel graphical user interface. Notice that the DNS information 192.168.1.1 is being learned by this client automatically using DHCP.

How do you verify that the Windows client can reach the DNS server and resolve domain names to IP addresses? One approach is to ping a known and reachable web server, using the friendly name. Example 19.2 demonstrates this approach.

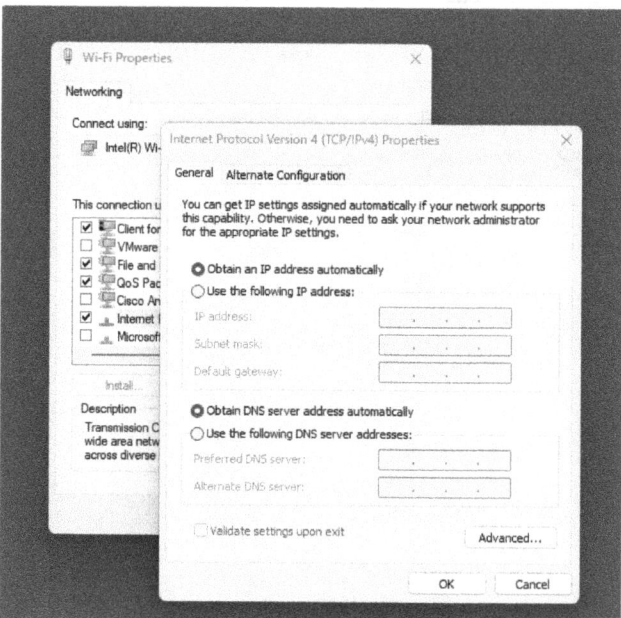

Figure 19.1 *DNS Settings in Windows*

Example 19.2   *Checking DNS Functionality by Using* ping

```
C:\Users\terry>ping www.cisco.com

Pinging e144.dscb.akamaiedge.net [23.202.192.170] with 32 bytes of data:
Reply from 23.202.192.170: bytes=32 time=35ms TTL=54
Reply from 23.202.192.170: bytes=32 time=37ms TTL=54
Reply from 23.202.192.170: bytes=32 time=36ms TTL=54
Reply from 23.202.192.170: bytes=32 time=35ms TTL=54

Ping statistics for 23.202.192.170:
    Packets: Sent = 4, Received = 4, Lost = 0 (0% loss),
Approximate round trip times in milli-seconds:
    Minimum = 35ms, Maximum = 37ms, Average = 35ms

C:\Users\terry>
```

Note   As discussed later in this chapter, you can configure a Cisco router or switch as a DNS client. Do not ignore the Windows client information, however.

If you would like to receive even more information about the DNS lookup process, you can use the **nslookup** command. Example 19.3 demonstrates this powerful tool.

Example 19.3   *Using* nslookup *to Verify DNS*

```
C:\Users\terry>nslookup www.cisco.com
Server:  ACME_Quantum_Gateway.my-router.home
Address:  192.168.1.1

Non-authoritative answer:
Name:    e144.dscb.akamaiedge.net
Addresses:  2600:1408:10:18c::90
         2600:1408:10:181::90
         23.202.192.170
Aliases:  www.cisco.Com
          www.cisco.com.akadns.net
          wwwds.cisco.com.edgekey.net
          wwwds.cisco.com.edgekey.net.globalredir.akadns.net
C:\Users\terry>
```

Just as it can be convenient for a Windows client to use DNS, it can also be beneficial for Cisco routers and switches to use DNS. Table 19.1 lists some of the commands available on these devices.

Table 19.1 *DNS-Related Commands on Cisco Devices*

Cisco Command	Description
`ip domain-lookup`	This command enables DNS-based hostname-to-address translation; it is enabled by default on Cisco devices. Note that this command is the legacy version of the `ip domain lookup` command (without the hyphen).
`ip name-server`	This command specifies the address(es) of the DNS server(s) for the device to use for DNS resolution.
`ip domain-name`	This command defines a default domain name that the Cisco IOS software uses to complete unqualified hostnames. An unqualified name is the leftmost part of the dotted hierarchical domain name. For example, www is the unqualified name of a web server, whereas www.cisco.com is the fully qualified hostname.

Topic Quiz

1. What is a common Windows client setting for IPv4 DNS?

   A. To use only Google DNS public servers

   B. To acquire DNS settings automatically via DHCP

   C. To use the public IP address of the ISP's router

   D. To use a local loopback address

2. What command enables DNS-based hostname translations on a Cisco router and is enabled by default on many Cisco routers?

   A. `ip domain-name`

   B. `ip name-server`

   C. `ip domain-list`

   D. `ip domain lookup`

Topic Quiz Answers

1. B is correct. A very common approach to DNS on Windows clients is to acquire this information dynamically.

2. D is correct. The `ip domain lookup` command enables DNS-based hostname resolution. This command is enabled by default.

Configure and Verify DHCP on a Router

Figure 19.2 shows a simple topology used in this section to configure a DHCP server using a Cisco router (R1) and to configure a Cisco router (R2) as a DHCP client.

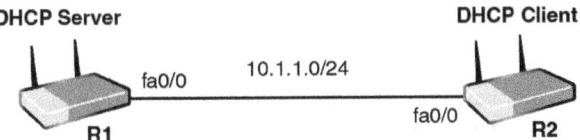

DHCP Server   **DHCP Client**

fa0/0   10.1.1.0/24

fa0/0

R1   R2

Figure 19.2   *The DHCP Server and Client Topology*

Example 19.4 shows the configuration of R1, the DHCP server.

Example 19.4   *The Configuration of the DHCP Server*

```
R1#
R1# configure terminal
Enter configuration commands, one per line. End with CNTL/Z.
R1(config)# interface fa0/0
R1(config-if)# ip address 10.1.1.1 255.255.255.0
R1(config-if)# no shutdown
R1(config-if)# exit
R1(config)#
%LINK-3-UPDOWN: Interface FastEthernet0/0, changed state to up
%LINEPROTO-5-UPDOWN: Line protocol on Interface FastEthernet0/0, changed state to up
R1(config)# ip dhcp excluded-address 10.1.1.1 10.1.1.10
R1(config)# ip dhcp pool CCNAEXAM
R1(dhcp-config)# default-router 10.1.1.1
R1(dhcp-config)# dns-server 8.8.8.8 1.1.1.1
R1(dhcp-config)# option 150 ip 10.10.10.2
R1(dhcp-config)# network 10.1.1.0 /24
R1(dhcp-config)# end
R1#
```

The commands in Example 19.4 that directly involve DHCP are as follows:

- **ip dhcp excluded-address 10.1.1.1 10.1.1.10**: This command tells the DHCP server *not* to assign the addresses from 10.1.1.1 to 10.1.1.10 to DHCP clients. For example, the 10.1.1.1 address is the static router interface address configured on R1's fa0/0 interface. Even though the router is smart enough to not offer its own IP addresses to DHCP clients, the dhcp excluded-address command is the router's only way to know not to offer statically configured IP addresses (of devices such as other routers, switches, printers, or file servers on the subnet).

- **ip dhcp pool CCNAEXAM**: This command creates a DHCP pool on R1. This pool of IP addresses will also contain the specific parameters to hand out to clients that lease addresses from the DHCP server.

- **default-router 10.1.1.1**: This command assigns the default gateway to clients of this DHCP pool.

- **dns-server 8.8.8.8 4.2.2.2**: This command sets a primary DNS server and a backup DNS server for the clients.

- **option 150 ip 10.10.10.2**: This command provides clients with the IP address of a TFTP server.

- **network 10.1.1.0 /24**: This command specifies the IP address assignments for the pool. Remember that we excluded a small portion of this network address space. As a result, we expect the first leased address to be 10.1.1.11/24.

> **Note**   The `network` command used in DHCP configuration accepts a subnet mask or CIDR notation in its syntax.

Example 19.5 shows the configuration of a DHCP client function on a Cisco router.

Example 19.5   *The Configuration of the DHCP Client*

```
R2#
R2# configure terminal
Enter configuration commands, one per line. End with CNTL/Z.
R2(config)# interface fa0/0
R2(config-if)# ip address dhcp
R2(config-if)# no shutdown
R2(config-if)# end
R2#
%SYS-5-CONFIG_I: Configured from console by console
R2#
%LINK-3-UPDOWN: Interface FastEthernet0/0, changed state to up
%LINEPROTO-5-UPDOWN: Line protocol on Interface FastEthernet0/0, changed state to up
R2#
```

Notice the very simple configuration in Example 19.5. The command **ip address dhcp** configures a DHCP client interface.

Next, let's begin verification on the server. Example 19.6 shows the use of the **show ip dhcp binding** command to verify the server's operation.

Example 19.6   *Verifying the DHCP Server*

```
R1#
R1# show ip dhcp binding
Bindings from all pools not associated with VRF:
IP address      Client-ID/         Lease expiration      Type
                Hardware address/
                User name
10.1.1.11       0063.6973.636f.2d63. 08:10 PM _____  Automatic
                6130.332e.3066.6330.
                2e30.3030.302d.4661.
                302f.30
R1#
```

Note   Notice that the default lease duration for Cisco DHCP servers is one day. To see any IP address conflicts in your Cisco DHCP environment, you can use the command **show ip dhcp conflict**.

Example 19.7 shows a simple verification on the client. The **show ip interface brief** command enables you to quickly view the DHCP-learned address on Fa0/0.

Example 19.7   *Verifying Dynamic Address Assignment on the DHCP Client*

```
R2#
R2# show ip interface brief
Interface       IP-Address OK? Method Status              Protocol
FastEthernet0/0 10.1.1.11 YES DHCP    up                  up
FastEthernet1/0 unassigned YES unset  administratively down down
FastEthernet1/1 unassigned YES unset  administratively down down
R2#
```

What happens if your DHCP server is not on the same subnet with the clients that need it? One option is to configure a DHCP relay agent. This is a router that hears the DHCP requests from clients and forwards them to the appropriate DHCP server. It is very simple to configure such a relay agent. Figure 19.3 and Example 19.8 show a sample topology and configuration. Note that the powerful **ip helper-address** *dhcp-server-ip* command gets the job done. The relay agent knows the address of the DHCP server, so it can successfully forward local DHCP traffic to the DHCP server.

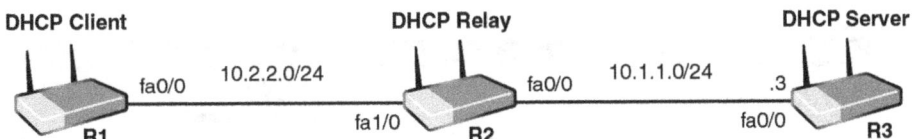

DHCP Client   fa0/0   10.2.2.0/24   **R1**   **DHCP Relay**   fa1/0   **R2**   fa0/0   10.1.1.0/24   .3   **DHCP Server**   fa0/0   **R3**

Figure 19.3   *The DHCP Relay Agent*

Example 19.8   *Configuring the DHCP Relay Agent*

```
R2#
R2# configure terminal
Enter configuration commands, one per line. End with CNTL/Z.
R2(config)# interface fa1/0
R2(config-if)# ip helper-address 10.1.1.3
R2(config-if)# end
R2#
```

Lab 19.1: Configuring DHCP

To complete this Hands-On Lab Practice Assignment, download the assigned Packet Tracer file from the book's companion website and perform the lab on your locally installed version of Packet Tracer. You will be following the instructions in the lab, and your performance will be evaluated.

In this lab, you will configure and verify DHCP using the topology shown in Figure 19.4.

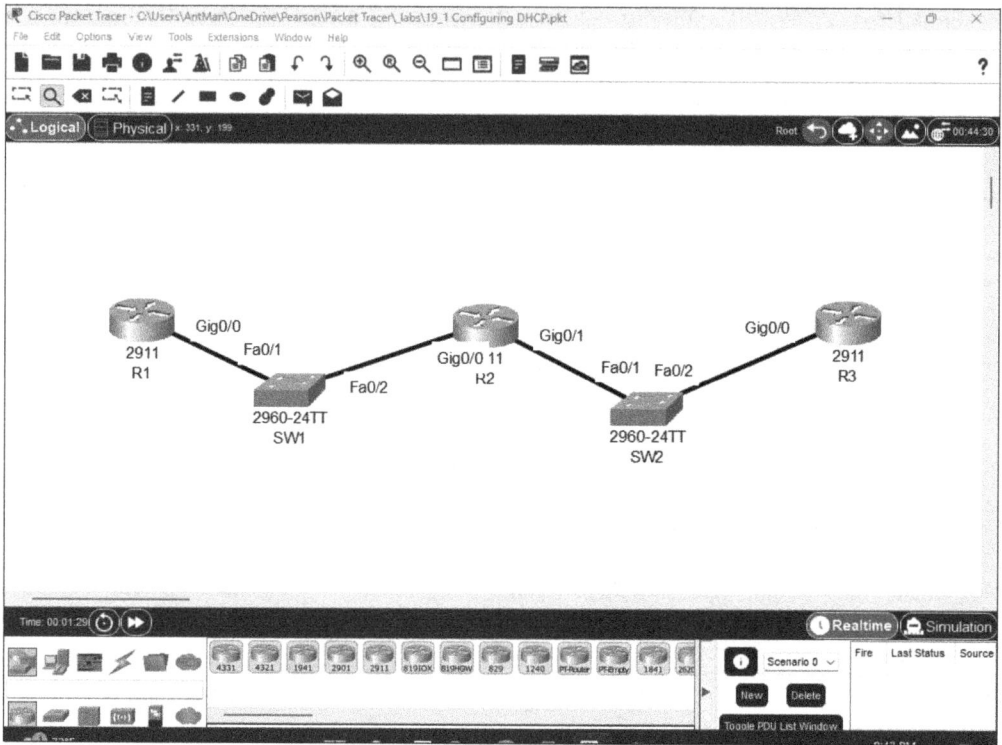

Figure 19.4   *The DHCP Lab*

Topic Quiz

1. What command ensures that a DHCP server does not lease out addresses you have statically configured elsewhere?

   A. `no dhcp-server assign-address`

   B. `no dhcp-lease address`

   C. `ip dhcp no-lease address`

   D. `ip dhcp excluded-address`

2. What command configures a default gateway in a DHCP server pool?

   A. `ip default-gateway`

   B. `ip default-router`

   C. `ip domain-server`

   D. `default-router`

3. What command configures a Cisco device as a DHCP client?

   A. `ip address auto`

   B. `ip address dhcp`

   C. `ip address learn`

   D. `ip address dynamic`

Topic Quiz Answers

1. **D** is correct. Use the `ip dhcp excluded-address` command to create a range of excluded addresses from a DHCP pool.

2. **D** is correct. Use the `default-router` command in the DHCP pool to set the default gateway address.

3. **B** is correct. `ip address dhcp`, used in interface configuration mode, sets the interface to act as a DHCP client.

Troubleshoot Client and Router-Based DHCP Connectivity Issues

Many issues can prevent proper DHCP connectivity. Here are just some issues you should be aware of:

- Errors in router or switch configurations

- DHCP server configuration

- DHCP relay agent configuration

- DHCP server scope configuration or software defect

Note   Although many possible errors can be addressed on the CCNA 200-301 exam, watch out for server or client misconfigurations because these are the most common.

Four steps of the DHCP process must succeed for a DHCP lease to be successful:

1. A Discover message from the client

2. An Offer message from the server

3. A Request message from the client

4. An Acknowledgment message from the server

Remember the key verification commands for DHCP. `show ip dhcp binding` is critical for the server, and `show ip interface brief` works well for the client.

Topic Quiz

The following configuration is related to the questions that follow:

```
R1# show running-config
Building configuration...


Current configuration : 1312 bytes
!
upgrade fpd auto
version 15.0
service time stamps debug datetime msec
service timestamps log datetime msec
no service password-encryption
!
hostname R1
!
...
!
!
ip dhcp excluded-address 10.1.1.1 10.1.1.10
!
ip dhcp pool CCNAEXAM
 network 10.1.1.0 255.255.255.0
 default-router 10.1.1.1
 option 150 ip 10.10.10.2
!
!
no ip domain lookup
no ipv6 cef
!
multilink bundle-name authenticated
!
!
```

```
redundancy
!
!
ip tcp synwait-time 5
!
!
!
interface FastEthernet0/0
 ip address 10.1.1.1 255.255.255.0
 duplex half
!
!
interface FastEthernet1/0
 no ip address
 shutdown
 duplex auto
 speed auto
!
!
interface FastEthernet1/1
 no ip address
 shutdown
 duplex auto
 speed auto
!
...


R1#
```

1. DHCP clients in the 10.1.1.0/24 subnet are complaining that they cannot access Internet resources. What is the most likely issue?

   A. The scope of addresses in the pool is not correct.

   B. There is no lease duration set.

   C. There are no DNS servers assigned to the clients.

   D. The default gateway is incorrect.

2. What is the second of the four steps of the DHCP process?

   A. Acknowledgment

   B. Request

   C. Offer

   D. Discover

Topic Quiz Answers

1. C is correct. This configuration is missing the assignment of DNS servers for the clients.

2. C is correct. The second step of the process is an offer.

Lab 19.2: Chapter Review

To complete this Hands-On Lab Practice Assignment, download the assigned Packet Tracer file from the book's companion website and perform the lab on your locally installed version of Packet Tracer. You will be following the instructions in the lab, and your performance will be evaluated.

In this lab, you will demonstrate your comprehension of the topics in this chapter using the topology shown in Figure 19.5.

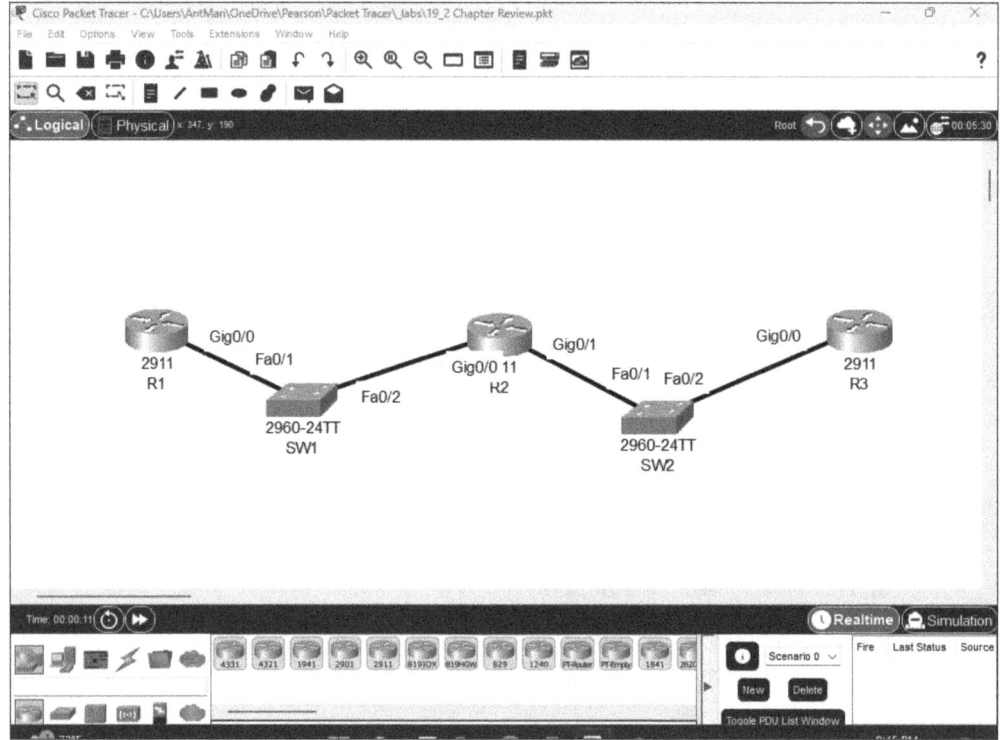

Figure 19.5   *The DHCP Chapter Review Lab*

Review Questions

1. What type of record is used in DNS for a mail server?

A. SOA

B. MX

C. NS

D. CNAME

2. Your junior network admin issues a ping to www.cisco.com, which is successful. What has been verified?

A. WINS

B. DNS

C. NTP

D. DHCP

3. What command sets the DHCP pool scope to 192.168.1.0/24?

A. `scope 192.168.1.0/24`

B. `network 192.168.1.0 255.255.255.0`

C. `subnet 192.168.1.0/24`

D. `addresses 192.168.1.0`

4. What command configures a DHCP relay agent?

A. `ip dhcp relay-agent`

B. `ip dhcp relay-agent enable`

C. `ip forward-address`

D. `ip helper-address`

Answers to Review Questions

1. B is correct. The MX record is for a mail server.

2. B is correct. DNS name resolution has been verified. For a client that receives its configuration via DHCP, the ping also verifies that the client received an IP address, the correct gateway, and DNS servers. But because it is possible to have all these settings statically configured, it is not possible to say that a ping to www.cisco.com will always verify proper DHCP operation. In some cases it might, but in others it may not. However, the ping will *always* verify DNS operation, making DNS the best answer.

3. B is correct. The `network` command sets this.

4. D is correct. To configure a relay agent, use `ip helper-address`.

Chapter 20

Configure Other Networking Services

This chapter covers the following official CCNA 200-301 exam topics:

- Describe the use of syslog and SNMP features

- Explain the forwarding per-hop behavior (PHB) for QoS, such as classification, marking, queueing, congestion avoidance, policing, and shaping

- Using SSH and FTP/TFTP in a network

This chapter rounds out the coverage of IP services by covering a variety of important topics you need to know for the CCNA 200-301 exam, including syslog, SNMP, FTP, TFTP, QoS, and remotely accessing devices by using SSH.

This chapter covers the following essential terms and components:

- Syslog

- SNMP version 2

- SNMP version 3

- PHBs

- Classification

- Marking

- Queueing

- Congestion

- Policing

- Shaping

- SSH
- FTP
- TFTP

Chapter Pretest

1. What is the default status of monitor and buffer logging on a Cisco network device such as a router?

_____

2. What syslog severity level is Emergency?

_____

3. What version of SNMP provides robust security mechanisms?

_____

4. What QoS approach ensures that resources are available for voice and video applications through the use of predetermined assignments?

_____

5. What QoS marking is used in Ethernet frames?

_____

6. What link QoS mechanism buffers traffic by default when it exceeds a certain rate?

_____

7. What is the secure alternative to the Telnet protocol for accessing devices remotely?

_____

8. TFTP relies on what transport layer protocol and port number?

_____

Answers

1. The default status of monitor and buffer logging is enabled.

2. Level 0

3. SNMP version 3

4. Integrated Services (IntServ) with Resource Reservation Protocol (RSVP)

5. Class of service (CoS)

6. Traffic shaping

7. The Secure Shell (SSH) protocol

8. UDP and port 69

Describe the Use of Syslog and SNMP Features

Network devices, including Cisco devices, typically engage in system-logging capabilities, commonly termed *syslog*. System logging allows devices to report on their health and important events that might be transpiring. In Cisco networking, we commonly call syslog simply *logging*. These log messages can vary from the mundane to the critical. Example 20.1 shows the default logging configuration on a Cisco router.

Note You can configure the timestamp information in your syslog messages by using the `Logging` command. You can ensure that the timestamps include detail down to the millisecond level, thanks to the `msec` optional keyword.

Example 20.1 *The Default Logging Configuration of a Cisco Router*

```
R2#
R2# show logging
Syslog logging: enabled (0 messages dropped, 2 messages rate-limited,
            0 flushes, 0 overruns, xml disabled, filtering disabled)

No Active Message Discriminator.

No Inactive Message Discriminator.

  Console logging: level debugging, 16 messages logged, xml disabled,
                filtering disabled
  Monitor logging: level debugging, 0 messages logged, xml disabled,
                filtering disabled
  Buffer logging: level debugging, 16 messages logged, xml disabled,
                filtering disabled
  Logging Exception size (8192 bytes)
  Count and timestamp logging messages: disabled
  Persistent logging: disabled

No active filter modules.

ESM: 0 messages dropped

  Trap logging: level informational, 19 message lines logged
```

```
Log Buffer (8192 bytes):

*Aug 28 15:54:39.063: %IFMGR-7-NO_IFINDEX_FILE: Unable to open nvram:/ifIndex-table
  No such file or directory
*Aug 28 15:54:56.991: %LINEPROTO-5-UPDOWN: Line protocol on Interface VoIP-Null0,
  changed state to up
*Aug 28 15:54:56.995: %LINK-3-UPDOWN: Interface FastEthernet0/0, changed state to up
*Aug 28 15:54:57.003: %LINK-3-UPDOWN: Interface FastEthernet1/0, changed state to up
...
```

Notice that, by default, logging is enabled, and syslog messages are stored in a buffer for later analysis. Specifically, notice that three forms of logging are enabled by default:

- **Console logging:** Console logging involves console syslog messages such as `*Aug 28 15:54:56.995: %LINK-3-UPDOWN: Interface FastEthernet0/0, changed state to up` that you see when you are connected to the device using the console port.

- **Monitor logging:** Monitor logging allows users who are connected remotely (using Telnet or SSH) into the device to see console messages as well.

- **Buffer logging:** Buffer logging stores logs in a buffer (local memory) and permits viewing of messages at a later date, as Example 20.1 demonstrates.

Note Even if a feature is typically on by default (for example, console logging), you should not make assumptions in the exam environment. Console logging might be disabled in a running configuration.

Notice from the sample log messages shown in Example 20.1 that syslog messages follow a specific format with fields including the following:

- **A timestamp:** In this case, `*Aug 28 15:54:57.003:`

- **The component that generated the message:** In this case, `%LINK` (technically termed the "facility")

- **A severity level:** In this case, `3`

- **A mnemonic for the message:** In this case, `UPDOWN`

- **A description:** In this case, `Interface FastEthernet1/0, changed state to up`

The possible severity levels for messages are very important, especially since you can filter the logging to the various destinations by using these levels. Table 20.1 shows the syslog severity levels used by Cisco equipment.

Table 20.1 *The Syslog Severity Levels*

Keyword	Level	Description
Emergency	0	System unusable
Alert	1	Immediate action required
Critical	2	Critical event
Error	3	Error event
Warning	4	Warning event
Notification	5	Normal but significant condition
Informational	6	Informational message
Debug	7	Used for debugging the software

Example 20.2 shows a sample configuration involving logging on a Cisco router.

Example 20.2 *A Sample Syslog Configuration on a Cisco Router*

```
R2#
R2# configure terminal
Enter configuration commands, one per line. End with CNTL/Z.
R2(config)# logging console 6
R2(config)# logging buffered 4
R2(config)# logging monitor warning
R2(config)# logging host 10.1.1.3
R2(config)# end
R2#
```

The commands in Example 20.2 have the following effects:

- `logging console 6`: Limits console syslog messages to levels 6 through 0.

- `logging buffered 4`: Limits buffer syslog messages to levels 4 through 0.

- `logging monitor warning`: Limits monitor syslog messages to levels 4 through 0; note that you can use the severity level's shorthand or the level number.

- `logging host 10.1.1.3`: Sends syslog messages to a syslog server (located at 10.1.1.3) for storage.

Simple Network Management Protocol (SNMP) eases the management of network devices. Monitoring and configuration are both possible using this technology.

SNMP version 2c is excellent and has been used for many years, but it lacks security features. In fact, it uses a simple plaintext community string (password) for security protection.

SNMP version 3 addresses the security concerns present in previous versions. This version provides robust authentication, authorization, and integrity verification—if desired. With SNMP version 3, you have several options for your security settings, as shown in Table 20.2.

Table 20.2   *SNMP Version 3 Security Levels*

Level	Authentication/Encryption	Description
noAuthNoPriv	Username/no encryption	Username match for authentication
authNoPriv	MD5 or SHA/no encryption	Authentication and no encryption
authPriv	MD5 or SHA/DES	Both authentication and encryption

Lab 20.1: Configuring Syslog

To complete this Hands-On Lab Practice Assignment, download the assigned Packet Tracer file from the book's companion website and perform the lab on your locally installed version of Packet Tracer. You will be following the instructions in the lab, and your performance will be evaluated.

In this lab, you will configure and verify syslog using the topology shown in Figure 20.1.

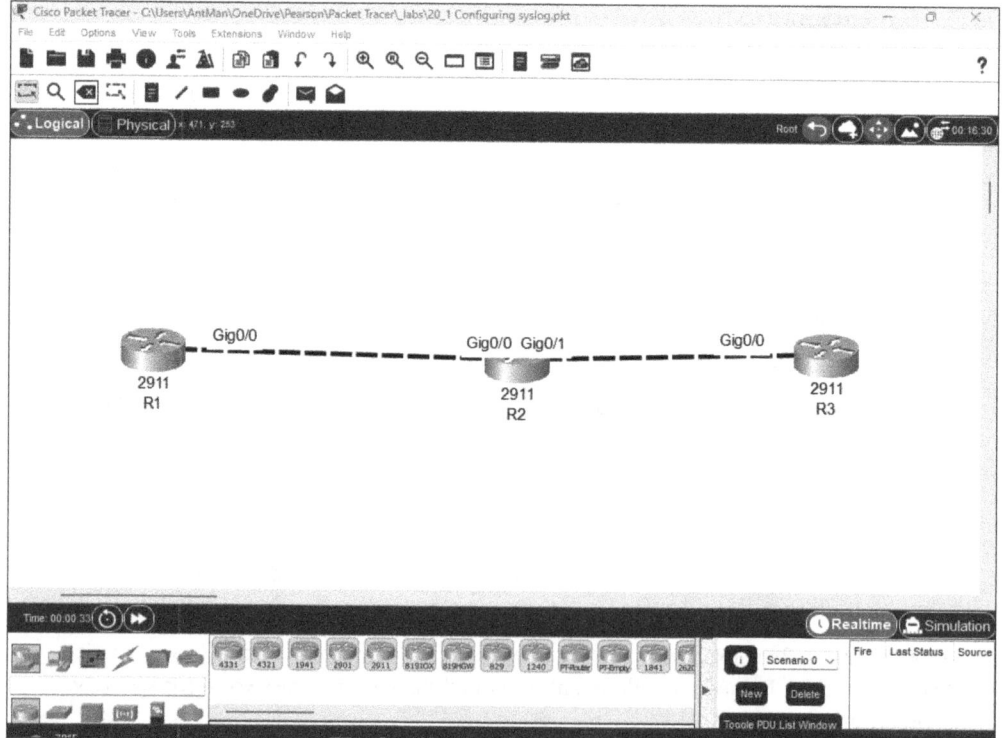

Figure 20.1   *The Syslog Lab*

Topic Quiz

1. What level of logging is appropriate for an event where an action is required immediately?

   A. Emergency

   B. Critical

   C. Error

   D. Alert

2. How can you configure your Cisco router so that log messages with severity levels 5 through 0 are stored in a buffer?

   A. `logging buffered 5`

   B. `logging level 5 buffer`

   C. `logging 5 buffered`

   D. `logging buffered 5 0`

3. What version of SNMP uses a simple plaintext password?

   A. Version 1

   B. Version 2c

   C. Version 3

   D. Version 4

Topic Quiz Answers

1. **D** is correct. The Alert syslog level in Cisco indicates that an action is required immediately.

2. **A** is correct. The command `logging buffered 5` enables you to filter the buffer for log messages at a level of 0 through 5.

3. **B** is correct. SNMP versions 2 and 2c use a simple plaintext password.

Explain the Forwarding Per-Hop Behavior (PHB) for QoS

There are three main approaches you can take to quality of service (QoS) in your organization:

- **Best effort (BE):** Using this approach, you overprovision the bandwidth in the network as you do not use any special QoS settings or tools; most Cisco devices default to a first-in, first-out (FIFO) approach to packet queueing and forwarding in the BE configuration.

■ **Integrated Services (IntServ):** With this approach, Resource Reservation Protocol (RSVP) is used to reserve resources on devices in the path to carry important or fragile traffic forms; this approach is no longer popular as it requires special signaling protocols and requires tight integration across the entire path of the traffic (which more often than not spans several non-homogeneously administered networks).

■ **Differentiated Services (DiffServ):** This approach is the most popular today; it begins with traffic marking and classification to identify and group traffic that must be treated in a special manner. Traffic receives special treatment in a hop-by-hop approach based on predefined and configured per-hop behaviors (PHBs).

Marking traffic for a certain QoS treatment can be done at several layers of the OSI model:

■ **Layer 2:** Class of service (CoS)

■ **Layer 2.5:** The Experimental Use field in MPLS

■ **Layer 3:** Type of service (ToS) for IPv4 and traffic class for IPv6

Should a router or switch trust the markings of incoming packets and frames? Is the directly connected device marking the packets properly? Such considerations are included in *device trust*. Devices you are trusting become the trust boundary in the network. Any packets arriving from outside the trust boundary should have any QoS marking ignored and cleared.

QoS seeks to control several potential issues in a network that is experiencing congestion. Prioritization of traffic is done in order to avoid problems with packet loss, packet delay (latency), and jitter (variations in delay).

QoS is very popular in networks today because more and more networks are converged. This means they feature two or more of the following traffic forms:

■ **Voice:** Voice over IP permits calls to occur over the same network as data traffic; no longer are special equipment and special links required for voice traffic.

■ **Video:** Video over IP is becoming more and more popular for the transmission of video traffic.

■ **Data:** Data traffic could include critical transactional data and scavenger class data, such as gaming or social media traffic.

Remember that with Differentiated Services, traffic is classified and marked, and then it is treated in a special manner on a hop-by-hop basis, based on the traffic's marking. Tools for this special treatment include the following:

■ **Shaping tools:** Shaping permits you to control the rate of traffic on a link; traffic above a specified threshold is buffered so it can be sent at a later time, when there is less traffic on the link.

- **Policing tools:** Policing is similar to shaping; with policing, however, traffic in excess of a specified rate is dropped by default.

- **Congestion management tools:** There are several tools in this category. Class-based weighted fair queueing (CBWFQ) seeks to prioritize traffic based on markings, while low-latency queueing (LLQ) adds to the CBWFQ system a strict priority queue (PQ) that is reserved for voice traffic in a typical implementation.

- **Congestion avoidance tools:** Tools in this category seek to avoid congestion altogether before it becomes an issue. Link fragmentation and interleaving (LFI) is a popular example of a congestion avoidance tool. Large packets are fragmented so that more importantly marked packets can be interwoven between the fragments. Another interesting approach is weighted random early detection (WRED). With WRED, low-priority packets are randomly dropped when interfaces start to approach a congested level, in the hopes that the traffic's sender will notice the drop and slow down.

Topic Quiz

1. What marking is done at Layer 3?

  A. Type of service

  B. Class of service

  C. Experimental bits

  D. BECN

2. What does it mean to trust a device in a QoS environment?

  A. To forward the traffic from the device, regardless of priority

  B. To honor the QoS markings

  C. To rewrite any Layer 2 markings

  D. To always provide LLQ to the device's traffic

Topic Quiz Answers

1. A is correct. The Type of Service field in an IPv4 header permits the marking of traffic at Layer 3.

2. B is correct. Device trust refers to honoring QoS markings of packets arriving from a trusted device.

Using SSH and FTP/TFTP in a Network

For a long time, Telnet was the method for remotely accessing a Cisco network device and applying a configuration at the command line of that device. Unfortunately, Telnet provides no security. In fact, the protocol sends the information from a local system to the remote Cisco device in plaintext. (Have you noticed by now that any time this book mentions *plaintext*, it is not a good thing?)

An alternative remote access protocol that is commonly used and recommended today is Secure Shell (SSH). Secure Shell takes care of secure authentication and encryption for the desired remote access.

Follow these steps to configure a Cisco device to support SSH:

Step 1.   Use the `hostname` command to ensure that the device has a hostname set.

Step 2.   Use the `ip domain-name` command to ensure that there is a domain name configured on the device.

Step 3.   Configure the required RSA key by using the command `crypto key generate rsa`.

Step 4.   In your VTY lines, ensure that SSH is the only supported method (instead of Telnet) by using the command `transport input ssh`. Take care to apply this command (or at least the `transport input none` command) to all the available VTY lines.

Step 5.   Use the command `ip ssh version 2` to ensure that the SSH version is 2.

For decades, File Transfer Protocol (FTP) was used to move files from one location to another over private intranets or even the public Internet. In fact, I still use this protocol today when delivering chapters of this text to Pearson for publishing. FTP uses the reliable TCP in its operation, along with ports 20 and 21.

You might think that FTP is of no use to Cisco networking devices, and you would be partially correct. Cisco devices to this day love to use a variation of FTP for downloading new IOS images and configuration files. This variation of FTP is called Trivial File Transfer Protocol (TFTP). It has far less overhead compared to FTP as it relies on UDP in its operation. It uses port 69.

Lab 20.2: Configuring SSH

To complete this Hands-On Lab Practice Assignment, download the assigned Packet Tracer file from the book's companion website and perform the lab on your locally installed version of Packet Tracer. You will be following the instructions in the lab, and your performance will be evaluated.

In this lab, you will configure and verify SSH using the topology shown in Figure 20.2.

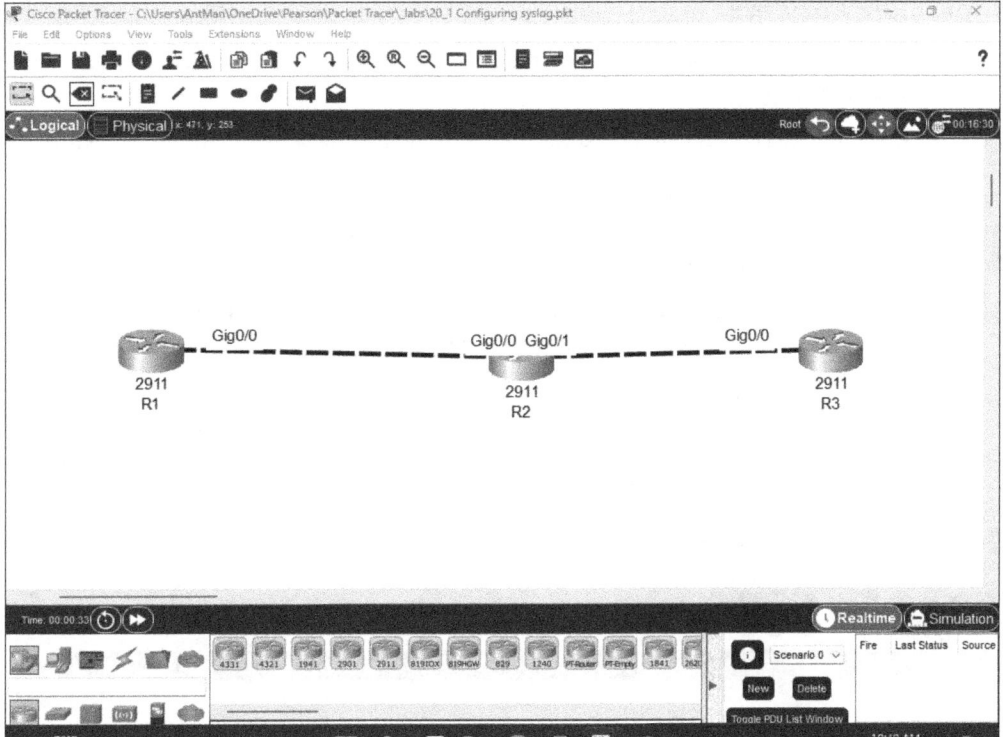

Figure 20.2 *The SSH Lab*

Topic Quiz

1. What command creates the RSA key for use with SSH?

    A. `crypto key generate rsa`

    B. `ssh key rsa generate`

    C. `get ssh key rsa`

    D. `ip ssh generate key rsa`

2. What is a typical use for TFTP in a modern Cisco network?

    A. To download the VLAN.dat file

    B. To download a startup configuration during a VoIP phone's bootup

    C. To download IOS images to the device

    D. To back up (upload) the current running configuration onto a TFTP server

Topic Quiz Answers

1. A is correct. You generate the required RSA key by using the command `crypto key generate rsa`.

2. C is correct. TFTP is often used for downloading IOS images and configurations to Cisco devices.

Lab 20.3: Chapter Review

To complete this Hands-On Lab Practice Assignment, download the assigned Packet Tracer file from the book's companion website and perform the lab on your locally installed version of Packet Tracer. You will be following the instructions in the lab, and your performance will be evaluated.

In this lab, you will demonstrate your comprehension of the topics in this chapter using the topology shown in Figure 20.3.

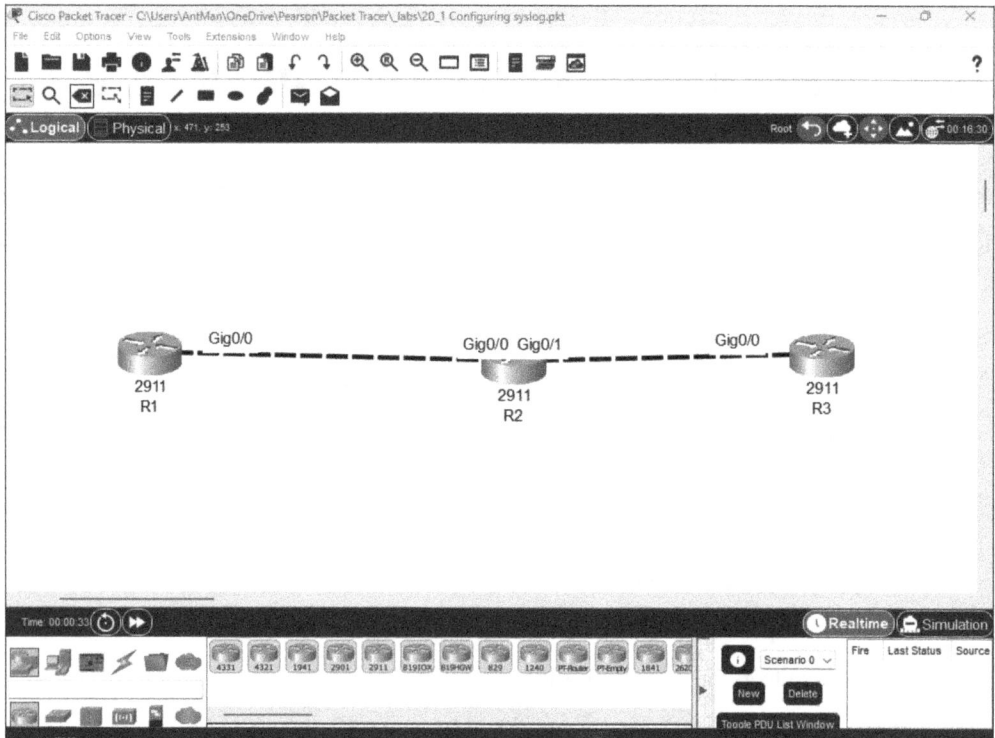

Figure 20.3 *The Networking Services Chapter Review Lab*

Review Questions

1. What command allows you to see the syslog configuration that is currently in place on a Cisco router?

   A. `show syslog`

   B. `show logging`

   C. `show logging enable`

   D. `show logging detail`

2. You see the syslog message `*Nov 16 00:23:23.003: %SYS-6-CLOCKUPDATE: System clock has been updated from 14:20:35 EDT Sun Aug 28 2023 to 19:23:23 EST Thu Nov 15 2023, configured from console by console`. What facility produced the message?

   A. `%SYS-6-CLOCKUPDATE`

   B. `CLOCKUPDATE`

   C. `%SYS`

   D. `6`

3. What command permits you to send log messages to a device at 10.1.1.3?

   A. `logging 10.1.1.3`

   B. `logging trap level 2 10.1.1.3`

   C. `logging host 10.1.1.3`

   D. `logging host send 7 host 10.1.1.3`

4. What approach to QoS involves marking and classifying traffic?

   A. IntServ

   B. DiffServ

   C. BE

   D. RSVP

5. What improvement does SNMP version 3 offer over SNMP version 2c?

   A. Monitoring with no overhead

   B. Increased security

   C. A reduction in server calls

   D. ICMP IP SLA

6. What is the term for variation in delay?

   A. Shaping

   B. Packet loss

   C. Latency

   D. Jitter

7. LLQ is a form of what type of tool in QoS?

   A. Congestion management

   B. Policing

   C. Shaping

   D. Marking

Answers to Review Questions

1. **B** is correct. Use the simple `show logging` command to verify syslog settings, as well as to view the contents of the logging buffer.

2. **C** is correct. The facility precedes the severity level.

3. **C** is correct. Use `logging host 10.1.1.3`.

4. **B** is correct. The Differentiated Services (DiffServ) approach features classification and marking as a first step.

5. **B** is correct. SNMP version 3 provides security enhancements over earlier versions.

6. **D** is correct. Jitter refers to variation in delay. Jitter is always present, but a large amount of jitter is a major problem for voice and video traffic.

7. **A** is correct. Examples of congestion management QoS tools are CBWFQ and LLQ.

PART VI

Security Fundamentals

We are facing more and more security attacks today from more and more diverse types of attackers. This part's four chapters all deal with security fundamentals.

In Part VI, you will learn valuable configurations that will help you secure device access, configure and verify access control lists, configure and verify Layer 2 security features, and configure wireless security protocols.

Part VI includes the following chapters:

Chapter 21

Configure Device Access Control

This chapter covers the following official CCNA 200-301 exam topic:

■ Configuring device access controls

A CCNA is responsible for helping secure traffic *through* Cisco devices and also for controlling traffic *to* these devices. For example, it is important to ensure that individuals attempting to access your devices to reconfigure them are the properly authenticated individuals and that they are correctly authorized to perform the actions they intend to perform. This chapter reviews many key aspects of configuring device access control.

This chapter covers the following essential terms and components:

■ AAA

■ TACACS+

■ RADIUS

■ Local authentication

■ Secure passwords

■ Device access

■ Source addressing

■ Telnet

■ Login banners

■ Password policy

Chapter Pretest

1. What single command allows you to create a local user account named JOHNS with the MD5 hashed password cisco123 and privilege level 15? (This command should be entered as efficiently as possible.)

———————

2. What password is used for backward compatibility with very old Cisco devices?

———————

3. What command can you use to apply weak encryption on plaintext passwords in a configuration?

———————

4. Examine the configuration that follows. List at least seven things that are problematic in this configuration from a device-hardening standpoint.

```
R1#
R1# show running-config
Building configuration...

Current configuration : 1113 bytes
!
version 15.4
service timestamps debug datetime msec
service timestamps log datetime msec
no service password-encryption
!
hostname R1
!
boot-start-marker
boot-end-marker
!
enable password cisco123
!

no aaa new-model
memory-size iomem 5
no ip icmp rate-limit unreachable
ip cef
!
!
!
no ip domain lookup
!
...
!
```

```
interface FastEthernet0/0
 ip address 10.10.10.1 255.255.255.0
 duplex auto
 speed auto
!
interface Serial0/0
 no ip address
 shutdown
 clock rate 2000000
!
interface FastEthernet0/1
 no ip address
 shutdown
 duplex auto
 speed auto
!
interface Serial0/1
 no ip address
 shutdown
 clock rate 2000000
!
ip forward-protocol nd
!
!
no ip http server
no ip http secure-server
!
...
!
line con 0
 exec-timeout 0 0
 privilege level 15
 logging synchronous
line aux 0
 exec-timeout 0 0
 privilege level 15
 logging synchronous
line vty 0 4
 password cisco
 login
 transport input telnet
!
!
end
R1#
```

_____

_____

_____

_____

_____

_____

_____

5. What AAA security protocol communicates from network devices to a central security server using TCP?

_____

Answers

1. `username JOHNS privilege 15 secret cisco123`

2. `enable password`

3. `service password-encryption`

4. There is no enable secret configured.

Telnet is allowed.

There is no banner message.

There is no service password encryption.

The console port never times out due to inactivity.

Simple passwords are in use.

Privilege level 15 is granted at the console without authentication.

5. TACACS+

Configuring Device Access Controls

AAA is an important concept for you to grasp as early as possible in your CCNA career. This important set of technologies seeks to ensure proper authentication, authorization, and accounting of access to and through devices. Remember that accounting means keeping records of what happens with a device and when it occurs (and maybe even for how long).

Some aspect of AAA is in use on a Cisco device even when you configure the device using local user accounts. Example 21.1 demonstrates such a configuration.

Example 21.1   *Configuring Local Authentication for the Console Line*

```
R1#
R1# configure terminal
Enter configuration commands, one per line. End with CNTL/Z.
R1(config)# aaa new-model
R1(config)# username JOHNS privilege 15 secret 1L0v3C1sc0Systems
R1(config)# line con 0
R1(config-line)# login local
R1(config-line)# end
R1#
```

The commands in Example 21.1 are as follows:

- **aaa new-model:** This command enables the AAA system on the router. Without this command, IOS uses the legacy enable and login passwords (as configured by the enable global and login vty line commands).

- **username JOHNS secret privilege 15 1L0v3C1sc0Systems:** This command creates a local user account with the name JOHNS; after the command is entered, the password is hashed using MD5 so it does not display as plaintext in the configuration. Note that the password keyword used in place of secret would not accomplish this hashing. The password itself for this user is 1L0v3C1sc0Systems. The privilege 15 portion of the command indicates the level of access for the user. The default privilege level for a user is privilege level 1.

- **login local:** This command requires authentication (based on the local configuration of user accounts) for a user to access this router through line console 0.

Obviously, configurations like the one in Example 21.1 are critical; misconfiguration can actually lead to device lockout. Therefore, it is important to be careful and always verify. Example 21.2 walks through the verification.

Example 21.2   *Verifying the Local Authentication Configuration*

```
R1#
R1# exit
R1 con0 is now available
Press RETURN to get started.
! Note: pressing enter will prompt for a username and password
User Access Verification
Username: JOHNS
Password:
R1#
```

Note   When creating local user accounts, you can assign privilege levels to those accounts with the `privilege` keyword. The default privilege for local users is 1, which is commonly referred to as *user mode*. Once a user is logged in, the user can move to privilege level 15 by using the `enable` command.

What if you are not going to use local user accounts for authentication and authorization but instead plan to use accounts that are stored in a remote authentication server of some kind? You need a protocol to communicate this account information across the network. Two popular protocols support AAA functions: TACACS+ and RADIUS.

Note   TACACS+ is often the security protocol used for authenticating administrators logging in to a Cisco device, whereas RADIUS is often the protocol used for authentication of users communicating through a Cisco device.

It is important to understand the key differences between TACACS+ and RADIUS. In addition to the ones provided in the preceding note, the differences include the following:

- RADIUS uses UDP, whereas TACACS+ uses TCP.

- RADIUS encrypts only the password in the access request packet from the client to the server, whereas TACACS+ encrypts the entire body of the packet.

- RADIUS combines authentication and authorization, whereas TACACS+ uses the AAA architecture, which separates authentication, authorization, and accounting functions.

- RADIUS is standardized by the IETF (in RFC 2865), whereas TACACS+ is a Cisco-proprietary protocol.

- TACACS+ supports per-command authorization, whereas RADIUS does not; this is why TACACS+ is preferred for administrator authentication and authorization.

Note that no matter how your user accounts are set up—whether they are stored on the local Cisco device or stored on a central authentication server—you should always use a well-designed password security policy. This policy should specify the minimum password length and complexity, it should dictate how often users must rotate their passwords, and it should also define the lockout procedures. Consideration must also be given to secure passwords on all your Cisco devices. Note that Example 21.1 uses a long string, simple character substitution, and a mix of case in order to set a fairly strong password. Cisco devices today can assist you with the implementation of your password security policy. They can enforce complexity and length requirements when passwords are set on the local devices. For example, with IOS you can enforce a password minimum length requirement of 10 by using the `security passwords min-length 10` command.

What about passwords that might appear in plaintext in the configuration? Cisco provides the **service password-encryption** feature to help with such cases. Example 21.3 shows the configuration and verification of this feature.

Example 21.3 *Configuring and Verifying the Service Password-Encryption Feature*

```
R1#
R1# configure terminal
Enter configuration commands, one per line. End with CNTL/Z.
R1(config)# enable password ThisIsmyPassw0rd
R1(config)# line vty 0 4
R1(config-line)# password ThisIsMyT3ln3tPassword
R1(config-line)# login
R1(config-line)# end
R1#
R1# show run
Building configuration...
Current configuration : 1370 bytes
. . .
enable password ThisIsmyPassw0rd
!
line vty 0 4
 password ThisIsMyT3ln3tPassword
 login
 transport input telnet
!
end
R1# configure terminal
Enter configuration commands, one per line. End with CNTL/Z.
R1(config)# service password-encryption
R1(config)# end
R1# show run
Building configuration...
Current configuration : 1413 bytes
. . .
service password-encryption
enable password 7 02320C52182F1C2C557E080A1600421908
!
line vty 0 4
 password 7 15260305170338093107662E1D54023300454A4F5C460A
!
end
R1#
```

The **enable password** command stores the enable password in plaintext in the configuration and is used for backward compatibility with very old Cisco devices that do not support the enable secret or other MD5 hashes. Passwords stored in plaintext are a security risk. Examples include the **enable password** and passwords configured on vty and console lines. Note that the **service password-encryption** command places a very weak level 7 Cisco-proprietary and well-known encryption on all passwords that are present in the running configuration. Although this is not a strong method of protecting the passwords, it does at least prevent them from appearing in plaintext. A decryption program for the encrypted passwords has been available since at least 1995, and according to Cisco, you "should treat any configuration file containing passwords as sensitive information, the same way they would treat a cleartext list of passwords."

Note If you use this **service password-encryption** command and then issue the command **no service password-encryption**, no future plaintext passwords are protected, but your existing passwords remain in their encrypted form.

Remember that the modern alternative to the **enable password** command is the **enable secret** command. This protects the privileged-mode password by storing only a hashed version of the password. If using both commands, the passwords must be different between the two, and only the secret is used for authentication.

Another important consideration with proper device hardening is physical security (device access). Someone who gains physical access to your Cisco equipment can easily recover the startup configuration or reset the equipment—and they can easily physically damage it as well.

Another important consideration for device hardening is source addressing specific traffic, such as management traffic. It is common to source traffic from a loopback address to improve reliability, consistency, and security by only allowing access from those loopback addresses. Example 21.4 provides an example.

Example 21.4 *Setting a Source Address for Network Communications*

```
R1#
R1# configure terminal
Enter configuration commands, one per line. End with CNTL/Z.
R1(config)# interface loopback 1
R1(config-if)# ip address 192.168.1.1 255.255.255.0
R1(config-if)# exit
R1(config)# snmp-server source-interface traps loopback 1
R1(config)# end
R1#
```

Example 21.4 uses the **source-interface** keyword to ensure that Simple Network Management Protocol (SNMP) traps are sent from a source address of the loopback interface.

Example 21.5 reviews the configuration of Telnet. Notice that the **service password-encryption** command encrypts the passwords stored in the configuration, as shown in this chapter. Remember, in production (non-lab environments) you should avoid the use of Telnet because it is never considered acceptable from a security standpoint as it sends all its payload in plaintext.

Example 21.5 *Configuring Telnet*

```
R1#
R1# configure terminal
Enter configuration commands, one per line. End with CNTL/Z.
R1(config)# line vty 0 4
R1(config-line)# password C1sc0I$Aw3some
R1(config-line)# login
R1(config-line)# transport input telnet
R1(config-line)# exit
R1(config)# service password-encryption
R1(config)# end
R1#
*Mar 1 00:01:34.131: %SYS-5-CONFIG_I: Configured from console by console
R1#
```

Note All the configuration examples in this chapter have shown manipulation of the default vty 0 4 (0 through 4) lines. Remember that there are other lines available, depending on the device. This means you can provide alternate configurations to different lines. Specifying `line vty 5 10`, for example, applies a specific configuration to vty lines 5 through 10. Most Cisco switches have vty lines 0 through 15 by default, so if you are configuring security on vty lines, apply it to all of them—and not just the first 5 lines. Pen testers often look for exactly this type of configuration neglect. They open 5 SSH sessions on a device (without ever logging in), thus reserving lines vty 0 through 4. Unless vty lines 5 through 15 have also been configured for SSH (which is easy for an attacker to verify), the next session only allows the default (Telnet) transport. It is quite easy at that point to open a ticket about connectivity issues and then wait. The administrator tries the default SSH client and can't log on to the device. The administrator then knows the problem is on this device (since the SSH server has crashed). Instinctively, the administrator tries other login methods (such as Telnet), and the pen tester sniffs the password off the wire (that is, off the plaintext Telnet traffic).

Telnet is insecure, and there is a secure remote access protocol alternative: Secure Shell (SSH). Example 21.6 shows a sample SSH configuration. (See Chapter 20, "Configuring Other Networking Services," for detailed coverage of the SSH configuration.)

Example 21.6   *Configuring SSH*

```
R2#
R2# configure terminal
Enter configuration commands, one per line. End with CNTL/Z.
R2(config)# ip domain-name lab.ajsnetworking.com
R2(config)# crypto key generate rsa
The name for the keys will be: R2.lab.cbtnuggets.com
Choose the size of the key modulus in the range of 360 to 2048 for your General
    Purpose Keys. Choosing a key modulus greater than 512 may take a few minutes.
How many bits in the modulus [512]: 768
% Generating 768 bit RSA keys, keys will be non-exportable...[OK]
R2(config)#
%SSH-5-ENABLED: SSH has been enabled
R2(config)# ip ssh version 2
R2(config)# line vty 0 4
R2(config-line)# transport input ssh
R2(config-line)# end
R2#
%SYS-5-CONFIG_I: Configured from console by console
R2#
```

The configuration commands in Example 21.6 are as follows:

- **ip domain-name lab.ajsnetworking.com**: The setting of a domain name on the device is required for the generation of the RSA key used for SSH security. Note that a hostname configuration is also required, but that is not shown here because it has already been done (on R2).

- **crypto key generate rsa**: This command triggers the generation of the RSA key for security. Notice that you must specify how many bits are in the modulus in order to control the strength of the security (where more is better); 768 is used here to specify SSH version 2 because at least 768 is required. On modern hardware, there is no reason not to use 2048.

- **ip ssh version 2**: This command specifies that version 2 of SSH should be used. Version 2 is more secure than the default version 1.

- **transport input ssh**: This command locks down the vty lines to the use of SSH and excludes the use of other protocols, such as Telnet.

Note   You can configure multiple protocols with the **transport input** command. For example, **transport input ssh telnet** specifies that SSH or Telnet may be used.

Another aspect of device hardening is the configuration of a login banner—a text message displayed to users when they log in to the device, just before the username and password prompt. The typical use of a banner is to provide a legal disclaimer indicating that access is restricted. A banner does not protect a device, but it prevents attackers from claiming in court that they didn't know they were not supposed to be taking over the device. Example 21.7 shows the configuration and verification of a login banner. (I am not an attorney, so be sure to check with your own legal team regarding the exact language of your banner!)

Example 21.7   *The Configuration and Verification of a Login Banner Message*

```
R2#
R2# configure terminal
Enter configuration commands, one per line. End with CNTL/Z.
R2(config)# banner login #
Enter TEXT message. End with the character '#'.
This router is for the exclusive use of ACME.INC employees.
Any other use is strictly prohibited.
Violators will be prosecuted to the full extent of the law.#
R2(config)# exit
R2# exit


R2 con0 is now available


Press RETURN to get started.


This router is for the exclusive use of ACME.INC employees.
Any other use is strictly prohibited.
Violators will be prosecuted to the full extent of the law.
User Access Verification


Username: JOHNS
Password:
R2#
```

Notice how simple the configuration is. The **banner login** # command gets the job done. The # symbol is a character chosen by the administrator, and when used again in the configuration of the banner, it triggers the end of the banner text. This allows you to insert carriage returns and even ASCII art, should you desire, into the banner text. The # in this case is called the *delimiter*. The delimiter delimits (that is, marks) the beginning and the end of the banner text. You therefore cannot use the delimiter within the banner's text.

Note   The login banner is only one type of banner possible on a Cisco device. For example, the **banner motd** command configures a message-of-the-day banner that is displayed to all the connected terminals. This banner is useful for sending messages that affect all users, such as messages about impending system shutdowns. When a user connects to the router, the MOTD banner appears.

Lab 21.1: Configuring Device Access Controls

To complete this Hands-On Lab Practice Assignment, download the assigned Packet Tracer file from the book's companion website and perform the lab on your locally installed version of Packet Tracer. You will be following the instructions in the lab, and your performance will be evaluated.

In this lab, you will configure and verify device access controls using the topology shown in Figure 21.1.

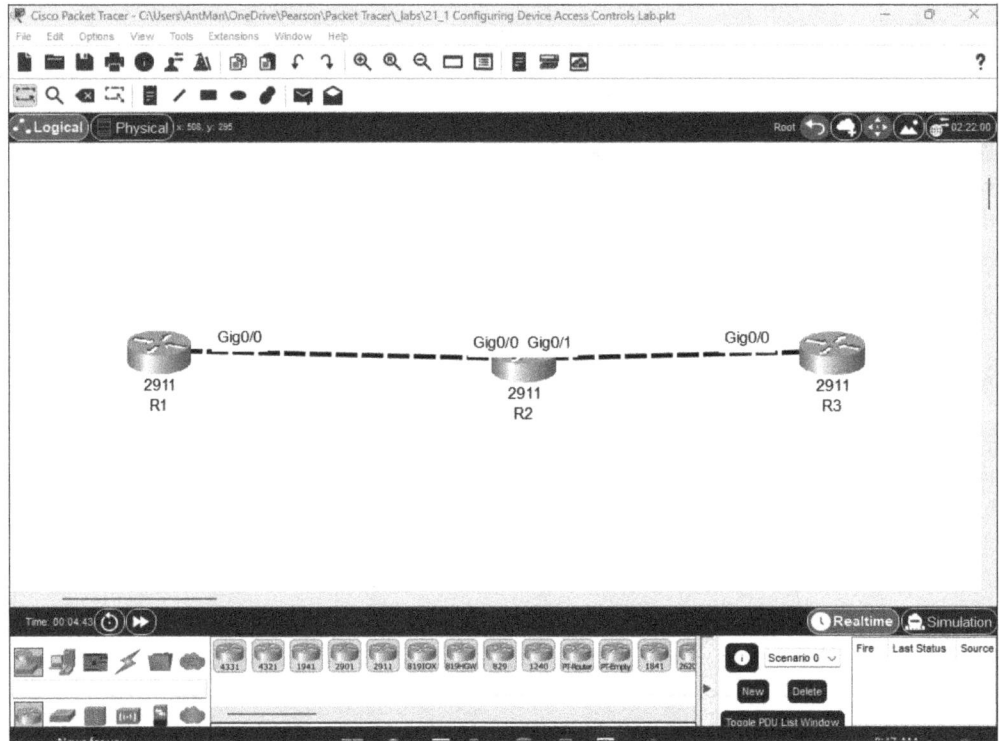

Figure 21.1 *The Configuring Device Access Controls Lab*

Topic Quiz

1. What is wrong with the command `username JOHNS password cisco123`? (Choose two.)

   A. The password is in plaintext if `service password-encryption` is not in use.

   B. The `username` command must be separate from the password assignment.

   C. The password is too simple.

   D. The privilege level must be set.

2. What command enables the use of AAA on a Cisco device?

A. `aaa enable`

B. `aaa run`

C. `aaa authentication`

D. `aaa new-model`

3. What command under the vty lines allows the checking of a local password?

A. `check-password`

B. `enable`

C. `login local`

D. `test`

4. What is the effect of the command `transport input ssh telnet`?

A. SSH is used instead of Telnet.

B. Telnet is used instead of SSH.

C. Telnet and SSH are restricted.

D. SSH and Telnet are allowed.

5. What is true about banner messages on Cisco routers? (Choose two.)

A. You must always use a # symbol to indicate the end of the banner.

B. Various types of banner messages appear at different times or for different conditions.

C. You can use ASCII art in them.

D. They typically are not used for legal warnings.

Topic Quiz Answers

1. A and C are correct. The password here will be in plaintext, and the password that is selected is much too simple. To store the password in encrypted form on the IOS device, use the `secret` keyword or configure the password encryption service. If the privilege level is not explicitly configured with the `username` command, it has a default value of 1.

2. D is correct. The `aaa new-model` command enables the use of AAA on the device.

3. C is correct. The `login local` command requires authentication using the local username and password configuration. The command `no login` on a vty line (when `aaa new-model` is not enabled globally) disables password checking before login and results in open access. The `login` command requires the administrator to enter the password as configured under the line configuration, without providing a username.

4. D is correct. `transport input ssh telnet` permits SSH and Telnet as a backup method.

5. B and C are correct. Various types of banner messages are used for different purposes. They can contain carriage returns and even ASCII art.

Lab 21.2: Chapter Review

To complete this Hands-On Lab Practice Assignment, download the assigned Packet Tracer file from the book's companion website and perform the lab on your locally installed version of Packet Tracer. You will be following the instructions in the lab, and your performance will be evaluated.

In this lab, you will demonstrate your comprehension of the topics in this chapter using the topology shown in Figure 21.2.

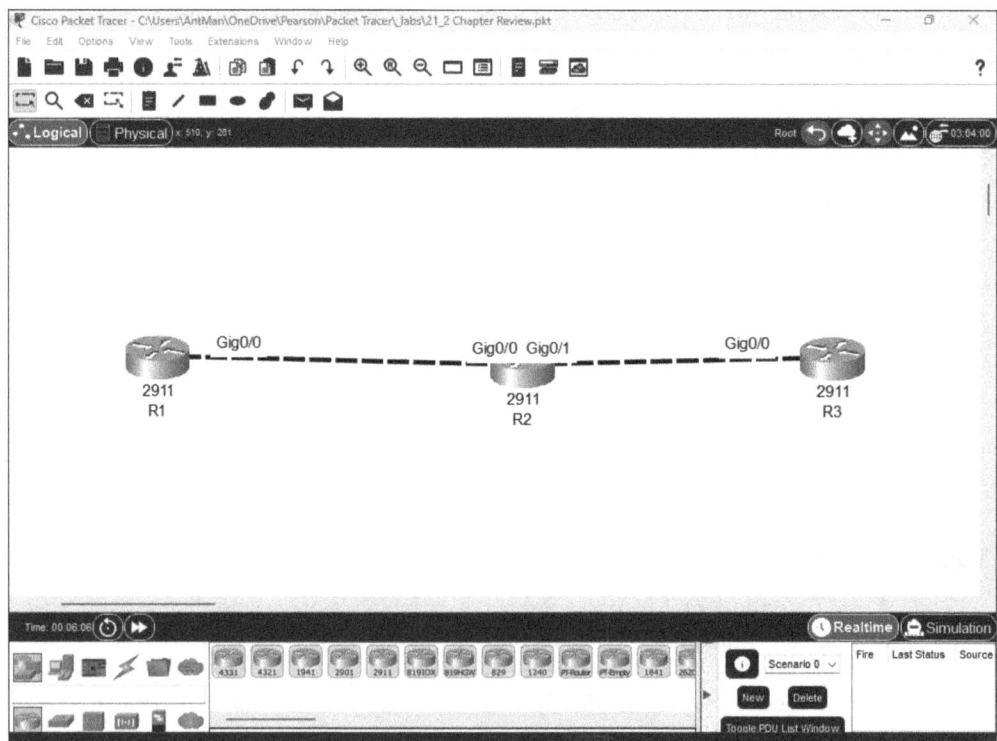

Figure 21.2   *The Device Access Controls Chapter Review Lab*

Review Questions

1. What is an alternative to using local authentication on a Cisco router?

    A. Centralized AAA

    B. A remote Telnet database

    C. SNMP for authentication

    D. FTP for authentication

2. What happens if you issue the command `no service password-encryption`?

    A. Encrypted passwords are reversed.

    B. The device no longer encrypts future passwords.

    C. The device removes all encrypted passwords.

    D. This command is not valid.

3. Why might you set the source interface in traffic? (Choose two.)

    A. In order to increase reliability

    B. In order to enhance processing speed

    C. In order to enhance security

    D. In order to eliminate the use of send buffers

4. What command do you use to create the public/private key pair for SSH?

    A. `crypto key ssh create`

    B. `crypto key generate ssh`

    C. `crypto key ssh`

    D. `crypto key generate rsa`

5. What AAA security protocol communicates from network devices to a central security server using UDP?

    A. TACACS+

    B. RADIUS

    C. Telnet

    D. SFTP

6. What security protocol does not encrypt the entire body of a packet?

    A. RADIUS

    B. TACACS+

    C. VTP

    D. STP

Answers to Review Questions

1. **A** is correct. The most common and most powerful configuration for authentication is to centralize this function with AAA.

2. **B** is correct. This command has no effect on passwords that have already been encrypted on the device. No passwords created in the future will be encrypted. All hashed passwords (MD5 hashed secrets) will remain hashed regardless of the `service password-encryption` command.

3. **A and C** are correct. Source address control is often used for enhanced reliability and security.

4. **D** is correct. This command creates the keying material needed by SSH.

5. **B** is correct. RADIUS provides low overhead. One of the ways it does this is by using UDP in its operations.

6. **A** is correct. RADIUS encrypts only the password in the access request packet from the client to the server.

Chapter 22

Configure and Verify Access Control Lists

This chapter covers the following official CCNA 200-301 exam topic:

- Configure, verify, and troubleshoot IPv4 standard numbered and named access lists for routed interfaces

The access control list (ACL) is a critical component of security in the Cisco world and beyond. Keep in mind that an ACL has other uses in Cisco networking, in addition to permitting or denying traffic through an interface for security reasons. For example, you might need to use an ACL to identify certain traffic forms on which you want to assure quality of service (QoS). Also keep in mind that ACLs are used in many other forms of technology. For example, in AWS, you work with network ACLs (NACLs), which permit or deny traffic between subnets in Virtual Private Cloud (VPC). This chapter is therefore very important when studying for the CCNA 200-301 exam.

This chapter covers the following essential terms and components:

- Access control list (ACL)
- Numbered ACL
- Named ACL
- Standard ACL
- Extended ACL
- Access control entry (ACE)
- Wildcard (inverse) mask
- Implicit deny all

Chapter Pretest

1. What ranges can be used for a standard numbered access control list (ACL)?

_____

2. What is implied at the end of every ACL?

_____

3. Examine the topology and configurations shown here. Why is R3 unable to ping R1? Be as specific as possible.

_____

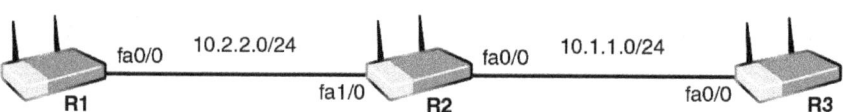

```
R1# show running-config
...
!
hostname R1
...
!
interface FastEthernet0/0
 ip address 10.2.2.1 255.255.255.0
 ip access-group 1 in
 duplex half
!
router rip
 version 2
 network 10.0.0.0
 no auto-summary
!
...
!
access-list 1 permit 10.1.1.0 0.0.0.255
access-list 1 permit 10.2.2.0 0.0.0.255
no cdp log mismatch duplex
!
...
!
line con 0
 exec-timeout 0 0
 privilege level 15
 logging synchronous
```

```
 stopbits 1
line aux 0
 exec-timeout 0 0
 privilege level 15
 logging synchronous
 stopbits 1
line vty 0 4
 login
!
end
R1#

R2# show running-config
...
!
hostname R2
!
...
!
interface FastEthernet0/0
 ip address 10.1.1.2 255.255.255.0
 ip access-group 1 in
!
!
interface FastEthernet1/0
 ip address 10.2.2.2 255.255.255.0
 duplex auto
 speed auto
!
!
router rip
 version 2
 network 10.0.0.0
 no auto-summary
!
...
!
access-list 1 deny 10.1.1.3
access-list 1 permit any
no cdp log mismatch duplex
!
...
!
line con 0
 exec-timeout 0 0
 privilege level 15
```

```
 logging synchronous
 stopbits 1
line aux 0
 exec-timeout 0 0
 privilege level 15
 logging synchronous
 stopbits 1
line vty 0 4
 login
!
end
R2#

R3# show running-config
...
!
hostname R3
!
...
!
interface FastEthernet0/0
 ip address 10.1.1.3 255.255.255.0
 duplex half
!
!
router rip
 version 2
 network 10.0.0.0
 no auto-summary
!
...
!
line con 0
 exec-timeout 0 0
 privilege level 15
 logging synchronous
 stopbits 1
line aux 0
 exec-timeout 0 0
 privilege level 15
 logging synchronous
 stopbits 1
 line vty 0 4
 login
!
end
R3#
```

4. Create a numbered access control entry (ACE) that permits Telnet traffic sourced from a server on network 10.10.10.0/24 destined for network 192.168.1.0/24. Use ACL 101.

Answers

1. Numbered standard ACLs use the ranges 1–99 and 1300–1999.

2. An implicit deny all ends an ACL.

3. There is an inbound ACL on R2 Fa0/0 explicitly denying traffic sourced from 10.1.1.3, which is R3's Fa0/0 interface. Unless R3 uses a loopback interface to source the ping to R1, it will use the Fa0/0 IP address as the source address.

4. `access-list 101 permit tcp 10.10.10.0 0.0.0.255 eq 23 192.168.1.0 0.0.0.255`

Configure, Verify, and Troubleshoot IPv4 Standard Numbered and Named Access Lists for Routed Interfaces

Access control lists (ACLs) are powerful tools for identifying traffic. This chapter examines a specific use of ACLs, based on the CCNA 200-301 exam blueprint: applying ACLs as a security filter to a routed interface.

There are two types of ACLs you need to be aware of:

- **Standard ACLs:** These lists can be named or numbered for identification. If numbered, you must use 1–99 or 1300–1999. Standard ACLs can only match on source IP address. As a result of this very limited matching criterion, Cisco recommends that, in general, standard ACLs be placed as close to the destination of the filtered traffic as possible.

- **Extended ACLs:** These lists can be named or numbered. If numbered, you must use 100–199 or 2000–2699. Extended ACLs can match on a wide variety of criteria, including source and destination IP addresses, protocol type, and specific port numbers. Because there are so many possible filtering criteria, Cisco recommends that, in general, extended ACLs be placed as close to the source of traffic as possible.

Entries in an ACL are called access control entries (ACEs). The order of these entries is critical because packets are processed in a top-down fashion, with a match resulting in the processing of the permit or deny action and the termination of further processing. Example 22.1 shows an example of the construction of a standard ACL that would function as desired if properly assigned to a routed interface. (This configuration is demonstrated later in this section.)

Example 22.1   *Building a Standard Numbered ACL*

```
R1#
R1# configure terminal
Enter configuration commands, one per line. End with CNTL/Z.
R1(config)# access-list 1 deny host 172.16.1.100
R1(config)# access-list 1 deny host 172.16.1.101
R1(config)# access-list 1 permit 172.16.1.0 0.0.0.255
R1(config)# end
R1#
```

Notice in Example 22.1 that the more specific entries are located above the more general entry, so the desired effect of blocking these two specific host source addresses would be achieved by the filter. Notice also the use of a wildcard (or inverse) mask in an access control list. This functions as the opposite of a subnet mask. So, in the entry **access-list 1 permit 172.16.1.0 0.0.0.255**, you match on the 172.16.1 portion of the address, and any value can appear in the fourth octet.

Notice the use of the keyword **host** in Example 22.1. This eliminates the requirement for the longer entry **access-list 1 deny 172.16.1.100 0.0.0.0**. Another shortcut keyword you can use is **any**. This eliminates entries such as **access-list 1 permit 0.0.0.0 255.255.255.255**; typing **access-list 1 permit any** is much easier.

Note   Every ACL ends with an implicit deny all entry that you cannot see. For this reason, when using an ACL as a routing interface filter, you must have at least one **permit** statement. Notice also in Example 22.1 that traffic sourced from 10.10.10.1 would be denied as a result of this implicit deny all entry that truly ends the ACL. You are likely to see the **deny any log** entry used to end an ACL. An administrator uses this entry to track how many packets are reaching the end of the ACL.

Verifying the creation of your ACL is simple, as you can see in Example 22.2.

Example 22.2   *Verifying a Standard ACL*

```
R1#
R1# show access-list
Standard IP access list 1
    20 deny    172.16.1.101
    10 deny    172.16.1.100
    30 permit 172.16.1.0, wildcard bits 0.0.0.255
R1#
```

Note You see from the output in Example 22.2 that the Cisco router numbers the entries for you, even though you did not specify sequence numbers during the construction of the ACL. This makes it easier for you to potentially edit an ACL.

Example 22.3 demonstrates the configuration of a standard named ACL.

Example 22.3 *Configuring a Standard Named ACL*

```
R1#
R1# configure terminal
Enter configuration commands, one per line. End with CNTL/Z.
R1(config)# ip access-list standard MYACL
R1(config-std-nacl)# deny 10.0.0.0 0.255.255.255
R1(config-std-nacl)# permit 192.168.1.0 0.0.0.255
R1(config-std-nacl)# end
R1#
```

Well-constructed ACLs are wonderful, but they're useless as routing filters unless they are applied to an interface. Example 22.4 demonstrates the assignment of numbered and named ACLs to interfaces.

Example 22.4 *Assigning Standard ACLs to Interfaces*

```
R1#
R1# configure terminal
Enter configuration commands, one per line. End with CNTL/Z.
R1(config)# interface fa0/0
R1(config-if)# ip access-group 1 in
R1(config-if)# exit
R1(config)# interface fa1/0
R1(config-if)# ip access-group MYACL out
R1(config-if)# end
R1#
```

As shown in Example 22.4, the `ip access-group` command is key, regardless of named or numbered ACL assignment. Notice that you must assign the filter for inbound traffic or for outbound traffic on the interface.

Note By default, an ACL does not impact traffic generated by the local router. So even if you place an ACL outbound on an interface, by default that ACL does not process or filter locally generated packets such as routing protocol updates. Remember that it is other devices' routed traffic, moving through a router, that ACLs can filter.

Is there a verification command you can use to see if an ACL is applied to an interface (other than **show run**, of course)? There is, as demonstrated in Example 22.5.

Example 22.5 *Verifying ACL Interface Assignment*

```
R1#
R1# show ip interface fa0/0
FastEthernet0/0 is up, line protocol is up
  Internet address is 10.1.1.1/24
  Broadcast address is 255.255.255.255
  Address determined by setup command
  MTU is 1500 bytes
  Helper address is not set
  Directed broadcast forwarding is disabled
  Outgoing access list is not set
  Inbound access list is 1
  Proxy ARP is enabled
  Local Proxy ARP is disabled
...
```

In Example 22.5, the **show ip interface** command verifies that there is an inbound access list set numbered 1. (The rest of this command's output was trimmed for the sake of brevity.)

Although Example 22.5 is great, what about verifying that an ACL is actually filtering traffic? This is possible with the **show access-list** command after the filter is assigned to an interface. Example 22.6 shows this. Notice that matches are being logged.

Example 22.6 *Using* show access-list *to Verify Matches*

```
R2#
R2# show access-list
Standard IP access list 1
    10 deny 10.1.1.3 (10 matches)
    20 permit any
R2#
```

Note Even though this topic deals with the specific case of ACLs used as filters, remember that ACLs can have other purposes as well. For example, you used ACLs in Chapter 17, "Configure and Verify Inside Source NAT," to simply identify traffic, not filter it. As stated earlier in this chapter, there are many additional uses for ACLs that are not covered on the CCNA 200-301 exam.

Thanks to extended access control lists, there are many parameters you can match, including the following:

- Source IP address

- Destination IP address

- Protocol

- Source port

- Destination port

Example 22.7 demonstrates the configuration of an extended ACL.

Example 22.7   *Configuring an Extended ACL*

```
R1#
R1# configure terminal
Enter configuration commands, one per line. End with CNTL/Z.
R1(config)# access-list 101 permit tcp 10.10.10.0 0.0.0.255 192.168.1.0 0.0.0.255 eq 23
R1(config)# access-list 101 permit tcp 10.10.10.0 0.0.0.255 192.168.1.0 0.0.0.255 eq 80
R1(config)# access-list 101 permit tcp 10.10.10.0 0.0.0.255 192.168.1.0 0.0.0.255 eq 21
R1(config)# interface gi0/1
R1(config-if)# ip access-group 101 in
R1(config-if)# exit
R1(config)# exit
R1#
R1# show access-list
Extended IP access list 101
  10 permit tcp 10.10.10.0 0.0.0.255 192.168.1.0 0.0.0.255 eq telnet
  20 permit tcp 10.10.10.0 0.0.0.255 192.168.1.0 0.0.0.255 eq www
  30 permit tcp 10.10.10.0 0.0.0.255 192.168.1.0 0.0.0.255 eq ftp
R1#
```

Lab 22.1: Configuring Access Control Lists

To complete this Hands-On Lab Practice Assignment, download the assigned Packet Tracer file from the book's companion website and perform the lab on your locally installed version of Packet Tracer. You will be following the instructions in the lab, and your performance will be evaluated.

In this lab, you will configure and verify access control lists using the topology shown in Figure 22.1.

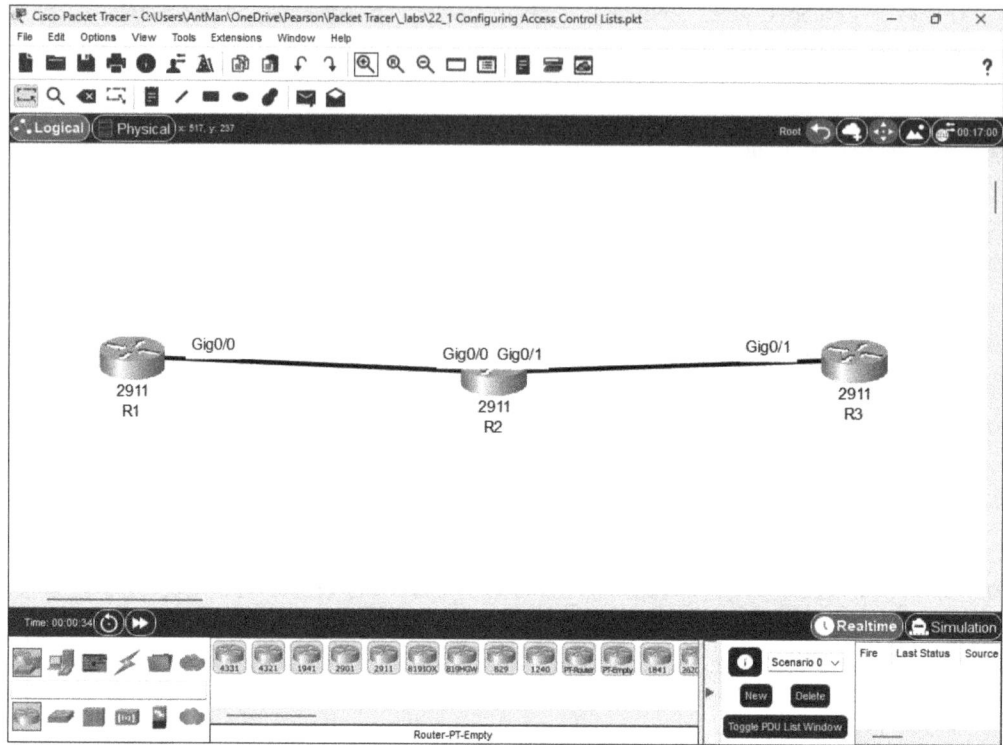

Figure 22.1   *The Configuring Access Control Lists Lab*

Topic Quiz

1. What ACL correctly denies traffic from 192.168.1.1 while permitting all other traffic?

   A. `access-list 1 permit 192.168.1.1 0.0.0.0`

   `access-list 1 permit 192.168.1.0 0.0.0.255`

   B. `access-list 1 deny 192.168.1.1 0.0.0.0`

   `access-list 1 permit 192.168.1.0 0.0.0.255`

   C. `access-list 1 deny 192.168.1.1 0.0.0.0`

   `access-list 1 permit any`

   D. `access-list 1 permit any`

   `access-list 1 deny host 192.168.1.1`

2. What command would you use to see the matches that an ACL would have?

    A. `show ip interface`

    B. `show ip interface brief`

    C. `show access-list hits`

    D. `show access-list`

3. What keyword can you use in place of a four-zeros wildcard mask?

    A. `device`

    B. `system`

    C. `host`

    D. `entry`

4. What does `eq` indicate in an ACL?

    A. You are matching a port or ports.

    B. You are using a standard ACL in place of an extended ACL.

    C. You are using only one ACE in the ACL.

    D. Your ACL is not a traffic filter.

Topic Quiz Answers

1. C is correct. The first entry denies 192.168.1.1, and the second ACE permits all other traffic.

2. D is correct. The `show access-list` command displays matches once the filter is in place.

3. C is correct. The `host` keyword allows you to eliminate the wildcard mask entry 0.0.0.0.

4. A is correct. `eq` is used to match port numbers.

Lab 22.2: Chapter Review

To complete this Hands-On Lab Practice Assignment, download the assigned Packet Tracer file from the book's companion website and perform the lab on your locally installed version of Packet Tracer. You will be following the instructions in the lab, and your performance will be evaluated.

In this lab, you will demonstrate your comprehension of the topics in this chapter using the topology shown in Figure 22.2.

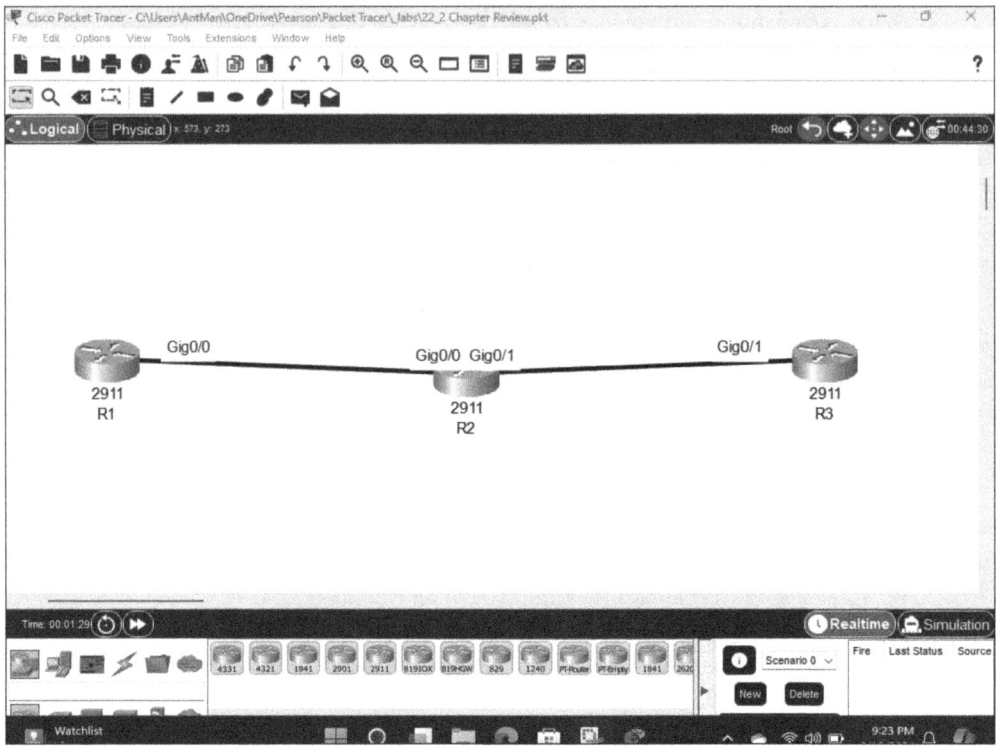

Figure 22.2   *The ACLs Chapter Review Lab*

Review Questions

1. What field can a standard ACL filter on?

   A. Protocol

   B. Port

   C. Destination IP

   D. Source IP

2. Why might **deny any log** appear at the end of an ACL?

   A. It is used to track traffic that matches no previous ACL entries.

   B. It is required as the final ACE.

   C. It ensures fast packet processing.

   D. It is used to send emails to security team members.

3. What command assigns a standard ACL for filtering on an interface?

   A. `ip access-group in|out`

   B. `ip access-bind in|out`

   C. `ip access-list in|out`

   D. `ip access-track in|out`

4. What command permits you to verify that an access list is assigned to an interface in a specific direction?

   A. `show access-list`

   B. `show access-list interface`

   C. `show ip interface`

   D. `show access-list assign`

Answers to Review Questions

1. D is correct. A standard ACL can filter on source IP address only.

2. A is correct. This is matched before the implicit deny all. An explicit deny all is used for tracking entries that match the end of the list.

3. A is correct. You use the `ip access-group` command in this case.

4. C is correct. You use `show ip interface` to verify assignment of ACLs to interfaces.

Chapter 23

Configure Layer 2 Security Features

This chapter covers the following official CCNA 200-301 exam topic:

■ Configuring Layer 2 security features

With so many new and emerging threats (and attackers) today, we love to build "defense in depth" into our networks. We include security at as many layers of the OSI model as we possibly can. Certainly, we begin security measures at Layer 1, the physical layer. We do this, of course, by keeping network equipment locked away and physically protected from attacks. This chapter focuses on several Layer 2 security mechanisms that go quite far in helping secure our networks and data: port security, DHCP snooping, and dynamic ARP inspection.

This chapter covers the following essential terms and components:

■ Port security

■ Static port security

■ Dynamic port security

■ Sticky learning

■ Maximum MAC addresses

■ Port security violation actions

■ **errdisable recovery**

■ 802.1x

■ DHCP snooping

■ Dynamic ARP Inspection (DAI)

Chapter Pretest

1. If you issue the `switchport port-security` command, what are the resulting port security mode, violation action, and maximum number of MAC addresses permitted?

   _____

   _____

   _____

2. What form of port security combines aspects of dynamic learning with static learning?

   _____

3. What command allows you to verify the port security settings of the Gi0/1 interface?

   _____

4. What is the default state of ports in a switched environment when you enable DHCP snooping on a switch?

   _____

5. What Layer 2 security feature does DAI rely on?

   _____

Answers

1. The mode is dynamic port security, the violation action is `shutdown`, and the maximum MAC addresses is 1.

2. Sticky MAC learning

3. `show port-security interface gi0/1`

4. Untrusted

5. DHCP snooping

Configure Layer 2 Security Features

Port security is a rather straightforward security idea. If a switch is excellent about transparently learning MAC addresses, wouldn't it be nice if you could ensure that the correct device connects to a switch, the correct MAC address is learned by the switch, and no one else with a different MAC address is allowed to connect? You can do all this and more with port security. In fact, locking down the port to a specific MAC address is not really the best that port security has to offer. Think about it: It is easy for an attacker to spoof a MAC address and pretend to be the authorized system. Port security is especially valuable because it protects against Content Addressable Memory (CAM) table overflow attacks and rogue devices being accidentally introduced into the network.

Example 23.1 shows how to enable port security on a switch port and verify the results.

Example 23.1   *Configuring and Verifying Port Security*

```
Switch# configure terminal
Enter configuration commands, one per line. End with CNTL/Z.
Switch(config)# interface gi0/1
Switch(config-if)# switchport mode access
Switch(config-if)# switchport port-security
Switch(config-if)# end
Switch#
%SYS-5-CONFIG_I: Configured from console by console
Switch# show port-security interface gi0/1
Port Security              : Enabled
Port Status                : Secure-up
Violation Mode             : Shutdown
Aging Time                 : 0 mins
Aging Type                 : Absolute
SecureStatic Address Aging : Disabled
Maximum MAC Addresses      : 1
Total MAC Addresses        : 0
Configured MAC Addresses   : 0
Sticky MAC Addresses       : 0
Last Source Address:Vlan   : 0000.0000.0000:0
Security Violation Count   : 0
Switch#
```

Notice how simple this basic configuration is. First, the port must be in access switchport mode. If it is not, the `switchport port-security` command cannot be entered. Notice also that a basic configuration involves just one simple command, without any additional parameters. This single command configures a basic and default dynamic port security configuration.

Let us examine some important sections of the `show port-security interface` output:

- Notice that port security is indeed enabled for the interface.

- The status indicates `Secure-up`, meaning that port security is functioning, and the port is not disabled due to a security violation.

- `Violation Mode` is set to the default, `Shutdown`. There are three options here that you can configure: `Protect`, `Restrict`, and `Shutdown`. `Shutdown` is the most severe, and `Protect` is the least. `Protect` is so lame that Cisco recommends you not use it. With `Protect`, offending MAC addresses are blocked from speaking on the port, but the administrator is never notified. `Restrict` blocks offending MAC addresses and causes the administrator to be notified. `Shutdown` is very severe indeed; with it, an offending MAC address causes the entire interface to be disabled.

As an administrator, you must manually reenable the port after correcting the security problem, or you can use the **errdisable recovery** command to cause the port to emerge from the error condition automatically after some time passes.

■ Notice that the default maximum MAC addresses permitted on the interface is one. So, in this very basic configuration, only one MAC address is dynamically learned on the interface, and no other MAC addresses are permitted. Notice that this default configuration would cause a massive problem in a VoIP environment because there would be no room on the port for a Cisco IP phone's MAC address.

Note   Know the defaults of the basic port security configuration for the CCNA 200-301 exam—and know them well!

Example 23.2 provides a very different configuration. This configuration involves static port security.

Example 23.2   *Configuring Static Port Security*

```
Switch# configure terminal
Enter configuration commands, one per line. End with CNTL/Z.
Switch(config)# interface gi1/0
Switch(config-if)# switchport mode access
Switch(config-if)# switchport port-security maximum 2
Switch(config-if)# switchport port-security mac-address fa16.3e20.58f1
Switch(config-if)# switchport port-security mac-address fa16.3e20.aabb
Switch(config-if)# switchport port-security
Switch(config-if)# end
%SYS-5-CONFIG_I: Configured from console by console
Switch# show port-security interface gi1/0
Port Security              : Enabled
Port Status                : Secure-up
Violation Mode             : Shutdown
Aging Time                 : 0 mins
Aging Type                 : Absolute
SecureStatic Address Aging : Disabled
Maximum MAC Addresses      : 2
Total MAC Addresses        : 2
Configured MAC Addresses   : 2
Sticky MAC Addresses       : 0
Last Source Address:Vlan   : fa16.3e20.58f1:1
Security Violation Count   : 0
Switch#
```

Notice that this configuration begins exactly the same as a dynamic configuration. You must set the port to access mode. This time, you quickly indicate that only up to two MAC addresses are permitted. Then things get really secure! You provide the exact MAC addresses expected. This is what makes the configuration static.

Note   Notice something interesting about this configuration: First, you set all the port security parameters, and then you actually enable port security. It is very easy to forget this last and critical step! This is one reason verification is always mandatory following your configurations, both for the CCNA 200-301 exam and in the real world.

I am betting that you are not a huge fan of running around your network, recording MAC addresses for your devices. I am not either. Thankfully, there is a nice combination approach to dynamic and static port security. It has one of the most colorful names in all of Cisco networking: sticky learning.

The idea with sticky learning is that you physically inspect to make sure the correct systems are connected to your switches. You then enable port security with the sticky learning feature. The static MAC address entries are dynamically inserted in the running configuration for you. All you need to do as the administrator is save the running configuration to the startup configuration. Example 23.3 demonstrates this configuration.

Example 23.3   *Configuring Sticky MAC Address Learning*

```
Switch# configure terminal
Enter configuration commands, one per line. End with CNTL/Z.
Switch(config)# interface gi0/2
Switch(config-if)# switchport mode access
Switch(config-if)# switchport port-security maximum 2
Switch(config-if)# switchport port-security mac-address sticky
Switch(config-if)# switchport port-security
Switch(config-if)# end
Switch#
%SYS-5-CONFIG_I: Configured from console by console
Switch# show port-security interface gi0/2
Port Security              : Enabled
Port Status                : Secure-up
Violation Mode             : Shutdown
Aging Time                 : 0 mins
Aging Type                 : Absolute
SecureStatic Address Aging : Disabled
Maximum MAC Addresses      : 2
Total MAC Addresses        : 2
Configured MAC Addresses   : 2
Sticky MAC Addresses       : 2
```

```
Last Source Address:Vlan    : 0000.0000.0000:0
Security Violation Count    : 0
Switch# copy running-config startup-config
Switch#
```

DHCP snooping is an excellent security feature that examines DHCP messages exchanged in a network to determine their validity. There are two DHCP trust states for every port: trusted and untrusted. By default, all ports are untrusted. This means that valid DHCP servers must be connected to certain ports, and then those ports must be explicitly trusted.

DHCP snooping provides the following benefits:

- Rogue DHCP servers are not permitted.

- DHCP database exhaustion attacks are prevented.

- IP address-to-MAC address security information can be maintained.

Another factor makes DHCP snooping great: The database it maintains of MAC address-to-IP address mappings can be used to fuel other great security mechanisms, such as dynamic ARP inspection (discussed later in this chapter).

DHCP snooping is very powerful and also very easy to configure. First, you enable DHCP snooping globally and then enable the feature for the VLANs you want to protect with it. Finally, you configure the trusted port(s) connected to the DHCP server(s). Example 23.4 shows this configuration.

Example 23.4 *Configuring DHCP Snooping*

```
Switch# configure terminal
Enter configuration commands, one per line. End with CNTL/Z.
Switch(config)# ip dhcp snooping
Switch(config)# ip dhcp snooping vlan 100,200,300
Switch(config)# interface range gi0/10 , gi0/12
Switch(config-if-range)# ip dhcp snooping trust
```

As mentioned earlier, while DHCP snooping is wonderful for protecting against rogue DHCP servers, it serves another very valuable function as well: It feeds other security features. As a CCNA, you need to be familiar with one such feature in particular: dynamic ARP inspection (DAI). This Layer 2 security mechanism seeks to guard against attackers that are spoofing a certain MAC address. (Remember that spoofing is a tech-centric word for forging.)

DAI protects against on-path attacks (formerly called man-in-the-middle attacks), where attackers send ARP replies or gratuitous ARP packets, claiming to own the victim's IP address and MAC address, thus placing themselves in the data path to the victim.

DAI guards against invalid ARP packets by comparing the MAC-to-IP mapping that was gathered during the DHCP snooping phase. Just as with DHCP snooping, offending packets can be dropped when they are discovered. Example 23.5 demonstrates the simple configuration of DAI.

Example 23.5 *Configuring DAI*

```
Switch# configure terminal
Enter configuration commands, one per line. End with CNTL/Z.
Switch(config)# ip arp inspection vlan 100,200,300
```

What if you have an interface where you do not want the overhead associated with checking the ARP packets for validity? No problem. You can set the trusted port state for DAI. Example 23.6 demonstrates the creation of a trusted port for the DAI feature. Notice how similar this is to the DHCP snooping configuration.

Example 23.6 *Configuring a DAI Trusted Port*

```
Switch# configure terminal
Enter configuration commands, one per line. End with CNTL/Z.
Switch(config)# interface gi0/10
Switch(config-if)# ip arp inspection trust
```

Lab 23.1: Configuring Layer 2 Security Features

To complete this Hands-On Lab Practice Assignment, download the assigned Packet Tracer file from the book's companion website and perform the lab on your locally installed version of Packet Tracer. You will be following the instructions in the lab, and your performance will be evaluated.

In this lab, you will configure and verify Layer 2 security features using the topology shown in Figure 23.1.

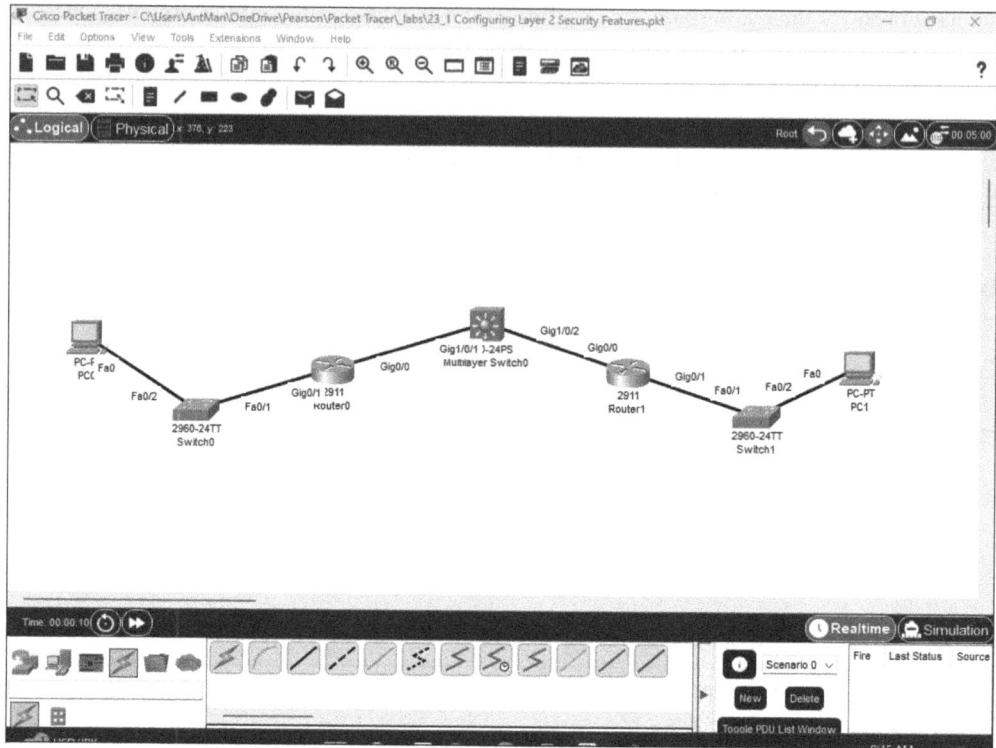

Figure 23.1   *The Configuring Layer 2 Security Features Lab*

Topic Quiz

1. What command typically precedes the `switchport port-security` command?

   A. `switchport port-security enable`

   B. `switchport mode access`

   C. `switchport mode secure`

   D. `switchport data enable`

2. What violation mode does Cisco not recommend?

   A. `Restrict`

   B. `Shutdown`

   C. `Error`

   D. `Protect`

3. What are the options for recovering from an error-disabled port due to port security? (Choose two.)

   A. Port Security Auto Recovery

   B. `errdisable recovery`

   C. Manual recovery

   D. `port security disable`

4. What is the default state when DHCP snooping port is enabled?

   A. Trusted

   B. Untrusted

   C. Permitted

   D. Disabled

5. What command would you use to configure DAI for VLAN 100?

   A. `ip dhcp snooping dai vlan 100`

   B. `ip dai vlan 100`

   C. `ip inspect mac vlan 100`

   D. `ip arp inspection vlan 100`

Topic Quiz Answers

1. B is correct. The `switchport mode access` command typically must precede `switchport port-security` as the port mode cannot be dynamic.

2. D is correct. Cisco does not recommend the `Protect` mode as the administrator is not alerted about any violations with this mode.

3. B and C are correct. You can have automatic recovery with `errdisable recovery`, or you can manually recover from the situation by flapping the port with the `shutdown` and `no shutdown` interface commands.

4. B is correct. By default, all ports in an environment are untrusted when you enable DHCP snooping. It is your job to indicate which ports connect to your DHCP server(s) and, therefore, which ports will be trusted.

5. D is correct. To enable dynamic ARP inspection for VLAN 100, you use the command `ip arp inspection vlan 100` in global configuration mode.

Lab 23.2: Chapter Review

To complete this Hands-On Lab Practice Assignment, download the assigned Packet Tracer file from the book's companion website and perform the lab on your locally installed version of Packet Tracer. You will be following the instructions in the lab, and your performance will be evaluated.

In this lab, you will demonstrate your comprehension of the topics in this chapter using the topology shown in Figure 23.2.

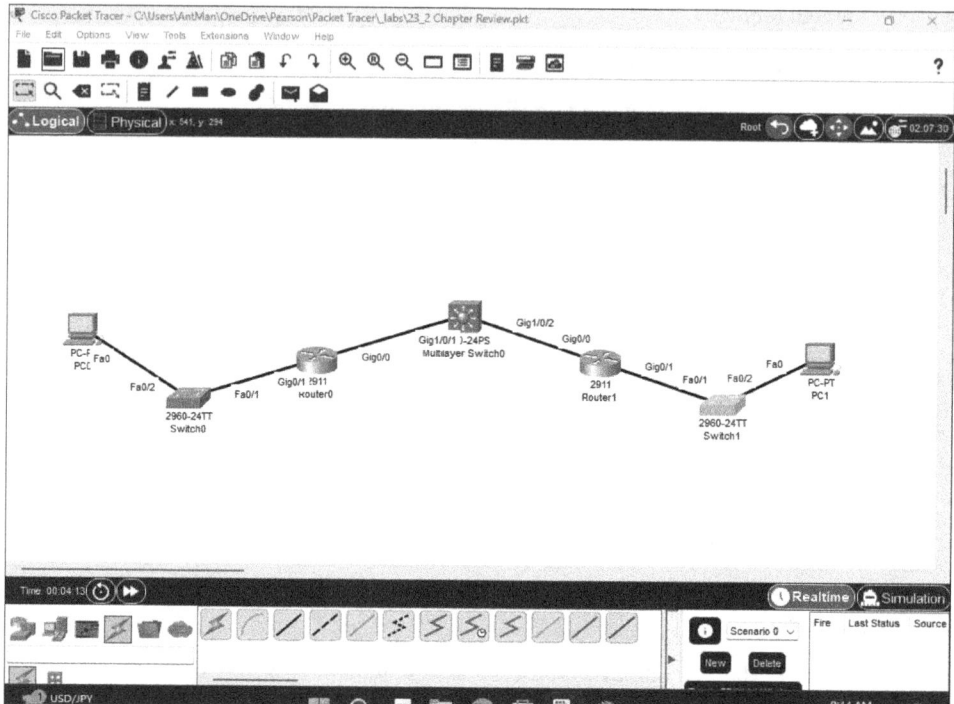

Figure 23.2   *The Layer 2 Security Chapter Review Lab*

Review Questions

1. What is the port status when there is no issue with the port but port security is enabled on it?

   A. Enabled-up

   B. Shutdown-up

   C. Secure-up

   D. Locked-safe

2. What command sets the maximum number of MAC addresses permitted to 4?

   A. set port-security max mac-address 4

   B. switchport port-security maximum 4

    C. `switchport port-security maximum mac-address 4`

    D. `switchport port-security 4`

3. What interface command creates a static entry to allow frames sources from MAC address aaaa.bbbb.cccc on an interface?

    A. `set port-security mac-address aaaa.bbbb.cccc`

    B. `switchport port-security mac-address aaaa.bbbb.cccc`

    C. `switchport port-security address aaaa.bbbb.cccc`

    D. `switchport port-security aaaa.bbbb.cccc`

4. Under which configuration mode is the command `ip dhcp snooping` used to enable DHCP snooping?

    A. Interface configuration mode

    B. Line configuration mode

    C. Security configuration mode

    D. Global configuration mode

5. What is the result of trusting an interface with the DAI feature?

    A. An automatic rate limit feature engages with the standard ARP inspection.

    B. The DAI functionality proceeds, and the DHCP snooping state changes to trusted.

    C. Trusted interfaces have no meaning for DAI; they have meaning only for DHCP snooping.

    D. Inspection of ARP packets does not take place on the interface.

Answers to Review Questions

1. C is correct. The state is `Secure-up`.

2. B is correct. The command is `switchport port-security maximum 4`.

3. B is correct. The command is `switchport port-security mac-address aaaa.bbbb.cccc`.

4. D is correct. As a first step with DHCP snooping, you must enable the feature globally in global configuration mode with `ip dhcp snooping`. This command is often the last command you enter after you have configured the VLANs for DHCP snooping and set your trusted interfaces. That way, when you actually turn on the feature globally, it is configured (and tuned) as you need it.

5. D is correct. Setting an interface as trusted for DAI disables the checking of ARP packets on that interface.

Chapter 24

Configure Wireless Security Protocols

This chapter covers the following official CCNA 200-301 exam topic:

■ Describe WPA, WPA2, and WPA3

Wireless cells seem to be available everywhere today—even on airplanes. We expect that protocols will accommodate strong security when needed. Fortunately, wireless security has evolved to provide strong and reliable security mechanisms.

This chapter covers the following essential terms and components:

■ WPA

■ WPA2

■ WPA3

■ PSK

Chapter Pretest

1. What security technology succeeded WEP as a result of the many vulnerabilities that were frequently being exploited in WEP?

_____

2. What improvement was introduced in WPA in order to provide security on a per-packet basis?

_____

Answers

1. WPA
2. TKIP

Describe WPA, WPA2, and WPA3

Wi-Fi Protected Access (WPA) was the much-hoped-for answer to the huge security issues presented by Wired Equivalent Privacy (WEP). Remember that WEP was the de facto Wi-Fi security approach for many years. Unfortunately, despite its bold name, Wired Equivalent Privacy had major weaknesses.

In more unfortunate news, its replacement technology, WPA, also had a number of weaknesses. Even though WPA featured much stronger public key encryption (256-bit WPA-PSK), it sadly still contained vulnerabilities that it had inherited from the WEP standard. Much of the issue stemmed from both protocols using the problematic stream encryption standard RC4. Although RC4 was once considered a strong security mechanism, vulnerabilities developed.

WPA introduced Temporal Key Integrity Protocol (TKIP), but it was deployed with the idea of maintaining support for older WEP devices. TKIP introduced some powerful feature improvements, such as permitting per-packet security on Wi-Fi communications.

WPA had a very short lifespan and was superseded by WPA2, which included some much-needed improvements. One of the most notable improvements is the use of Advanced Encryption Standard (AES) for encryption. This workhorse encryption protocol is used in many different scenarios today, including protecting data at rest in the cloud.

WPA2 also introduced CCMP (Counter Cipher Mode with Block Chaining Message Authentication Code Protocol), which replaced the need for TKIP and eliminated the vulnerabilities related to TKIP as well.

Note You can still use TKIP with WPA2. Why would you want to? Perhaps you have some WPA-only devices still in the network, or maybe you would like to use TKIP as a fallback in case issues arise with CCMP.

Things were going quite well for WPA2 until a major discovery was made. The Key Reinstallation Attack (KRACK) permitted systems to inject themselves into the four-way handshake of WPA2. The attacker could then manipulate the encryption key creation.

Note   It did not take long for the Wi-Fi Alliance to respond with WPA3, with Protected Management Frames (PMF) and the requirement of AES-192. WPA3 also provides protection against brute-force attacks targeted toward users with weak passwords.

WPA2 is typically very simple to configure on a wireless access point (AP). Figure 24.1 shows just how simple it is to use the GUI of a wireless AP. Here you can see that I am working with the Basic Settings options for the Wireless Configuration tab.

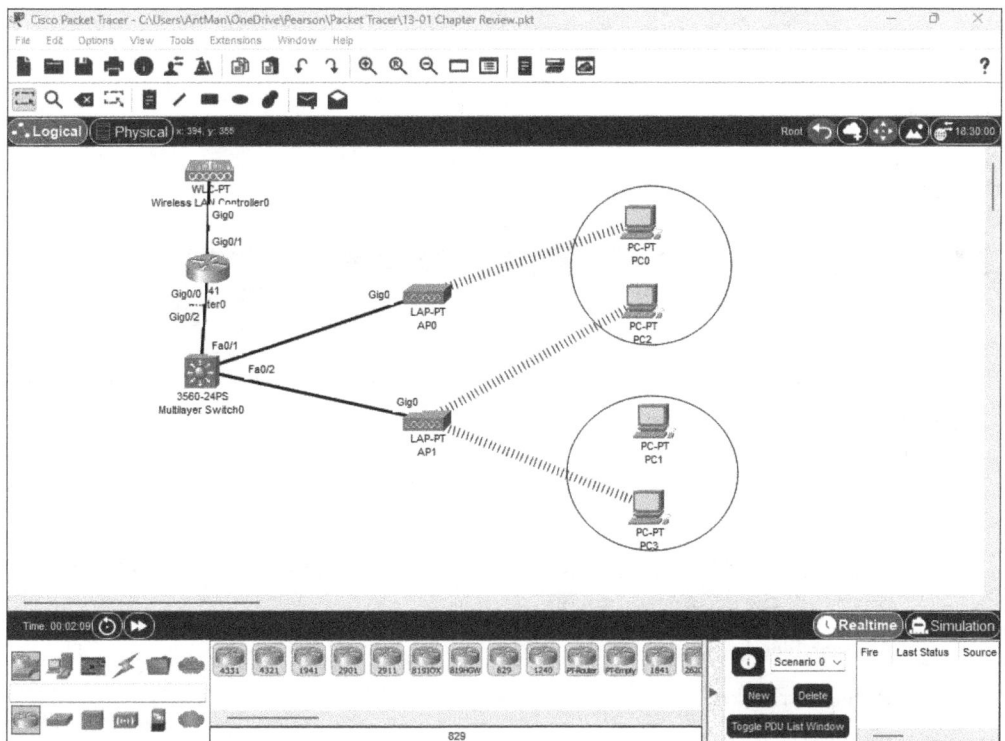

Figure 24.1   *Configuring WPA2 in the GUI*

Lab 24.1: Configuring Wireless Security

To complete this Hands-On Lab Practice Assignment, download the assigned Packet Tracer file from the book's companion website and perform the lab on your locally installed version of Packet Tracer. You will be following the instructions in the lab, and your performance will be evaluated.

In this lab, you will configure wireless security using the topology shown in Figure 24.2.

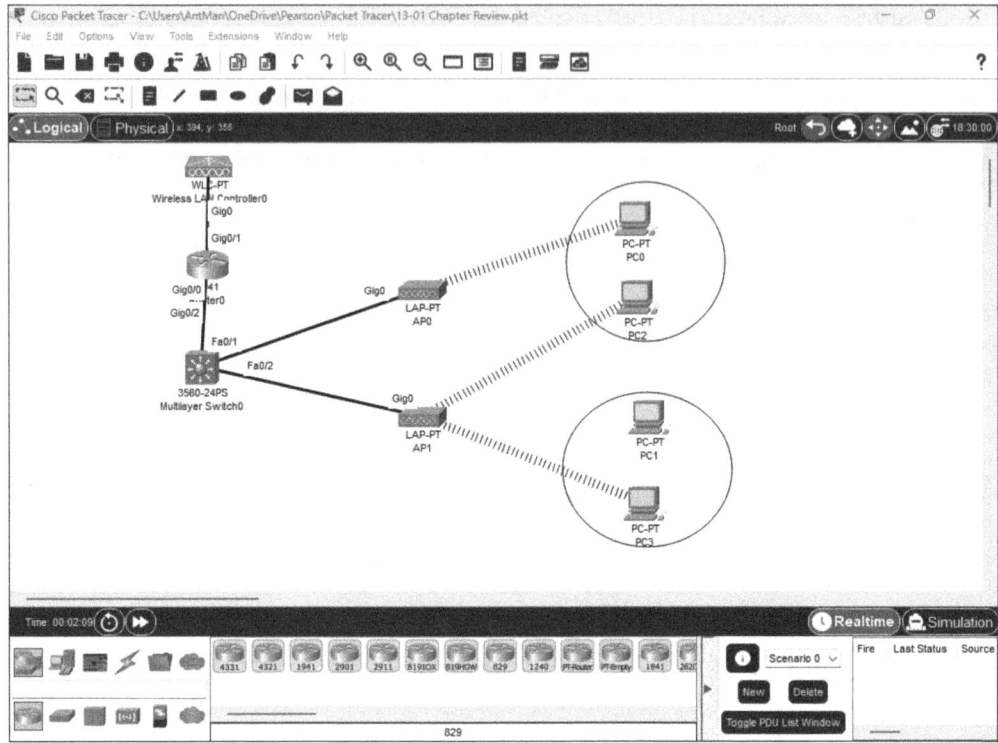

Figure 24.2   *The Wireless Security Lab*

Topic Quiz

1. What exploit of WPA2 demonstrated vulnerabilities in the four-way handshake process of the security protocol?

   A. Heartbleed

   B. ShadowBroker

   C. KRACK

   D. EternalBlue

2. What technology can replace TKIP and is found in WPA2?

   A. CCMP

   B. SAE

   C. RC4

   D. AES

Topic Quiz Answers

1. **C** is correct. The KRACK attack against WPA2 demonstrated how the four-way handshake could be compromised to permit an attacker to manipulate the encryption process.

2. **A** is correct. WPA2 introduced CCMP, which replaced the need for TKIP.

Notice that this example shows WPA2 being configured in personal mode. In this configuration, you can use a simple Pre-Shared Key method. WPA2 features an enterprise mode that uses even stronger security mechanisms.

Lab 24.2: Chapter Review

To complete this Hands-On Lab Practice Assignment, download the assigned Packet Tracer file from the book's companion website and perform the lab on your locally installed version of Packet Tracer. You will be following the instructions in the lab, and your performance will be evaluated.

In this lab, you will demonstrate your comprehension of the topics in this chapter using the topology shown in Figure 24.3.

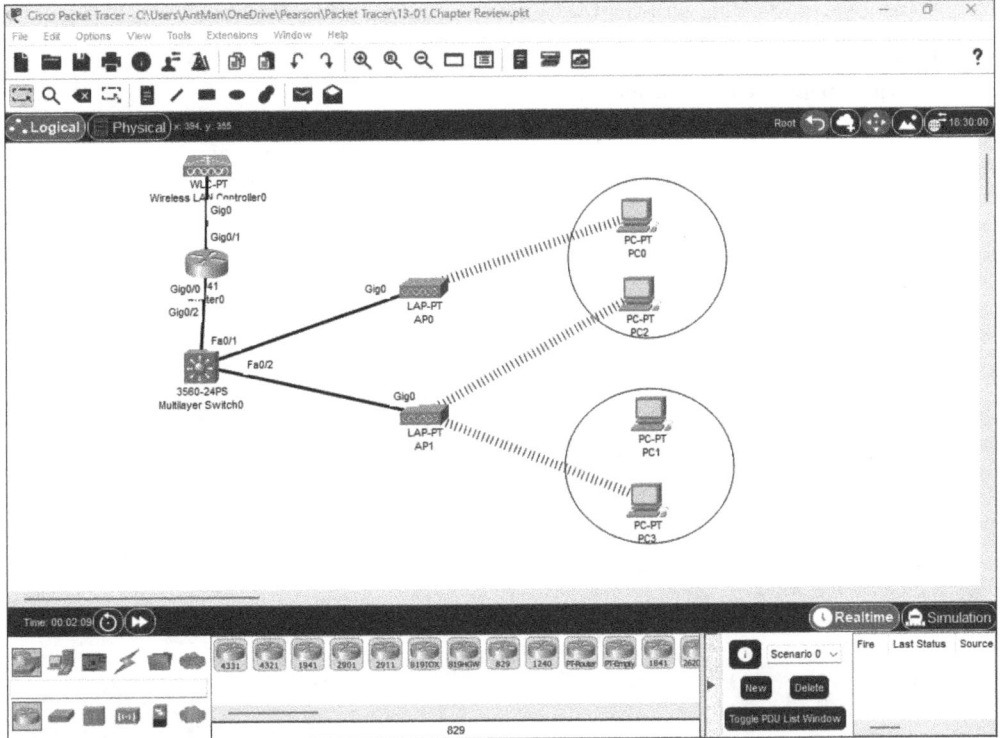

Figure 24.3 *The Wireless Security Chapter Review Lab*

Review Questions

1. What approach is used with WPA2 in personal mode?

A. SAE

B. 3DES

C. MD5

D. PSK

2. If you are running WPA3 in enterprise mode, what is the required version of AES?

A. AES-32

B. AES-64

C. AES-128

D. AES-192

Answers to Review Questions

1. **D** is correct. A Pre-Shared Key (PSK) approach can be configured with WPA2 in personal mode. This is fitting for its ease of configuration.

2. **D** is correct. WPA3 provides AES-192 as an option in personal mode and as a requirement in enterprise mode.

Appendices

Other CCNA Topics

The Role and Function of Network Components

This section covers the following official CCNA 200-301 exam topics:

- Explain the role and function of network components
- Next-generation firewalls and IPS
- Controllers (Cisco Catalyst Center and WLC)

There are many different network components (devices) you can encounter in a modern network. This section ensures you are familiar with some of the most important. This includes next-generation firewalls, Layer 2 and Layer 3 switches, and many more.

This section covers the following essential terms and components:

- Next-generation firewalls and IPSs
- Access points (APs)
- Wireless LAN controllers (WLCs)
- Layer 2 and Layer 3 switches
- Cisco Catalyst Center (formerly Cisco DNA Center)
- Endpoints
- Servers

Section Pretest

1. What networking term can be used for devices such as PCs, laptops, and mobile phones used by end users?

   _____

2. Name a network device that features many ports for high-speed connectivity of endpoints and offers high-speed routing capabilities.

   _____

3. Name a network device that connects users to a network using multiple radio frequency bands.

   _____

4. What modern security device can perform deep packet inspection and match packets against known security attacks?

   _____

5. What next-generation firewall feature used to be implemented in a separate appliance?

   _____

6. Why might AI be used in a next-generation firewall?

   _____

7. What modern Cisco controller can be set up to provision, configure, and monitor all your network devices in minutes and can even use AI and ML?

   _____

8. What type of appliance is designed to configure and manage Cisco wireless networks?

   _____

Answers

1. Endpoints (or end hosts, hosts, or end systems)
2. Layer 3 switch
3. Access point
4. Next-generation firewall (NGFW)
5. Intrusion prevention system (IPS)
6. To dynamically analyze network behaviors and learn about brand-new attacks without the need to manually code in the attack's signature

7. Cisco Catalyst Center (formerly Cisco DNA Center)

8. Wireless LAN controller (WLC)

Explain the Role and Function of Network Components

Networks today are growing in complexity. New devices are appearing and playing critical roles in the network infrastructure and functionality. Although there are many specialized devices, the CCNA 200-301 exam blueprint calls out specific devices that you need to understand. This topic examines four of them:

- **L2 and L3 switches:** Remember that L2 and L3 stand for Layer 2 and Layer 3 of the OSI model. An L2 switch is typically a low-cost switch whose job is to switch frames as quickly as possible from one port to another to direct traffic from device to device. The most common of these switches, the Layer 2 transparent Ethernet switch, quietly learns MAC address–to–port mappings by "learning" the MAC addresses of endpoints from the many frames that inevitably arrive on the various switch ports.

  A Layer 3 switch takes things up a notch (layer). These popular devices not only switch frames but also route (Layer 3) packets between different subnets. Remember that, in the Cisco world, a subnet is defined as a VLAN in the infrastructure.

  Layer 3 switches offer some of the most blazing speeds when it comes to moving packets from one subnet to another. In addition, Layer 3 switches eliminate the need for the old-fashioned router-on-a-stick configuration for the purpose of routing between VLANs. A router-on-a-stick configuration features a Layer 2 switch that trunks to an external router that provides the required routing functions.

- **Access points:** It seems like you cannot go anywhere today without being in a wireless cell for Internet access. Some cities around the world (including my own) provide complimentary Internet access using Wi-Fi throughout the entire city downtown area. One of the key devices that make this a reality is the access point.

  Access points are often *dual band*, supporting two of the most popular unlicensed frequency bands, as defined in various iterations of the 802.11 wireless standards. Most Wi-Fi implementations use one or both of the two unlicensed spectrum bands. The role of an AP is simple: Connect users to the network as quickly and efficiently as possible with *some* level of security. This might be no security at all in the case of an open guest network, or it might mean the highest levels of security available in the wireless segment for a protected business network. For corporate environments, Cisco manufactures "lightweight" access points that rely on a wireless LAN controller for their configuration and management.

> **Note**   Wireless networks often use an older method of allowing multiple devices to access the infrastructure "at the same time." They use carrier-sense multiple access with collision avoidance (CSMA/CA). CSMA/CA uses carrier sensing, but nodes attempt to avoid collisions by transmitting only when the channel is sensed to be idle. Nodes also transmit in order and in predetermined time slots. This "ordered" transmission does not guarantee that there will not be collisions, but it significantly reduces the probability that they will occur. Contrast this to what happened in older hub-based local-area networks (LANs) with Ethernet cables, where no effort was made to *avoid* collisions: There was only a mechanism to detect collisions and recover from them when they occurred. Ethernet uses carrier-sense multiple access with collision detection (CSMA/CD). This is a media access control method that uses a carrier-sensing scheme in which a transmitting data station listens for other signals while transmitting a frame. If it detects that two devices are sending at the same time, the device stops transmitting that frame, transmits a jam signal, and then waits for a random time interval before trying to re-send the frame.

- **Endpoints:** Why do we work so hard to build great networks? Well, one main reason is that we are doing it for the many different endpoints in our environment. An endpoint is a computing device that communicates back and forth with our network to reach resources such as data storage or other endpoints. Examples of endpoints include desktop PCs and Macs, laptops, smartphones, tablets, and workstations. Thanks to the Internet of Things (IoT), this list just keeps getting longer.

- **Servers:** Technically, servers in a network are also considered endpoints, but Cisco places them in a category by themselves. Perhaps this is because endpoints can be thought of as devices that are using the network to enjoy resources, while servers are serving up resources on the network. Servers can provide file and print resources, websites, compute horsepower for applications, security software, and much more.

  Just as there are many different purposes for a server in a network, there are many different operating systems to choose from. Servers can run Windows, UNIX, Linux, and even macOS for various purposes. Did you know that the dominant web server in the world is Apache running on Linux?

Topic Quiz

1. What technology is used with half-duplex Ethernet networks?

   A. CSMA/CA

   B. CSMA/CD

   C. CSMA/CC

   D. CSMA/CQ

2. What network infrastructure component is now frequently a replacement for a router-on-a-stick configuration?

   A. Access point

   B. Endpoint

   C. L2 switch

   D. L3 switch

Topic Quiz Answers

1. **B** is correct. Half-duplex Ethernet LANs use carrier-sense multiple access with collision detection in order to guard against collisions.

2. **D** is correct. An L3 switch can both switch frames and route packets, replacing the functionality of a router-on-a-stick configuration.

Next-Generation Firewalls and IPS

Firewalls have been around a long time and come in many different shapes and sizes. In fact, firewalls might be physical appliances "racked and stacked" in your data center right along with routers and switches, or they might be software implementations tucked inside your operating system. The built-in Windows Firewall is a great example of this latter type.

No matter its form, the firewall's job is always the same: Protect one portion of a network or computer system from another portion. The classic example is the network firewall. This device connects to "inside" protected networks and protects them from "outside" networks (such as the Internet). A shining example of a network firewall appliance from Cisco Systems was the Adaptive Security Appliance (ASA). There was even a virtual version (ASAv) that you could connect to a virtualized (VMware) network. Amazingly, these ASA and ASAv devices are already considered legacy Cisco devices.

Cisco is very excited about its latest next-generation firewalls. These devices go far beyond the simple inspection of the source/destination IP addresses and ports used in packets. NGFW devices can perform deep packet inspection for a detailed analysis of application layer information.

In fact, NGFWs can now perform the functions of intrusion prevention systems (IPSs). In the past, IPS technology was implemented (most often) through distinct appliances. Such devices used a variety of methods (such as signatures) to recognize attacks and drop packets that were part of attacks. Because most modern malware uses strong encryption, NGFWs also use heuristics to detect malware traffic.

Today NGFWs often call upon external signature databases of new and emerging attacks, so they are constantly getting smarter and more skilled at learning what traffic to deny. Due to the speed with which malware spreads today and the increasing severity of the damage it can cause, the speed with which vendors update their signature databases is no longer considered sufficient to protect networks from the latest threats. Interestingly, artificial intelligence (AI) in the form of machine learning (ML) is often put to use in detecting and thwarting new attacks that have never been seen before (zero-day attacks)—without the need for downloading signatures.

To function as an NGFW, a Cisco appliance requires a special term-based software license and Internet connectivity to download the signatures that Cisco updates daily and to validate its license. Without valid special NGFW licenses, the devices revert to classic firewall functionality. Keeping track of licenses in a large network is a full-time job in itself.

> **Note** The Cisco Firepower NGFW devices were originally produced by a company called Sourcefire. Cisco bought that company in 2013 for $2.7 billion. Think there is a lot of money in cybersecurity?

Topic Quiz

1. What are the latest NGFW devices from Cisco called?

    A. Sourcefire

    B. Firepower

    C. TrendMicro

    D. Prime

2. A network firewall often connects the protected inside network to the outside network. What does the outside network typically consist of?

    A. A server cluster

    B. Another subnet of the protected network

    C. A partner network

    D. The Internet

Topic Quiz Answers

1. B is correct. Firepower is the name for a large number of security devices from Cisco Systems.

2. D is correct. A classic network firewall implementation connects the protected corporate inside network to the outside public Internet.

Controllers

Cisco Catalyst Center (Formerly Cisco DNA Center)

For many years, Cisco was not very well respected when it came to management software for the networks it was building and maintaining. In the early 2000s, I was teaching about a product Cisco offered called CiscoWorks. As you might guess, a frequent joke surrounding this product was the fact that it did not *work* all that well.

Certainly much has changed, and today Cisco offers a very well-received controller for just about everything in your network. It is Cisco Catalyst Center.

The goals of Catalyst Center are lofty ones. The product seeks to:

- Simplify network management
- Deploy networks in minutes
- Lower costs
- Incorporate cloud services and third-party integrations

Cisco Catalyst Center provides what the industry likes to term a "single pane of glass" for all of this. It offers a single web-based graphical user interface (GUI) with plenty of tabs and command options to permit you to interact with a network in many different ways, all within the Cisco Catalyst Center software.

Wireless LAN Controllers (WLCs)

Large environments that are more complex than home networks might need many access points to fulfill the needs of the organization. A wireless LAN controller (WLC) is ideal in such a situation, to manage the many APs (access points) that exist. A WLC often acts as the brains of the operation and controls aspects such as security and frequency usage as well as transmission power. As you might guess, Cisco is in the business of wireless controllers.

When the APs in a wireless network do not require a WLC in order to work their magic, they are referred to as *autonomous* access points. If they do require a WLC in order to be configured and managed, they are referred to as *lightweight* access points. You should also note that many of the Cisco APs can actually function in either mode, and this is completely configurable.

Note   Wireless LAN controllers from Cisco are capable of many advanced features, including the following:

- Configuration of wireless policy, management, or security settings at any time through centralized provisioning and management

- Faster response to business needs through central management of wireless networks

- Standardized access point configuration for software versioning

- Wireless intrusion prevention system (wIPS) capabilities

- Network-wide quality of service (QoS) for voice and video across wired and wireless networks

- Network-wide centralized security policies across wired and wireless networks

- Mobility, security, and management for IPv6 and dual-stack clients

- Tight integration with Cisco Catalyst Center

Topic Quiz

1. What is the term for an access point that does not require a WLC for its operation?

   A. Autonomous

   B. Lightweight

   C. Distributed

   D. Mesh

2. What is the term for an access point that relies on a WLC for its configuration and management?

   A. Lightweight

   B. Autonomous

   C. Distributed

   D. Mesh

Topic Quiz Answers

1. A is correct. An autonomous access point does not require a WLC.

2. A is correct. A lightweight access point is an AP that requires a WLC for its configuration and operation.

Review Questions

1. What security device tends to be implemented in many different forms, including hardware and software?

   A. WLC

   B. Firewall

   C. Access point

   D. Router

2. What device is designed to be a high-speed, low-cost method of connecting endpoints to a network?

   A. WLC

   B. NGFW

   C. L2 switch

   D. L3 switch

3. Why are access points often referred to as dual band?

   A. Because they can also service LAN clients

   B. Because they support multiple frequency bands

   C. Because they offer multiple security settings

   D. Because they are capable of operating in lightweight or autonomous modes

4. What is the typical method of communication used in wireless networks?

   A. CSMA/CW

   B. CSMA/CQ

   C. CSMA/CD

   D. CSMA/CA

5. Deep packet inspection often refers to which layer of the OSI model?

   A. Layer 3

   B. Layer 4

   C. Layer 5

   D. Layer 7

6. In addition to replacing your legacy firewall, a Cisco Firepower device can also replace what other physical appliance?

   A. Web server

   B. L2 switch

   C. IPS

   D. Content caching system

Answers to Review Questions

1. **B** is correct. A firewall protects some part of a system or network from another part of the system or network. Firewalls come in many different varieties. Some firewalls are hardware based, whereas others are software based.

2. **C** is correct. An L2 switch connects endpoints to a network in a cost-effective yet very efficient manner.

3. **B** is correct. Most APs support multiple frequency bands. They are therefore often referred to as *dual-band devices*.

4. **D** is correct. Wireless networks often use CSMA/CA, which means nodes send traffic only when the network is sensed to be idle.

5. **D** is correct. Deep packet inspection refers to the NGFW being able to inspect deep inside a packet, all the way to the application payload (Layer 7 information).

6. **C** is correct. NGFWs often feature replacement technology for legacy IPS appliances.

The Characteristics of Network Topology Architectures

This section covers the following official CCNA 200-301 exam topics:

■ Two-tier architectures and two-tier spine-leaf

■ WANs and SOHOs

■ On-premises and cloud

While there is tremendous variety in the topologies in use today in modern networks, this section covers some classic and some newer layouts you will discover. Different topologies have different strengths and weaknesses. Matching these topologies to network requirements can go a long way toward creating efficient network infrastructures.

This section covers the following essential terms and components:

■ Three-tier network designs

- Collapsed core network designs

- Two-tier spine-leaf topologies

- Network topologies

- WANs

- SOHOs

- Point-to-point topologies

- Full-mesh topologies

- Hub-and-spoke topologies

- Single-homed topologies

- Dual-homed topologies

- Cloud resources

- On-premises resources

Section Pretest

1. What are the three tiers of the classic hierarchical Cisco network design?

_____

_____

_____

2. What layer of the classic hierarchical Cisco network design is typically eliminated in a collapsed two-tier design?

_____

3. What new network architecture is often found in a data center with Cisco's celebrated SDN solution?

_____

4. What WAN topology involves two devices on the link?

_____

5. What topology is often used in connecting a headquarters and many branch offices?

_____

6. What technology forms a MAN using Ethernet?

_____

7. What Cisco technology permits the dynamic creation of hub-to-spoke and even spoke-to-spoke tunnels?

_____

8. Name at least three characteristics of cloud computing IT services.

_____

_____

_____

9. What cloud model is often used to help enterprises develop and deploy software applications?

_____

10. What kind of cloud computing organization connects to multiple cloud providers and multiple customers and creates a private network as a service?

_____

Answers

1. Core, distribution, and access

2. Distribution

3. Two-tier spine-leaf

4. P2P (point-to-point)

5. Hub-and-spoke

6. Metro Ethernet

7. DMVPN

8. They can be requested on demand, they can dynamically scale, they use a pool of resources, they offer a variety of network access options, and their usage can be measured and billed to the user.

9. Platform as a service (PaaS)

10. Intercloud Exchange

Two-Tier Architectures and Two-Tier Spine-Leaf

For years, Cisco has suggested that we break up our networks into easy-to-understand and easy-to-manage layers or tiers (not to be confused with OSI or TCP/IP model layers). The classic three-layer model consists of the following:

- **Access layer:** This layer provides workgroup/user access to the network; as a result, this layer is sometimes called the workstation layer.

- **Distribution layer:** The layer provides policy-based connectivity and controls the boundary between the access and core layers; it is also sometimes referred to as the aggregation layer.

- **Core layer:** This layer provides fast transport between distribution switches within the enterprise campus; it is sometimes called the backbone layer.

Note   You should be aware of particular functions that most often occur at different layers. Here are some examples:

Access layer:

- Layer 2 switching

- Spanning tree

- Power over Ethernet (PoE) and auxiliary VLANs for VoIP

- QoS classification and marking and trust boundaries

- Port securityAddress Resolution Protocol (ARP) inspection

- Virtual LAN access control lists (VACLs)

Distribution layer:

- Aggregation of LAN or WAN links

- Policy-based security in the form of access control lists (ACLs) and filtering

- Routing services between LANs and VLANs and between routing domains

- Redundancy and load balancing

- A boundary for route aggregation and summarization configured on interfaces toward the core layer

- Broadcast domain boundary

Core layer:

- High-speed transport

- Reliability and fault tolerance

If you are in charge of a small, simple network right now, you might be thinking, "Really??? You expect me to buy all this equipment to make all of that happen in layers?" This is where the two-tier collapsed core design might come in.

Note   The collapsed core (two-tier) design takes the functions of the distribution layer and moves them (or collapses them) into the core layer. So you can dramatically simplify a network by using a core layer and an access layer only. Keep in mind that this also might be done in larger networks, especially when the core/distribution equipment is so sophisticated that it provides the required throughput while at the same time performing all the distribution layer functions.

The Two-Tier Spine-Leaf

Yes, there is a new network topology architecture in town, and it means business! The two-tier spine-leaf is now a widely recommended data center design that is not necessarily applicable in the enterprise campus. In fact, it is the shining star in the Cisco software-defined networking (SDN) solution called Cisco ACI (Application Centric Infrastructure). Figure A.1 shows this new spine-leaf topology as it looks with Cisco ACI.

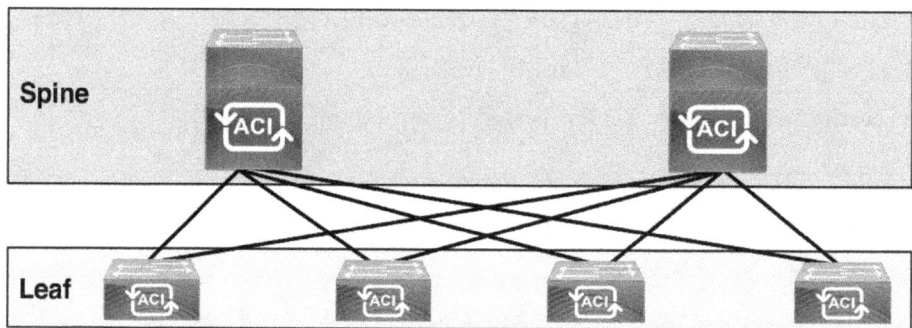

Figure A.1   *The Two-Tier Spine-Leaf Topology*

Notice that with this topology, each leaf device is connected to every spine device in a full mesh. The spine is considered the backbone (how appropriate), or the core of the network. Notice how critical the spine is in a two-tier spine-leaf topology: It is the glue that enables communications between leaf devices. If one leaf needs to send traffic to another leaf (and they almost always do), it must send the traffic through the spine—unless, of course, the leaf device is sending traffic to a device that is connected to that very leaf device.

How could such a simple topology be featured with some of Cisco's most advanced technologies? This simple topology presents many advantages, including the following:

- Network design that is as simple as possible while meeting business requirements

- Simpler, deterministic load balancing between core devices

- Low latency

- Simple scalability through the addition of spine devices

- Support for overlay networks to add a virtualization layer(s)

Topic Quiz

1. At what layer of the Cisco network model might you expect to find port security?

   A. Distribution

   B. Internet

   C. Access

   D. Core

2. At what layer of the Cisco network model is speed most important?

   A. Distribution

   B. Internet

   C. Access

   D. Core

3. Which statement about leaf devices in the two-tier spine-leaf architecture is true?

   A. Each leaf device connects to every spine device.

   B. Each leaf device connects to exactly one spine device.

   C. Each leaf device connects to exactly two spine devices.

   D. Each leaf device must connect to every other leaf device directly.

Topic Quiz Answers

1. C is correct. The access layer is where we find mechanisms such as port security, QoS classification and marking, and Power over Ethernet, to name just a few.

2. D is correct. The core layer is where speed is of critical importance. In fact, speed is so important at this layer that it is why we often move functions such as QoS and security out of the core layer.

3. A is correct. Each leaf in the spine-leaf topology connects to each of the spine devices, forming a full mesh between the spines and leafs.

WANs and SOHOs

WANs

It is great if you have an awesome network built in your small office/home office (SOHO). But unfortunately today, more than ever, many (if not most) of the resources you are going to want to access are in the cloud (Internet). This makes the wide-area network (WAN) more important than ever before. A WAN provides connectivity outside your local LAN when you need to reach resources on the Internet or another office location that is not local to you.

There are many possible WAN topologies. Let's quickly review the most popular of them:

- **Point-to-point:** This simple WAN topology connects two devices over a single connection.

- **Hub-and-spoke:** This WAN topology features a central hub device (typically at a network headquarters, for example) that makes WAN connections out to branch offices (the spokes).

- **Full mesh:** This WAN topology is the most expensive and complex to maintain because it has all devices making connections to all other devices. Although a full mesh can be complex and expensive, it provides excellent redundancy of WAN paths through the network.

- **Single homed and dual homed:** A single-homed WAN topology makes a connection to a single ISP, and a multi-homed WAN makes connections to multiple ISPs. A dual-homed configuration is very powerful because if one ISP completely fails to be able to route traffic for the customer, the customer can dynamically fail over to the surviving ISP.

Today, customers have more technological options than ever before for client connectivity to the WAN. Here is a review of the options you should know for the CCNA 200-301 exam:

- **MPLS:** Multiprotocol Label Switching (MPLS) is a data-carrying technique for high-performance telecommunications networks that directs data from one network node to the next based on short path labels rather than long network addresses. This provides many advantages, including the elimination of complex lookups in a routing table. The labels identify virtual links (paths) between remote nodes rather than endpoints. MPLS can encapsulate packets of various network protocols, hence the "Multiprotocol" part of its name. MPLS supports a range of access technologies, including Ethernet, T1/E1, ATM, and DSL. Most (if not all) ISPs run MPLS internally.

- **Metro Ethernet:** A Metro Ethernet network is a metropolitan-area network (MAN) that is based on Ethernet standards. Such a network is commonly used to connect subscribers to a larger service network or the Internet. Businesses can also use Metro Ethernet to connect their own offices to each other. An Ethernet interface is much cheaper than a synchronous digital hierarchy (SONET/SDH) or plesiochronous digital hierarchy (PDH) interface of the same bandwidth. Another distinct advantage of an Ethernet-based access network is that it can be easily connected to the customer network due to the prevalent use of Ethernet in corporate and residential networks. Metro Ethernet service is typically implemented by ISPs using MPLS.

- **Broadband PPPoE:** Point-to-Point Protocol over Ethernet (PPPoE) is a network protocol for encapsulating PPP frames inside Ethernet frames. It appeared in 1999, in the context of the boom of DSL, as a solution for tunneling packets over a DSL connection to an ISP's IP network and from there to the rest of the Internet. Typical use of PPPoE involves leveraging the PPP facilities for authenticating the user with a username and password, predominately via PAP and less often via CHAP.

■ **Internet VPN (DMVPN, site-to-site VPN, client VPN):** Dynamic Multipoint VPN (DMVPN) is a Cisco invention for creating hub-and-spoke topologies with ease, including the dynamic creation of spoke-to-spoke tunnels in order to reduce the burdens on busy HQ (hub) devices. In the context of DMVPN, dynamic refers to virtual private network (VPN) tunnels being established whenever required and torn down when they are not required. Site-to-site VPNs permit the creation of VPN links between locations that client devices can use to send protected data over an untrusted network (such as the Internet). Finally, client VPN software can be used to permit remote access to corporate resources. The client VPN software can be a standalone complex client app, or it can be as simple as a web browser.

SOHOs

Many of us today work in SOHO environments (I certainly do). In fact, these networks are often filled with technology that used to be so sophisticated that it was used only in data centers. For example, my SOHO features a fiber-optic connection into my home for high-speed WAN connectivity, and it features a 10 Gbps LAN network for ultra-high speed locally. Typical SOHOs contain routers, switches, access points, firewalls, and wired and wireless endpoints.

However, as great as a SOHO is, we are all the time needing access to more and more resources that are not within the confines of the SOHO.

Topic Quiz

1. Which topology requires the highest costs and administrative overhead?

   A. Full-mesh topology

   B. Hub-and-spoke topology

   C. Point-to-point topology

   D. Single-homed topology

2. If your WAN client actually makes connections to two separate ISPs, what kind of topology is this?

   A. Single-homed topology

   B. Dual-homed topology

   C. Point-to-point topology

   D. Full-mesh topology

3. What technology uses simple labels instead of complex routing tables for the forwarding of traffic?

   A. Broadband PPPoE

   B. Client VPN

    C. Metro Ethernet

    D. MPLS

  4. What technology might use a web browser to form a secure VPN connection?

    A. Broadband PPPoE

    B. Client or SSL VPN

    C. Metro Ethernet

    D. MPLS

Topic Quiz Answers

  1. **A** is correct. The full-mesh topology involves the highest cost due to the very large number of links and node interfaces required.

  2. **B** is correct. Making a WAN connection to different providers requires a dual-homed topology.

  3. **D** is correct. MPLS uses labels to forward traffic.

  4. **B** is correct. A client SSL VPN might come in the form of a web browser.

On-Premises and Cloud

On-Premises

All the IT resources (computing, storage, network) at your SOHO or enterprise network are referred to as *on-premises* (or *on-prem*) resources.

Many organizations are eager to take advantage of the many benefits of cloud technology, and more and more tools are being developed to help migrate and/or sync on-premises IT solutions with the cloud. Amazon Web Services (AWS) DataSync and the AWS Database Migration Service are just two that come to mind.

Cloud

Cloud services are incredibly popular today. From companies relying on Dropbox Business and Gmail to enterprises building their own cloud services, it seems that everyone wants to adopt some aspect of IT as a cloud service. What does it mean for IT services to really be considered cloud technology? Here is an important list of criteria:

- These services can be requested on demand from clients by using an API.
- The services offer dynamic scaling (often referred to as *elasticity*).
- These services rely on resource pooling in the data center.
- These services provide a wide variety of network access options.

- The use of these services can be easily measured; customers can be billed for usage according to agreements with the cloud provider. (Google Cloud Platform's Compute Engine, for example, has a per-second billing model.)

Some larger enterprises develop their own cloud services in their own privately controlled data centers. Such a setup is known as a *private cloud*. In contrast, a *public cloud service* is one that is external to the organization. Public cloud providers (such as Google with Gmail) offer cloud services to many private enterprises and persons all over the globe.

Today, an increasing number of enterprises are using a hybrid cloud approach, in which an organization relies on private clouds for some resources and public clouds for other IT services.

Cloud technologies have given rise to the virtual service model. Here are some important examples of cloud technology *as a service* terms you should commit to memory:

- **Infrastructure as a service (IaaS):** With IaaS, the cloud provider makes available to the customer the hardware, software, servers, storage, and other infrastructure components; IaaS providers can also host clients' applications and handle tasks such as system maintenance, backup, and resiliency planning. Amazon Web Services (AWS) is one of the pioneers in the IaaS cloud space.

- **Software as a service (SaaS):** With SaaS, the cloud provider makes powerful software available to clients. A prime example of SaaS is Gmail, through which Google provides rich email services to worldwide clients.

- **Platform as a service (PaaS):** With PaaS, the cloud provider makes virtual machines (VMs) available to clients so that they can develop software applications in a test environment; it is typical for a PaaS provider to also make available software development tools as part of the platform. An example of PaaS is an AWS Drupal instance.

- **X as a service (XaaS):** These days, it seems like anything and everything is being offered "as a service," and that is exactly what XaaS (or EaaS) refers to: any aspect of IT that is delivered through a cloud model.

This list is not definitive, and there is a continuum of XaaS offerings, blurring any delineations between the above definitions, with each cloud vendor defining these terms loosely and differently.

Just as there are many virtual service offerings, there are many ways clients can connect. Remember that an aspect of cloud technologies is to enable many different network access options. For public cloud services, most people immediately think of the Internet as the connection path. This certainly provides ease of use, convenience, and reduced costs. Unfortunately, it does come with disadvantages, such as security concerns as well as quality of service issues. VPN technologies can address most security concerns and are another pathing option.

Some organizations rely on cloud services so heavily that they purchase private WAN connections to these services. This permits much greater security and control, but it tends to come with higher costs. Intercloud exchanges have appeared to make these

private WAN connections more affordable and flexible. Intercloud exchanges connect to multiple
public cloud providers via dedicated high-speed links and make it simple for their end users to pay for only a single private connection to the exchange and then allow users to switch between the various public clouds to which the exchange is connected.

Virtual network services are becoming more and more common in making cloud-based data centers a reality. Just as VMs revolutionized the computer industry, so has virtual networking changed traditional networking. More and more functions of the network are moving to virtual implementations, including the functions of the following:

- Firewalls

- Routers

- Switches

- DNS services

Virtualization of network services leads to more flexibility and more cloud-like scaling possibilities for a data center. Of course, this also leads to more programmability.

Topic Quiz

1. Which of the following is not a common characteristic of cloud services?

   A. On demand

   B. Dynamic scaling

   C. Auto-administration

   D. Resource pooling

2. Gmail is an example of what type of *as a service* model?

   A. TaaS

   B. SaaS

   C. IaaS

   D. PaaS

3. You have several application solutions and many terabytes of data in your local enterprise. What is the term for this location of technology?

   A. On-premises

   B. Legacy stored

   C. Data laked

   D. Cloud bursted

Topic Quiz Answers

1. C is correct. Auto-administration is not one of the five common characteristics of cloud services.

2. B is correct. Gmail is a prime example of software as a service.

3. A is correct. In a world that is now dominated by cloud technology, our local resources are now referred to as on-premises.

Review Questions

1. What pathing option for public cloud provides the most security and control for an organization?

   A. Private WAN

   B. Internet access

   C. Internet access with VPN

   D. Cisco Cloud Connect

2. In what layer of a two-tier architecture is speed most important?

   A. Workstation layer

   B. Access layer

   C. Backbone layer

   D. Distribution layer

3. If you are using Cisco ACI in your data center and notice that you are starting to run out of overall bandwidth and capacity, what is often the solution to provide the required scalability?

   A. Upgrade to 1 Gbps links

   B. Add access devices

   C. Add spine devices

   D. Add leaf devices

4. Which WAN topology is often the most expensive and difficult to maintain?

   A. Hub-and-spoke topology

   B. Full-mesh topology

   C. Point-to-point topology

   D. Single-homed topology

5. A major reason that many companies are excited about moving to the cloud is that they gain the ability to dynamically resize resources based on demand. What is the term for this ability?

A. Elasticity

B. Cloud-bursting

C. Scalability

D. Immutability

Answers to Review Questions

1. A is correct. The private WAN option provides the most control and security, but it often comes with a much higher cost.

2. C is correct. In the backbone layer (also termed the spine or core) of the network architecture, speed is absolutely critical.

3. C is correct. The two-tier spine-leaf topology of Cisco ACI is very easily scaled. You simply need to add devices to the spine of the infrastructure.

4. B is correct. While a full-mesh WAN topology is excellent for redundancy, throughput, and high availability, it can be very costly and difficult to operate and maintain.

5. A is correct. Elasticity refers to a cloud-provided ability to use features such as auto-scaling to dynamically reduce and expand resources as needed based on demand. Note that scalability refers to simply growing the architecture as needed. It does not refer to dynamically reducing the size of the architecture.

Describe TCP and UDP

This section covers the following official CCNA 200-301 exam topics:

■ Compare and contrast the OSI and TCP/IP models

■ Compare and contrast TCP and UDP

There are two main options at the Transport Layer of the OSI model when it comes to sending data; these are Transmission Control Protocol (TCP) and User Datagram Protocol (UDP). As you will learn, one of these provides for reliable delivery, while another sacrifices reliability for less overhead.

This section covers the following essential terms and components:

■ The Open Systems Interconnection (OSI) model

■ Transmission Control Protocol/Internet Protocol (TCP/IP) model

- Transmission Control Protocol (TCP)
- User Datagram Protocol (UDP)

Section Pretest

1. Fill in the missing levels of the OSI model, from top to bottom.

   Application

   _____

   _____

   _____

   _____

   _____

   _____

2. Name the four layers of the TCP/IP model, from top to bottom.

   _____

   _____

   _____

   _____

3. Name the PDUs of the bottom four layers of the OSI model, from top to bottom.

   _____

   _____

   _____

   _____

4. What protocol maps Layer 3 addresses to Layer 2 addresses in Ethernet local-area networks (LANs)?

   _____

5. What two layers of the OSI model are associated with the network interface layer of the TCP/IP model?

   _____

   _____

6. Name at least four key characteristics of UDP.

_____

_____

_____

_____

7. Name at least four key characteristics of TCP.

_____

_____

_____

_____

Answers

1. Presentation

Session

Transport

Network

Data Link

Physical

2. Application

Transport

Internet

Network Interface

3. Segments

Packets

Frames

Bits

4. ARP (Address Resolution Protocol)

5. Data link layer and physical layer

6. UDP is connectionless.

UDP has very little overhead.

UDP is often used for voice and video traffic.

UDP can multiplex using port numbers to work with multiple applications.

7. TCP is connection oriented.

TCP has more overhead than UDP.

TCP uses features like sequencing and acknowledgments to ensure reliable and ordered delivery of segments and implements end-to-end flow control to maximize throughput over an unreliable and dynamic network without overwhelming the receivers with data they cannot process.

TCP can multiplex using port numbers to work with multiple applications.

Compare and Contrast the OSI and TCP/IP Models

Figure A.2 shows the classic OSI and TCP/IP models for networking. Notice how the layers compare between the two models.

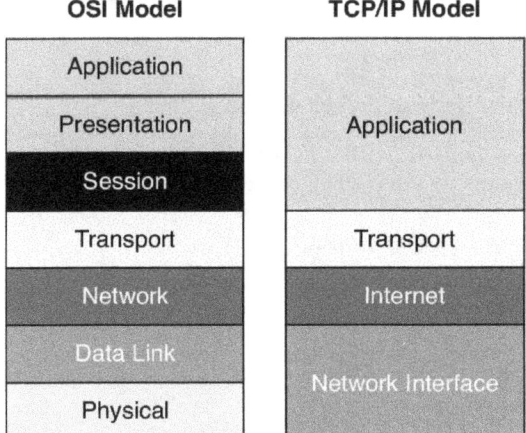

Figure A.2   *The OSI and TCP/IP Models*

> **Note**   You might be wondering why this appendix presents the OSI and TCP/IP models when the CCNA 200-301 exam blueprint from Cisco Systems does not explicitly include these topics. This text follows the approach of almost all the other books in the industry on the latest CCNA exam and includes this coverage because it is very valuable and is basically assumed knowledge at this point.

To remember the layers of the OSI model in a top-down fashion, use the mnemonic device **All People Seem to Need Data Processing.** From the bottom up, the popular memory tool is **Please Do Not Throw Sausage Pizza Away.** (Since pizza is my favorite food, this is the one I use!) Here is a recap of the major functions of the layers of the OSI model, starting from the lowest layer and climbing up:

- **Physical (Layer 1):** Defines the electrical and physical specifications.

- **Data Link (Layer 2):** Detects and, when possible, corrects errors found at the physical layer; defines the Layer 2 protocols to establish and terminate a connection between two physically connected devices.

- **Network (Layer 3):** Provides for logical network addressing. Address Resolution Protocol (ARP) is used to resolve Layer 3 network IP addresses to Layer 2 MAC addresses on Ethernet LANs.

- **Transport (Layer 4):** This layer optionally (potentially) implements/offers reliability of communications through acknowledgments and optionally implements flow control mechanisms on end hosts. Important examples of protocols used at this layer are Transmission Control Protocol (TCP) for reliable delivery and User Datagram Protocol (UDP) for unreliable delivery.

Note To establish a TCP connection before the transmission of data, TCP uses a three-way handshake. This process is as follows:

1. **SYN:** The client sends a SYN to the server.

2. **SYN-ACK:** In response, the server replies with a SYN-ACK.

3. **ACK:** Finally, the client sends an ACK back to the server.

At this point, the client and server have both received acknowledgments from each other regarding the connection.

- **Session (Layer 5):** This layer controls the logical connections between two systems; it establishes, manages, and terminates the connections between the local and remote systems. The functions of the session layer are implemented by TCP in the TCP/IP stack.

- **Presentation (Layer 6):** This layer is sometimes called the syntax layer because it ensures that network formats are converted in such a way that the application layer can understand them.

- **Application (Layer 7):** This layer provides services for end-user applications so that communication with another application across the network is possible.

Note Network engineers mostly deal with the bottom four layers intensely. As a result, you often hear them discussed as simply Layers 1 through 4. For example, you might simply say "Layer 2" instead of "the data link layer."

The data and header information (protocol data units [PDUs]) that are built at each of the bottom four layers of the OSI model have special names. Figure A.3 shows the specific PDU names for the layers.

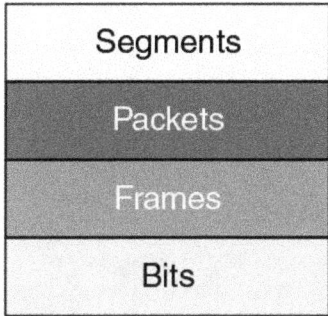

Figure A.3   *The PDUs of the Bottom Four Layers of the OSI Model*

Note   Be prepared to be tested on the PDU names for the bottom four layers of the OSI model. An easy way to remember them is by using the memory tool **Some People Fear Birthdays**. By the way, we tend to reference the information above Layer 4 as simply *data*.

Another important skill is identifying the sample technologies we work with every day and at what layer of the OSI model they exist. Table A.1 provides important sample information in this regard.

Table A.1   *Protocols at Various Layers*

Layer	Protocol Examples
Application	FTP, HTTP, SMTP
Presentation	JPEG, MPEG
Session	NetBIOS, PPTP
Transport	TCP, UDP
Network	IP, ICMP
Data link	PPP, ATM
Physical	Ethernet, USB

Note that protocols rarely implement all the functions that a layer defines, and they often implement functions of several layers.

Topic Quiz

1. What protocol does a host use to discover the L2 address of the next device in the path toward a remote destination?

   A. TCP

   B. UDP

   C. ICMP

   D. ARP

2. What layer of the OSI model corresponds to the transport layer of the TCP/IP model?

   A. Network

   B. Transport

   C. Session

   D. Presentation

Topic Quiz Answers

1. **D** is correct. Neighbor solicitation is the job of ARP in IPv4 networks and ICMPv6 in IPv6 networks.

2. **B** is correct. The transport layer of the TCP/IP model corresponds directly with the transport layer of the OSI model.

Compare and Contrast TCP and UDP

Transmission Control Protocol (TCP) and User Datagram Protocol (UDP) are both protocols that operate at the transport layer (Layer 4). TCP is used for reliable, connection-oriented communications, whereas UDP is used for connectionless transport. It might seem as if you would *never* want to send information in an unreliable manner using UDP, but keep in mind that TCP adds overhead and some inefficiencies to the process. Therefore, UDP is often used for things like voice and video communications, where minimization of delay of packets is key and worth the sacrifice of reliability mechanisms. In fact, sometimes applications use UDP and then use their own application layer mechanisms for reliability. For example, whenever possible, Chrome uses QUIC. Table A.2 lists some applications that rely on TCP compared to applications that rely on UDP.

Note Remember that not all traffic relies on TCP or UDP at the transport layer. Forms of traffic that do not use TCP or UDP typically have their own protocol identifiers. Here is a list of examples of protocol identifiers from the IP header:

1—ICMP

6—TCP

17—UDP

88—EIGRP

89—OSPF

Table A.2 *Applications That Rely on TCP and on UDP*

Use TCP	Use UDP
HTTP	DHCP
FTP	RIP
Telnet	SNMP
SSH	TFTP
SMTP	DNS*
	Multicast applications

* DNS also uses TCP in some instances, such as with a DNS zone transfer, but DNS is mainly considered a UDP example.

TCP and UDP can both multiplex using port numbers to work with multiple applications. For example, DHCP uses UDP ports 67 and 68, RIP uses UDP port 520, and HTTP uses TCP port 80. The overhead of TCP is due to its use of reliable delivery. For example, TCP enables the following:

- Error recovery
- Flow control using windowing
- Connection establishment and termination
- Ordered data transfer
- Data segmentation

Note You never know when Cisco might need you to prove that you know a TCP or UDP port number. This might even come up in a sneaky way on the CCNA 200-301 exam, such as with a requirement to build a firewall statement. I encourage you to make flash cards to learn the well-known ports shown in Table A.3.

Table A.3 *Port Numbers and Protocols*

Port Number	TCP or UDP?	Protocol
20	TCP	FTP data
21	TCP	FTP control
22	TCP	SSH
23	TCP	Telnet
25	TCP	SMTP
53	UDP and TCP*	DNS
67 and 68	UDP	DHCP
69	UDP	TFTP
80	TCP	HTTP
110	TCP	POP3
161	UDP	SNMP
443	TCP	SSL/TLS (HTTPS)
514	UDP	Syslog
520	UDP	RIP

Topic Quiz

1. What transport layer protocol does EIGRP rely on in its operation?

   A. TCP

   B. UDP

   C. ICMP

   D. None of these answers are correct.

2. What protocol does RIP use, and what port does it use? (Choose two.)

   A. TCP

   B. UDP

   C. 514

   D. 520

Topic Quiz Answers

1. **D** is correct. EIGRP does not rely on TCP or UDP in its operation. The protocol encapsulates inside IP and provides its own reliable mechanisms for delivery from router to router. Note that ICMP is not a transport layer protocol but a network layer protocol. Interestingly, ICMP does not rely on TCP or UDP to function but rather has its own protocol number.

2. **B** and **D** are correct. RIP relies on the connectionless UDP protocol, and RIP messages are sent to port number 520. Note that RIPng (the IPv6 version of RIP) uses UDP port 521.

Review Questions

1. What port number does SNMP use, and what protocol does it use? (Choose two.)

   A. TCP

   B. UDP

   C. 161

   D. 514

2. What layer of the OSI model exists just above the network layer?

   A. Session

   B. Presentation

   C. Application

   D. Transport

3. What form of flow control is used with TCP?

   A. None

   B. Random

   C. Windowing

   D. Explicit buffering

4. What are the terms for the four PDUs that exist at the bottom of the OSI model? Name them in order, from bottom to top.

   A. Segments, frames, packets, bits

   B. Bits, frames, packets, segments

   C. Packets, frames, bits, segments

   D. Segments, packets, frames, bits

5. Which of the following are transport layer protocols? (Choose two.)

   A. ICMP

   B. TCP

   C. UDP

   D. FTP

6. What protocol uses windowing to implement flow control?

   A. ICMP

   B. TCP

   C. UDP

   D. RIP

7. What port number does SSH use, and what protocol does it use? (Choose two.)

   A. TCP

   B. UDP

   C. 22

   D. 23

Answers to Review Questions

1. B and C are correct. SNMP relies on UDP port 161 in its operations.

2. D is correct. The transport layer exists just above the network layer in the OSI model.

3. C is correct. TCP uses a process called windowing to provide flow control.

4. B is correct. From the bottom to the top, the PDUs are bits, frame, packets, and segments.

5. B and C are correct. Both TCP and UDP implement transport layer features.

6. B is correct. Transmission Control Protocol uses the sliding window mechanism to control the flow between hosts. It also uses several other mechanisms to maximize throughput and avoid congestion.

7. A and C are correct. SSH uses TCP and port 22 in its operations.

Describe the Purpose of First Hop Redundancy Protocols

This section covers the following official CCNA 200-301 exam topic:

- Describe the purpose and functions of first hop redundancy protocols

With most traffic flows today directed off local networks to reach remote destinations (or even the cloud), reaching a healthy default gateway is more important than ever. In this section, you will learn services that help ensure gateway availability. They are called First Hop Redundancy Protocols (FHRPs).

This section covers the following essential terms and components:

- First hop redundancy protocols (FHRPs)
- Hot Standby Router Protocol (HSRP)
- Virtual Router Redundancy Protocol (VRRP)
- Gateway Load Balancing Protocol (GLBP)

Section Pretest

1. What is the main purpose of an FHRP?

   _____

2. Which FHRP is an open standard?

   _____

Answers

1. To ensure reachability to the default gateway

2. VRRP

Describe the Purpose and Functions of First Hop Redundancy Protocols

Have you ever thought about how important it is to reach the Internet? Such reachability is more important today than it's ever been as we are relying more and more on cloud-based resources. The first hop when reaching these resources is the default gateway. How can we help ensure that a default gateway is always available? One method is to use a first hop redundancy protocol (FHRP). An FHRP ensures that at least one of multiple default gateways can be reached by clients that rely on them for access beyond their local network—even in the presence of some failures.

There are three FHRPs you should be knowledgeable about as you prepare to take the CCNA 200-301 exam:

- **Hot Standby Router Protocol (HSRP):** This is the Cisco invention that basically gave rise to the world of FHRPs. With HSRP, you configure the default gateway on hosts with a "phantom" IP address that the healthy default gateway in the HSRP group can respond to.

- **Virtual Router Redundancy Protocol (VRRP):** This is the open standard version of HSRP. There are more similarities between VRRP and HSRP than there are differences.

- **Gateway Load Balancing Protocol (GLBP):** This Cisco invention is super clever. GLBP not only allows a healthy default gateway to respond to clients but also permits dynamic load balancing between the multiple healthy default gateways that might exist. Load balancing is technically possible in HSRP and VRRP, but the configuration of such load balancing is laborious and unnecessarily complex, especially compared to the simplicity of GLBP.

As I am sure you know, HSRP allows multiple default gateways to respond to clients and route traffic onto and off their LAN segment.

With HSRP, each router presents a virtual IP address to the LAN segment. The active router can respond to ARP requests to this virtual IP address and forward traffic. The device that forwards traffic is called the *active router*, and the other devices in the group are called *standby routers*.

The HSRP routers communicate with each other every 3 seconds by default to ensure that they are up. There is also a dead timer, which is by default 10 seconds.

Note   Remember that HSRP is a Cisco-proprietary FHRP—and so is GLBP. There is one standards-based FHRP: VRRP.

As mentioned earlier, VRRP is almost identical to HSRP. The biggest difference between them is that VRRP is not a Cisco-proprietary invention but an open standard. Like HSRP, VRRP dynamically allows several routers on a multiaccess link to use the same virtual IP address. In a VRRP configuration, one router is elected as the virtual router master, and the other routers act as backups in case the virtual router master fails.

Note   Use of the terms *master* and *slave* is ONLY in association with the official terminology used in industry specifications and standards and in no way diminishes Pearson's commitment to promoting diversity, equity, and inclusion and challenging, countering, and/or combating bias and stereotyping in the global population of the learners we serve.

Realizing that improvements were needed in the HSRP approach to first hop reachability, Cisco Systems worked hard on GLBP and succeeded in delivering a much more flexible and clever protocol. Once again, multiple first hop routers on the LAN combine to offer a single virtual first hop IP router; however, with GLBP, load balancing with other healthy routers is possible.

GLBP provides load balancing over multiple routers using a single virtual IP address and multiple virtual MAC addresses. These multiple virtual MAC addresses are the magic behind the scenes that permit all of the healthy routers to help share the forwarding load.

Members of a GLBP group elect one gateway to be the active virtual gateway (AVG) for that group. Conveniently, the other group members provide backup for the AVG in the event that the AVG becomes unavailable.

The AVG assigns a virtual MAC address to each member of the GLBP group. Each gateway assumes responsibility for forwarding packets sent to the virtual MAC address assigned to it by the AVG. Each of these gateways is known as the active virtual forwarder (AVF) for its virtual MAC address.

The AVG is responsible for answering Address Resolution Protocol (ARP) requests for the virtual IP address. Load sharing is achieved by the AVG replying to the ARP requests with different virtual MAC addresses.

Topic Quiz

1. What does FHRP stand for?

   A. First hop redundancy protocol

   B. First HSRP Router Protocol

   C. First hop routing protocol

   D. Final hop routing protocol

2. Which FHRP seeks to bring load sharing to the redundant gateways in a network without requiring difficult configuration?

   A. VRRP

   B. GLBP

   C. HSRP

   D. IS-IS

Topic Quiz Answers

1. A is correct. FHRP stands for first hop redundancy protocol.

2. B is correct. GLBP makes it simple to balance the load between the healthy default gateways.

Review Questions

1. What is the name for the router that is responsible for assigning traffic to routers in GLBP?

   A. AVF

   B. AVR

   C. AVG

   D. AVA

2. How is the load sharing of GLBP ultimately accomplished?

   A. Using a round robin approach based on the physical IP addresses of gateways

   B. Using virtual MAC addresses

   C. Using multiple virtual IP addresses

   D. Using the routing table of the IGP

3. In HSRP, what is the term for routers that are not forwarding traffic for the LAN but are waiting to see if they are needed?

   A. Distinct routers

   B. Backup routers

   C. Standby routers

   D. Secondary routers

4. In VRRP, what is the name of the router that is forwarding traffic for the clients?

   A. Virtual router master

   B. Main router

   C. Active router

   D. Primary router

Answers to Review Questions

1. C is correct. The active virtual gateway (AVG) responds to ARP requests with the different virtual MAC addresses of the healthy gateways (AVFs). This creates the load balancing.

2. B is correct. Virtual MAC addresses are used to distribute the load from clients among healthy routers in the infrastructure.

3. C is correct. HSRP uses the concept of active routers and standby routers.

4. A is correct. The forwarding device in VRRP is termed the virtual router master.

Describe Key Security Concepts

This section covers the following official CCNA 200-301 exam topics:

- Describe modern threats, vulnerabilities, and exploits
- Describe common mitigation techniques and security program elements

It is often tempting to drill right down into the specific technologies that you use to secure network devices, but it is important to take a high-level look at the problems you are striving to guard against. This section examines the modern information technology security landscape. It also speaks in general terms about common mitigation and prevention techniques.

This section covers the following essential terms and components:

- Threats
- Vulnerabilities
- Exploits
- Mitigation
- Security program

Section Pretest

1. You notice many ping sweeps against your perimeter devices. What form of attack is this most likely to be?

   _____

2. What type of attack uses botnets?

   _____

3. What is often the best approach to mitigating the impacts of social engineering?

   _____

4. What are three common types of characters you can require in a password in order to make the password more secure?

   _____

   _____

   _____

Answers

1. Reconnaissance

2. DDoS attack

3. End-user training

4. Mixed case, numerals, and special characters

Describe Modern Threats, Vulnerabilities, and Exploits

Modern networks are undergoing more attacks than ever before, and these attacks are of a wider variety and from more sources than in the past. Today, there are huge variations in the motivations of attackers. At one time, fame, curiosity, and the desire for easy money primarily motivated computer criminals. Today, entire nation-states, with seemingly infinite resources, field attackers for political reasons.

Here is just a partial list of some of the most common threats in cybersecurity today that you should be aware of for the CCNA 200-301 exam:

- **Computer viruses:** Viruses are some of the oldest threats, and they persist today. Viruses are code pieces or entire applications that seek to install on systems to do damage or steal data in some way.

- **Malware:** The industry needed a very broad term to describe the many different types of attacks that are intentionally designed to disrupt, damage, or gain unauthorized access to a computer, server, client, or computer network. *Malware* is the awesome word the industry came up with. Malware is an umbrella term for viruses, ransomware, Trojan horses, adware, and so on.

- **Trojan horse:** With this type of threat, the code that attacks or steals data from a system is hidden behind what appears to be a legitimate application or website. Often, these types of attacks spread via email. An application is sent for you to download, you download the application and install it, and the attacking code is then executed.

- **Adware and spyware:** Adware may sneak onto your computer or trick you into installing it while appearing to be some useful little utility or full program. This software then presents ads in the forms of banners or popup windows. Spyware is even more evil. This software watches and records your actions and is often a critical facet of a larger attack against a system.

- **Worm attack:** In this type of attack, malicious code spreads from system to system in the network. It does this by replicating itself onto another system from the system where it was originally running. Worms can spread and cause damage, such as conducting denial-of-service (DoS) attacks or stealing data.

- **Distributed denial-of-service (DDoS) attack:** DDoS attacks are feared today. Such an attack attempts to make services or entire systems unavailable. DDoS attacks often employ botnets (also called zombie systems) that have no idea they are taking part in the attacks. Over the years, DDoS attacks have succeeded in taking down major portions of the public Internet. Note that parts of the Internet have also often gone offline not as a result of DDoS attacks but as a result of fat fingering or non-malicious mistakes.

■ **Phishing:** Phishing is a popular social engineering attack. In this type of attack, a malicious party sends an email that is carefully constructed to look legitimate. It might pretend to be from a bank and ask the recipient to enter a username and pass-word on a website linked in the email. Of course, this website is also constructed to appear completely legitimate. Spear phishing is a phishing attack that is customized for and targets a particular person.

■ **Rootkit:** A rootkit is a collection of software tools that is installed on a system to ultimately provide the attacker with full administrative control over a device.

■ **SQL injection attack:** This type of attack leverages the fact that most applications and sites are powered by SQL-based databases and do not filter user input. In a SQL injection attack, malicious SQL code is injected into the system through a form, with the goal of extracting data or simply denying service to the system.

■ **On-path attack:** In this type of attack (formerly called a man-in-the-middle attack), a system intercepts communication between devices. The difference between an on-path attack and simple eavesdropping is that the on-path attack also impersonates the end devices in order to terminate encrypted sessions and get access to the data exchanged, whereas an eavesdropper would also have to decrypt the encrypted traf-fic first.

■ **Ransomware:** This is software that encrypts a system's data and then offers decryption keys for a fee.

■ **Data exfiltration:** In this type of attack, a system's data is copied to an external system by an unauthorized attacker or by malware.

Note   This is a partial list of modern attacks. There are currently more variations than this, and new attack types are invented all the time. Any one attack may involve several of the above terms and attack types. For example, malware may be placed onto a network by a phishing attack and spread on the network as a worm. It may then install a rootkit, exfil-trate data, and encrypt all the data in order to ask for ransom. The ransom could include a fee for decryption keys as well as for not publicly releasing the exfiltrated data.

In addition to understanding the modern threats against you and your systems, you should also be aware of several other terms in cybersecurity:

■ **Vulnerability:** A vulnerability is a bug or a misconfiguration of a computer system that could lead to a successful attack. Defending systems today involves efficiently and effectively scanning these systems for vulnerabilities and keeping them patched.

- **Exploit:** An exploit involves software written specifically to utilize a vulnerability to execute an attack. Standalone exploits are often software version specific, which is why cybercriminals have developed exploit kits, which are toolkits that can leverage a whole slew of vulnerabilities, across platforms and operating systems.

- **Zero-day attack:** A zero-day attack is a previously unknown vulnerability, especially one that has previously been exploited to perpetrate an attack. Ethical actors (such as security researchers, ethical hackers, and companies) are constantly combing through networks and source code to identify vulnerabilities, but so are unethical actors. An ethical actor who identifies a new vulnerability usually follows a "responsible disclosure" process so that a patch is developed and deployed quickly, before a public disclosure of the vulnerability. On the other hand, a malicious actor is likely to develop an exploit of the vulnerability identified and use the exploit to attack victims or sell the exploit on the black market. There is no way to completely protect against zero-day attacks.

Topic Quiz

1. What type of attack involves emails that appear to be sent from legitimate sources?

   A. Rootkit

   B. On-path attack

   C. Phishing

   D. DoS attack

2. What set of tools seeks to gain full administrative access to a system?

   A. Rootkit

   B. On-path

   C. Ransomware

   D. Spyware

Topic Quiz Answers

1. **C** is correct. Phishing attacks, which are very common today, involve emails pretending to be from legitimate sources.

2. **A** is correct. A rootkit is used to gain administrative access to a system.

Describe Common Mitigation Techniques and Security Program Elements

Mitigation techniques greatly outnumber the types of attacks that are common—thanks to the move to provide "defense in depth" in a highly secured network environment.

Security mitigation begins at the end user, in the form of specialized training, and continues to the host workstation, the switch or access point the user connects to, and onward to the routers and various devices and media handling the traffic from that point forward.

Cisco devices have inherent network security features, and there are also specialized technologies you can add to a network. Here are some that you should be familiar with for the CCNA 200-301 exam:

- **AAA (authentication, authorization, and accounting):** Authentication deals with the attempt to prove a user's identity, authorization tries to dictate what a user can do, and accounting seeks to carefully track and measure what a user does.

- **ACLs (access control lists):** ACLs provide additional layers of security and can be applied in many different precise locations in a network. ACLs act as firewalls, filtering out unwanted traffic.

- **Security management features:** Cisco devices offer various built-in mechanisms to assist with securing the required management network traffic and helping to keep the devices secure. Mechanisms include SSH, SNMPv3, RADIUS, TACACS+, and many others. Be sure you are aware of versions on your devices. For example, SNMP v2c does not offer nearly the security of SNMP v3.

- **Cryptographic features:** SSH, IPsec, and SSL support are built in to many IOS images.

- **Security appliances and applications:** You can add many different variations of these technologies to the network. Common additions include NGFWs, IPSs, and IDSs. IPSs analyze traffic and identify attacks and drop these packets. IDSs excel at detecting these attacks and notifying administrators.

Another important ingredient in the overall security posture of an organization is the security policy. It is actually quite frightening to think about the number of organizations that don't have such policies today! Common (and important) elements of a security policy for an enterprise include the following:

- End-user security awareness training

- End-user security policy training

- Physical access control

- Patch management

- Audits

- Backups (specifically for protection against ransomware)

Of course, an important component of most security policies and training programs for the enterprise is the security password policy. Such a policy spells out how passwords must be used in the organization as well as password complexity rules. A password security policy typically includes the following:

- A password length requirement

- A password expiration requirement

- A unique password over time requirement

- A complexity requirement (for example, requiring mixed case, special characters, and numerics)

Topic Quiz

1. What secure option exists for remote access to a Cisco device?

    A. Telnet

    B. Syslog

    C. FTP

    D. SSH

2. What version of SNMP is considered the most secure?

    A. SNMPv2c

    B. SNMPv2

    C. SNMPv3

    D. SMTPv4

Topic Quiz Answers

1. **D** is correct. Secure Shell (SSH) is commonly used to securely access a CLI on a network device for remote access.

2. **C** is correct. SNMPv3 adds many robust security options to SNMP, including authentication and encryption options.

Review Questions

1. What attack method locks out a system or even encrypts it and then offers to unlock it in exchange for money?

    A. Worm

    B. On-path

    C. Phishing

    D. Ransomware

2. What is a bug in a system that might be a target of an exploit?

   A. Vulnerability

   B. Rootkit

   C. SSH

   D. IPsec

Answers to Review Questions

1. **D is correct.** Ransomware is an attack that locks a system or encrypts it. The attacker then offers to accept payment to unlock the affected system.

2. **A is correct.** A vulnerability is a weakness or a break in a system that can be exploited.

Describe Remote Access and Site-to-Site VPNs

This section covers the following official CCNA 200-301 exam topics:

- VPN types

- Virtual private network (VPN) basics (including cryptography)

A virtual private network (VPN) is a common component of networking today. Interestingly, a VPN involves hardware, software, and many specific technologies. This section provides a review of these CCNA topics. This appendix does not go deeper than it needs to (as some other texts do) into this vast topic.

This section covers the following essential terms and components:

- VPN

- Remote access VPN

- Site-to-site VPN

- IPsec

- Cryptography

Section Pretest

1. SSL has effectively been replaced by what technology?

   _____

2. What are two major forms of VPNs that an enterprise typically uses?

   _____

   _____

3. What aspect of security means that a sender cannot claim not to have sent something?

_____

4. What aspect of security indicates that data has not been tampered with?

_____

Answers

1. TLS

2. Site-to-site and remote access

3. Nonrepudiation

4. Integrity

VPN Types

Today, most communication over the Internet happens over Transport Layer Security (TLS), which has superseded Secure Sockets Layer (SSL). Typically, a browser process initiates a TLS session with a web server thread, and HTTP traffic is tunneled through a TLS tunnel. This is essentially interprocess communication over a *secure tunnel*. A VPN is a secure tunnel between a device and a network. We call the network to which a VPN facilitates access the *internal network*.

All processes running on a device that is attached to a VPN may communicate securely with other processes residing on the internal network, without the need for each inter-process communication to be secured separately. When a VPN is established, the VPN is indistinguishable from a cable directly attached to a switch in the internal network.

VPNs come in two major varieties: remote access VPNs and site-to-site VPNs.

A remote access VPN connects a single device, such as a laptop or smartphone, to an internal network. This is most useful for remote workers who need access to internal resources through an Internet connection. Another use case for remote access VPNs is the enforcement of a security policy for all communications from and to a remote corporate asset.

Remote access VPNs exist to help remote employees securely connect to remote locations (such as a home office) while they are traveling or "dialing in" from home. Remote access VPNs are hugely popular thanks to robust client software that vendors provide to seamlessly make the connections on behalf of users. Cisco Mobility AnyConnect is a great example of this software.

A site-to-site VPN is a VPN between two *sites*, usually established between two edge devices, one on each site. A site-to-site VPN interconnects two internal networks over an untrusted underlay.

A site-to-site VPN connects many more users and devices simultaneously than does a remote access VPN. For example, you might have a branch office with hundreds of employees who all need access to vital resources stored at the HQ location. In such a scenario, you can establish a site-to-site VPN between the branch office and HQ and permit many different users to connect over this connection. Oftentimes, the VPN end devices are integrated services routers, multilayer switches, or specialized security devices that form the VPN connection and then permit the sharing of this connection by those who need it.

Topic Quiz

1. What type of VPN is typically used between an HQ site and a branch office?

  A. Remote access

  B. Clientless

  C. Plaintext

  D. Site-to-site

2. What is tunneled through a TLS tunnel?

  A. ICMP

  B. NTP

  C. HTTP

  D. HSRP

Topic Quiz Answers

1. D is correct. A site-to-site VPN is often used between locations of an enterprise.

2. C is correct. Typically, HTTP is tunneled through a secure TLS tunnel over the Internet.

Virtual Private Network (VPN) Basics (Including Cryptography)

The services offered by VPNs are similar to those offered by most other secure tunnels:

- Data confidentiality

- Data integrity

- Data origin authentication

- Anti-replay

- Nonrepudiation

VPNs use technologies such as an authentication infrastructure, encryption protocols, and (for remote access VPNs) security policy enforcement tools.

An authentication infrastructure may include RADIUS, LDAP integration, or Cisco Identity Services Engine (ISE). The dominant encryption protocol for VPNs is IPsec, but TLS can be used in some VPN solutions as well (especially those that need to blend in with the rest of the Internet traffic).

Cisco ISE provides a solution for enforcing a security policy on remote access devices. ISE can also be part of an overarching Cisco AnyConnect deployment that enforces a security policy on all devices connected to the internal network, whether over a VPN or otherwise.

Another key concept here is cryptography. This technology continues to evolve and forms the basis for encrypting data so that it cannot be read or successfully processed by anyone who is not intended to be able to work with the data.

Cryptography began very early on in human history. Simple "classic cryptography" approaches engaged in simple techniques such as substituting pieces of data for other pieces of data to make the end result incomprehensible. As you would guess, modern approaches are much more sophisticated.

Remember that, with cryptography, we like to call the password used for encryption (and decryption) the *key*. In symmetric-key algorithms, the same key is used for encryption and decryption. In public key cryptography (also known as asymmetric cryptography), there are two mathematically related, yet different, keys: the public key and the private key. Anyone can have the public key, but if they don't also possess the private key, it is impossible for them to decrypt the data.

VPNs often use the IPsec suite of protocols in their operation. IPsec provides flexibility in the configuration of a VPN. You can choose different protocols for authentication and encryption, which means you can configure the precise level of security required for different environments.

Any text discussing VPNs would be remiss to not mention Dynamic Multipoint VPN (DMVPN), Cisco's crown jewel of site-to-site VPN solutions. DMVPN allows for the rapid provisioning of VPN connections from new remote sites and simplified configuration; it also makes possible an on-demand full mesh of site-so-site IPsec tunnels. DMVPN leverages IPsec, Multipoint Generic Routing Encapsulation (mGRE), and Next Hop Resolution Protocol (NHRP) to achieve all these capabilities.

Topic Quiz

1. Which of the following is not a technology that DMVPN requires?

    A. mGRE

    B. NHRP

    C. IPsec

    D. OSPF

2. What Cisco appliance is used to assist with AAA functions in a network?

    A. ISE

    B. ESA

    C. PIX

    D. ACI

Topic Quiz Answers

1. D is correct. OSPF can certainly function with DMVPN, but it is not required.

2. A is correct. The Cisco Identity Service Engine (ISE) is the replacement device for the Cisco Access Control Server (ACS). These devices are used to promote secure AAA in the organization.

Review Questions

1. What type of key technology is used with public key cryptography?

    A. Single key

    B. Prime factor

    C. Asymmetric

    D. Symmetric

2. What types of keys are used in public key cryptography? (Choose two.)

    A. Private key

    B. Prime key

    C. Public key

    D. Secondary key

Answers to Review Questions

1. C is correct. Public key cryptography uses an asymmetric key approach.

2. A and C are correct. Private and public keys are the primary mechanisms through which asymmetric (public key) cryptography functions.

Automation

This section covers the following official CCNA 200-301 exam topics:

■ Explain how automation impacts network management

■ Controller-based networking and software-defined architectures (overlay, underlay, and fabric)

■ Compare traditional campus device management with Cisco Catalyst Center–enabled device management

One of the most exciting and compelling areas in modern networking today is automation. Automation involves creating tasks that can perform jobs for us on the network and free us from repetitive administration. Automated tasks can often then be orchestrated to create almost completely autonomous systems.

This section covers the following essential terms and components:

■ Automation

■ Controller-based networking

■ SDN

■ Overlay

■ Underlay

■ Fabric

■ Cisco Catalyst Center

Section Pretest

1. What is the term for a system that coordinates the application of many different automated tasks?

   _____

2. Name at least three advantages presented by the use of automation.

   _____

   _____

   _____

3. What are two approaches to SDN that vary in terms of where the intelligence about the network is stored?

   _____

   _____

4. What is an example of an overlay technology in SDN?

_____

5. What is a modern Cisco management tool that is cloud based, acts as a single pane of glass, and offers automation capabilities that include machine learning for the management of Cisco enterprise infrastructure?

_____

6. What type of networking does Cisco Catalyst Center try to help you achieve? (_Hint:_ _____-based networking)

_____

Answers

1. Orchestration

2. Increased throughput and/or productivity

Improved quality

Improved consistency of processes or products

Increased consistency of output

Reduced labor costs

Reduced time to complete tasks

Tasks completed with a higher degree of accuracy

3. Controller-based versus controller-less

4. VXLAN

5. Cisco Catalyst Center

6. Intent-based networking

Explain How Automation Impacts Network Management

Network management is being revolutionized thanks to automation. As you implement more and more automation for your everyday tasks, you get more time to dedicate to evolving and improving the network. These are the major benefits of automation:

- Increased throughput and/or productivity

- Improved quality

- Improved consistency of processes or products

- Increased consistency of output

- Reduced human labor costs

- Reduced time to complete tasks

- Tasks completed with a higher degree of accuracy

Things get really exciting in this area with *orchestration*, in which a system coordinates many different automated tasks. Orchestration is being used more and more in technology systems today. For example, in AWS a powerful tool called CloudFormation can automate the construction of entire IaaS infrastructures.

Cisco Systems has created a really amazing technology that helps with automation in the network management space: Cisco Catalyst Center (formerly named Cisco DNA Center). You'll learn more about Cisco Catalyst Center later in this appendix.

Topic Quiz

1. Which of the following is not a valid benefit of automation?

    A. Sacrifice of accuracy for speed

    B. Reduced labor costs

    C. Reduced time required for tasks to complete

    D. Increased consistency

2. What Cisco network management product helps to bring automation into your management workflows?

    A. Cisco Configuration Professional

    B. CiscoWorks

    C. Catalyst Center

    D. Prime

Topic Quiz Answers

1. A is correct. There tends to be no sacrifice of accuracy for speed. In fact, automation should help you experience an increase in accuracy as well as an increase in the speed at which you can enact configurations.

2. C is correct. The Cisco Catalyst Center product has a definite focus in the area of network automation. Remember that it also serves as a powerful design and monitoring tool, among other potential functions.

Controller-Based Networking and Software-Defined Architectures (Overlay, Underlay, and Fabric)

Software-defined networking (SDN) is all the rage in networking today. Everyone wants to implement SDN solutions as quickly as possible to make networks more flexible and to have them respond to new applications and services with ease.

Many students struggle with just what SDN is because many definitions are written by the marketing teams of companies that are making their technologies sound as complex as humanly possible. Simply put, software-defined networking involves controlling network devices by using centralized workstations that are pushing the appropriate configuration commands down to the devices. For example, you might sit in front of Cisco Catalyst Center and graphically configure new VLANs and then ensure that those VLANs appear on the network devices you selected. Does this sound like an approach you have used before? It sure does. In fact, many elements of SDN have been with us for a very long time in networking. Granted, some of the newer aspects of SDN are quite exciting. For example, there is now a standardization that is taking place on the use of RESTful APIs that is making it easier than ever before to automate and even orchestrate many of the tasks that had to be performed manually in the past.

One of the biggest decisions your IT team needs to make early in the process of moving to SDN is whether to take a controller-based approach to SDN or implement a controller-less design.

Cisco Systems is big on controller-based SDN. In Cisco's SDN solution, Application Centric Infrastructure (ACI), a centralized (redundant) controller is the brains of the operation. It provides the instructions to the nodes it manages so that they can automatically provision the required network resources. Other SDN products offered by Cisco include the Cisco Open SDN Controller and the Cisco APIC Enterprise Module (APIC-EM).

An SDN controller maintains a complete picture of the network at all times. It knows the state information for all devices all the time.

While the Cisco ACI solution works very well if implemented properly, it does present some challenges. Enter controller-less SDN, which marketing teams often term "next-generation SDN." With this approach, there is a shared management plane between the devices, and this information is not centrally stored, as it is in a controller-based design.

With Cisco's controller-based SDN, ACI, what is the glue that allows the SDN architecture to function so well? It is a communication process between the control and data planes that involves the use of application programming interfaces (APIs).

A classic example of a southbound API in the SDN world is OpenFlow. The OpenFlow specification defines both a protocol between the control and data planes and an API by which the control plane can invoke the OpenFlow protocol.

An API is implemented by writing a function call in a program. This provides the linkage to the required subroutine for execution. An open or standardized API can ensure the portability of the application code and the vendor independence of the called service.

SDN controllers can be implemented directly on a server or on a virtual server. OpenFlow or some other open API is used to control the switches in the data plane. In addition, controllers use information about capacity and demand obtained from the networking equipment through which the traffic flows.

SDN controllers also expose northbound APIs. Developers and their network engineers can therefore deploy a wide range of off-the-shelf and custom-built network applications. Obviously, many of these applications were not possible before SDN.

As of yet, there is no standardized northbound API, nor is there consensus on an open northbound API or the capabilities that SDN controllers should expose through such an API. A vendor may offer a representational state transfer (REST)–based API to provide a programmable interface to its SDN controller.

Also envisioned but not yet defined are horizontal APIs (eastbound/westbound), which would enable communication and cooperation among groups or federations of controllers to synchronize state for high availability.

At the application plane are a variety of applications that interact with SDN controllers. An SDN application may use an abstract view of the network for its decision-making goals. Such programs convey their network requirements and desired network behavior to the SDN controller via a northbound API. Examples of applications of these controllers are for energy-efficient networking, security monitoring, access control, and network management.

The architectures found with SDN in today's networks include technologies like these:

- **Overlay:** These networks allow simple virtualization of the underlying physical network. VXLAN is an example of an SDN overlay network. It permits the creation of millions of virtual networks.

- **Underlay (fabric):** Cisco and other vendors are creating very high-speed physically connected networking components to build an underlay (often termed the network fabric). Cisco ACI offers the advantage of tight integration of overlay technologies and the underlay fabric.

Topic Quiz

1. Where does a northbound API exist in an SDN network?

   A. Between the controller and the network management applications

   B. Between the controller and the network devices being managed

   C. Between the controller and the public cloud

   D. Between the controller and the access layer

2. What is a common API category for the northbound protocols?

   A. Python

   B. ASCI

   C. REST

   D. Ruby

Topic Quiz Answers

1. A is correct. The northbound APIs exist between the controller and the software managing the network.

2. C is correct. A vendor may offer a RESTful API to provide a programmable interface to its SDN controller. Note that REST is basically a method of passing calls to software. These calls are encapsulated within an HTTPS request. The data passed within a RESTful call is defined within the API.

Compare Traditional Campus Device Management with Cisco Catalyst Center–Enabled Device Management

Automation can revolutionize network management and development, so it is no surprise that a management product from Cisco Systems, Cisco Catalyst Center, emphasizes automation.

What separates Cisco Catalyst Center from other network management solutions that Cisco has given us in the past? Cisco Catalyst Center strives to provide us with a concept called *intent-based networking*. What does this mean? It means that the solution does the following:

■ Cisco Catalyst Center accomplishes translation and validation. For example, you provide high-level commands that you want accomplished, and the solution from Cisco translates these commands into the software instructions required by the various systems.

■ Cisco Catalyst Center implements the changes you require in the network by using (surprise, surprise) automation.

■ Cisco Catalyst Center accomplishes much of what it can do for you because it is constantly aware of device state; the system tirelessly and continuously gathers information from the systems it manages so that it is always up to date in its awareness of the state of your systems.

■ Cisco Catalyst Center calls on machine learning (ML) to ensure that it is not only state aware but can take actions in an automated fashion if you must maintain devices in a certain state.

As you might guess, there are times when Cisco Catalyst Center cannot achieve these lofty goals alone. Fortunately, it can easily integrate with many third-party tools to permit a wider variety of supported devices and higher levels of intelligence and automation.

As this book went to press, Cisco Catalyst Center included the following main features:

- **Management:** Catalyst Center provides granular views of all major networking components and technologies, full life cycle management features, multidomain integration, and an open and extensible framework.

- **Automation:** Devices are discovered automatically, and policy can be created and deployed with point-and-click and drag-and-drop. In addition, Catalyst Center enables zero-touch device deployment and life cycle management, as well as automated QoS.

- **AI/ML analytics:** Everything functions as a sensor, and Catalyst Center offers context-guided analytics and local and cloud-based AI analytics.

- **Security:** Catalyst Center enables group-based policy, third-party policy servers, AI analytics, and secure segmentation.

Topic Quiz

1. How can you discover devices with Cisco Catalyst Center?

   A. Using ping sweeps

   B. Using static import

   C. Using DHCP snooping

   D. Automatically

2. What very modern tool is used to assist in network analytics?

   A. SNMPv2c

   B. AI

   C. SNMPv3

   D. Syslog

Topic Quiz Answers

1. D is correct. Cisco Catalyst Center permits the dynamic discovery of managed devices.

2. B is correct. AI, specifically machine learning (ML), is used to assist with analytics against the massive amount of information collected by Cisco Catalyst Center.

Review Questions

1. Which of these statements is false regarding the Cisco ACI solution?

   A. ACI controls the network and uses state awareness with a controlled device.

   B. ACI offers robust support for a wide range of APIs.

   C. ACI uses a high-speed fabric underlay.

   D. ACI is an example of controller-less SDN.

2. VXLAN is an example of what type of SDN technology?

   A. Fabric

   B. Underlay

   C. Overlay

   D. API

Answers to Review Questions

1. D is correct. Cisco ACI uses a controller-based approach to SDN.

2. C is correct. VXLAN technology permits the virtualization of the underlying physical network. VXLAN is used to build an overlay architecture.

Programmability

This section covers the following official CCNA 200-301 exam topics:

- Describe characteristics of REST-based APIs (CRUD, HTTP verbs, and data encoding)

- Explain AI (generative and predictive) and machine learning in network operations

- Recognize the capabilities of the configuration management mechanisms such as Ansible and Terraform

- Interpret JSON-encoded data

No, Cisco does not expect you to leave the CCNA experience a well-versed programmer. Cisco does, however, expect you to have a good understanding of key principles related to programmability. This appendix covers those key principles.

This section covers the following essential terms and components:

- REST

- API

- CRUD

- HTTP verbs
- Data encoding
- AI
- Terraform
- Ansible
- JSON

Section Pretest

1. What does CRUD stand for?

_____

2. What HTTP request method can perform the U in CRUD?

_____

3. Name two popular configuration tools that help automate modern server infrastructures.

_____

_____

4. Of the tools that you just listed, which tool does not ever feature the use of agent software on the managed node?

_____

5. JSON is very similar to what other encoded data format?

_____

6. What symbol does JSON code begin and end with?

_____

Answers

1. Create, Read, Update, Delete

2. PUT

3. Ansible and Terraform

4. Ansible

5. XML

6. A curly brace

Describe Characteristics of REST-Based APIs (CRUD, HTTP Verbs, and Data Encoding)

Application programming interfaces (APIs) permit software to communicate with other software components, as well as with users and engineers in charge of maintaining the software. Today, in our cloud-dominated world, APIs that follow a style called representational state transfer (REST) are most popular. As their name implies, RESTful APIs use REST conventions that follow a particular set of software rules.

RESTful APIs often use HTTP, and this makes them a great choice for the networking and cloud technologies that often leverage HTTP. Specifically, REST and HTTP share three very important aspects that enable them to work well together:

■ Both follow a client/server model

■ Both follow a stateless model

■ Both indicate whether an object is cacheable or not

Another important reason that REST and HTTP work so well together is that HTTP uses verbs in its operations (request methods) that nicely mirror the CRUD operations performed with APIs in software. CRUD stands for the following actions:

■ Create

■ Read

■ Update

■ Delete

Just look at how nicely the verbs used by HTTP for its actions mirror these CRUD requirements:

■ Create: POST

■ Read: GET

■ Update: PUT

■ Delete: DELETE

In addition to using HTTP verbs, you use URIs to indicate what resource to act on. For example, http://api.ciscospark.com/v1/rooms creates an HTTP GET request for the /v1/rooms resource at the server api.ciscospark.com.

Here is an example of a REST API request that uses HTTP and AWS S3 in the cloud:

http://s3-eu-west-1.amazonaws.com/ajs/me.jpg

This example performs the HTTP GET against an S3 storage bucket named ajs and asks for the resource (JPG) named me.jpg. Notice how incredibly simple HTTP and the REST API make this access.

Note that REST defines the standard set of operations that a RESTful API has to offer as access methods. The payload of the API calls is defined per service and/or (in the case of networking devices) per device. For example, the RESTful API of IOS XE uses JSON to encode its payload (as documented at https://www.cisco.com/c/en/us/td/docs/routers/csr1000/software/restapi/restapi/RESTAPIglobal.html).

Topic Quiz

1. What does the URI in a REST API call indicate?

A. The latency acceptable for the response

B. The security protocol for authentication

C. The resource being acted upon

D. The protocol variant used

2. Which of the following is not a valid similarity between REST APIs and HTTP?

A. Both indicate whether a resource can be cached

B. Both are stateless approaches

C. Both are client/server models

D. Both feature connectionless communications

Topic Quiz Answers

1. C is correct. You use the URI information to indicate what resource the API call impacts.

2. D is correct. HTTP relies on TCP, which is a connection-oriented protocol.

Explain AI (Generative and Predictive) and Machine Learning in Network Operations

Artificial intelligence (AI), including generative and predictive models, alongside machine learning (ML), is increasingly being integrated into network operations to enhance efficiency, security, and performance. Let's look at how they play their roles.

Generative AI models, such as generative adversarial networks (GANs) and variational autoencoders (VAEs), are used in network operations to simulate and generate data that mirrors real-world network conditions. This capability is crucial for scenarios like network planning and simulation, where accurate modeling of network traffic, user behavior, and potential failure modes are required, without disruption to the actual network. For example, generative AI can create synthetic network traffic patterns to test and optimize network configurations or develop realistic cybersecurity scenarios to train systems and personnel in identifying and responding to potential threats. The ability to generate realistic data allows network operators to preemptively address issues and refine their networks in a controlled environment, leading to more robust and resilient network infrastructures.

Predictive AI focuses on anticipating future network conditions and behaviors by analyzing historical and real-time data. Techniques such as time series forecasting, anomaly detection, and predictive maintenance are used to monitor network performance and health. For instance, predictive AI can analyze trends in network traffic to forecast demand spikes and optimize resource allocation to prevent congestion. It can also predict potential equipment failures by identifying patterns and anomalies in sensor data, allowing for proactive maintenance and reducing downtime. In cybersecurity, predictive AI models can detect unusual activity that may indicate a security breach, enabling swift intervention before any significant damage occurs. By predicting and mitigating issues before they impact the network, predictive AI enhances the overall reliability and efficiency of network operations.

Machine learning, a subset of AI, involves algorithms that learn from data to make informed decisions and improve network operations over time. ML can be used for tasks such as dynamic routing, where algorithms learn the most efficient paths for data packets based on current network conditions and past performance, leading to improved latency and bandwidth utilization. In security, ML algorithms can analyze vast amounts of network traffic data to identify and respond to threats more quickly than traditional methods. ML is also critical for network management and automation, where it can optimize configurations, balance loads, and even predict and adjust to user behavior patterns in real time. This ability to adapt and optimize based on learned insights helps ensure that network operations are continuously aligned with evolving demands and challenges.

Topic Quiz

1. What type of AI can be instrumental in creating realistic synthetic traffic for testing your network equipment?

A. Ruby

B. Terraform

C. Predictive

D. Generative

2. What type of AI can be instrumental in anticipating future network conditions?

A. Ansible

B. Ruby

C. Predictive

D. Generative

Topic Quiz Answers

1. D is correct. Generative AI can be very useful in creating realistic synthetic traffic for testing.

2. C is correct. Predictive AI can be very useful for anticipating future network conditions.

Recognize the Capabilities of the Configuration Management Mechanisms of Ansible and Terraform

The creation of more virtualization technologies and the cloud fostered the development of new technology in the area of configuration control and management. Two pioneering companies (and software packages) rose to the top in this area: Ansible and Terraform.

Ansible, which is installed on a Linux system, can configure and manage devices without ever requiring that an "agent" software package be installed on the systems it is controlling. This is a great advantage because installing agent software on all the systems you want to control can be a huge undertaking.

How does the Ansible system control a node if there is no agent software installed on that system? It uses an SSH connection to pass the required instructions.

Ansible is run using simple components (such as text files) that control its behavior and abilities. These are the main components:

- **Inventory:** A list of nodes that Ansible is set to manage
- **Modules:** The units of code that Ansible executes
- **Tasks:** The units of action in Ansible
- **Playbooks:** Ordered lists of tasks that permit the future execution of the sequence

Ansible relies heavily on Python. The increase in popularity of Python is another strong selling point for those considering the various automation tools.

Terraform is an open-source infrastructure as code (IaC) tool developed by HashiCorp that is designed to enable users to define and provision infrastructure resources across a wide range of cloud providers and on-premises environments in a declarative configuration language. At its core, Terraform allows users to write configuration files that describe the desired state of their infrastructure, which it then translates into API calls to create, manage, and modify resources like virtual machines, storage, and networking components. This approach promotes consistency and repeatability, ensuring that infrastructure can be easily replicated and maintained across different environments, such as development, staging, and production.

One of Terraform's key strengths is its ability to work across multiple cloud platforms, including AWS, Azure, Google Cloud Platform, and many others, as well as on-premises systems like VMware and OpenStack. This multi-cloud support is facilitated through a system of providers that enable Terraform to interface with various APIs and services, allowing for a unified approach to infrastructure management regardless of the underlying technology stack. Users can define resources from different providers within a single configuration, making Terraform an excellent choice for hybrid and multi-cloud deployments where consistency and integration are critical.

Terraform also emphasizes modularity and reusability through its support for modules, which are reusable packages of Terraform configurations that can be shared and versioned. Modules enable organizations to create standardized templates for common infrastructure components, promoting best practices and reducing the time needed to deploy and manage complex environments. In addition, Terraform's state management feature keeps track of the current state of the infrastructure, allowing it to detect changes and apply updates in a controlled manner. This stateful approach ensures that changes are predictable and auditable, helping teams maintain control over their infrastructure and minimizing the risk of configuration drift or unintended disruptions.

Topic Quiz

1. What language is instrumental for Ansible?

   A. Ruby

   B. C#

   C. Java

   D. Python

2. What is the term used with Ansible for the text file that lists the nodes that Ansible can manage?

   A. Runbook

   B. Playbook

   C. Recipe

   D. Inventory

Topic Quiz Answers

   1. D is correct. Python is the key language used in the development of Ansible.

   2. D is correct. Ansible uses an inventory file to list the nodes that are managed by the software.

Interpret JSON-Encoded Data

JavaScript Object Notation (JSON) is a very common data format today that has many potential uses. From feeding commands to Cisco devices to creating entire infrastructures in the cloud, JSON is versatile and very easy for humans to read and work with.

Note   JSON is often compared to XML. This is a very valid comparison. However, JSON script is much, much easier to read than XML.

JSON has many potential uses. Here are a few examples:

- It is used with many web technologies like public cloud

- It can be used to provide the details needed to construct a cloud infrastructure through code

- It can provide the details needed to configure data for local projects

- It can be used to power automation software

- It can be used with Ansible for the configuration of devices

As you examine this list, remember that JSON is not the executable code that makes the magic happen. It is just a standardized data format for feeding the required data into an application.

Note   JSON is often the data format used when extracting data from an application.

Examine this JSON and make some observations about it:

```
{
  "response": [
    {
      "id": "d4b33d28-04dd-4733-a6de-8877ec26c196",
      "tag": "campus",
      "networkDeviceId": "e5f93514-3ae5-4109-8b52-b9fa876e1eae",
      "attributeInfo": {}
    },
    {
      "id": "d4b33d28-04dd-4733-a6de-8877ec26c196",
      "tag": "campus",
      "networkDeviceId": "da733ffb-e34b-4733-bd85-b615fb7e61f3",
      "attributeInfo": {}
    },
    {
```

```
      "id": "d4b33d28-04dd-4733-a6de-8877ec26c196",
      "tag": "campus",
      "networkDeviceId": "f8c3fc68-cd26-4576-bcec-51f9b578f71e",
      "attributeInfo": {}
    }
  ],
  "version": "0.0"
}
```

Notice that this JSON code begins and ends with the curly braces, which denote a JSON object. Notice that the JSON code also consists of simple key/value pairs (for example, the key version and the value 0.0). Notice that values can be objects, strings, numbers, Boolean values, and more.

Keep in mind that indentation in JSON is not required, but it is strongly encouraged since it makes the data much more human readable.

I think it is worth repeating one more time for emphasis: JSON does not contain executable code. It is a powerful format for data that we tend to move into and out of applications.

Topic Quiz

1. What does a JSON object consist of?

   A. Arrays

   B. Subobjects

   C. If-Then statements

   D. Key/value pairs

2. Which statement about JSON is false?

   A. JSON does not require the use of indenting.

   B. JSON consists of groupings of executable code.

   C. JSON is often used to provide the required data for cloud infrastructure construction.

   D. JSON is considered more human readable than XML.

Topic Quiz Answers

1. D is correct. A JSON object consists of key/value pairs.

2. B is correct. JSON does not consist of executable code.

Review Questions

1. What type of APIs are often used with networking and cloud technologies?

   A. JSON-RPC

   B. XML-RPC

   C. REST

   D. SOAP

2. Which is not a term in the acronym CRUD?

   A. Request

   B. Create

   C. Update

   D. Delete

3. What technology is used to permit Ansible to connect to managed nodes for configuration purposes?

   A. SSH

   B. TFTP

   C. IPsec

   D. HTTP

4. What is the name for an ordered list of tasks in Ansible?

   A. Cookbook

   B. Playbook

   C. Story

   D. Task list

5. What character is used to separate a key from its value in JSON?

   A. :

   B. ,

   C. [

   D. {

Answers to Review Questions

1. **C** is correct. REST APIs work very well with HTTP and therefore are often used with networking and cloud technologies.

2. **A** is correct. The R in CRUD stands for Read, not Request.

3. **A** is correct. Ansible uses SSH to connect to and configure managed nodes in a secure fashion.

4. **B** is correct. Ansible uses playbooks in order to run many automation tasks together.

5. **A** is correct. A colon (:) separates the key from the value in a key/value pair in the JSON format.

Practice Exams

Are you ready to assess your preparedness for the CCNA 200-301 exam? Practice Exam 1 and Practice Exam 2 are here to help.

As you take these practice exams, consider the following test-taking tips:

- **Read each question twice if necessary:** Be sure to read each question carefully so that you fully understand it. You may need to read some questions twice.

- **Read the answers starting from the bottom:** When you read the answers from the bottom, you force yourself to carefully read each answer. If you read the answers from the top, you might find yourself quickly selecting an answer that looks right and skipping over the other answers. This is dangerous as there might be a better answer later in the options.

- **Time yourself:** The CCNA 200-301 exam is a 90-minute exam. Time yourself during each practice exam to make sure you stay within this time limit.

- **If you do not know the answer to a question, make a note of it:** Go back and review any trouble areas later. Be sure that you are fully comprehending each topic area, not just looking up the answers to individual questions. If you are unsure about one aspect of a topic, chances are you might be unsure about other areas related to that same topic.

- **Prepare mentally to take a test:** To properly assess yourself, take each practice exam as you would take the real exam: Find a quiet place without any distractions so that you can focus on each question and equip yourself with scratch paper and a pen or pencil. For the actual exam, you will be allowed no other tools (such as calculators), so you shouldn't use additional tools for the practice exams either.

- **If you cannot determine the correct answer(s), begin by eliminating incorrect answer(s):** If there are four options, and you know that three are absolutely wrong, the fourth option has to be the correct one.

- **Consider taking each of these practice exams multiple times until you get perfect scores:** Consistently scoring high on these practice exams is a good indication that you're ready to take the actual exam.

- **Pay close attention to the Answer Key:** The answers to the practice exam questions include explanations, which often bring up related important information. Even if you answered a question correctly, be sure to read the explanation in the Answer Key.

- **Use the online materials:** There are even more practice exams waiting for you on the Pearson Test Prep software that is available to you either online or as an offline Windows application. Be sure to use those materials as well.

- **Don't despair:** Do not be overly upset if you do not score well on your first attempt at the practice exam. It only means that you need to continue studying. Be glad that you can spot your weak areas now and not after getting into the actual exam. Go back through and review your problem areas now to ensure that you are ready!

Congratulations on your pursuit of this valued IT certification!

Practice Exam 1

1. What transport layer protocol features the use of sequencing and synchronization methods?

    A. ICMP

    B. TCP

    C. UDP

    D. ARP

2. Examine the figure. If devices 1, 2, and 3 are all Cisco Layer 2 switches in their default configurations, how many collision domains exist in this network?

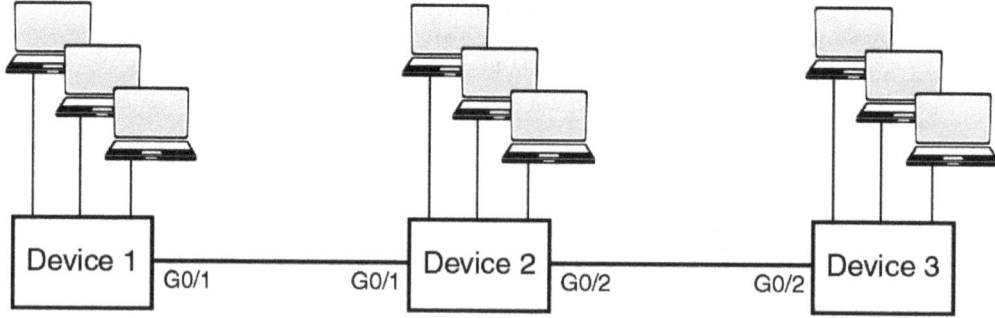

3. You have configured your gi0/1 Cisco switch port as follows:

```
interface gi0/1
switchport mode accesss
witchport port-security
```

Which of the following statements is true?

A. The default violation mode is `Restrict`.

B. The mode must be `Trunk` for port security to be used.

C. The default number of dynamic MAC addresses is one.

D. This configuration prevents the logging of port security violations.

E. The violation mode in use here is `Protect`.

4. What protocol is used with an Integrated Services approach to QoS?

A. ICMP

B. VTP

C. SPAN

D. NTP

E. RSVP

5. What is the default administrative distance for OSPF?

A. 20

B. 120

C. 110

D. 200

E. 90

6. What is the IPv4 address range 224.0.0.0 to 239.255.255.255 used for?

A. To send a packet to all systems

B. To send a packet to a group of systems

C. To send a packet to a single specific system

D. To send multiple packets to only a single specific system

7. Which RF band is used with 802.11ac?

A. 2.4 GHz

B. 5 GHz

C. Both 2.4 GHz and 5 GHz

D. 7 GHz

8. What is the privilege level for the user in the command `username johns secret cisco123`?

    A. 0

    B. 1

    C. 15

    D. 8

9. What character is used to signify an object in JSON?

    A. Square bracket

    B. Curly brace

    C. Colon

    D. Semicolon

10. Examine the figure. What is the Layer 2 destination address?

```
Ethernet II, Src: ca:00:1a:a4:00:1c (ca:00:1a:a4:00:1c), Dst: IntelCor_12:34:56 (00:1b:77:12:34:56)
  Destination: IntelCor_12:34:56 (00:1b:77:12:34:56)
  Source: ca:00:1a:a4:00:1c (ca:00:1a:a4:00:1c)
  Type: IP (0x0800)
Internet Protocol Version 4, Src: 198.133.219.25 (198.133.219.25), Dst: 10.0.0.2 (10.0.0.2)
Transmission Control Protocol, Src Port: http (80), Dst Port: d-cinema-rrp (1173), Seq: 0, Ack: 1, Len: 0
```

11. Examine the code shown here. What format is in use?

```
"templateConfig":{
              "vInfraPolicy":"cloud82",
              "networks":[
                    {
                        "networkName":"lan0",
                        "networkType":1000,
                        "vlanIDPool":"100-199",
                        "networkPool":1000,
                        "ipSubnetPool":1000,
                        "networkIP":"10.10.10.0",
                        "networkMask":"255.255.255.0",
                        "gatewayIP":"10.10.10.1"
                    },
```

    A. XML

    B. YAML

    C. JSON

    D. PBF

12. What technology provides multiple default gateways in a redundant manner and automates load sharing?

    A. FHRP

    B. HSRP

    C. VRRP

    D. GLBP

13. Which of the following features is designed to prevent a switch port from becoming a root port in the Spanning Tree Protocol (STP) by placing it into a "root-inconsistent" state if a superior BPDU is received?

    A. Loop Guard

    B. BPDU Guard

    C. BPDU Filtering

    D. Root Guard

14. How is a playbook expressed in Ansible?

    A. YAML

    B. XML

    C. JSON

    D. HTML5

15. Create an extended ACE that permits Telnet traffic from a Telnet server on the network 10.10.10.0/24, going to a host on network 192.168.1.0/24. Use ACL 101.

    _____

16. What keyword enables the use of PAT in a NAT configuration?

    A. `load`

    B. `ports`

    C. `overload`

    D. `pool`

17. How many syslog levels are there with Cisco equipment?

    A. 8

    B. 6

    C. 4

    D. 16

18. What wireless security standard replaces PSK with SAE?

   A. WPA3

   B. AES

   C. TKIP

   D. WPA2

19. Examine the topology shown here. How many collision domains exist between the PC and Router 1?

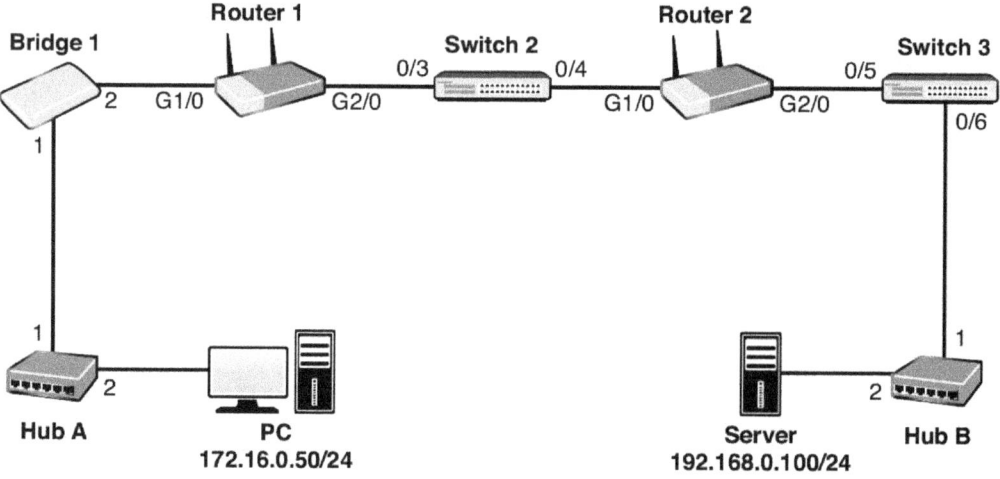

   A. 0

   B. 1

   C. 2

   D. 3

20. Which of the following provides a secure method to transfer files in a Cisco network?

   A. TFTP

   B. FTP

   C. Telnet

   D. SCP

21. Examine the topology shown in the figure. The PC has sent a ping request to the server. Which devices in the network operate only at the physical layer of the OSI reference model? (Choose two.)

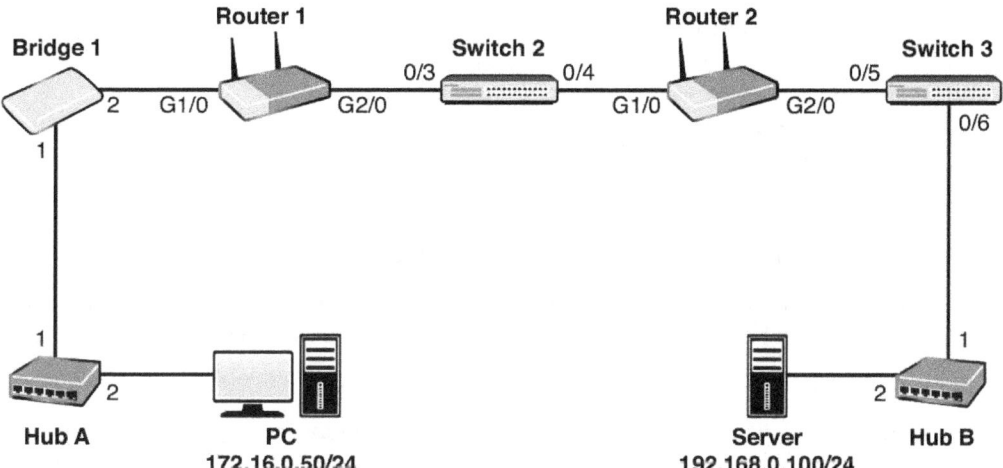

A. Ethernet cabling

B. Bridge 1

C. Router 2

D. Hub A

E. Switch 3

F. PC network interface card

22. Which of the following are true on a typical Cisco access layer switch? (Choose two.)

A. It can have IP routing enabled.

B. It can have an IP address configured for management.

C. It can be used for NAT or PAT.

D. A default gateway allows the switch to access remote networks.

E. Ports default to no switchport mode.

23. What feature does DAI rely on?

A. ACLs

B. DHCP snooping

C. QoS DiffServ

D. NBAR

E. OSPF

24. Examine the switch configuration shown. What problem exists with this configuration?

```
SW1
configure terminal
interface fa0/10
switchport trunk encapsulation isl
switchport mode trunk
switchport port-security
switchport port-security max 2
no shutdown
```

   A. Port security can support only a single secure MAC address.

   B. Port security can be used on trunks (depending on the switch), but it is likely that there will be many more than two learned MAC addresses on that port.

   C. Port security can only be used with 802.1Q trunks.

   D. A violation mode for port security must be selected.

25. Which of the following is not an HTTP method used with REST APIs?

   A. PUT

   B. POST

   C. SEND

   D. GET

   E. DELETE

26. Examine the topology shown in the figure. If OSPF, EIGRP, and RIPv2 were all enabled on each interface on each router, which routing protocol would R4 use to determine the best route to 10.77.67.0/24?

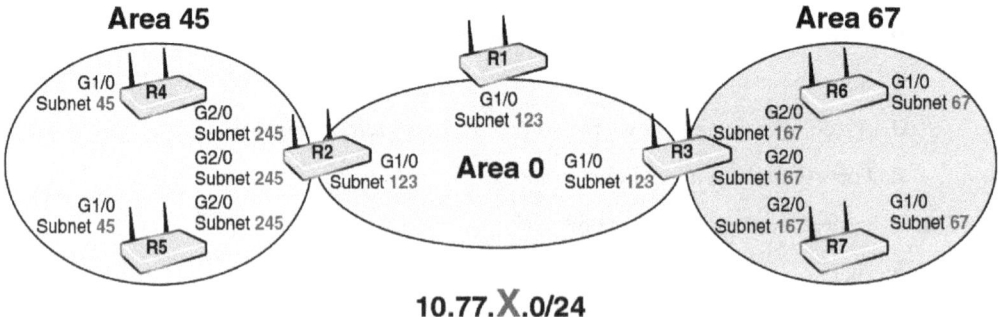

   A. EIGRP because its metric considers bandwidth and delay

   B. OSPF because its cost is derived from bandwidth and delay

C. OSPF because it is an advanced distance-vector routing protocol

D. EIGRP because of administrative distance

27. You decided to reduce the size of your existing Layer 2 broadcast domains by creating new VLANs. What network device that forwards packets between those VLANs would be operating (at a minimum), and at which OSI layer?

A. A switch at Layer 1

B. A switch at Layer 2

C. A router at Layer 2

D. A router at Layer 3

28. Examine the topology shown in the figure. Provide the Router 2 configuration for OSPFv2 to enable OSPF area 0 for process 100 on G2/0. The G2/0 IP address is 192.168.0.1/24. Do not use the interface-level OSPF command and ensure that OSPF runs on no other interface.

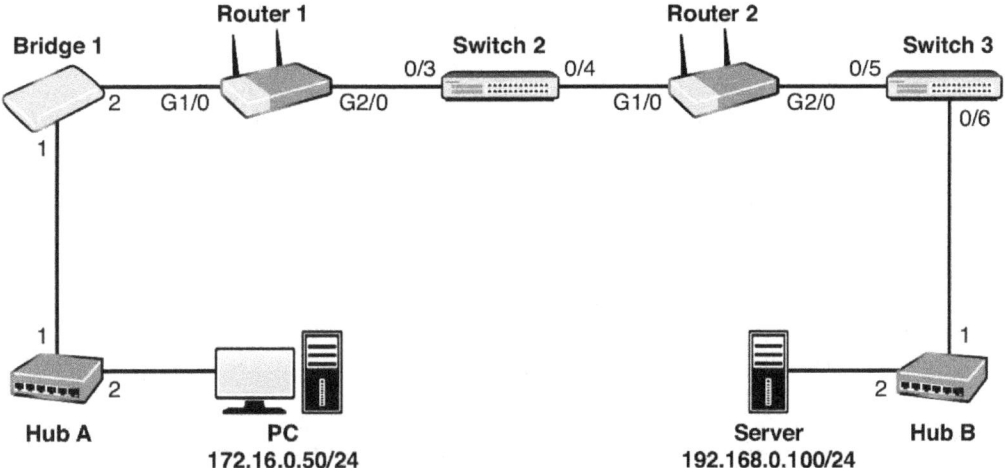

29. Which of the following statements regarding ICMP is correct?

A. ICMP functions at the network layer of the OSI model.

B. ICMP relies on TCP for reliable packet delivery.

C. ICMP relies on UDP for efficient packet delivery.

D. ICMP functions at the session layer of the OSI model.

30. What device can use a dual-band approach and 802.11 standards for connecting end users to the network?

A. Firewall

B. WLC

C. AP

D. Router

31. Which of the following best describes the primary purpose of Terraform?

A. To automate the monitoring of network traffic

B. To automate the provisioning and configuration of cloud infrastructures

C. To automate the testing of software applications

D. To automate the creation of CI and CD pipelines

32. What is the last usable host address, given the IP address and subnet mask 172.16.10.101 with 255.255.224.0?

_____

33. What command produced the following output?

```
MK5 unit 0, NIM slot 1, NIM type code 7, NIM version 1
  idb = 0x6150, driver structure at 0x34A878, regaddr = 0x8100300
IB at 0x6045500: mode=0x0108, local_addr=0, remote_addr=0
N1=1524, N2=1, scaler=100, T1=1000, T3=2000, TP=1
buffer size 1524
DTE V.35 serial cable attached
RX ring with 32 entries at 0x45560 : RLEN=5, Rxhead 0
  00 pak=0x6044D78 ds=0x6044ED4 status=80 max_size=1524 pak_size=0
```

_____

34. What is a potential underlay protocol for a VXLAN EVPN fabric?

A. VTP

B. eBGP

C. RIP

D. EIGRP

35. Which of the following addresses is a private-use-only address?

A. 12.43.56.120

B. 177.12.34.19

C. 201.92.34.100

D. 10.123.23.104

36. What must be in place before you can route other devices' IPv6 traffic through a Cisco router?

   A. The command `dual-stack routing`

   B. A loopback 0 interface with an IPv4 address assigned

   C. IPv4 interfaces

   D. The `ipv6 unicast-routing` global configuration command

37. Which command displays a quick view of OSPF neighbor status?

   A. `show ip ospf neighbor`

   B. `show ospf peers`

   C. `show ip ospf routers`

   D. `show ospf peers`

38. What are two reasons a duplex mismatch can be difficult to find? (Choose two.)

   A. Users are presented with an error message that varies by operating system.

   B. Connectivity is typically intermittent.

   C. Users cannot communicate on the network at all.

   D. Connectivity might be slow.

39. What command would you use on a Cisco Layer 2 switch to verify errors regarding sending or receiving frames?

   A. `show controllers`

   B. `show interface`

   C. `show collisions`

   D. `show version`

40. A Cisco switch is currently in VTP Client mode. You issue the `vlan 100` command in global configuration mode to create a new VLAN. What is the result?

   A. The switch produces an error message.

   B. The switch sends VLAN 100 configuration information to the VTP server.

   C. The switch reverts to Transparent mode.

   D. The switch configures the VLAN but on the local device only.

41. What traditional 802.1D STP port state does not exist in 802.1w RSTP?

   A. Discarding

   B. Listening

C. Learning

D. Forwarding

42. What global configuration command allows you to disable CDP on an entire Cisco switch?

    A. `no cdp`

    B. `no cdp enable`

    C. `no cdp run`

    D. `no cdp search`

43. When you enable port security for a switch port, what is the default violation mode?

    A. `Restrict`

    B. `Shutdown`

    C. `Protect`

    D. `Passive`

44. What is the default administrative distance for internal EIGRP?

    A. 20

    B. 110

    C. 120

    D. 90

45. What architectural model is used with Cisco ACI?

    A. Two-tier spine-leaf

    B. Two-tier collapsed core

    C. Three-tier

    D. Concentric

46. In the configuration that follows, what is the next hop for 10.10.20.0/24?

```
ip route 10.10.20.0 255.255.255.0 172.16.1.1
```

    A. 255.255.255.0

    B. 10.10.20.1

    C. 172.16.1.1

    D. 0.0.0.0

47. What command permits you to see your locally used OSPF routes?

   A. `show ip ospf database local`

   B. `show ospf all`

   C. `show ip route ospf`

   D. `show ospf routes local`

48. Which of the following is the best example of the use of generative AI in modern computer networking?

   A. Generating random network configurations for testing purposes

   B. Predicting network traffic patterns and optimizing routing algorithms

   C. Automatically configuring network devices with known best practice configurations

   D. Automatically generating last known good configurations for network devices

49. What tool produced the output shown?

```
Server:          8.8.8.8
Address:         8.8.8.8#53

Non-authoritative answer:
www.yahoo.com canonical name = fd-fp3.wg1.b.yahoo.com.
Name: fd-fp3.wg1.b.yahoo.com
Address: 98.139.183.24
Name: fd-fp3.wg1.b.yahoo.com
Address: 98.139.180.149
```

   A. `netstat`

   B. `nbtstat`

   C. `nslookup`

   D. `msconfig`

50. What interface configuration mode command configures a Cisco router as a DHCP client?

   A. `ip address auto`

   B. `ip address enable dhcp`

   C. `dhcp address`

   D. `ip address dhcp`

51. What command allows you to confirm the IP address and mask assigned to an interface?

    A. `show interfaces terse`

    B. `show addresses`

    C. `show ip interface brief`

    D. `show ip interface`

52. What is the stratum of a Cisco router if you use the command `ntp master` to configure it to use its internal clock as a time source?

    A. 0

    B. 1

    C. 2

    D. 8

    E. 13

Note Use of the terms *master* and *slave* is ONLY in association with the official terminology used in industry specifications and standards and in no way diminishes Pearson's commitment to promoting diversity, equity, and inclusion and challenging, countering, and/ or combating bias and stereotyping in the global population of the learners we serve.

53. Examine the access list shown here. What is the issue with this access list?

```
access-list 1 permit any
access-list 1 deny host 10.10.10.1
access-list 1 deny host 10.10.10.2
access-list 1 deny host 172.16.1.1
access-list 1 deny any log
```

    A. The access list cannot end with a `deny` statement.

    B. The access list permits the traffic before it denies any traffic.

    C. The access list is not named, and naming is required.

    D. Standard access lists do not support logging.

54. What do you use in dynamic NAT configuration in order to identify the traffic you intend to translate?

    A. An access list

    B. A pool

    C. A NAT list

    D. An interface reference

55. What is the name of the "database" used with SNMP?

    A. AGENT

    B. MIB

    C. TREE

    D. VARSTORE

56. What suite of protocols is often found in use with modern VPN connections?

    A. IPsec

    B. SLA

    C. DNSSEC

    D. PGP

57. Which of the following is not a step for supporting SSH connections on a Cisco router?

    A. Configure a DNS domain.

    B. Generate the SSH key.

    C. Configure the `hostname` command.

    D. Enable SSH globally.

58. Examine the configuration shown here. Which statement is false?

```
no service password-encryption
!
enable secret rtYHS3TTs
!
username admin01 privilege 15 secret Cisco123
!
line vty 0 4
password ChEeEs&WiZ
login
transport input telnet
```

    A. Telnet users will be required to provide a password for Telnet access.

    B. Telnet users will be required to provide the password ChEeEs&WiZ for access to privileged mode.

    C. The account password of the admin privilege-level user is not very secure.

    D. New plaintext passwords will not be encrypted.

59. A new Layer 2 switch in its default configuration has just been powered up. In addition to a console connection, there are two Windows hosts and an IP phone (using PoE) connected to its Ethernet ports. Which of the following are true? (Choose two.)

    A. If either Windows host has successfully completed an ARP resolution, the switch will have learned the MAC addresses of both Windows hosts.

    B. The switch would see the two Windows hosts' directly connected devices from CDP.

    C. The switch would not know if the IP phone is a Cisco IP phone or a third-party IP phone until a call is initiated from the phone.

    D. The switch can be configured with an IPv4 address on interface VLAN 1.

60. Refer to the network topology that follows. Your senior network administrator is concerned about network security. He has asked you to ensure that the PC-10 device in VLAN 10 does not overflow the switch's CAM table. How should you respond? (Choose two.)

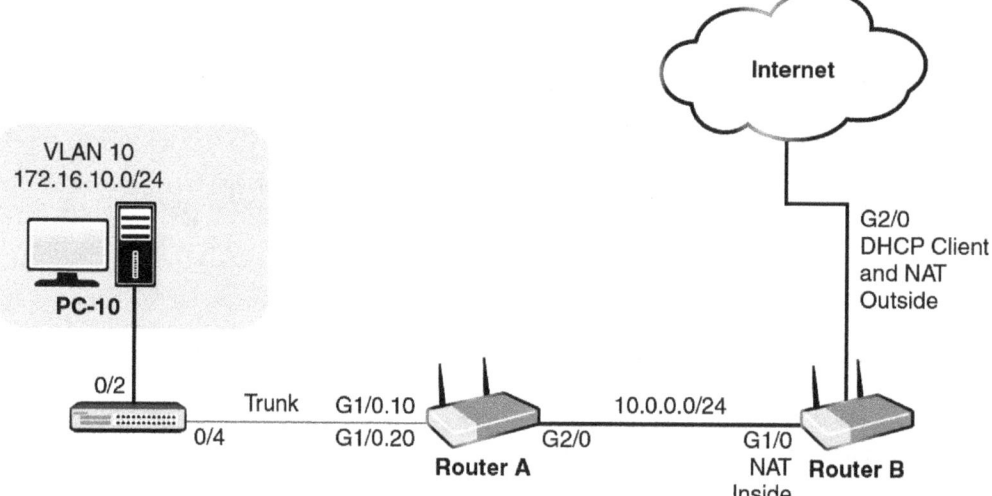

    A. Configure OSPF on all network devices and use MD5 authentication.

    B. Configure the `service password-encryption` command on the switch.

    C. Configure port security on interface 0/2 of the switch.

    D. Configure Router A to route traffic sourced from any device other than PC-10 to Null0.

    E. Configure a static MAC address as part of port security.

Practice Exam 1 Answer Key

Practice Exam 1 Answers at a Glance

1. B

2. 11

3. C

4. E

5. C

6. B

7. B

8. B

9. B

10. 00:1b:77:12:34:56

11. C

12. D

13. D

14. A

15.
```
access-list
101 permit
tcp 10.10.10.0 0
0.0.255 eq
23 192.168.1.0
0.0.0.255
```

16. C

17. A

18. A

19. C

20. D

21. A, D

22. B, D

23. B

24. B

25. C

26. D

27. D

28.
```
router ospf
100 network
192.168.0.1
0.0.0.0 area 0
```

29. A

30. C

31. B

32. 172.16.31.254

33. `show controllers`

34. B

35. D

36. D

37. A

38. B, D

39. B

40. A

41. B

42. C

43. B

44. D

45. A

46. C

47. C

48. B

49. C

50. D

51. D

52. D

53. B

54. A

55. B

56. A

57. D

58. B

59. A, D

60. C, E

Answers with Explanations

1. **Answer B is correct.** There are two transport layer protocols listed here. Therefore, you should be able to narrow down this question to two options immediately: B (TCP) and C (UDP). Of these two, TCP provides reliability features such as sequencing of packets and synchronization. UDP does not.

2. **The correct answer is 11.** Every port on a Layer 2 switch creates a collision domain by default. Here we have 9 workstations connected, creating 9 collision domains, and we have a collision domain for each of the 2 interswitch links. This makes a total of 11 collision domains. This Layer 2 switch concept is often called *microsegmentation*. Keep in mind that the term *microsegmentation* also refers to other aspects of information technology. For example, the term is frequently used in security architectures and network fabric designs.

3. **Answer C is correct.** Notice that this is a default configuration of port security. Every value is set to the default. This means the default number of MAC addresses is one, and the default violation mode is Shutdown, which logs violations.

4. **Answer E is correct.** RSVP sends signals to reserve resources in the devices along a path.

5. **Answer C is correct.** The default administrative distance for routes learned by OSPF is 110. Contrast this to RIP's default administrative distance of 120.

6. **Answer B is correct.** 224.0.0.0 to 239.255.255.255 is the IPv4 multicast address range. This range permits the sending of a single packet to a group of machines that "subscribe" to the traffic. This is unlike a broadcast, where a single packet is sent to all systems. In IPv6, broadcast traffic is eliminated in favor of multicast.

7. **Answer B is correct.** 802.11ac uses the 5 GHz band.

8. **Answer B is correct.** The username command defaults to privilege level 1 for the user when a level is not specified.

9. **Answer B is correct.** JSON uses curly braces to signify JSON objects. It uses square braces to signify arrays.

10. **The correct answer is 00:1b:77:12:34:56.** The Layer 2 addressing information appears under the Ethernet II section. The output of the packet capture shown includes Src for source and Dst for destination.

11. **Answer C is correct.** This is an example of the JSON file format. Notice how much more readable it is compared to XML.

12. **Answer D is correct.** The FHRPs you should know are HSRP, VRRP, and GLBP. GLBP is a Cisco invention that automates load balancing with redundant gateways.

13. **Answer D is correct.** Root Guard reacts to superior BPDUs that arrive on an interface.

14. **Answer A is correct.** Ansible playbooks are expressed in YAML format, which was chosen, in part, for its readability. For more information, see https://docs.ansible.com/ ansible/latest/user_guide/playbooks_intro.html.

15. **The correct answer is** `access-list 101 permit tcp 10.10.10.0 0.0.0.255 eq 23 192.168.1.0 0.0.0.255`. This ACE meets the criteria given. In particular, this ACE would be an entry in an ACL that permits the traffic that is allowed to be leaving the server in the 10.10.10.0/24 subnet.

16. **Answer C is correct.** The `overload` keyword implies the use of Port Address Translation.

17. **Answer A is correct.** Syslog levels 0 through 7 are available on most Cisco devices.

18. **Answer A is correct.** WPA3 introduces many improvements over WPA2, including the replacement of the PSK authentication method.

19. **Answer C is correct.** There are two collision domains. The hub does not create collision domains off its ports. The bridge does. So there are two collision domains created by the bridge.

20. **Answer D is correct.** Secure Copy Protocol (SCP) relies on SSH technology for its operation. It is the only protocol listed here with security and encryption capabilities for file transfer.

21. **Answers A and D are correct.** The cabling and the hub are Layer 1 components. Bridges and switches are Layer 2 components. A router may be a Layer 2 or Layer 3 component.

22. **Answers B and D are correct.** Layer 2 access switches typically have IP addresses assigned for management purposes. A default gateway permits a managed switch to access remote networks, again for management purposes.

23. **Answer B is correct.** The dynamic ARP inspection security feature relies on DHCP snooping for its operation.

24. **Answer B is correct.** Port security can be used on configured access or trunk ports but not on a dynamic port. When used on a trunk, it is likely that many devices' MAC addresses will cross the trunk, so the limit of two MAC addresses would likely be too restrictive.

25. **Answer C is correct.** SEND is not an HTTP method.

26. **Answer D is correct.** Here EIGRP is preferred due to its lower administrative distance.

27. **Answer D is correct.** A router at Layer 3 provides the inter-VLAN communication. Note that this routing function can also be implemented by a route processor inside a multilayer switch.

28. **The correct answer is** the following configuration:

```
router ospf 100
network 192.168.0.1 0.0.0.0 area 0
```

29. **Answer A is correct.** ICMP operates at the network layer of the OSI model. It is encapsulated directly in IP packets and does not rely on UDP or TCP for its operation. Note that ICMP has been assigned its own Internet Protocol number by IANA, just like OSPF and EIGRP, which also do not rely on TCP or UDP. ICMP is essentially a suite of services, some of which affect the routing of packets and some of which offer diagnostic and informational services. Since some ICMP services affect L3 forwarding, we often say that ICMP is an L3 protocol, comparable to OSPF, which populates the routing table and also affects L3 forwarding. On the other hand, other ICMP functions resemble application layer services more than L3 services. For example, the echo service could easily have been written as an L7 function, running over UDP, without any difference in behavior or appearance. So in this context, some ICMP functions are more comparable to those of an L7 application that runs directly (and relies) on the network layer.

30. **Answer C is correct.** A wireless access point (AP) is a device designed to connect users to the network. Modern APs are typically dual band, using both the 2.4 GHz and 5 GHz bands for access by several different 802.11 standards, including 802.11n, 802.11ac, and others.

31. **Answer B is correct.** Terraform is an open-source infrastructure as code (IaC) tool created by HashiCorp that is designed to automate the provisioning and management of cloud, on-premises, and hybrid infrastructure resources. It allows users to define infrastructure configurations by using a declarative configuration language, typically in HashiCorp Configuration Language (HCL) or JSON format.

32. **The correct answer is 172.16.31.254.** There are 3 subnet bits. The increment is 32. The host range for this subnet is 172.16.0.1 to 172.16.31.254.

33. **The correct answer is** `show controllers`. This is output from `show controllers`. Note the type of cable connected displayed is a serial cable, indicating a serial interface.

34. **Answer B is correct.** eBGP is an excellent choice for the underlay in this case.

35. **Answer D is correct.** The private IPv4 address ranges are 10.0.0.0: 10.255.255.255, 172.16.0.0: 172.31.255.255, and 192.168.0.0: 192.168.255.255.

36. **Answer D is correct.** Cisco routers are able to support IPv6 on interfaces by default. They cannot, however, route other devices' IPv6 traffic without the global `ipv6 unicast-routing` command.

37. **Answer A is correct.** You use `show ip ospf neighbor` to quickly verify peer OSPF devices.

38. Answers B and D are correct. This issue is difficult to pinpoint because communication is intermittent or slow.

39. Answer B is correct. The `show interface` command is very valuable for troubleshooting issues such as collisions and also for verifying the overall status of a switch or a router interface.

40. Answer A is correct. VLANs cannot be created on VTP client devices. If you attempt to create a VLAN on a VTP client device, you receive an error message.

41. Answer B is correct. The listening state does not exist in RSTP.

42. Answer C is correct. `no cdp run` is used to disable CDP globally on a device. To disable CDP on just a single interface, use the `no cdp enable` command in interface configuration mode.

43. Answer B is correct. When you configure port security, the default violation mode is `Shutdown`.

44. Answer D is correct. The default admin distance for internal EIGRP is 90.

45. Answer A is correct. The architectural model Cisco ACI uses is the two-tier spine-leaf. The leaf devices connect to all spine devices in a full mesh.

46. Answer C is correct. The static route is `ip route 10.10.20.0 255.255. 255.0 172.16.1.1`. The next hop is the last IP address shown in this command. On a point-to-point link, the local exit interface can be used as part of the command instead of the next-hop address of the next router in the path. The local exit interface can also be used in a multi-access scenario, but this use is discouraged in most cases due to the potential overhead of the Layer 2–to–Layer 3 name resolution that takes place.

47. Answer C is correct. Use `show ip route ospf` to see the OSPF routes in your local routing table.

48. Answer B is correct. A great example of the use of generative AI in computer networking today is to have the tool predict network patterns and optimize routing algorithms based on machine learning of the current network.

49. Answer C is correct. The `nslookup` tool is a common Windows utility for investigating DNS issues. The tool is excellent and displays information that you can use to diagnose Domain Name System (DNS) infrastructure problems and misconfigurations.

50. Answer D is correct. It is simple to configure a Cisco device to acquire an address via DHCP. In interface configuration mode, after bringing up the interface, use the `ip address dhcp` command.

51. Answer D is correct. The `show ip interface brief` command provides a nice summary of the IP addresses assigned to interfaces and their status. It does so in an easy-to-read, table-like format. This command is often typed as simply `sh ip int br`. This command does not provide mask information, however. For that, you use `show ip interface`.

52. Answer D is correct. A stratum 1 device is the most authoritative time server on a network. When you use the command `ntp master` and do not specify the stratum, the default stratum is 8.

53. Answer B is correct. The order of access list statements is very important; they are processed from top to bottom. Here, the `permit` statement that begins the list permits all traffic before the `deny` statements are processed. On many IOS routers, the subsequent "deny" access control entries wouldn't even be allowed and would generate a message indicating a conflict due to the `permit any` entry already being in place.

54. Answer A is correct. Dynamic NAT uses an ACL to identify the addresses to translate. The NAT commands also can include a pool to indicate the addresses that will be used for the translations.

55. Answer B is correct. SNMP relies on a Management Information Base (MIB) for storing variables and their values.

56. Answer A is correct. IPsec is often used with VPNs.

57. Answer D is correct. SSH is not enabled globally on the device.

58. Answer B is correct. Here the Telnet password will be `ChEeEs&WiZ`, but to access privileged mode, `rtYHS3TTs` is required.

59. Answers A and D are correct. When the Windows hosts send at least one frame into the network, the switch learns the MAC address of each host. The switch can be configured with a management VLAN 1 IP address for the benefit of management of the switch. You can also choose another VLAN ID for your management network. A default gateway is also required for the switch to communicate back to the management computer if that management computer is not on the same IP subnet as the switch.

60. Answers C and E are correct. Here, a solution is to configure port security with a static port security MAC address assignment.

Practice Exam 2

1. Examine the following NAT configuration. What is the problem with this configuration?

```
interface gi0/0
 ip address 10.10.10.1 255.255.255.0
 ip nat inside
!
interface gi0/1
 ip address 10.10.20.1 255.255.255.0
 ip nat inside
!
interface serial 0/0
 ip address 172.16.10.64 255.255.255.0
!
ip nat pool MYPOOL 172.16.10.1 172.16.10.1 prefix 24
```

```
ip nat inside source list 7 pool MYPOOL overload
access-list 7 permit 10.10.10.0 0.0.0.31
access-list 7 permit 10.10.20.0 0.0.0.31
```

_____

2. Which wireless security protocol makes the use of CCMP mandatory?

A. DAI

B. IPsec

C. WPA2

D. WEP

3. The user at the PC shown in the figure is copying a file from the server by using a program that uses a connectionless transport protocol. Which protocols on the left match up to the layers on the right regarding the encapsulation done by the PC? (Note that not all the protocols are used.)

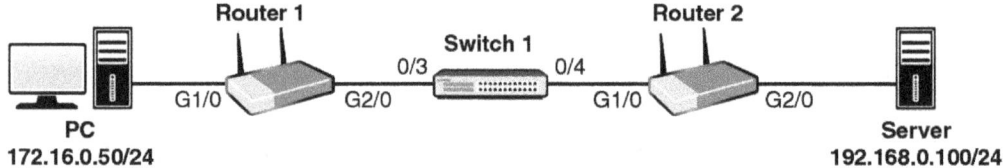

Protocols	Layers
UDP	Application
Serial	
TFTP	Transport
ICMP	
TCP	
Ethernet	Internet
IP	
FTP	Network Access

4. What symbol do you use in JSON in order to indicate an array?

A. Curly brace

B. Square bracket

C. Colon

D. Semicolon

5. How are the connections made between devices in the spine-leaf architecture of Cisco ACI?

A. Each leaf device connects to every other leaf device.

B. Each spine device connects to every other spine device.

C. Exactly one spine device connects to exactly one leaf device.

D. Each leaf device connects to every spine device.

6. Examine the configuration shown here. Why is this configuration producing an error when it is pasted into the CLI?

```
Current configuration : 2945 bytes
!
...
hostname Router-A
!
...
!
interface GigabitEthernet0/0
no ip address
shutdown
duplex auto
speed auto
media-type rj45
!
interface GigabitEthernet0/1
ip address 172.16.1.64 255.255.255.224
duplex auto
speed auto
media-type rj45
!
ip forward-protocol nd
!
!
no ip http server
no ip http secure-server
ip route 10.10.10.0 255.255.255.0 172.16.1.2
!
!
!
access-list 101 permit ip 10.10.0.0 0.0.255.255 any
access-list 101 deny ip host 10.10.10.1 any
access-list 101 deny ip any any log
!
...
!
end
```

A. There is no enable password set.

B. The hostname is not legal.

C. The hostname contains an invalid character.

D. There is a bad IP address and mask combination.

E. The second entry of ACL 101 will in effect not deny anything more than the next ACE.

7. What information for a wireless network can you choose not to broadcast?

A. SSID

B. The AP's MAC address

C. Type

D. Version

8. What QoS technology is often used for congestion management in VoIP environments?

A. LLQ

B. CBWFQ

C. WFQ

D. FIFO

9. What is smaller and more efficient than a virtual machine (VM)?

A. Bucket

B. Cluster node

C. API

D. Container

10. What is true regarding a network device that receives the packet shown in the protocol analyzer output that follows? (Choose two.)

```
Ethernet II, Src: ca:00:1a:a4:00:1c (ca:00:1a:a4:00:1c), Dst: IntelCor_12:34:56 (00:1b:77:12:34:56)
  Destination: IntelCor_12:34:56 (00:1b:77:12:34:56)
  Source: ca:00:1a:a4:00:1c (ca:00:1a:a4:00:1c)
  Type: IP (0x0800)
Internet Protocol Version 4, Src: 198.133.219.25 (198.133.219.25), Dst: 10.0.0.2 (10.0.0.2)
Transmission Control Protocol, Src Port: http (80), Dst Port: d-cinema-rrp (1173), Seq: 0, Ack: 1, Len: 0
```

A. A bridge would forward the packet based on the Layer 1 destination address.

B. A hub would forward the packet based on the Layer 2 destination address.

C. A switch would forward the frame based on the Layer 2 destination address.

D. A router would forward the packet based on the Layer 2 source address.

E. A router would forward the packet based on the Layer 3 source address.

F. A router would forward the packet based on the Layer 3 destination address.

11. Which RSTP port role functions to provide a fast-converging replacement for the current root port?

  A. Disabled

  B. Alternate

  C. Backup

  D. Designated

12. Map the layers on the left to the protocols on the right. Note that not all layers are used, and some layers may be used more than once.

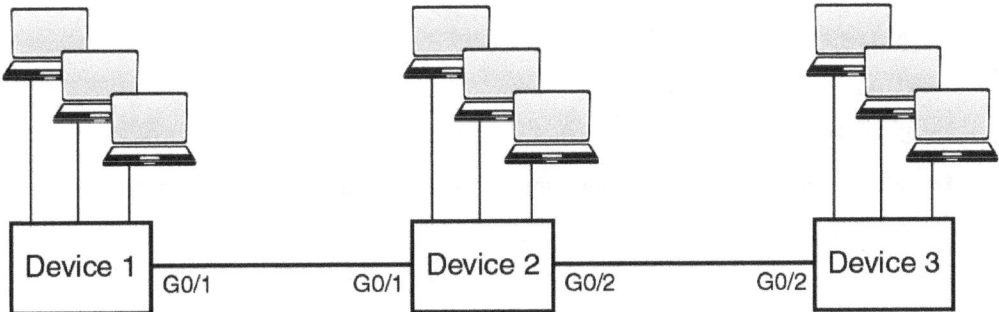

13. What Cisco wireless controller feature simplifies controller configuration by no longer requiring the setup of primary and secondary ports for each interface?

  A. RSTP

  B. SNMP

  C. VTP

  D. LAG

14. What transport layer protocol provides sequencing and synchronization?

  A. HTTP

  B. TCP

  C. ICMP

  D. UDP

15. What device protects "internal" networks from "external" networks?

  A. WLC

  B. Firewall

C. AP

D. Layer 2 switch

16. What layer of the classic Cisco network model is typically not collapsed in a simplified two-layer design?

A. Access

B. Internet

C. Core

D. Distribution

17. You are examining the interfaces on a Cisco WLAN controller. You observe an interface named Students-VLAN. What is most likely the type of this interface?

A. Service port interface

B. User-defined dynamic interface

C. Management interface

D. AP-Manager interface

18. What is the standard maximum frame size (in bytes) in a typical Ethernet network?

A. 1500

B. 1600

C. 1900

D. 9000

19. In the network depicted, the user at PC1 has asked which program to use to copy a file from the server to PC1 using a reliable Layer 4 transport protocol. Which of the following would meet both requirements? (Choose two.)

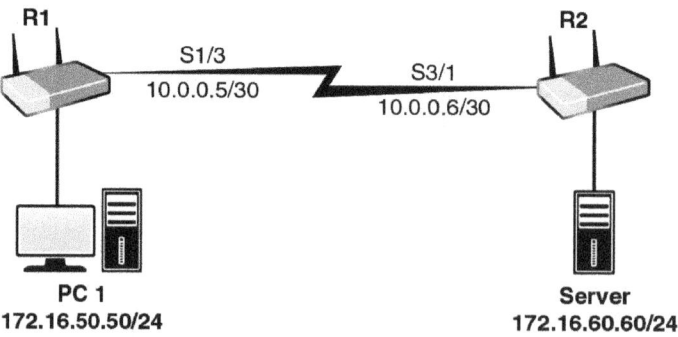

A. OSPF

B. TFTP

C. FTP

D. SCP

E. DNS

20. Which statement about PortFast on Cisco switches is incorrect?

    A. PortFast is used exclusively on trunk ports.

    B. PortFast speeds up convergence.

    C. PortFast is supported in STP and RSTP.

    D. PortFast is designed for use on edge ports.

21. What technology is used to allow a switch port to carry the traffic of multiple data VLANs from one device to another in a Cisco network?

    A. VLAN hopping

    B. Trunking

    C. Port security

    D. VTP

22. Examine the following MAC addresses on two switches:

    SwitchA: c001.3412.9301

    SwitchB: 0019.e728.8101

    In a tiny network with only these two switches, which switch becomes the root bridge if the default STP priority values are in place?

    A. SwitchA

    B. SwitchB

    C. Neither of these switches

    D. Both devices

23. What port security approach is considered a mix of dynamic and static configuration?

    A. Trunking

    B. Violation null

    C. Sticky learning

    D. Blocked learning

24. Your junior administrator is examining the routing table on a Cisco router and asks you what is the meaning of the D she sees in routing table entries. What does this indicate?

    A. OSPF

    B. BGP

C. RIP

D. EIGRP

25. What prefix is reserved for IPv6 link-local addresses?

    A. fe80::/10

    B. fec0::/10

    C. fe80::/8

    D. fec0::/8

26. Examine the command shown here. What is the purpose of the last argument in this command (121)?

```
ip route 10.10.10.0 255.255.255.0 172.16.1.1 121
```

    A. This is a sequence number.

    B. This is the metric value for the route entry.

    C. This is an administrative distance value to create a floating static route.

    D. This is a weight value.

27. Which of the following is used by an IPv6 multicast address?

    A. f080::/10

    B. ff00::/8

    C. fc00::/8

    D. f008::/10

28. What networking device provides instructions to APs?

    A. Router

    B. Firewall

    C. Switch

    D. WLC

29. Which of the following parameters does not need to match on your routers when configuring an OSPF version 2 peering?

    A. The local process ID

    B. The hello and dead timers

    C. The area ID

    D. Authentication

30. What type of modern computer threat involves the use of zombies or botnets?

    A. Reconnaissance

    B. On-path attack

    C. DDoS attack

    D. Trojan horse

31. In the network depicted, the server is sending HTTP content back to the PC that requested it. Which of the following is true as the packets are forwarded over the network?

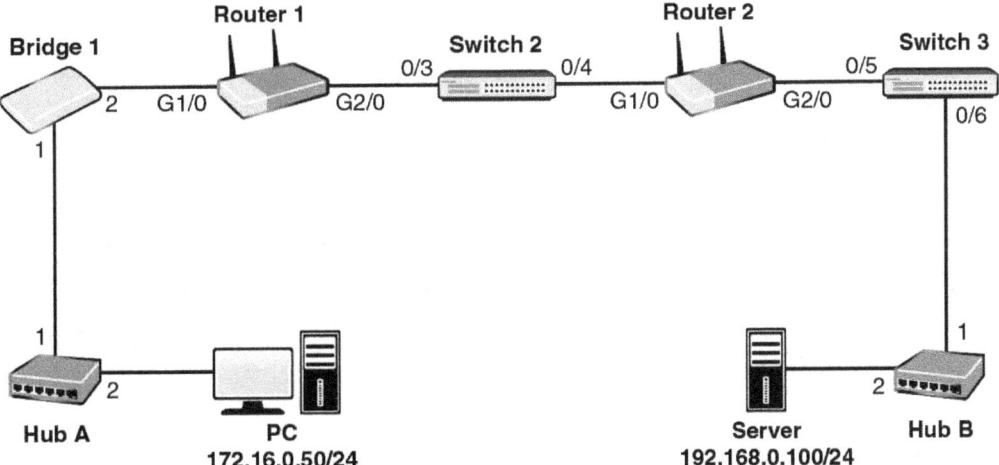

    A. The bridges and switches use Ethernet addresses to make forwarding decisions.

    B. The hubs, bridges, and switches use Ethernet addresses to make forwarding decisions.

    C. The routers, bridges, and switches use Ethernet addresses to make forwarding decisions.

    D. The hubs, routers, bridges, and switches use Ethernet addresses to make forwarding decisions.

32. Based on the network depicted, provide the complete syntax for a standard ACL for Router 2 G2/0 that permits traffic sourced from the PC but denies all other traffic. This ACL must use the number 10 and must use the most efficient syntax possible.

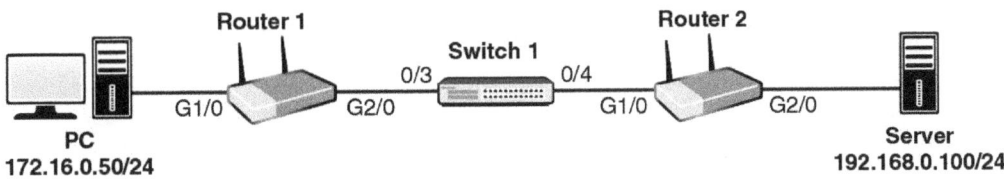

33. After identification has been accomplished with a DDoS attack, what is typically the next step in mitigation?

A. Forwarding

B. Filtering

C. Monitoring

D. Redirection

34. Which of the following is essentially a standards-based version of HSRP?

A. OSPF

B. SNMP

C. VRRP

D. GLBP

35. Examine the topology shown. Given that the IP address assigned to R2 fa1/0 is 10.2.2.2, provide a default static route on R1 that uses R2 as the default gateway.

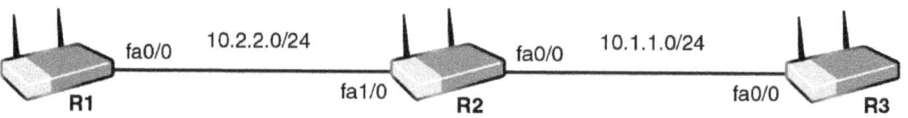

36. Your junior admin notes that when he just performed a ping, one of the packets failed. What is the most likely cause of the following results?

```
Router1# ping 10.255.0.126
Type escape sequence to abort.
Sending 5, 100-byte ICMP Echos to 10.255.0.126, timeout is 2 seconds:
.!!!!
Success rate is 80 percent (4/5), round-trip min/avg/max = 35/72/76 ms
```

A. Load balancing, with one of the next hops being unavailable

B. ARP resolution

C. Half-duplex operation

D. 10 Mbps being used instead of Fast Ethernet or Gigabit Ethernet

37. Router A is assigning IP addresses to hosts in VLAN 10, as shown in the network depiction. The user powers up PC-10 and checks https://www.reuters.com for news. What are the first four protocols used by PC-10 when it powers up, in order?

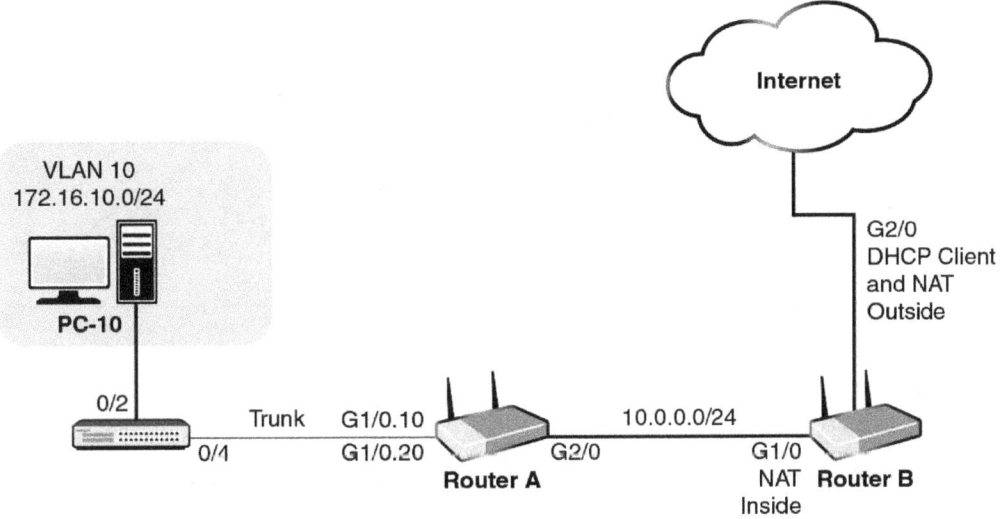

Protocol	Order
OSPF	1st
ARP	
HTTP	2nd
DNS	
DHCP	3rd
ICMP	4th

38. Given the following address and the mask 172.16.10.1 255.255.248.0, what is the broadcast address for the subnet?

A. 172.16.15.255

B. 172.16.8.0

C. 172.16.16.255

D. 172.16.255.255

E. 172.16.10.255

39. What is the authentication method used in many RADIUS environments today?

A. EAP

B. PAP

C. Telnet

D. MD5

40. What is the term for an API that communicates from a network management station to the SDN controller?

A. Westbound

B. Eastbound

C. Southbound

D. Northbound

41. What is the purpose of the command `service timestamps log datetime msec`?

A. To prevent attackers from manipulating the time in syslog messages

B. Not applicable as this command is not valid

C. To mark syslog messages with the data and time, including the milliseconds

D. To indicate the time of transference for syslog messages to the server

42. What command does a client use to enable stateless autoconfiguration of IPv6 address information on an interface?

A. `ipv6 address autoconfig`

B. `ipv6 address dhcp`

C. `ipv6 address enable`

D. `ipv6 enable`

43. OSPF is properly configured and working on both routers shown in the depicted network. The following is added to Router X: `ip route 10.255.0.128 255.255.255.224 10.255.0.75 89`. What will be the result?

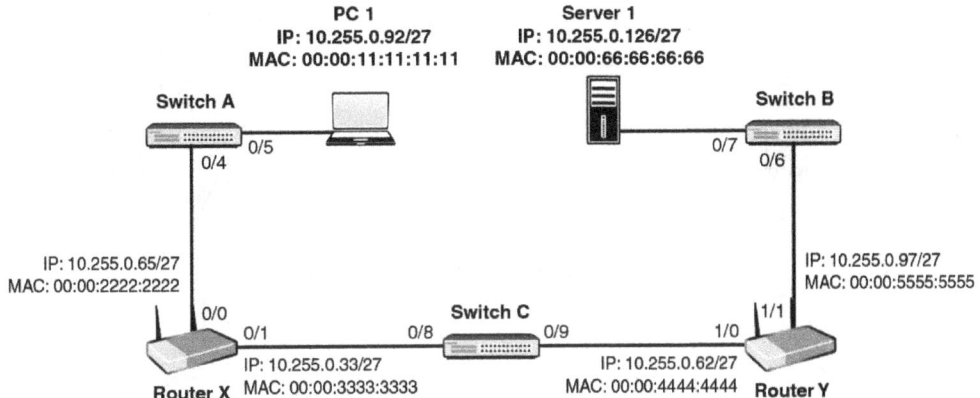

A. The static route will have an administrative distance that is better than that of OSPF.

B. There will be a Layer 2 loop.

C. Router X will attempt to send to PC 1 packets destined to subnet 10.255.0.128/27.

D. A broadcast storm will occur.

44. Examine the topology shown here. PC1 is sending an HTTP packet to Server 1. What is true about this traffic as it is forwarded through Switch C? (Choose three.)

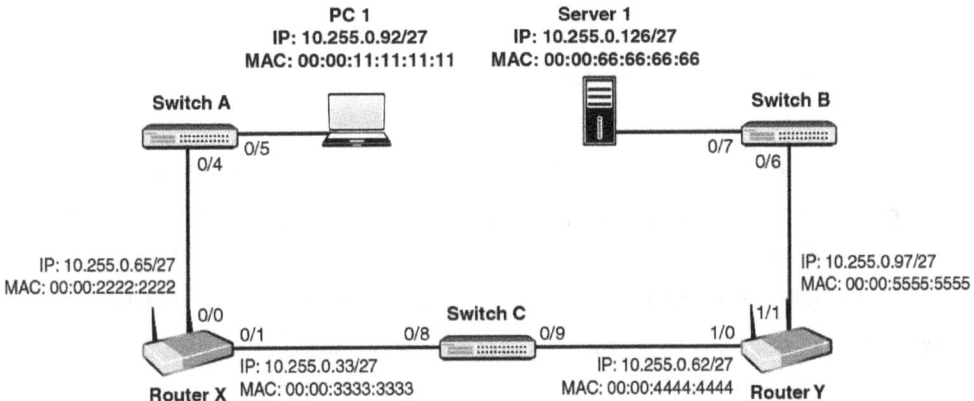

A. The source physical address will be 0000.3333.3333.

B. The source Layer 2 address will be 00:00:11:11:11:11.

C. The source address will be 10.255.0.92.

D. The destination physical address will be 00:00:66:66:66:66.

E. The destination address will be 0000.4444.4444.

45. As shown in the switch MAC address table below the topology depicted, PC 1's ARP cache is empty, and the user at PC 1 uses `ping` to test the IP address reachability of Server 1. Which of the following is true when the user presses Enter?

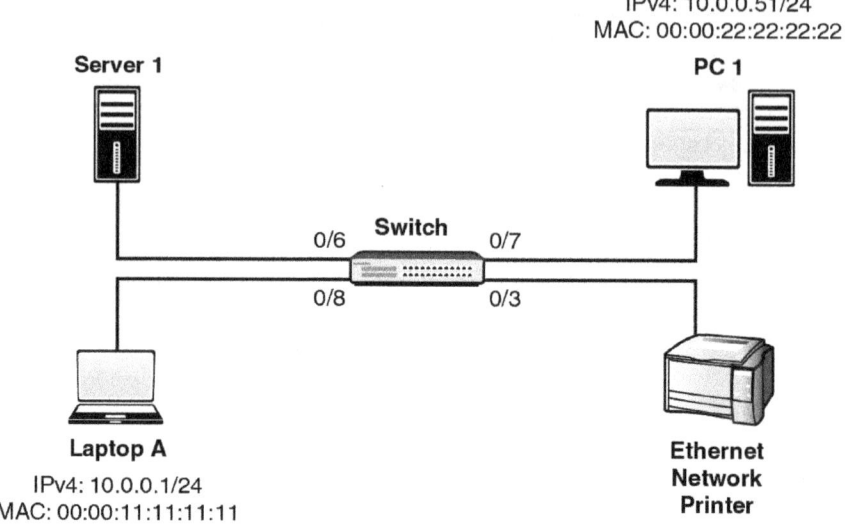

MAC Address	VLAN	Port
0000.1111.1111	1	0/8
0000.2222.2222	1	0/7
0000.6783.BEEF	1	0/6

A. The first frame will be sent out port 0/6 only.

B. The switch will add the printer's MAC address to the MAC address table.

C. The first frame from PC1 will be forwarded out all ports except 0/7.

D. The reply to the ping request will cause the server's MAC address to be added to the table.

E. The first frame will use Server 1's MAC address as the destination MAC address.

46. A host runs the command `ipconfig` on the local system. The output is as follows:

```
Ethernet adapter:
 Connection-specific DNS Suffix . :
 IPv4 Address. . . . . . . . . . . : 172.18.62.255
 Subnet Mask . . . . . . . . . . . : 255.255.248.0
 Default Gateway . . . . . . . . . : 172.18.63.254
```

Which of the following are true? (Choose two.)

A. The broadcast address for the host's subnet is 172.18.71.255.

B. The host is attached to a subnet of a Class B private network.

C. The subnet the host is connected to can support up to 2048 hosts.

D. The host with IP address 172.18.64.5 would be on the same network as the host in the question.

E. The host address is on the 172.18.56.0/21 network.

47. Which of the following are valid host addresses when using the mask 255.255.248.0? (Choose three.)

A. 34.45.56.0

B. 40.50.60.0

C. 50.60.70.255

D. 51.61.71.255

E. 60.70.80.0

F. 60.70.80.255

48. Refer to the depicted network. All the switches and R1 have had their startup configurations deleted and then were rebooted before saving to NVRAM. These devices are now running in their default configuration. Which of the following are true? (Choose three.)

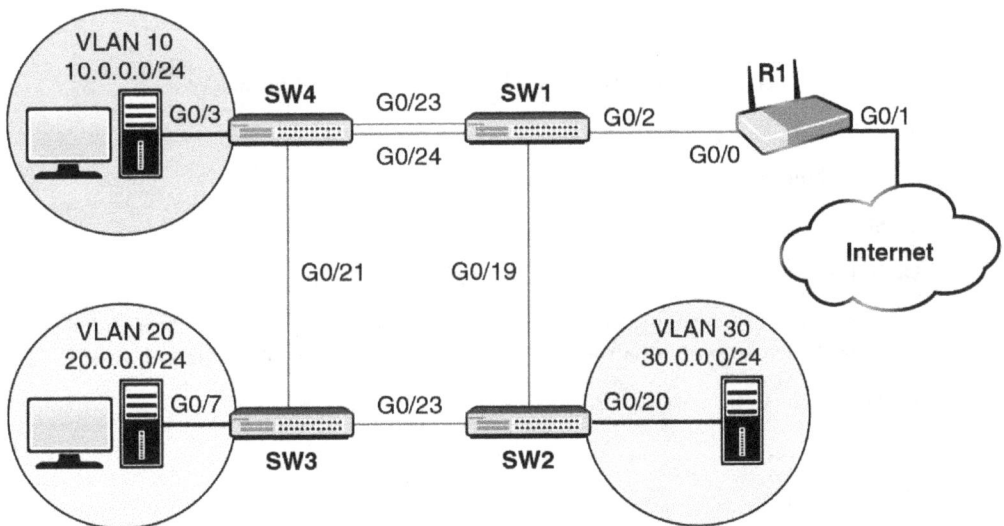

A. Clients shown in the diagram as being on VLANs 10, 20, and 30 will now all be on the same VLAN.

B. SW1 will see CDP neighbors on at least three interfaces.

C. The command `show protocols`, `show ip interface`, `show interface`, or `show ip interface brief` can be used to confirm that R1 G0/0 is up/up.

D. If the command `ip address 10.0.0.1 /24` were added for G0/0 on R1, SW1 would learn that IP address within 60 seconds.

E. SW2 will see two CDP neighbors.

49. Provide the switch configuration to meet these requirements:

The user account BOB should be created with the password `ToUgH1!23`, which is stored using MD5.

Telnet should be disabled on the switch.

SSHv2 should be enabled on the switch.

The local user accounts should be used to authenticate on the vty lines.

Existing and future plaintext passwords should be encrypted.

The password to get into privileged mode should be `iTsMe@HeRe$`, and it should be stored using MD5.

The management interface should use the default VLAN and have the IP address 10.20.30.75/27.

The default gateway should be set to 10.20.30.94.

_____

50. CSMA/CD technology is critical for what type of Ethernet network?

A. Full mesh

B. Partial mesh

C. Star

D. Half-duplex

51. You are interested in having your switch ports automatically disabled if an end user plugs in their own switch on their local access port. What tool should you use?

A. This needs to be Loop Guard

B. BPDU Guard

C. Root Guard

D. Port Security

52. How is CDP carried on the network?

    A. Using 802.1Q messages

    B. Using VTP messages

    C. Using Layer 2

    D. Using Layer 1

53. What is the default administrative distance of iBGP?

    A. 20

    B. 90

    C. 120

    D. 200

54. What options exist for the next-hop information in a static route? (Choose two.)

    A. Specifying the next-hop IP address

    B. Specifying the next-hop MAC address

    C. Specifying the next-hop CDP ID

    D. Specifying the exit interface

55. What is the default lease duration for a Cisco DHCP server?

    A. One hour

    B. One day

    C. One week

    D. One month

56. How do you configure a Cisco router to use its internal clock as the reference time source and then become an NTP server?

    A. Use the `ntp server` command.

    B. Use the `ntp master` command.

    C. Use the `ntp source` command.

    D. Use the `ntp clock` command.

57. What is the default privilege level for a local user account created with the `username` command?

    A. 0

    B. 1

    C. 8

    D. 15

58. What vty line command causes the local username database to be checked for remote access?

   A. `login`

   B. `local`

   C. `login local`

   D. `aaa login local`

59. Which format is a popular method of providing the instructions for cloud infrastructure construction in Terraform?

   A. XML

   B. JSON

   C. Python

   D. C#

60. What component does Ansible use to gather plays that perform tasks on a network?

   A. Playbook

   B. Inventory

   C. Cookbook

   D. Runbook

Practice Exam 2 Answer Key

Practice Exam 2 Answers at a Glance

   1. This configuration fails to define the outside NAT interface.

   2. C

   3. Application layer: TFTP; transport layer: UDP; Internet layer: IP; network access layer: Ethernet

   4. B

   5. D

   6. D

   7. A

   8. A

   9. D

   10. C, F

11. B

12. CDP: data link; TCP: transport; PPP: data link; SMTP: application; Serial: physical; IP: network

13. D

14. B

15. B

16. A

17. B

18. A

19. C, D

20. A

21. B

22. B

23. C

24. D

25. A

26. C

27. B

28. D

29. A

30. C

31. A

32.
```
access-list 10
permit host
172.16.0.50
access-list 10
deny any
interface
gi2/0
ip access-group 10 out
```

33. B

34. C

35.

```
ip route
0.0.0.0
0.0.0.0
10.2.2.2
```

36. B

37. DHCP, ARP, DNS, HTTP

38. A

39. A

40. D

41. C

42. A

43. A

44. A, C, E

45. C

46. B, E

47. B, C, F

48. A, B, E

49.

```
username
BOB secret
ToUgH1!23
!
line vty 0 15
transport
input ssh
login local
!
service password-encryption
!
enable secret
iTsMe@HeRe$
!
interface
vlan 1
ip address
10.20.30.75
255.255.255.224!
ip default-gateway
10.20.30.94
```

50. D

51. B

52. C

53. D

54. A, D

55. B

56. B

57. B

58. C

59. B

60. D

Answers with Explanations

1. **The correct answer is that this configuration fails to define the outside interface, and the `access-list 7` wildcard masks are too short.** Notice that this configuration performs dynamic NAT and that it overloads a single routable address. This means it is doing Port Address Translation (PAT). This configuration is fine, except it does not specify the outside NAT interface (serial 0/0). In addition, the wildcard mask /27 does not cover all the subnets attached to Gigabit 0/0 and Gigabit 0/1.

2. **Answer C is correct.** WPA2 uses TKIP and CCMP, and the implementation of CCMP is mandatory.

3. **The correct is application layer: TFTP; transport layer: UDP; Internet layer: IP; network access layer: Ethernet.** Here the connectionless application is TFTP. UDP is the connectionless transport protocol used by TFTP. IP is the Internet layer protocol, and Ethernet is used at the network access layer.

4. **Answer B is correct.** JSON uses square brackets when it comes time to indicate an array.

5. **Answer D is correct.** With the spine-leaf architecture, each leaf device connects to each and every spine device in a full mesh.

6. **Answer D is correct.** A valid IP address can't have all zeros for the host portion, which is the problem with this attempted configuration for the Gigabit 0/1 interface. As a side note, on some Cisco devices, a hostname must begin with a letter, end with a letter or digit, and have as interior characters only letters, digits, and hyphens. A name must be 63 characters or fewer. In this example, the hostname is not the problem. Another (minor) issue with the particular configuration script when pasted directly into the configuration mode CLI of an IOS device is that the first line (`Current configuration : 2945 bytes`) produces the error `Invalid input detected at '^' marker`.

7. Answer A is correct. You can choose not to broadcast the name of the network (that is, the SSID). Note that not broadcasting the SSID does not add to the overall security of the implementation.

8. Answer A is correct. LLQ is the most common congestion management mechanism in VoIP environments today. It provides a strict priority queue for voice traffic, alongside CBWFQ for other traffic forms.

9. Answer D is correct. Containers are an evolution in virtualization. They are similar to virtual machines but are smaller and more efficient as a container does not have an entire operating system in the virtualized object.

10. Answers C and F are correct. Switches forward based on the destination MAC (Layer 2) address, whereas routers forward based on the destination Layer 3 address (the IP address).

11. Answer B is correct. The alternate port is a fast-converging alternative to the current root port.

12. The correct answer is CDP: data link; TCP: transport; PPP: data link; SMTP: application; Serial: physical; IP: network. Be prepared to map technologies to the correct layers of the OSI model, as in this question.

13. Answer D is correct. Link aggregation (LAG) is a feature available on most Cisco wireless controllers. This feature permits the bundling of ports into a port channel and eliminates the need for creating primary and secondary ports.

14. Answer B is correct. TCP at the transport layer provides connection-oriented, reliable features, including the sequencing and synchronization of packets.

15. Answer B is correct. Firewalls are specialized devices that protect internal networks from external networks. Keep in mind that they can be software implementations or hardware appliances. These days, they can even be virtual.

16. Answer A is correct. A collapsed core design is one where distribution layer functions are implemented in the core. You often see this in smaller networks, where the complexity of a three-layer design really is not needed.

17. Answer B is correct. In typical Cisco WLAN deployments, the WLAN is mapped to a dynamic interface on the WLAN controller.

18. Answer A is correct. The standard frame size and MTU in Ethernet networks is 1500 bytes.

19. Answers C and D are correct. OSPF is a routing protocol and not a file transfer protocol. TFTP uses UDP for transport and does not provide reliability. DNS is used for domain name resolution.

20. Answer A is correct. PortFast is commonly used on edge ports that connect to endpoints in the network. This feature causes fast convergence for these ports, which should never connect to other switches. PortFast is a feature that is independent from STP and RSTP, and it can be applied on ports regardless of the version of STP that is running on a switch.

21. **Answer B is correct.** Trunking, specifically 802.1Q, permits the transport of multiple data VLANs between devices across a single interface.

22. **Answer B is correct.** In the case of equal priority values, the lowest MAC address wins the STP root bridge election. In this case, Switch B has a lower MAC address. Remember that the hex values (in ascending order) are 0, 1, 2, 3, 4, 5, 6, 7, 8, 9, A, B, C, D, E, F.

23. **Answer C is correct.** Port security sticky learning means the port will initially dynamically learn the MAC addresses and add them to the running configuration. After this, this updated running config can be saved (using the command `copy running-config startup-config`) in the startup configuration as a static MAC address assignment for port security for when the switch reboots.

24. **Answer D is correct.** EIGRP routes appear in the routing table with a D designation.

25. **Answer A is correct.** fe80::/10 is the prefix reserved for link-local addressing in IPv6.

26. **Answer C is correct.** Administrative distance is added to the `ip route` command in order to create floating static routes. If the administrative distance value is lower than another source of information for the same destination prefix, the static route replaces the other route. (The static route is only floating as long as there is a source offering a path to the destination prefix with a lower AD than the static route's configured AD. Configuring an AD to a static route doesn't automatically make the static route floating.)

27. **Answer B is correct.** Multicast addresses in IPv6 use the ff00::/8 prefix (per RFC 4291, section 2.7).

28. **Answer D is correct.** A wireless LAN controller is a device in a modern network that controls and manages access points.

29. **Answer A is correct.** Many values must match in order for an OSPF peering to form. The local process ID is not one of them.

30. **Answer C is correct.** Distributed denial-of-service (DDoS) attacks typically feature the use of zombies or botnets that help carry out the attacks.

31. **Answer A is correct.** Switches and bridges use Layer 2 Ethernet addresses to forward traffic. Routers use L3 addresses to make forwarding decisions. Hubs do not make forwarding decisions; they just flood any Ethernet frames out all their ports.

32. **The correct syntax is as follows:**

```
access-list 10 permit host 172.16.0.50
interface gi2/0
ip access-group 10 out
```

33. **Answer B is correct.** Filtering typically follows the identification phase for DDoS mitigation.

34. **Answer C is correct.** VRRP is very similar to HSRP. This FHRP is standards based.

35. The correct answer is the following default static route:

```
ip route 0.0.0.0 0.0.0.0 10.2.2.2
```

36. Answer B is correct. Initial ping packets might fail as a result of the initial ARP resolution that must be performed.

37. The correct order is DHCP, ARP, DNS, HTTP. As soon as its operating system loads, PC-10 broadcasts DHCP Discover messages, looking for its local DHCP server. It then performs ARP for its default gateway (or the DNS server, if it's local). Finally, this device uses DNS for domain name resolution and HTTP to access the website.

38. Answer A is correct. Here the increment is on 8 because there are 5 bits used for subnetting. The host range of this subnet is 172.16.8.1 to 172.16.15.254. The broadcast address for the 172.16.8.0/21 subnet is 172.16.15.255.

39. Answer A is correct. EAP is an authentication framework used in many RADIUS environments. PAP is an older authentication scheme that was popular in the days of dialup.

40. Answer D is correct. The northbound APIs are used to communicate between those configuring the network and the SDN controller. The southbound APIs represent the communications from the controller to the network devices.

41. Answer C is correct. This command ensures that syslog messages are timestamped to the millisecond.

42. Answer A is correct. The `ipv6 address autoconfig` command is used on the client. The `ipv6 address enable` command does not exist. The `ipv6 enable` command enables IPv6 and configures only an IPv6 link-local address using EUI-64 on the interface. The `ipv6 address dhcp` command relies on a DHCP server to determine configuration information in order to assign an IPv6 address to the interface. The `ipv6 address autoconfig` command only relies on a router transmitting RAs to determine a global IPv6 address.

43. Answer A is correct. Here the AD of the static route (89) is less (better) than the default AD of OSPF, which is 110. Note that unless an exam question explicitly states otherwise, you must consider only default settings. As a result of the static route, packets destined to 10.255.0.128/27 will be forwarded to the router 10.255.0.75 (not shown in the diagram, so it might not exist). As long as there is no ARP reply from the router at 10.255.0.75 (the static route's target), Router X will keep sending out ARP requests, looking for 10.255.0.75. This continuous stream of ARP requests is not a broadcast storm.

44. Answers A, C, and E are correct. Without NAT, the source and destination IP addresses never change. The Layer 2 header information as the frame goes through Switch C will show a source MAC address of Router X and a destination MAC address of Router Y. Note that MAC addresses are also often called *physical* *addresses*, especially since in earlier NIC implementations, they were burned into the Ethernet hardware and could not be modified in software—not because they were physical layer addresses.

45. Answer C is correct. The first frame would be an ARP request, sent as an L2 broadcast (with destination MAC address ffff.ffff.ffff), and it is sent out all ports for that VLAN except the switch port where the original frame entered the switch.

46. Answers B and E are correct. This host is on the 172.18.56.0/21 network with host range 172.18.56.1 to 172.18.63.254. The subnet's broadcast address is 172.18.62.255, and it can support up to 2046 hosts. The private address 20-bit block ranges from 172.16.0.0 to 172.31.255.255. This means the 172.18.56.0/21 subnet is part of the 20-bit block of private addresses.

47. Answers B, C, and F are correct. Host addresses can't have all 1s or all 0s for the host portion of the address. The following is the breakdown for the relevant networks, given a subnet mask of 255.255.248.0, or /21 in CIDR notation:

Subnet	Range of Valid Host Addresses	Broadcast Address
x.x.56.0	x.x.56.1–x.x.63.254	x.x.63.255
x.x.64.0	x.x.64.1–x.x.71.254	x.x.71.255
x.x.72.0	x.x.72.1–x.x.79.254	x.x.79.255
x.x.80.0	x.x.80.1–x.x.87.254	x.x.87.255
x.x.88.0	x.x.88.1–x.x.95.254	x.x.95.255
x.x.96.0	x.x.96.1–x.x.103.254	x.x.103.255
x.x.104.0	x.x.104.1–x.x.111.254	x.x.111.255

48. Answers A, B, and E are correct. The clients are now on the same VLAN, the default VLAN 1. Even though the vlan.dat has not been explicitly deleted, it does not matter in this case because every port's VLAN membership is stored in the running configuration. So upon restart, VLANs 10, 20, and 30 might actually be defined and have configured names on the switches, but all of the switch's ports will be assigned to VLAN 1. SW1 will see SW4, SW2, and R1 via CDP. SW2 will see SW1 and SW3 via CDP. The commands `show protocols`, `show ip interface`, `show interface`, and `show ip interface brief` can be used to confirm that R1 G0/0 is administratively down, not that it is up/up. The default state of router interfaces is to be administratively down, so that is the only state any command can be used to verify. And without turning on the G0/0 interface (with the `no shutdown` command) on R1, adding an IP address to the interface will not enable it. If the interface is enabled and an IP address is configured on G0/0, SW1 will learn of R1 and a lot of information about R1 through CDP messages, which might include the G0/0 IP address.

49. The correct answer is the following configuration:

```
username BOB secret ToUgH1!23
!
line vty 0 15
transport input telnet ssh
login local
!
service password-encryption
!
enable secret iTsMe@HeRe$
!
interface vlan 1
ip address 10.20.30.75 255.255.255.224
no shutdown
!
ip default-gateway 10.20.30.94
```

50. **Answer D is correct.** CSMA/CD allows devices to react properly when collisions occur on half-duplex network connections. A star topology could have a hub in the center, for which CSMA/CD would also be critical. But because the links are full duplex when using a switch in the center, answer D is better than C.

51. **Answer B is correct.** BPDU Guard is a feature in Cisco networking devices that is designed to enhance network stability and security by preventing the accidental or unauthorized connection of rogue switches to the network. When enabled on an interface, BPDU Guard monitors incoming bridge protocol data units (BPDUs), which are messages exchanged between switches to establish and maintain network topology information. If BPDU Guard detects the receipt of a BPDU on a port configured as an access port (that is, a port intended for end devices), it immediately puts the port into an error-disabled state, effectively disabling network connectivity on that port.

52. **Answer C is correct.** CDP is transported directly over Layer 2. This ensures that CDP messages can be exchanged even before any L3 protocols are configured on an interface. Even though VTP (and DTP, PAgP, and UDLD) frames use the same destination MAC address as CDP, they are different protocols and use different messages.

53. **Answer D is correct.** iBGP is not considered comparable to IGPs for distribution of prefixes inside an AS. As a result, it has a very high admin distance of 200.

54. **Answers A and D are correct.** The next-hop property can take an IP address of the next router or the local exit interface of the sending router. Setting a multi-access interface (such as an Ethernet interface) as a next hop is not recommended and should be avoided. Just because you can do something doesn't mean you should.

55. **Answer B is correct.** The default lease duration is one day.

56. Answer B is correct. The `ntp master` command sets the local device's internal clock to act as a time source for the network. Any Cisco router that has a time source to synchronize to (either an internal clock using the `ntp master` command or an external NTP server configured with the `ntp server` command) will act as a time source for any other NTP clients that try to get time from the local device.

57. Answer B is correct. The default privilege level is very low: 1 (although 0 also exists). This permits user mode access only.

58. Answer C is correct. The `login local` command ensures the use of the local user account's database on the device when connecting to the vty lines.

59. Answer B is correct. The primary data format used with Terraform is the HashiCorp Configuration Language (HCL), a simple, declarative language specifically designed for defining infrastructure as code. HCL offers a concise and human-readable syntax that allows users to describe resources, variables, and configurations in a clear and structured manner. In addition, Terraform also supports JSON (JavaScript Object Notation) as an alternative data format, enabling users who are more familiar with JSON to define their infrastructure configurations in this format. JSON provides a widely accepted standard for data interchange and is often preferred in environments where interoperability with other tools and systems is crucial.

60. Answer A is correct. Ansible uses a component called a *playbook* to enable automation on a network. This playbook consists of a list of tasks, known in Ansible as *plays*.

Glossary

Numerics

2-tier spine-leaf topology A newer network topology design from Cisco Systems that is used in technologies such as Cisco ACI. The two tiers are called spine and leaf. Each leaf device is connected to every spine device in a full mesh. The spine is considered the backbone or the core of the network. The spine is the glue that allows for the communications between leaf devices. If one leaf needs to send traffic to another leaf, it must send the traffic through the spine.

802.1Q A technology that inserts tags into frames in order to identify the virtual local-area network (VLAN) to which traffic belongs when traveling over a trunk link.

802.1x A security protocol suite for authentication of local-area network (LAN) and wireless local-area network (WLAN) users.

A

access control entry (ACE) A permit or deny statement in an access control list (ACL).

access control list (ACL) A list of access control entries (ACEs) that are checked to match traffic on a Cisco device; ACLs are often used to filter traffic assigned to an interface.

access point (AP) A device that connects an end user to a network by using IEEE wireless technologies; APs are often dual band.

address resolution protocol (ARP) A protocol used to map a known logical address to a physical address. A device performs an ARP broadcast to identify the physical Layer 2 address of a destination device on an Ethernet network. This physical address is then stored in local cache memory for later use.

administrative distance A value that ranges from 0 through 255 that determines the believability of a source's routing information; a lower value is preferred.

advanced distance vector protocol A routing protocol that combines some of the characteristics of both distance vector and link-state routing protocols. Cisco's Enhanced Interior Gateway Routing Protocol (EIGRP) is considered an advanced distance vector protocol.

alternate port A backup port that provides an alternate path to the root bridge and transitions to forwarding state if the designated port fails.

Ansible An automation and orchestration tool that is a very popular open-source offering. Ansible is written in Python and uses playbooks written in YAML to carry out the automation. It is unique in that it is agentless. The control node uses Secure Shell (SSH) to manage systems, and these systems do not require any special agent software in order to be configured and maintained.

anycast The ability to assign identical IP addresses to different nodes. The network then calculates and forwards traffic to the "closest" device to respond to client requests.

AP modes Different modes available with Cisco Access Points for various functions; for example, to have the access point assist with WLAN troubleshooting or security.

application layer The highest layer of the Open Systems Interconnection (OSI) model (Layer 7), which represents network services to support end-user applications such as email and File Transfer Protocol (FTP).

application programming interface (API) A set of options that permits simplified access to the functions of a software application or infrastructure.

Application Virtualization Technology Software that separates applications from the underlying operating system running on the host system.

artificial intelligence (AI) A branch of computer science focused on creating systems capable of performing tasks that typically require human intelligence, such as learning, reasoning, and problem solving.

attenuation The reduction in strength of a signal whenever it travels through a medium. Attenuation occurs with any type of signal, whether electromagnetic or audio. Sometimes referred to as signal loss.

Authentication, Authorization, Accounting (AAA) Security protocols that assist with proving identity, assigning permissions, and tracking access and actions performed.

automation The ability to dynamically carry out tasks on a network. For example, a network device might monitor itself (based on the configuration) and then automatically purge files when a storage facility is nearly full.

Auto MDI-X A feature that many Cisco devices support on ports. These ports can detect whether a connection would require a crossover cable instead of a straight-through cable and can manipulate the port settings to function with either cable that is connected.

autonomous system (AS) A group of networks under common administration that share a routing strategy.

B

backup configuration The version of a Cisco device configuration stored in the nonvolatile random-access memory (NVRAM) of a system; also called the startup configuration. Also, a copy of a configuration that exists on a remote Trivial File Transfer Protocol (TFTP) or File Transfer Protocol (FTP) server.

backup port A redundant port that provides an alternate path to the root bridge in case the primary path fails.

bandwidth The capacity of a network link that is available to carry traffic over a physical medium.

bidirectional network address translation (NAT) A form of NAT that features address translation from the inside network to the outside network as well as translation of traffic flowing from the outside network to the inside network.

boot field   The lowest 4 bits of the 16-bit configuration register in Cisco IOS devices. The value of the boot field determines the order in which a router searches for Cisco IOS software.

Border Gateway Protocol (BGP)   An exterior routing protocol that exchanges route information between autonomous systems.

BPDU filter   A feature in Spanning Tree Protocol (STP) that prevents bridge protocol data units (BPDUs) from being sent or received on a port, effectively disabling STP on that port.

BPDU guard   A Spanning Tree Protocol (STP) security feature for blocking rogue switches.

bridge   A device used to segment a local-area network (LAN) into multiple physical segments. A bridge uses a forwarding table to determine which frames need to be forwarded to specific segments. Bridges isolate local traffic to the originating physical segment but forward all nonlocal and broadcast traffic.

broadcast   A data frame that is sent to every node on a local segment.

C

carrier-sense multiple access with collision avoidance (CSMA/CA)
A physical specification used in wireless networks to provide contention-based frame transmission. A sending device first verifies that data can be sent without contention before it sends the data frame.

carrier-sense multiple access with collision detection (CSMA/CD)   A

physical specification used by Ethernet to provide contention-based frame transmission. CSMA/CD specifies that a sending device must share physical transmission media and listen to determine whether a collision occurs during or after transmitting. In simple terms, this means that an Ethernet card has a built-in capability to detect a potential packet collision on the internetwork.

channel   A single communications path on a system. In some situations, channels can be multiplexed over a single connection.

chassis aggregation   A technology that allows many switches to act as a single switch.

checksum   The result of a calculation used to ensure the integrity of data. Many protocols include checksum fields to verify that no errors are introduced during transmission.

Chef   A configuration management tool written in Ruby and Erlang. It uses a Ruby domain-specific language for writing system configuration recipes. Chef is used to streamline the task of configuring and maintaining a company's servers and can integrate with cloud-based platforms such as Amazon EC2, Google Cloud Platform, Oracle Cloud, OpenStack, SoftLayer, Microsoft Azure, and Rackspace to automatically provision and configure new machines.

Cisco Catalyst Center   The new name for the Cisco DNA Center.

Cisco Discovery Protocol (CDP)
A Cisco-proprietary protocol for discovering information about neighbors.

Cisco DNA Center   A network management and command center for provisioning and configuring many network devices using a single graphical user interface (GUI). It can utilize advanced artificial intelligence (AI) and machine learning (ML) to proactively monitor, troubleshoot, and optimize a network. Cisco DNA Center also integrates with third-party systems for improved operational processes. Note that in 2024, Cisco renamed the Cisco DNA Center to the Cisco Catalyst Center.

classful addressing   A type of addressing that categorizes Internet Protocol (IP) addresses into ranges that are used to create a hierarchy in the IP addressing scheme. The most common classes are A, B, and C, which can be identified by looking at the first three bits of an IP address.

classless addressing   A type of addressing that does not categorize addresses into classes and that is designed to deal with wasted address space.

classless interdomain routing (CIDR) A process implemented to resolve the rapid depletion of Internet Protocol (IP) address space on the Internet and to minimize the number of routes on the Internet. CIDR provides a relatively efficient method of allocating IP address space by removing the concept of classes in IP addressing. CIDR enables routes to be summarized on powers-of-two boundaries; therefore, it reduces multiple routes into a single prefix.

client DNS configuration   Configuration of DNS on a client that permits the device to resolve fully qualified domain names (such as www.yahoo.com) to the Internet Protocol (IP) addresses needed for network communication.

cloud services   Resources that exist on the Internet for use by several customers.

collapsed core network design   A simplified version of the three-layer network model from Cisco Systems that collapses the distribution layer into the core layer, resulting in two layers: core and access.

collision   The result of two frames colliding on a transmission medium. In modern Ethernet networks, this condition is avoided through the use of switches.

configuration register   A 16-bit storage location that is set as a numeric value (usually displayed in hexadecimal form) and used to specify certain actions on a router, such as where to look for the IOS image and whether to load the startup configuration from NVRAM (nonvolatile random-access memory).

congestion   A situation that occurs during data transfer when one or more computers generate network traffic faster than it can be transmitted through the network.

congestion management   A quality of service (QoS) category for dealing with network congestion.

console   A direct access to a router for configuring and monitoring the router.

container   A newer virtualization technology that permits the virtualization of applications (or services) without requiring the complete virtualization of an underlying operating system.

content-addressable memory (CAM)   The specialized memory used to store a CAM table, which is a dynamic table in a network switch that maps Media Access Control (MAC) addresses to ports. It is the essential mechanism that separates network switches from hubs; the CAM table is often considered to be synonymous with the MAC address table.

Control and Provisioning of Wireless Access Points (CAPWAP)   An Internet Engineering Task Force (IETF) standard that Cisco lightweight access points (APs) use to communicate between the controller and other lightweight APs on the network. CAPWAP, which is based on Lightweight Access Point Protocol (LWAPP), is a standard, interoperable protocol that enables a controller to manage a collection of wireless APs.

control plane   A category of network processing that involves control protocols such as routing protocols.

controller   A software-defined networking control plane device.

convergence   The result when all routers within an internetwork agree on routes through the internetwork.

Create, Read, Update, Delete (CRUD)   The basic functions of persistent storage.

cryptography   The practice and study of techniques for secure communication in the presence of third parties called adversaries.

cyclic redundancy check (CRC)   An error-checking mechanism by which the receiving node calculates a value based on the data it receives and compares it with the value stored within the frame from the sending node.

D

data access port   A port on a switch that is used to accept traffic from a single VLAN from workstations (or up to two VLANs if an IP phone is also attached to the port). Contrast this with a trunk port that is carrying the traffic of many VLANs.

data plane   A category of network processing that involves the movement of user traffic.

de-encapsulation   The process by which a destination peer layer removes and reads the control information sent by the source peer layer in another network device.

default mask   A binary or decimal representation of the number of bits used to identify an Internet Protocol (IP) network. The class of the IP address defines the default mask. The mask can be presented in dotted-decimal notation or as the number of bits making up the mask.

default route   A network route used for destinations that don't have a better match in the routing table.

default routing   The process of creating a default gateway for unknown destinations.

default virtual local-area network (VLAN)   A VLAN that permits all ports to participate in it by default. By default, access ports are assigned to the default VLAN. In a Cisco switch with the default factory configuration, the default VLAN is VLAN 1.

delay   The amount of time necessary to move a packet through an internetwork from source to destination.

demarc   The point of demarcation between a carrier's equipment and the customer premises equipment (CPE).

designated port   A network port on a switch that is chosen to forward frames toward the root bridge in a Spanning Tree Protocol (STP) topology, ensuring there are no loops in the network.

device access   The ability to connect to a Cisco device for management using a wide variety of methods, including Secure Shell (SSH), Telnet, and the console.

device trust   Trust for the quality of service (QoS) markings sent from a device.

DHCP   A technology for eliminating rogue DHCP servers in a network.

distance vector protocol   An interior routing protocol that relies on information from immediate neighbors only instead of having a full picture of the network. Most distance vector protocols involve each router sending all or a large part of its routing table to its neighboring routers at regular intervals.

Domain Name System (DNS)   A system used to translate fully qualified hostnames or computer names into Internet Protocol (IP) addresses.

dotted-decimal notation   A method of representing binary IP addresses in decimal format. Dotted-decimal notation represents the four octets of an IPv4 address in four decimal values separated by dots (that is, periods or decimal points).

dynamic ARP inspection (DAI)   A technology made possible by Dynamic Host Configuration Protocol (DHCP) snooping that helps guard against Media Access Control (MAC) address spoofing in the network. It also helps guard against many different MAC-related attacks, such as MAC flooding.

Dynamic Host Configuration Protocol (DHCP)   A communication protocol that permits a server to automatically assign the IP address information required by clients on the network, along with a slew of other useful information (such as default gateway and Domain Name System [DNS] server). DHCP servers and DHCP clients are involved in the process.

Dynamic Host Configuration Protocol (DHCP) relay   A device on a network that forwards DHCP requests from clients as unicast traffic to a DHCP server on a remote network segment.

Dynamic Multipoint Virtual Private Network (DMVPN)   A Cisco technology for dynamically connecting spokes to the hub over a public network.

dynamic Network Address Translation (NAT)   A form of NAT that uses a pool of addresses for translation and access lists to define the addresses that will be translated.

dynamic port security   A variation of port security that features Media Access Control (MAC) addresses that are dynamically learned and allowed on the switch port.

dynamic route   A network route that adjusts automatically to changes within the internetwork. These routes are learned dynamically via a routing protocol.

dynamic routing   Using routing protocols to dynamically share prefix and next-hop information.

E

EIGRP for IPv6   A protocol for IPv6 routing based upon EIGRP.

encapsulation   The process of wrapping data in a particular protocol header. In the context of the Open Systems Interconnection (OSI) model, encapsulation is the process by which a source peer layer includes header and trailer control information with a protocol data unit (PDU) destined for its peer layer in another network node. The information that is encapsulated instructs the destination peer layer how to process the information. Encapsulation occurs as information is sent down the protocol stack.

endpoint   A generic term used to describe an entity in an internetwork that is using the network to communicate. Examples of endpoints include end-user workstations, network printers, and file servers.

Enhanced Interior Gateway Routing Protocol (EIGRP)   A Cisco-proprietary routing protocol that includes features of both distance vector and link-state routing protocols. EIGRP is considered an advanced distance vector protocol.

Enhanced Interior Gateway Routing Protocol (EIGRP) for IPv4   A hybrid routing protocol designed by Cisco in an attempt to address scalability while offering ease of configuration.

errdisable recovery   A Cisco device feature that permits automatic recovery from error conditions after a set duration of time.

error   One of the many different error conditions that might occur in an Ethernet network. The `show interface` command is used to see the errors for an interface.

escalation   The process of taking a troubleshooting issue to other parties for their assistance.

EtherChannel   The bundling of links together for shared bandwidth.

Ethernet frame format   The common fields in modern Ethernet frames, including a source Media Access Control (MAC) address and destination MAC address, which are critical fields for Ethernet switches.

Ethernet switching   A process that permits full-duplex communication that is collision free in modern local-area networks (LANs).

EXEC   The user interface for executing Cisco router commands.

exploit   A piece of software or another mechanism that leverages a vulnerability in a system in order to carry out an attack.

extended access control list (ACL)   An ACL that permits the matching of traffic using many different criteria, including source Internet Protocol (IP) address and destination IP address.

extended options   Extra options used by commands such as ping and traceroute for adjusting various parameters when running network tests using Internet Control Message Protocol (ICMP).

exterior gateway protocol (EGP)   A protocol designed to route traffic between autonomous systems (ASs).

External Border Gateway Protocol (eBGP)   A form of BGP that involves peering with a remote autonomous system (AS).

F

fault isolation   The process of determining exactly where a problem exists in a network.

file system management   The process of managing the various storage facilities within a Cisco device, including components such as random-access memory (RAM), nonvolatile random-access memory (NVRAM), flash, and universal serial bus (USB).

File Transfer Protocol (FTP)   A protocol used to copy a file from one host to another host, regardless of the physical hardware or operating system of each device. FTP identifies a client and server during the file transfer process. In addition, it provides a guaranteed transfer by using the services of Transmission Control Protocol (TCP).

firewall   A hardware or software device that seeks to protect a network or device at specific points in the network.

first hop redundancy protocol (FHRP)   A protocol such as Hot Standby Router Protocol (HSRP), Virtual Router Redundancy Protocol (VRRP), or Gateway Load Balancing Protocol (GLBP) that is used to make multiple default gateways available to client systems.

flash   Router memory that stores the Cisco IOS image and associated microcode. Flash is erasable, reprogrammable read-only memory (ROM) that retains its content when the router is powered down or restarted.

floating static route   A route that has an artificially high administrative distance value in order to make dynamic routes more preferred. Such routes are used as backup routes when the dynamic routing protocol fails to determine a path to a destination.

flow control   A mechanism that throttles back data transmission to ensure that a sending system does not overwhelm the receiving system with data.

frame check sequence (FCS)　Extra characters added to an Ethernet frame for error control purposes. FCS is the result of a cyclic redundancy check (CRC).

frame flooding　A process in which a switch sends traffic out all ports except for the port where the traffic entered. This is done for broadcast frames and unknown unicast frames.

frame rewrite　A process in which routers manipulate address information inside the packets they are sending. Specifically, they rewrite MAC address information.

frame switching　The processes used on an Ethernet switch to efficiently forward and filter traffic in the LAN.

frame tagging　A method of tagging a frame with a unique user-defined virtual local-area network (VLAN). The process of tagging frames allows VLANs to span multiple switches.

full-duplex　The physical transmission process on a network device by which one pair of wires transmits data while another pair of wires receives data. Full-duplex transmission is achieved by eliminating the possibility of collisions on an Ethernet segment, thereby eliminating the need for a device to sense collisions.

G

gateway of last resort　The router to which traffic is sent when a more exact destination of the traffic is not in the local routing table.

generative AI　A subset of artificial intelligence that focuses on creating models capable of producing new content, such as text, images, or music, by learning patterns from existing data.

global configuration mode　An IOS CLI mode that enables simple device configuration commands—such as router names, banners, and passwords—to be executed. Global configuration commands affect the whole device rather than a single interface or component.

global unicast　The IPv6 address type that is used for Internet routing.

GRE (generic routing encapsulation)　A process used for tunneling IPv4 traffic.

H

half-duplex　A physical transmission process in which only a single device in the broadcast domain can send data at a time. In a half-duplex Ethernet network, CSMA/CD is used.

header　Control information placed before the data during the encapsulation process.

hierarchical routing protocol　A routing environment that relies on several routers to compose a backbone. Most traffic from non-backbone routers traverses the backbone routers (or at least travels to the backbone) to reach another non-backbone router.

hop count　The number of routers a packet passes through on its way to the destination network.

host route　The most specific route possible in the routing table. This route features a 32-bit or 128-bit mask, depending on whether IPv4 or IPv6 is used.

hostname　A logical name given to a network device.

Hot Standby Router Protocol (HSRP)　A first hop redundancy protocol (FHRP) that permits multiple default gateways in the network.

hybrid cloud　Cloud technology that includes internal and external cloud components.

hybrid topology   A network that features the use of multiple topologies, such as a star topology connected to a full mesh topology.

hypervisor   Software that makes virtualization of servers possible. A Type 1 hypervisor runs directly on top of host hardware (bare metal), and a Type 2 hypervisor runs within an operating system.

I

implicit deny all   A statement that ends every ACL. It is an implied deny statement, which ensures that packets not matching an explicit entry are denied. It does not appear as a separate ACE when listing an ACL.

initial configuration dialog   The dialog used to configure a router the first time it is booted or when no configuration file exists. The initial configuration dialog is an optional tool used to simplify the configuration process. It is often called setup mode.

initial device onfiguration   Configuration provided by an administrator or provided by the Cisco factory default of the basic parameters of a device.

inside global   The inside addresses after they have been translated with Network Address Translation (NAT). Inside global addresses are registered addresses that represent inside hosts to outside networks.

inside local   The addresses on the inside of a network before they are translated with Network Address Translation (NAT).

Institute of Electrical and Electronics Engineers (IEEE)   An organization with many functions, activities, and objectives, including defining standards for many local-area networks (LANs), including Ethernet (802.3), wireless LANs (802.11), Zigbee (802.15.4), WiMax (802.16), and many more.

interface   A router component that provides network connections to an external transmission medium. Depending on the model of router, interfaces exist either on the motherboard or on separate, modular interface cards. Interfaces can also be logical, such as loopback interfaces or 802.1Q subinterfaces.

inter-VLAN routing   The process of using a routing engine (RE) to move packets from one VLAN to another. Remember that VLANs usually have a one-to-one correlation with IP subnets.

Interior Border Gateway Protocol (iBGP)   A form of BGP that involves peering within an autonomous system (AS).

interior routing protocol   A routing protocol that exchanges information within an autonomous system (AS). Routing Information Protocol (RIP) and Open Shortest Path First (OSPF) are examples of interior routing protocols.

Internet Control Message Protocol (ICMP)   A protocol that communicates error and control messages between Internet Protocol (IP) devices. Multiple types of ICMP messages are defined. ICMP enables devices to check the status of other devices and is used with ping and traceroute.

Internet Protocol (IP)   One of the many protocols maintained in the Transmission Control Protocol/Internet Protocol (TCP/IP) suite of protocols. IP is the Layer 3 network-level mechanism used for Transmission Control Protocol (TCP) and User Datagram Protocol (UDP). IP comes in two versions: version 4 (IPv4) and version 6 (IPv6).

Internet Protocol version 6 (IPv6) autoconfiguration   The ability of an IPv6 device to receive its IPv6 address information automatically, with little to no administrator intervention.

intrusion prevention system (IPS)
A specialized security device that can recognize attack traffic and drop that traffic before it reaches critical parts of the network. Cisco next-generation firewalls often have built-in IPS capabilities.

IOS recovery   The process of copying a valid IOS image to a Cisco device that has a troubled operating system. This is often done from a Trivial File Transfer Protocol (TFTP) server that stores backup or upgraded IOS files.

IOS tool   One of the many powerful troubleshooting and monitoring tools built into IOS.

IP Security (IPsec)   A suite of protocols that provides security over a network to Internet Protocol version 4 (IPv4) or Internet Protocol version 6 (IPv6) packets. IPsec is often used with virtual private networks (VPNs) today.

IP service-level agreement (SLA)   A tool for testing a network and monitoring its health and performance over time.

IP standard access list   An access list that provides a way of filtering IP traffic on a router interface based on only the source IP address or range.

IPv6 (stateless address autoconfiguration)   The IPv6 process for assigning full IPv6 address information to devices that require it.

J

JavaScript Object Notation (JSON)   An open-standard file format that uses human-readable text to transmit data objects consisting of attribute/value pairs and array data types. It is a very common data format, with a diverse range of applications, such as serving as a replacement for XML in AJAX systems.

K

keepalive frame   A protocol data unit (PDU) transmitted at the data link layer that is used for multiple purposes, including verifying that an interface is up and available.

L

Layer 2 EtherChannel   The bundling of links together at Layer 2 for switching traffic.

Layer 2 protocol   A protocol such as Cisco Discovery Protocol (CDP) that operates at Layer 2 of the Open Systems Interconnection (OSI) model.

Layer 3 EtherChannel   The bundling of links together at Layer 3 for routed traffic.

Layer 3 switch   Another name for a multilayer switch. Layer 3 switch indicates that the device has routing intelligence (capabilities) built inside it, permitting it to both switch and route traffic.

licensing   The process of acquiring the legal permission required to run a particular software product on a device.

link aggregation (LAG)   A form of link aggregation found on many Cisco devices, including many wireless LAN controllers (WLCs). LAG permits the sharing of bandwidth for multiple ports and also offers fault tolerance in the event of a LAG link failure.

Link Aggregation Control Protocol (LACP)   A protocol that can dynamically create EtherChannels.

Link Layer Discovery Protocol (LLDP)   An open-standard Layer 2 technology that permits devices to learn information about each other over the local link.

link-local address A special IPv6 address used to permit communication between devices sharing the same data link.

link-state advertisement (LSA) A data structure in OSPF that contains the status of a router's links or network interfaces. LSAs are carried in link-state updates (LSUs).

link-state protocol An interior routing protocol in which each router sends the state of its own network links across the network to every router within its autonomous system (AS) or area. This process enables routers to learn and maintain full knowledge of the network's exact topology and how it is interconnected. Link-state protocols, such as Open Shortest Path First (OSPF), use a "shortest path first" algorithm.

local-area network (LAN) protocol A set of rules used for the transmission of data within a LAN. A popular LAN protocol is Ethernet.

local authentication A process in which a Cisco device performs the security checks required to prove the identity of a user requesting access to the device, using its running configuration on the local router.

local SPAN A monitoring tool for a local switch.

log event Information recorded about the health and operation of a device, thanks to the local syslog system.

logging The process on a Cisco router of using syslog to report about the operation and health of the local device.

logical addressing Network layer IP addressing (as opposed to the physical addressing of the data link layer). A logical address consists of two parts: the network and the node.

logical link control (LLC) sublayer A sublayer of the data link layer that provides some of the functions needed to support the data link layer.

login banner A message presented to a user just before the username prompt on the device. Such banners are often used for security warnings.

loop guard A network protocol feature that prevents network loops by disabling a port if a unidirectional link failure is detected, ensuring the port does not transition to a forwarding state.

loopback A virtual interface that is used for many maintenance and monitoring techniques. It can also provide a stable connection between devices that have multiple physical paths in the event that one of those paths goes down, since loopbacks should always be available as long as one physical path between the devices remains functional.

M

MAC address table The database on a Layer 2 switch that lists the MAC addresses known by the device and the ports these MAC addresses are attached to.

MAC aging The process of removing stale MAC addresses from a Layer 2 switch.

MAC learning The process of recording the source MAC addresses for incoming frames on a Layer 2 switch.

machine learning A subset of artificial intelligence that enables systems to learn and improve from experience without being explicitly programmed by analyzing and identifying patterns in data.

marking The tagging of traffic with an identifier to be used for quality of service (QoS).

Maximum MAC Addresses A port security feature that permits you to restrict the total number of Media Access Control (MAC) addresses associated with a port in the MAC address table.

MD5 Verify   A Cisco device feature that permits the integrity verification of an IOS image.

Media Access Control (MAC) address   A physical Layer 2 address used to define a device uniquely on a data link.

mesh topology   A network topology that features full connections or partial connections between all network nodes.

metric   The relative cost of sending packets to a destination network over a specific network route. Examples of metrics include hop count and cost.

Metro Ethernet   A version of Ethernet used for the creation of a metropolitan-area network (MAN).

mitigation   The actions and technologies that are put in place in order to help guard against security attacks to systems.

Modified EUI-64   A method of assigning an IPv6 node with its host address portion; this is one of the many time-saving features of IPv6.

multi-area Open Shortest Path First (OSPF)   A feature of OSPF that divides a routed system into hierarchical areas, allowing greater control over routing update traffic. Router loads are generally reduced, as is the frequency of SPF recalculation. Multi-area OSPF can scale to large deployments.

multicasting   A process of using one IP address to represent a group of IP hosts. Multicasting is used to send messages to a subset of IP addresses in a network or networks.

multipath routing protocol   A routing protocol that load balances over multiple optimal paths to a destination network. This is often used when the costs of the paths are equal. (EIGRP can load balance across unequal-cost paths.)

multiplexing   A transport layer method in which application conversations are combined over a single channel by interleaving packets from different segments and transmitting them.

Multiprotocol Label Switching (MPLS)   The switching of traffic using labels instead of IP address information. Typically used within provider networks.

N

named ACL (access control list)   An ACL that uses a name instead of a number as an identifier.

native VLAN   A VLAN on a trunk link that is not tagged with an 802.1Q VLAN identifier. All untagged traffic on a trunk link belongs to the native VLAN.

Network Address Translation (NAT)   The process of translating internal IP addresses to routable registered IP addresses on the outside of a network.

network command   The command Border Gateway Protocol (BGP) uses to advertise a local prefix.

network interface card (NIC)   An adapter or circuitry that allows a network host to attach to a data link.

network mask   The subnet mask used with an IP address.

Network Time Protocol (NTP)   A protocol that provides IP network-based synchronization of device clocks, facilitating log and transaction analysis, and improving quality-of-service (QoS) responsiveness in voice and video over IP systems.

next-generation firewall   The latest firewalls from Cisco Systems, which feature cutting-edge technologies and capabilities, thanks in great part to the Cisco acquisition of Sourcefire in 2013.

next hop   The next device in a path to reach a network destination.

nonvolatile random-access memory (NVRAM)   A memory area of a router that stores permanent information, such as the router's backup configuration file. The contents of NVRAM are retained when the router is powered down or restarted.

northbound API (application programming interface)   The communications in SDN from the management station to the SDN controller.

numbered ACL (access control list)   An access control list (ACL) identified by a number instead of a name.

O

Open Shortest Path First (OSPF)   A hierarchical link-state routing protocol that was developed as a successor to the distance vector protocol Routing Information Protocol (RIP).

Open Systems Interconnection (OSI) model   A layered networking framework developed by the International Organization for Standardization that describes seven layers that correspond to specific networking functions.

OSPFv2 (Open Shortest Path First version 2)   OSPF for IP version 4 (IPv4).

OSPFv3 (Open Shortest Path First version 3)   OSPF for IP version 6 (IPv6).

P-Q

packet switching   A process by which a router moves a packet from one interface to another.

passive-interface   A routing protocol command that places a router interface into "receive-only" mode so that no routing

updates are sent out, but those that are received are processed. This allows the passive interface's network to be advertised out other interfaces without generating unnecessary routing protocol traffic on the passive interface network.

password recovery   The process of resetting the password on a Cisco device in order to permit access to the device. This typically requires physical access to the device. On newer Cisco devices, password recovery usually involves totally wiping any stored configuration.

peer-to-peer communication   A form of communication that occurs between the same layers of two different network hosts.

peerings   A term for BGP adjacencies.

Per VLAN Spanning Tree (PVST)+   A Cisco implementation of STP that provides an STP topology for each VLAN in your infrastructure.

ping   A software tool for testing IP connectivity between two devices. ping is used to send multiple Internet Control Message Protocol (ICMP) packets to a receiving device. The destination device responds with another ICMP packet to notify the source device of its existence.

policing   A quality of service (QoS) technique that involves dropping traffic that exceeds a certain rate.

Port Address Translation (PAT)   A form of NAT that allows many different inside devices to share a single global address for translation.

Port Aggregation Protocol (PAgP)   A protocol for dynamically bundling EtherChannels.

port security   A system of MAC-based switch port security capabilities that can limit or deny access to certain hosts attempting to connect to a switch port.

port security violation actions   The various actions that can be taken when there is a port security violation.

PortFast   A Spanning Tree Protocol (STP) feature that transitions a port to forwarding almost immediately.

Power over Ethernet (PoE)   A series of standards that deliver power to end devices using the Ethernet connection the device is already using for data. PoE is often used to power APs, VoIP phones, and video over IP cameras.

predicitive AI   A type of artificial intelligence that uses data analysis and machine learning algorithms to forecast future events or trends based on historical data.

preemption   The ability of a Hot Standby Router Protocol (HSRP) device to take over as the active forwarder.

prefix   The network portion of a Layer 3 logical address.

presentation layer   Layer 6 of the Open Systems Interconnection (OSI) model, which is concerned with how data is represented to the application layer.

prioritization   A quality of service (QoS) feature that permits some traffic to receive better treatment compared to other traffic.

priority   The process of giving certain traffic forms preferential treatment over other traffic forms.

private cloud   Cloud technology that resides internal to a company.

private IPv4 (Internet Protocol version 4) address   An IPv4 address that is for use in internal networks only. Private IPv4 addressing allows for the duplication of addresses behind corporate network boundaries and was created to help ward off the IPv4 address shortage. RFC 1918 lists most of the private IPv4 address space.

privileged mode   An extensive administrative and management mode on a Cisco router. This CLI mode permits testing, debugging, and commands to modify the router's configuration.

protocol   A formal description of a set of rules and conventions that defines how devices on a network must exchange information.

protocol data unit (PDU)   A unit of measure that refers to data that is transmitted between two peer layers in different network devices. Segments, packets, and frames are examples of PDUs.

public cloud   Cloud technology that exists external to a company.

Puppet   An open-core software configuration management tool. It runs on many UNIX-like systems as well as on Microsoft Windows and includes its own declarative language to describe system configuration. It is written in C++, Clojure, and Ruby, and its free-software version is released under the Apache License 2.0.

R

random-access memory (RAM)   A memory area of a router that serves as a working storage area. RAM contains data such as routing tables, various types of caches and buffers, and input and output queues and the router's active configuration file. The contents of RAM are lost when the router is powered down or restarted.

Rapid Spanning Tree Protocol (RSTP)   A newer version of Spanning Tree Protocol (STP) that provides very fast convergence due to the many enhancements over the original protocol, including a new proposal and agreement mechanism that uses the point-to-point links between switches.

read-only memory (ROM)   A type of memory that stores the bootstrap program and power-on diagnostic programs.

representational state transfer (REST)   A software architectural style that defines a set of constraints to be used for creating web services. Web services that conform to the REST architectural style, called RESTful web services, provide interoperability between computer systems on the Internet. RESTful APIs are now hugely popular, thanks to the explosion in cloud technology.

ROM Monitor mode   A mode on a Cisco router that allows basic functions such as changing the configuration register value or loading an IOS image to Flash from a Trivial File Transfer Protocol (TFTP) server.

root bridge   The central reference point in a Spanning Tree Protocol (STP) network topology from which the shortest path to all other devices is calculated.

root guard   A Spanning Tree Protocol (STP) feature that prevents designated ports from becoming root ports, ensuring the stability and integrity of the network's root bridge.

root port   A network port on a switch that has the least path cost to reach the root bridge in a Spanning Tree Protocol (STP) topology.

route aggregation   The process of combining multiple IP networks into one superset of those networks. Route aggregation is implemented to reduce the number of routing table entries required to forward IP packets accurately in an internetwork.

routed protocol   A protocol that can be routed, such as Internet Protocol (IP).

router mode   A mode that enables the execution of specific router commands and functions. User and privileged are examples of router modes that allow you to perform certain tasks.

router-on-a-stick   A router attached to a trunk link that is used to route between the VLANs on the trunk.

routing algorithm   Well-defined rules that aid routers in the collection of route information and the determination of the optimal path.

Routing Information Protocol (RIP)
A distance vector routing protocol that uses hop count as its metric.

routing protocol   A protocol that uses algorithms to generate a list of paths to a particular destination and the cost associated with each path. Routers use routing protocols to communicate with each other the best route to use to reach a particular destination.

routing table   An area of a router's memory that stores route forwarding information. Routing tables contain information such as destination network, next hop, and associated metrics.

running configuration   The configuration in RAM on a Cisco device that is currently being used by the device.

S

Secure Copy Protocol (SCP)   A protocol that permits the secure transfer of files in a network. SCP relies upon Secure Shell (SSH) for the security mechanisms.

Secure Shell (SSH)   A protocol that allows for secure communication between a client and a router. It is a secure alternative to Telnet.

service set identifier (SSID)   A 32-byte unique identifier that is used to name a wireless network.

session layer   Layer 5 of the Open Systems Interconnection (OSI) model, which establishes, manages, and terminates sessions between applications on different network devices.

setup mode   The router mode triggered on startup if no configuration file resides in nonvolatile random-access memory (NVRAM).

shaping   The quality of service (QoS) process of buffering traffic that goes over a certain rate.

Simple Mail Transfer Protocol (SMTP)   A protocol used to pass mail messages between devices; SMTP uses Transmission Control Protocol (TCP).

Simple Network Management Protocol (SNMP)   A standards-based protocol that allows remote monitoring and management of networked devices.

sliding window   A method by which TCP dynamically adjusts the window size during a connection, enabling the receiving device involved in the communication to slow down the sending data rate. The purpose of the sliding window mechanism is to maximize throughput through a network and between two hosts.

SNMP (Simple Network Management Protocol) version 2c   A version of SNMP that does not provide sophisticated security.

SNMP (Simple Network Management Protocol) version 3   A version of SNMP that provides sophisticated security.

socket   The combination of the source and destination Transmission Control Protocol (TCP) or User Datagram Protocol (UDP) port numbers and the source and destination Internet Protocol (IP) addresses. A socket can be used to define any UDP or TCP connection uniquely.

software-defined networking (SDN)   An approach to network management that enables dynamic, programmatically efficient network configuration. The goals of SDN are to improve network performance and monitoring, as well as quickly deploy changes to meet business requirements.

source addressing   The management technique of specifying the source IP address of traffic coming from a router. This often allows for more consistent or reliable traffic management.

source NAT (Network Address Translation)   A type of NAT that uses the source address in traffic packets.

southbound API (application programming interface)   The communication protocol that allows communication between a software-defined networking (SDN) controller and network devices.

Spanning Tree Protocol (STP)   A technology used to prevent Layer 2 loops.

standard ACL (access control list)   An ACL that can filter using source Internet Protocol (IP) address information.

star topology   A topology with a switch connecting workstations. If this topology is drawn with the switch in the center of the network diagram, it resembles a star.

startup configuration   The configuration of a device that is stored in nonvolatile random-access memory (NVRAM) for booting a system.

startup configuration file   The backup configuration file on a router, stored in nonvolatile random-access memory (NVRAM).

static EtherChannel   The manual configuration of an EtherChannel without the use of dynamic protocols.

static NAT (Network Address Translation)   A type of NAT in which a single source address is mapped to a specific translated address.

static port security   The manual configuration of a MAC address or addresses on a switch port with port security enabled.

static route   A network route that is manually entered into a routing table. Static routes function well in simple and predictable network environments.

static routing   The creation of static route entries for routing purposes.

sticky learning   The process of recording dynamically learned MAC addresses as static entries in the running configuration of a switch running port security.

STP (Spanning Tree Protocol) optional features   Additional STP features that help secure and optimize the protocol.

STP (Spanning Tree Protocol) root bridge selection   The process by which STP elects a root device.

stratum   A measure of the "distance" from an authoritative time source.

subinterface   One of possibly many virtual interfaces on a single physical interface.

subnet mask   The network mask associated with an IP address. The purpose of this value is to distinguish between the network and host portions of the address.

subnetting   A process of splitting a classful range of IP addresses into multiple Internet Protocol (IP) subnetworks to allow more flexibility in IP addressing schemes. Subnetting overcomes the limitation of address classes and allows network administrators the flexibility to assign multiple networks with one class of IP addresses.

switch   A network device that provides increased port density and forwarding capabilities compared to a bridge. The increased port densities of switches enable Ethernet LANs to be segmented, thereby increasing the amount of bandwidth delivered to each device.

switch stacking   The process of grouping physical switches together to allow them to act as one virtual switch.

switched virtual interface (SVI)   A Layer 3 interface defined on a switch. SVIs are also called VLAN interfaces because there is usually one defined for each VLAN, allowing inter-VLAN routing to be performed by a Layer 3 switch instead of by a router. A Layer 2 switch can have only one SVI configured, and it is used for switch management.

syslog   A network protocol and service that provides centralized log message archiving.

T

TCP (Transmission Control Protocol) three-way handshake   A three-step process whereby a TCP session is established. In the first step, the sending device sends the initial sequence number with the SYN bit set in the TCP header. The receiver sends back a packet with the SYN and ACK bits set. In the third and final step, the sender sends a packet with the ACK bit set.

TCP (Transmission Control Protocol) windowing   A method of increasing or reducing the number of acknowledgments required between data transmissions. See also sliding window.

Telnet   A standard protocol that provides a virtual terminal and enables a network administrator to connect to a device's CLI remotely.

Terminal Access Controller Access Control System Plus (TACACS+)   A security protocol that provides authentication, authorization, and accounting (AAA) for Cisco devices.

terminal monitor   Functionality that permits a user with a Telnet or Secure Shell (SSH) session to a Cisco device to see logging messages produced by that local device.

Terraform   An open-source infrastructure as code (IaC) tool that allows users to define and provision data center infrastructure using a high-level configuration language.

three-tier network design   This classic Cisco networking model defines three layers: the access, distribution, and core layers.

Timezones   A clock setting that is possible on a Cisco device.

traceroute   An IP service on a Cisco router that uses User Datagram Protocol (UDP) and Internet Control Message Protocol (ICMP) to identify the hops between sending and receiving devices and the paths taken from the sending devices to destinations. Typically, traceroute is used to troubleshoot Internet Protocol (IP) connectivity between two devices.

trailer   Control information placed after the data in packets during the encapsulation process. See encapsulation for more detail.

Transmission Control Protocol (TCP)   One of the many protocols maintained in the Transmission Control Protocol/Internet Protocol (TCP/IP) suite of protocols. TCP provides transport layer connection-oriented and reliable service to the applications that use it.

Transmission Control Protocol/Internet Protocol (TCP/IP) model   A model that represents the protocols used in the Internet Protocol (IP) protocol suite, including those at the application, transport, network, and data link layers.

transport layer   Layer 4 of the Open Systems Interconnection (OSI) model, which is concerned with segmenting the upper-layer application data stream and, in the case of TCP, is concerned with establishing end-to-end connectivity through the network, sending segments from one host to another, and ensuring the reliable transport of data.

Trivial File Transfer Protocol (TFTP)   A protocol used to copy files from one device to another. TFTP is a stripped-down version of File Transfer Protocol (FTP).

troubleshooting methodology   An approach to troubleshooting using a defined sequence of steps.

trunk   A communications line or link that supports multiple virtual local-area networks (VLANs) on a single physical interface.

The standardized protocol for Ethernet trunks is 802.1Q.

U

unicast   A method of data transfer from one specific system on a network to another specific system on the network.

unidirectional NAT (Network Address Translation)   NAT that occurs in one direction (for example, inside addresses being translated for outbound traffic but no translation occurring for source addresses in the return path).

unique local addressing   An IPv6 approach to private addressing that is similar to IPv4's RFC 1918 private addressing.

User Datagram Protocol (UDP)   One of the many protocols maintained in the Transmission Control Protocol/Internet Protocol (TCP/IP) suite of protocols. UDP is a Layer 4, best-effort delivery protocol and, therefore, provides connectionless network services.

user mode   A display-only mode on a Cisco router. Only limited information about the router can be viewed within this router mode, and no configuration changes are permitted. User mode often refers to privilege level 1, which is the default for a new user account created on the local router.

V

variable-length subnet masking (VLSM)   A process that provides flexibility in assigning Internet Protocol (IP) address space. Routing protocols that support VLSM allow administrators to assign IP networks with different subnet masks. This increased flexibility saves IP address space because administrators can assign IP networks based on the number of hosts on each network.

virtual local-area network (VLAN) A technique that involves assigning devices to specific LANs based on the port to which they attach on a switch rather than the physical location. VLANs can extend the flexibility of LANs by allowing devices to be assigned to specific LANs on a port-by-port basis rather than on a per-device basis.

virtual machine (VM) A server running in a virtual environment, which might be an on-premises VMware environment or a VM running in a cloud service.

virtual network infrastructure (VNI) An infrastructure that includes virtualized network devices in the enterprise.

virtual network service A network service that has been virtualized (for example, a virtual security service).

virtual private network (VPN) A very common type of network used to send confidential information over a public network. There are two major categories of VPNs: Site-to-site VPNs are used to connect different offices together securely, and a remote access VPN is used to connect a remote user to a central network.

virtual terminal line (vty) A virtual access port on a Cisco device that allows connectivity using protocols such as Telnet and Secure Shell (SSH).

VLAN Trunking Protocol (VTP) A protocol for configuring and administering virtual local-area networks on Cisco network devices. With VTP, an administrator can make configuration changes centrally on a single Catalyst Series switch and have those changes, such as the addition of VLANs, automatically communicated to all the other switches in the network.

voice port A switch port that has been configured to carry voice traffic in addition to data.

vulnerability A misconfiguration or bug in a system that might permit security attacks to succeed. Many vulnerability scanners in the industry now are specialized devices for checking systems for such problems. A popular example is Nessus.

W-Z

well-known port One of a set of ports between 1 and 1023 that are reserved for specific Transmission Control Protocol/Internet Protocol (TCP/IP) protocols and services.

wide-area network (WAN) A network that uses data communications equipment to connect multiple local-area networks (LANs). Examples of WAN connectivity options include Metro Ethernet and L3 virtual private networks (VPNs).

Wi-Fi channel overlap A situation in which wireless networks interfere with each other due to potential conflicts in the 2.4 GHz band. To avoid problems when you are setting up wireless access points (APs) in the 2.4 GHz band, you should be sure to use the non-overlapping channels 1, 6, and 11.

Wi-Fi Protected Access (WPA) The main security technology in use today for Wi-Fi networks. Versions WPA, WPA2, and WPA3 are in use today, and each successive version introduces security improvements over previous versions.

wildcard (inverse) mask A technique that is used in access control lists (ACLs) to mark bits as not being required to match. For example, the wildcard mask 0.0.0.255 means the last octet of the associated Internet Protocol (IP) address doesn't have to match.

wireless LAN controller (WLC) A device used to control and manage wireless access points (APs) in a network.

Index

Numerics

802.1Q, 128-130, 429
802.1X, 429

A

AAA (authentication, authorization, and accounting), 266, 353, 430
  local authentication
    configuring, 267
    verifying, 267
  RADIUS, 268
  TACACS+, 268
aaa new-model command, 267
access layer, 325
access points, 168–169, 315, 429
accessing
  CLI, 35
  Packet Tracer, 4–9
ACEs (access control entries), 283, 429
ACL (access control list), 283, 353
  configuring, 287–288
  extended, 283, 287, 435
  implicit deny entry, 284

  keywords, 284
  numbered, 284
  standard, 283
    assigning to an interface, 285–286
    configuring, 285
    verifying, 284
  wildcards, 284
administrative distance, 181, 183, 429
adware, 350
AES (Advanced Encryption Standard), 306
AI (artificial intelligence), 367, 429
  generative, 370–371
  machine learning, 371
  predictive, 371
alternate port, 429–430
Ansible, 372, 430
anycast, 87, 430
API (application programming interface), 364, 430
  RESTful, 363, 367, 369
  southbound, 363
application layer, 430
Application Virtualization Technology, 430

O

P